SHIPBROKING
AND
CHARTERING
PRACTICE

FOURTH EDITION

SHIPBROKING AND CHARTERING PRACTICE

By

LARS GORTON
Professor of Law and legal consultant

ROLF IHRE
Advocate

ARNE SANDEVÄRN
Shipping Consultant and Trainer
Shipbroker and Sale/Purchase Adviser

FOURTH EDITION

LONDON   NEW YORK   HAMBURG   HONG KONG
LLOYD'S OF LONDON PRESS LTD
1995

Lloyd's of London Press Ltd.
Legal & Business Publishing Division
27 Swinton Street
London WC1X 9NW

USA AND CANADA
Lloyd's of London Press Ltd.
Suite 308, 611 Broadway
New York, NY 10012, USA

GERMANY
Lloyd's of London Press GmbH
59 Ehrenbergstrasse
2000 Hamburg 50
Germany

SOUTH EAST ASIA
Lloyd's of London Press (Far East) Ltd.
Room 1101, Hollywood Centre
233 Hollywood Road
Hong Kong

© Liber Hermods, Malmö, Sweden 1980, 1984, 1990, 1995
First English edition 1980
Second edition 1984
Third edition 1990
Fourth edition 1995

British Library Cataloguing in Publication Data
A catalogue record for
this book is available from
the British Library

ISBN 1-85044-971-6

Text set in 10 on 12pt Times by
The Eastern Press Limited
Reading, Berkshire
Printed in Great Britain by
WBC Ltd., Bridgend, Mid-Glamorgan

PREFACE

This book was originally based upon a project launched by the Swedish Shipowners' Association in conjunction with Liber Hermods, a Swedish publisher. The volume (called in Swedish *Befraktning*) was intended as a basic textbook for persons working in shipping (brokers, exporters, agents, shipowners, sea and land personnel). The first edition of the English version was rather different from the Swedish basic book.

This fourth edition has been largely updated and rewritten in certain parts, several adjustments have been made to adapt it to the occurrences of the last few years. We have received a number of letters giving us new ideas, and we have had the opportunity to discuss with several persons different problems which have arisen. We thank all those who have shared with us their experience in the field and will appreciate it if readers will continue to do so and let us know if there are parts which are superfluous, incorrect, too superficial, etc. Please send all such information to Lloyd's of London Press Ltd., or directly to the authors at the following address: Lars Gorton, Institute of Business Law, Stockholm School of Economics, Box 6501 S-11383, Stockholm, Sweden.

We feel that it is necessary to emphasize that this book is a basic textbook which does not contain any legally sophisticated information on interpretation of clauses. From the third edition we have introduced some short case notes which are intended to illustrate certain principles. Our cases have been mainly selected from English and American case law. The intention is that the reader should be given a general idea of what chartering is about from a practical economic-administrative and, to some extent, legal point of view. On the subjects of the sale/purchase of ships and ships' financing there are excellent modern textbooks available, so we have restricted ourselves here to examining only some of the practical day-to-day matters, and especially those which are related to chartering work. If more illustrative cases are required in a future edition we shall gladly introduce such. Also, if there are topics which need more elaboration, we shall do our best to achieve that.

LARS GORTON, ROLF IHRE, ARNE SANDEVÄRN

INTRODUCTION

The shipping company has undergone a gradual structural change. In earlier days a shipping company was involved in all operations relating to a vessel: owning, manning, technical operation and commercial operation. A number of circumstances have led up to a division of functions: the *owning* function (including financing); the *management* function (manning, technical super-vision, spares, bunkers, etc.), and sometimes, the *operational* function (daily routines concerning the vessel); and the *commercial* function (mainly the employment of the vessel). These functions are normally connected with particular documentation and, nowadays, the functions are often divided between different companies, frequently in different countries.

Often a shipowner is established in one country, where for example the financing matters are handled, but owns or controls subsidiaries in various countries each with their own function. It is likely the fleet will be owned through single-vessel companies.

Shipowners co-operate through different types of joint ventures known as *shipping pools*. By this means certain resources, such as manning, technical development or marketing, can be pooled. Further savings are made if the activities are channelled through a jointly-owned company situated in a tax haven. In liner shipping a particular type of cartel has developed known as *liner conferences* during the hundred-year period.

It should be mentioned that both the US and the European Union has legislation prohibiting certain types of co-operation agreements, and to some extent also shipping activities may be embraced by such rules.

The activities of a shipping company normally start with a shipbuilding contract (or memorandum of agreement (MOA) for the purchase of a second-hand vessel). The documentation for the financing of a ship is routinely extensive and comprises various documents, particularly in respect of financial security, such as the ship mortgage. Upon delivery of the vessel a bill of sale will be handed over from the seller to the buyer. The management function is documented in a *management agreement* between the owner and the manager spelling out the manager's duties. A particular operations agreement may be concluded between the owner and the operator. Commercial activities may be carried out by a broker normally working in close co-operation with the owner but on an *ad hoc* basis and without particular authority to bind the owner. Sometimes a particular chartering agreement may give a particular organization authority to employ the vessel for the owner and the chartering will then be performed by this organization for the owner.

Shipping is an international business and a person dealing with chartering has to work with the conditions prevailing day by day in the international freight market. A large number of customs and rules of the trade have been established through the years all over the world, and strict business ethics have developed which should be observed in the professional shipping business.

Chartering work is essentially a form of exchange of information. It is really one of the trades where the right information at the right moment is essential to be successful. Everyone involved in chartering acts, to a large extent, as a collector, judge and distributor of information. A great deal of the flow of information consists of, e.g., notes on fixtures all over the world. "Making a fixture" means that the parties interested in a specific sea transport, through negotiations, reach a mutual agreement on all details in a charter.

The parties involved in a charter deal are, on the one hand, someone who owns or operates a ship (owner, time chartered owner or disponent owner), and, on the other hand, someone who requires a sea transport to be carried out (normally but far from always the cargo owner—in a charter-party the counterpart of the shipowner is called the charterer). Both parties normally negotiate through the intermediary of representatives called shipbrokers or booking agents. The owner of the cargo (often the shipper or the consignee) is frequently also the charterer.

The document drawn up after conclusion of the negotiations is called a charter-party (C/P), or if booking of general cargoes is concerned, a booking note (B/N). In most cases the brokers representing the charterers draw up the original documents, which are often signed by the respective brokers on behalf of the parties (sometimes only with the name of the brokers "As Agents only"). Subsequently, upon the receipt of goods or their loading onto the vessel, a *bill of lading* is normally issued by or on behalf of the carrier.

Chartering negotiations are carried out day and night and nearly always under pressure of time. Frequently it does not take more than a day from the time a shipping order has been placed on the market until a fixture has been confirmed. The negotiations are normally conducted over telephone, telex and telefax.

In practice and by law all agreements, whether given in writing or by word of mouth, are with certain exceptions of equal value. As early as the beginning of the century the expression "our word is our bond" was coined among those dealing with professional chartering in London. For the sake of evidence, however, it goes without saying that it is appropriate to have the agreements drawn up in writing.

CONTENTS

CHAPTER 11. COMMON CLAUSES AND CONCEPTS   150

CHAPTER 12. THE VOYAGE CHARTER-PARTY   178

LIST OF ILLUSTRATIONS

BIBLIOGRAPHY

Books

Alderton, *Sea Transport*
Branch, *Economics of Shipping Practice and Management*
Carver's *Carriage by Sea*
Cooke *et al.*, *Voyage charters* (1993)*
Fairplay, *World Shipping Directory*
Gilmore & Black, *The Law of Admiralty*
Gorton, Ihre, *Contracts of Affreightment and Hybrid Contracts* (2nd edition, 1990)*
Gram on Chartering Documents (2nd edition by S. Bonnick, M.C.I.T., 1988)*
Gray, *Futures and Options for Shipping* (1987)*
Hazelwood, *P & I Clubs—Law and Practice* (1989)*
Hill, *Maritime Law* (3rd edition, 1989)*
Hill, Robertson and Hazelwood, *An Introduction to P & I* (1989)*
Lopez, *Bes' Chartering and Shipping Terms*
Mitchellhill, *Bills of Lading, Law and Practice*
Packard, *Sale and Purchase*
Packard, *Sea Trading I–III*
Powers, *A Practical Guide to Bills of Lading*
Scrutton on Charter-parties and Bills of Lading
Schofield, *Laytime and Demurrage* (1986)*
Spencer, *Spencer on Ships*
Stopford, *Maritime Economics*
Summerskill, *Laytime*
Tetley, *Marine Cargo Claims*
Tiberg, *The Law of Demurrage*
Veldhuizen, *Freight Futures—Targeting the 90s* (1988)*
Wilford, Coghlin and Kimball, *Time Charters* (3rd edition, 1989)*
Wramfelt, *The Shipbrokers' Register*

Newspapers/magazines, periodicals and reports giving information about the freight market, legal decisions, arbitration awards, insurance and legal matters

American Maritime Cases
BIMCO publications
Droit Maritime Français
European Transport Law
Fairplay International Shipping Weekly

Journal of Maritime Law and Commerce
*Lloyd's Law Reports**
Lloyd's List (daily)*
*Lloyd's Maritime and Commercial Law Quarterly**
*Lloyd's Maritime Law Newsletter**
Seatrade (monthly)
The Journal of Business Law
Market reports and statistics supplied by international shipbroking firms, like I.A.
Clarkson, Eggar Forrester, Fearnleys, Galbraiths, Simpson Spence & Young.

  * Published by Lloyd's of London Press Ltd.

CHAPTER 1

THE FREIGHT MARKET

The freight market is not a uniform market where the trend is entirely up or down. It consists rather of a number of different part markets that are not necessarily dependent on each other but can often develop very differently. The freight market does not have a homogeneous connection with a specific geographical area but rather with ships that can carry similar types of cargoes.

The current trend or state of the market is determined by the balance between the supply and demand of shipping services of various kinds. A measure of the state of the market is the freight level which a certain type of vessel can obtain in various standard trades. The freight market is, of course, dependent on the state of the world trade market but is sometimes strongly influenced by circumstances like war, widespread strikes, bad harvests, ice-bound waters, etc. Another important factor which affects the freight market is the granting of government subsidies to shipyards. It goes without saying that there is an interrelation between the newbuilding market, the second-hand tonnage market and the freight level, although these are not synchronized in detail. This also means that, like newbuilding, scrapping also affects the freight market.

Contact between the different freight markets may be more or less extensive. This depends on the type and size of ships, the commodities involved, and to a certain extent on the distance of transportation. Each freight market has, however, different interested parties and has thus often separate networks of information and information channels.

The world fleet of merchant ships consists of some 35,000–40,000 vessels, with a total tonnage of about 600–650 million tons deadweight. About half of this total tonnage comprises ships of under 10,000 tons d.w. Tankers represent only about 8,000 units, but account for about half the total tonnage. Disregarding some 2,000 vessels employed in other markets, the number of ocean-going ships in the typical dry cargo market is still large—roughly 14,000 to 15,000 units.

A basic division into principal freight markets may be made as follows:
—the dry cargo market
—the tanker market

1

—the reefer market
—the car carrier market
—the passenger market.

THE DRY CARGO MARKET

With respect to types of trade as well as types of ships the dry cargo market is the most diversified. Some parts of this market may at times show a market picture which is quite different from the dry cargo market in general.

What are common to the various sectors are information centres and information channels. To be able to consider alternative employment for the ships, to judge newbuilding requirements, to develop new types of vessels, to attempt solutions to transportation problems and to seek new trading opportunities, the dry cargo owners must follow what is happening within the dry cargo market as a whole and what happens from day to day in important shipping centres like London, Oslo, New York, Tokyo and Hamburg. This is done through specialized shipbrokers as well as through direct contacts between owners and charterers. The charterers, also, have to follow what is taking place within the whole dry cargo area to be able to obtain optimum solutions to their transportation problems.

The dry cargo market may be subdivided into the following sectors:
—bulker
—'tweendecker
—container
—ro/ro
—liner
—small ships
—special.

The bulk and 'tweendecker market

The vessels operating in this market vary greatly in size—from about 10,000 tons d.w. up to 170,000 tons and more. Although a division into size-class cannot be very distinct, there are certain differences which are recognized in day-to-day market discussions. A standard type 'tweendecker means now generally a vessel of 17,000–23,000 tons with her own gear of derricks and/or cranes and with one 'tweendeck throughout. In bulk carriers there is a diminishing class of smaller size vessels, of about 16,000–20,000 tons, very often employed in the logs section of the timber trade (log carriers). These ships have their own gear like the big and very important group of bulk carriers within the 20,000–40,000-tons bracket, which are referred to as "handysize bulkers".

During the past few years a new class of bulk carrier has emerged and established a position in the market. These ships can best be described as enlarged handysize vessels of about 40,000–50,000 tons, so-called "handy-max" mostly built with good gear and sophisticated hatch arrangements.

In the next big group of bulkers, taking a step up in size, we find the so-called "Panamax bulkers", which means vessels representing the largest measurements allowed in length, beam and draught for passage through the Panama Canal in loaded condition. The deadweight range is about 50,000–80,000 tons with a concentration within the 68,000–73,000-tons bracket. These ships are mostly gearless and are busy in the main grain, coal and ore trades.

The important size-class of bigger ore and coal carriers, in sizes from 80,000 tons and upwards, are frequently referred to as "Cape-size" vessels. In the daily communication brokers sometimes use a subdivision of this class, like "handycape" 80,000–120,000, "cape" 120,000–170,000 and "large cape" over 170,000 d.w. and reserving VLO or VLOO for sizes above 200,000 tons.

Within the bulk sector one has to follow the variations in supply of the important bulk cargoes like coal, grain, ores and concentrates, scrap, steel, cement, phosphates and fertilizers.

Owners of specially equipped vessels also have to keep in touch with the market for the shipment of, for example, lumber, woodchips and cars. Modern bulk carriers, with technically sophisticated equipment, can also be used for the transportation of unitized cargoes of various kinds, like paper and pulp and also for containers, etc. All ships able to carry these commodities are competitors within the same market sector. This means that when making voyage calculations one has to calculate on all the various cargo combinations or chartering alternatives and set the freight or daily hire at a level with the current market conditions within the entire market sector in question.

Ships fitted with specialized equipment or designed for a particular area have to look to their own specific section of the market in order to charge the extra rate on top of the current freight rate which is required to pay off investments in equipment and construction. Examples of these are vessels equipped with their own grabs for discharge of bulk commodities ("self-dischargers"), vessels specially constructed with the measurements and fittings required for passage through the St Lawrence Seaway during the season ("Lakes traders" or "Lakes-fitted vessels") and vessels built to "ice-class", which are suitable for trading into the Baltic or to Canada during winter conditions.

Even the 'tweendeckers carry bulk cargoes, but the number of such vessels in the bulker trade diminishes continuously in favour of genuine bulk carriers. The most important employment possibilities for 'tweendeckers are, on the one hand, shipments of all kinds of bagged commodities, for example sugar, rice, cement and fertilizers, and, on the other hand, employments as supplementary or "extra" vessels for the regular lines. This latter possibility for employment of the older conventionally built 'tweendeckers, of 12,000–

17,000 d.w. sizes, has actually diminished rapidly during the past years, as most liner trades are now fully containerized.

The cargoes not suitable for containerization or otherwise left over by the regular lines, as well as the lines' continued requirement of "extra" ships for trip or short period, have become an interesting market for the modern sophisticated handysize bulkers often referred to as "multi-purpose" vessels, and for the standardized types of modern 'tweens in the 17,000–25,000 tons sizes.

The market variations for bulkers and 'tweendeckers follow each other to a great extent. Both groups of ships also normally use the same brokers, although the individual shipbroker is often a specialist within each sector.

The container market

In the 1960s a widespread opinion prevailed that containerships of the lo/lo type (Lift on/Lift off) would totally knock out the conventional liners from the important trades. This did not occur and, instead, there developed pure container trades parallel to conventional liner traffic or rather to a traffic of semi-liner character employing modern standard-type 'tweendeckers as well as sophisticated handysize bulkers.

The container ship has long established its place, especially in traffic plying between highly industrialized areas with a technically advanced inland transportation system in both the exporting and the importing areas. This traffic requires large investment in specially equipped vessels, port installations and terminal equipment. Container ships are often operated by international joint venture organizations and pools, partly because of the high investment costs involved and also for multi-national marketing purposes but nowadays there seems to be a development where these pools disintegrate.

The time charter market (T/C market) for container ships has proved to be the market sector which often is the first to react to a change in the state of the world trade market and this is probably so because these ships are employed in the worldwide movement of finished high-technology products. The container ships are subject to competition from modern 'tweendeckers of standard type as those vessels, to some extent, can also carry containers. Competition is also felt from bulk carriers constructed to be suitable for container handling.

The market for container ships is limited and there is only a small number of brokers who are specialized in the chartering of such vessels.

The ro/ro market

For the ro/ro ships (roll on/roll off) the development has been very special during the past two decades. From the beginning, these ships were typical short trade carriers in trades between highly industrialized countries. Several circumstances have, however, caused these vessels to participate as a natural part of ocean traffic.

During the 1970s the movement overseas of industrial products, machinery, vehicles and building material increased considerably, especially from Europe and the United States to the Middle East countries, as well as to West Africa from Europe. The ports in the importing countries had a low capacity at the time and therefore ran into serious congestion caused by too many vessel arrivals and the inability to cope with the increasing quantity of cargo. At the same instance the time had become ripe for the liner companies trading to these areas with conventional general cargo ships to renew their fleets.

One solution to these problems was the ocean-going ro/ro ship, a type of ship which can carry all sorts of commodities placed on wheeled platforms or flats that may be handled by the use of fork-lift trucks and, of course, containers and trailers. Thus we are talking about a type of vessel which does not require any port installation other than a stretch of quay with a length equal to the width of the ship, where the ramp can be lowered for rolling on or off the cargo units. The handling is very fast and a vessel may be totally emptied of cargo within a few hours.

In the mid 1970s this led to the development of a completely new market with orders being placed on a world-wide basis so there are also brokers who since then specialize and concentrate their activities on ro/ro chartering. With the easing of the congestion problems previously mentioned (in some cases congestion has disappeared altogether) ro/ro ships are encountering competition from modern 'tweendecker and bulker vessels as well as from the pure containerships. The ocean-going ro/ro vessel has, however, clearly proved its worth and will provide competition both in the established and the new markets.

The liner market

Liner traffic is a firmly controlled activity where remuneration is geared more to the long term rather than to single voyages. The freight rates in the tariff are by definition not subject to the large variations that characterize the so-called open market. Nevertheless, liner traffic is susceptible to market variations, depending on availability of cargo and load factors on each voyage.

$$\text{Load factor} = \frac{\text{Loaded cubic}}{\text{Available cubic}} \times 100(\%)$$

The load factor indicates how much of the available cubic capacity is made use of.

There is an intermittent need for time-chartered tonnage, which will be either expensive or cheap depending on the supply of ships and employment terms, especially the point of redelivery. When the market is low such extra vessels may be trip-chartered at a low daily hire, but the availability of cargo for the scheduled sailing, which has to be performed anyway, may not be very good. During such market conditions the competition from so-called outsiders often gets stronger, as these may enter a liner trade for only a number of trips, accepting freight rates that are lower than the liner tariff rates just to keep the ships going until the open market conditions improve again.

Liner shipping is often carried out within a liner conference, which is a type of cartel for a particular market, see further below, page 79.

Liner vessels get the larger share of their cargo through contracted liner agents who mostly do not work as shipbrokers in the dry cargo market. A liner company may also book basic part cargoes and interesting special commodities in order just to fill empty space. This is often done on charter-party terms through broker connections in the open market. Imbalance in cargo volumes between the outward and homeward legs of a round voyage often makes the lines competitors with the 'tweendecker tonnage working the open market from the same areas.

Liner operators are usually more involved than other shipowners in the improvement of cargo handling techniques and they often participate actively in developing those ports at which they call regularly.

The small ship market

As mentioned previously there is a large number of vessels of 10,000 tons and under. Most of this tonnage is engaged in short-sea and coastal trading, and this market has its own information system and channels of communication which function independently, the market variations not necessarily coinciding with those of the market affecting the ocean-going tonnage. Coastal shipping is often particularly reserved for vessels of the coastal state. Many shipping companies carry on independent trading with smaller-sized vessels, but the trend is now to employ small single and 'tweendeckers in some sort of regularly scheduled feeder traffic. The result is that these vessels find themselves in competition with other carriers in the short-sea trade, including larger ships carrying part-cargoes as well as road and rail traffic.

One may find typical feeder companies looking for employment in the open market depending on the casual need. It is, however, also common for ocean liner companies or a forwarding agent or a charterer shipper who trades with his own products to operate feeder ships as a part of his transport scheme.

Owners and operators of coasters and feeder vessels are frequently working together and are pooling their fleets and administrative resources in order to undertake contracting and to optimize scheduling, employment distribution and earnings.

Some owners specialize in tailoring their ships and operation for so-called industrial shipping, in close co-operation over a longer period of time with a big exporter/importer or industry to provide an integrated link in the industry's overall logistics system.

Special markets

In addition to the above-mentioned types of vessels there are quite a number of special ships which meet various special needs. Among such vessels the following can be mentioned:

Heavy-lift carriers

Some companies have specialized in heavy-lift cargoes and technically complicated transports where the movement between quay and ship is the most difficult part of the operation. For such purposes the vessels must be built with the special demands on stability and constructional strength in mind.

Barges and pontoons

These carriers are also used for the transport of heavy material, for example built-up drilling rigs, but they are also used as floating quays, as feeders in short-sea traffic and as discharging platforms between an ocean-going ship and the quay.

Tugs

The demand for towing vessels has increased with the increased use of barges and pontoons. At the same time, towing work for the merchant fleet is becoming more frequently demanded.

Barge carriers, etc.

In this context the system with barge carrying ships must also be mentioned, for example the LASH system (Lighter Aboard Ship). This method is based on cargo being loaded into barges which are towed up to and loaded into an ocean-going vessel. At the port of destination the barges are again launched and towed, for example up a river, to the final place of reception. A combination of logistics is the tug-barge system where a detachable pushing tug unit is used as an engine for a number of "cargo-hold" units.

THE TANKER MARKET

One characteristic of the tanker market has been the dominating position held by a comparatively small number of big charterers: the large oil companies. The number of smaller private firms (often known as "traders") and State organizations engaged in the chartering of tankers has increased considerably during the last 10 or 15 years. The small number of loading areas and the off-shore loading terminals is also typical of the tanker market. From the early 1990s we have also seen increasing national and international concern over tanker safety and environmental aspects, resulting in new rules and conditions for tanker owners (notably by IMO and by the USA's OPA 90) which long-term will affect the market and the marketing of tankers, especially older vessels.

Tankers—especially those carrying crude oil—practically never get any return cargoes and are therefore normally forced to proceed in ballast over an ocean-route to a loading area. Many shipowners prefer to place their ships on time charter for a long period, but there is also an important spot market. It is typical that the volume of spot business becomes comparatively larger during a low-market period.

Since the tanker market back in the 1950s divided into one "crude" or "dirty" sector and one "product" sector there was a continuous trend towards increasingly larger tankers, a development which levelled out during the late 1970s. The largest ones are usually called VLCC and ULCC (Very Large Crude Carriers, in sizes of about 200,000–300,000 d.w. tons and Ultra Large Crude Carriers, of more than 300,000 tons) which are used for the transport of crude oil. The classes of smaller and moderate sizes (Panamax of 55,000–70,000 tons, Aframax of 70,000–100,000 tons and Suezmax of 100,000–150,000 tons) may be used for either "dirty" or product cargoes depending on the ship's age and status of cleanness. The smaller coaster tankers are used to carry refined products. Since the late 1970s there has been an increase in demand for handysize tankers within the 30,000–100,000 tons range and lately also for sizes up to Suezmax. Since the late 1980s there have been a few orders for VLCC tankers.

The international regulations for tanker ship safety have become much stricter and oil pollution in any form is not acceptable—all these rules and regulations are followed by the majority of tanker shipowners competing for charters. Also, from a technical point of view, the sea transport of oil is carried out in virtually the same way all over the world. Tanker charterers, tanker owners and tanker brokers are also working with elaborate and standardized documents, the design of which has been influenced by the oil companies over the years and which may be used on, more or less, a take-it-or-leave-it basis. The negotiations for a tanker charter are therefore less complicated than, for example, negotiations in dry cargo chartering and are normally carried out within a very short space of time.

The problems encountered in tanker chartering are, however, even greater than those found in other forms of chartering. The art is to hit the right time for the fixture at a freight level well in tune with the prevailing market. The daily fluctuations, as well as the periodical changes, normally occur very rapidly and with strong deflections which may cause the situation to change radically from one hour to the next. Due to the comparatively limited number of parties involved in the tanker market every occurrence has a great effect, which sometimes means that one single fixture may affect the total state of the market for the day. Day-to-day communication between the parties involved is frequently done with the aid of computers.

Within the tanker market there are also special carriers, for example solvent and parcel tankers for liquid chemicals of various kinds. These ships can often carry a great number of such chemical products of different kinds at the same time. The size of this type of vessel about equals that of the product tanker. There are also small chemical tankers for coastal trading. A solvent tanker may also be used for the carriage of refined petroleum products of various kinds. The gas tankers form a special class and the vessels are called LPG (Liquefied Petroleum Gas) and LNG (Liquefied Natural Gas) tankers in accordance with the product the ships are constructed to carry.

Beside the combination carriers (see below) the conventional tankers may compete in the dry cargo market, for example for the transportation of grain.

A field which is related to the tanker market is the *Offshore sector*, concerned with exploration and exploitation of oil in the open sea with more or less permanently anchored drilling vessels and drilling rigs. During the last decade a special freight market has developed for such "ships" and for their offshore servants, the supply ships.

The activity on the offshore market varies and consequently so does the market for supply vessels. To some extent these ships can compete for cargoes with smaller tonnage in the short-sea trade and they may also be used for towing work.

THE "COMBOS"

The combination carriers of Ore/Oil type and Ore/Bulk/Oil (OBO) have a special market position, although not always in the way intended originally. The intention was that those ships would perform combined voyages in a trade with, for example, dry bulk cargo in one direction and with tanker cargo for the return leg, thus improving the roundvoyage result by reducing the time in ballast and increasing the earning time. Such an operation requires a high degree of flexibility and skill in owner's management and teamwork of staff, and indeed there are owners and operators specialising in such trading. The great majority of "Combo" owners, however, prefer to use their ships either as pure tankers or as pure bulk carriers, depending on which market is offering the best revenue at the moment. This development was also created by the difficulty in combining freight contracts and also by such practical problems as costs for cleaning the ships' holds between the different commodities. Thus the combination carriers increase the supply of tonnage on the market where they are being worked for the moment and can therefore contribute to weaken an upward trend in freight levels or to strengthen a downward trend. This impact of the tanker on the dry markets—albeit that a relatively small number of ships is concerned (300–350 units)—makes the operators of pure tankers or dry bulk vessels watch carefully to try to predetermine the next move by the Combo-owners.

THE REEFER MARKET

Big scale reefer (refrigerated ship) trading is basically a worldwide operation, but this market is nevertheless very much a closed one. There are only a few owners, operators and reefer brokers who devote themselves to this freight market which employs some 500–600 ocean-going ships. The charterers are often very large organizations, privately owned as well as governmental. In contrast to what is normally the method in dry cargo chartering, a reefer charter is frequently made directly between owners and charterers without the assistance of brokers. Nevertheless, there are many connections and similarities between the reefer and the dry cargo markets.

Reefer ships are employed in contract trading to a large extent, but there is also an important spot market. The operation is strongly influenced by large seasonal variations in the supply of cargoes. The reefer market is, however, also characterized by sudden changes and at the same time the contractual engagements require very strict and careful scheduling.

The loading areas are scattered all over the world but the discharging areas are concentrated mainly in Northern Europe and Japan. Bananas, fish and meat are transported the year round, while citrus and other fruits, vegetables and potatoes are seasonal. The demand for reefer tonnage normally reaches a peak during the first half of each year when the products of the Southern Hemisphere are bound for shipment to Europe.

Reefer trades are practically always one-way routes and generally speaking there is a huge imbalance, not only geographically in the distribution of the loading/discharging areas, but also seasonally with the so-called high season during the first half of a year and a low season during the balance of the year. In addition to this there are weekly and daily variations in demand for transport depending on crop outcome in the various areas. Sudden problems in some supplying areas may cause drastic rerouteing of reefer vessels more or less overnight but at the same time the shipping programmes for the individual routes follow very strict schedules and require perfect timing in arrivals and departures. Of course, reliable technical equipment and great skill in cargo handling and treatment during the sea voyage are also necessary.

Economy is achieved by reducing ballasting to a minimum and by always using a vessel's maximum cargo capacity. In order to reduce the time and costs in port, all the major reefer trades are now based on palletization.

Comparatively large quantities of reefer cargoes, for example meat, are being carried by containerships in reefer-containers, but also by combined reefer-dry cargo ships in liner service or by conventional general cargo liners. When the freight level of the dry cargo market is equivalent to that of the reefer market, the reefer ships may be used in the dry cargo market. It is customary for reefers to carry cars and tractors and, if the freight levels permit, even bagged cargoes, paper, lightweight unitized cargoes, etc., and also containers. The vessels will then compete with the 'tweendeckers and multi-purpose ships operating in the open market.

THE CAR CARRIER MARKET

There are many similarities between the reefer market and the market for car-carrying vessels. The number of vessels employed on a world-wide basis is about 500 to 600. It is a very closed market using very little broker assistance and business is concluded mostly on the basis of long-term contracts between a few operators and exporting companies. The market variations, however, are generally non-seasonal and follow a rhythm of their own with rather big differences—not so much in freight levels but in demand for shipping space. So far the market cycles have been of about two to four years' duration.

The most important trades with fully assembled vehicles are from Japan to the United States and Europe and from Europe to the United States and there is also an inter-European trade covering important volumes. Secondary trades in respect of volumes carried are from Europe and the United States to countries in Africa and the Middle East and Central and South America and from Japan to the same areas, plus Australia.

Most vehicles are medium size passenger cars but lorries, trucks, tractors and buses are also carried. This sector of the market is increasing. In addition and parallel to the trade of fully assembled vehicles there is an increasing volume of car parts, so-called "cars knocked down" (CKD) for assembly in factories in the receiving countries. These cargoes so far have been carried by the lines.

The overseas transportation of vehicles in the big-volume trades is taken care of by very large purpose-built vessels, so-called "pure car carriers" (PCC) and the car carriers especially built to accommodate large vehicles (PVHCC or PCTC), each with a capacity of about 2,000 to 6,000 units. The loading/unloading of a PCC is done by roll on/roll off methods and is extremely fast.

Until the introduction of the first PCCs in the late 1950s and thereafter throughout the 1960s, an important part of the traffic was performed by so-called car-bulkers. These vessels of about 20,000–30,000 tons were conventional bulk carriers fitted with hoistable or folding car decks of a lightweight construction, giving a vessel a car-carrying capacity of some 1,000–2,000 units. The cars were mostly handled by a lift on/lift off method which is slower and more liable to incur damage to the cargo than ro/ro handling. Such vessels could entertain combination contracts by taking normal bulk commodities one way and cars on the return run. Special car-bulkers are no longer purpose-built and all mass transportation of fully built-up vehicles is done by the ro/ro mode in PCCs, ro/ro ships and ferries. One good reason for this being that shippers of cars normally refuse shipment by lo/lo-tonnage when ro/ro is available.

Smaller volumes of cars (from just a few up to about 100–150 per shipment) are taken care of by the lines at liner tariff freights, but for trades where the volumes are increasing up to anything between 200 and 900 units per shipment the charterers will frequently employ reefer tonnage, which, with many 'tweendecks ("multi-deckers"), can provide the deck space required.

THE PASSENGER MARKET

The big passenger ships in transoceanic liner traffic have now, in practice, vanished. Large size tonnage with accommodation only for passengers is now primarily engaged in cruising. Most passenger vessels are operated in short-distance trade with consecutive trips on tight schedules—the so-called ferry traffic. These ships mostly have a good capacity for rolling goods and they are a supplement to the pure cargo ro/ro ships operating in the same trading area.

The market for passenger ships is very much dependent on seasonal variations and the working of those vessels in the open market is often done with the assistance of the brokers specialized in ro/ro chartering and employment is practically always fixed on a time charter basis.

THE SALE AND PURCHASE MARKET

An important part of shipping concerns the sale and purchase of ships. The general freight market and the so-called second-hand market for ships have a considerable mutual influence. It is important to follow the day-to-day level of the second-hand market as well as the state of the freight market for a specific type of vessel.

The owners watch the offers from the shipyards of newbuildings but also the supply of vessels on the second-hand market, as well as the development of scrap prices for old ships. Such details give useful information about the supply of tonnage for a few years ahead and may have a decisive influence on the long range development of the freight market. During a period of low market activity it is especially interesting to observe if the existing tonnage is laid up, is sold for trading under low-cost flags, or is scrapped.

The second-hand market varies largely in conjunction with the freight market for each specific type of ship. Theoretically, an owner would buy ships during a low market period and sell vessels when the freight market rose. Owners, however, tend to do the reverse and there are several reasons for this. Among other things, this has to do with the need during a period of recession to sell in order to strengthen the liquidity position.

CHAPTER 2

THE STATE OF THE MARKET

There is a difference between the liner-bound freight market and the open freight market. The latter market is the market where tonnage is fixed voyage by voyage—the so-called spot market—where the buyers of sea transport find the additional tonnage required to comply with all the occasional increases in demand for transport. The open market also includes a time charter sector and the important sector covering other more long range contractual engagements of various natures.

It has been calculated that about 70% of the volume of goods transported at sea in the world is fixed in the open market. The balance is taken care of by the liner services in their strictly directed and scheduled traffic with controlled freight terms and conditions and freight levels. It is estimated that the spot market volume is about five to 10% of the total open market volume. This sector gets an increasing supply of ships during periods of general economic recession, when there is a low demand for sea transport.

The open market is influenced by the "law" of supply and demand, but it would be an over-simplification to state that the market is generated and directed by this. The variations in freight levels are very large and this is easily seen in the diagram (page 15) showing the tanker market fluctuations during a quarter of a century. The diagram would largely be the same if notations are made for one of the important dry cargo commodities, for example coal. Diagrams for the dry cargo market (page 25) covering a period of about 15 years illustrate how the market conditions follow on the one hand a long-wave system, which tends to coincide—but not always—with diagrams for the world industrial output, and on the other hand a short-wave system, which is irregular, but not entirely, as one can find by inspection that there are yearly seasonal variations. The connection to the world industrial activity is reflected by market rates for the two so-called leading commodities iron ore and coal (raw materials for the steel industry), and seasonal variations are influenced by demand for ships to carry grain, which is the third leading commodity in the dry cargo sector.

An illustration will show how operative forces work in practice in a miniature market. If for a specific loading date within a limited area there are 10 ships open for employment, but there are only nine cargoes offered, then it is very likely that

14

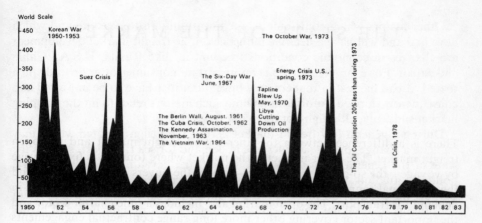

World Scale

Korean War 1950-1953

The October War, 1973

Suez Crisis

The Six-Day War June, 1967

Energy Crisis U.S., spring, 1973

Tapline Blew Up May, 1970

Libya Cutting Down Oil Production

The Berlin Wall, August, 1961
The Cuba Crisis, October, 1962
The Kennedy Assasination, November, 1963
The Vietnam War, 1964

The Oil Consumption 20% less than during 1973

Iran Crisis, 1978

Various events of world-wide importance often have a great influence on freight levels. (Tanker market.)

none of the vessels will obtain a higher freight rate than the lowest rate any one of the respective shipowners is willing to accept. In the reverse situation, where there are 10 cargoes available but only nine ships one can expect every ship which is fixed to obtain better terms than the preceding one.

Factors influencing the general freight situation and the development of the open market are, except for the general state of the world economy, sudden changes in demand for specific commodities, an economic boom within special limited market areas, state of war, closure of important routes, crop failure, extreme congestion in important ports, oversupply of specific types of ships, unusually late or early closure of icebound waters, etc.

It is practically impossible to predict with any degree of certainty future developments in the freight market. In general, periods of low freight market conditions are substantially longer than periods when high freight rates can be obtained. There is really no such thing as a "normal" market level and it would be more accurate to say that the freight market constantly oscillates between extremes. Certain factors, for example political involvement in the shipping field, sometimes make it possible for those concerned in the main bulk trades to anticipate a reduction in the open market's share of the total transport volume to the advantage of enclosed, strictly controlled, transportation systems.

There are always, even during periods of general economic recessions, areas where there is a more or less temporarily high demand for tonnage. In 1977, for instance, there was a great excess of tonnage in the dry cargo and tanker markets. A tendency to improvement in the state of the dry cargo market was counteracted, for example, by continuing deliveries of bulk carriers from the shipyards. At the same time, however, there was a strong demand for ocean-going ro/ro vessels and reefer ships, which thus obtained very high time charter rates.

Other factors which contribute to the uncertainty in forecasting and which have had and will have a decisive influence on the freight market development are changes in economic conditions in countries like Russia, U.S.A., China and Japan. For example, Russia is an important consumer of grain and when there is a bad harvest in that country huge quantities have to be imported and consequently shipped. Information about such matters tends to hit the shipping market suddenly, although not quite unexpectedly.

During a general low freight market period every sign is noted which may indicate a change towards an increase in demand for sea transport, such as the state of the general economic world market, the development of the general political situation, the market trends within special sectors, for example steel output, the production of cars and the outcome of the harvest in important consuming areas. When there seem to be small but firm indications of higher freight rates shown simultaneously by most important market indicators, an exception is created which in the beginning is weak but which grows stronger and stronger among the parties in the shipping business. It is in the interests of charterers and shippers to try to belittle such signs of forthcoming changes, while shipowners then take an attitude of wait and see. If it becomes evident that there is substance in these market trends, charterers get more and more active in the time charter markets trying to secure long term contractual engagements at low freight levels. Thereby the supply of tonnage on the spot market will decrease and the freight levels generally start to rise slowly.

If there arises a sudden increase in demand for tonnage in a special trade, as for instance the grain trade between the U.S. or Canada and Russia, a scarcity of tonnage will occur in other areas and in other trades dependent on the same types and sizes of ships. The rising trend in freight levels will then become further accentuated. At this moment certain psychological factors will start to contribute to the development of the market. Charterers, in fear of running into a situation of acute scarcity of tonnage, will try to conclude their shipping arrangements as soon as possible. Owners can ask for increasingly higher freight rates and if, in addition, a sudden political crisis arises, then those interested in the shipping market may find themselves in a real freight boom.

A consequence of such a development is often that the owners of older vessels which have been laid up during the low market period will start trading their ships again instead of sending them to the scrapyards. Little by little owners and charterers will now start realizing that they can dispose of transport capacity which is too big and which is at the same time too expensive. They will now start to offer part of the previously time chartered tonnage for employment on the spot market or for time charter engagements. Another factor which will affect the market with a delay of some two or three years is that a number of owners will now order newbuildings, which if they have bad luck, will be delivered during the next period of a low freight market thus perhaps contributing to a further deterioration in the prevailing level of the market.

A recession in the shipping market is now predictable although its precise timing may not be possible. Owners will show an increasing interest in fixing their ships for long term engagements and freight levels will move downwards. Charterers will hold out to obtain even lower freight levels and as suddenly as the freights start to rise to very high levels, the market will now drop.

CHAPTER 3

SHIPOWNING CONDITIONS AND MARKET ACTIVITIES

Besides keeping themselves well informed at all times, a great deal of flexibility is required from companies and organizations engaged in shipping. Apart from the daily fluctuations in freight levels and other trading conditions depending on the supply-demand situation, there is a constant development towards new techniques in shipbuilding and propulsion, cargo handling and terminal operation. Due to the ever-changing conditions for international commerce the overseas trading patterns are changing and new cargoes and loading-discharging areas will be developed—sometimes this will quite drastically diminish the importance of previously very active ports and cargo movements. Such changes will occur over periods of a few years or maybe several times during a vessel's technical lifespan of 15 to 20 years. Irrespective of the freight market being very active or depressed there are seasonal changes in volumes to be shipped and there are also variations in quantities of certain important commodities being bought or sold. So the operators of fleets of vessels have to gear themselves to be able to take advantage of new opportunities simply to survive and stay on in the business of shipping.

In order to maintain maximum flexibility on both a daily and a long-term basis—and thereby stay safe and sound economically—owners have to renew their fleets at intervals. They have to operate the number, types and sizes of vessels necessary to meet the minimum requirements of their contract engagements. They have to hire extra tonnage and to reschedule the fleet whenever their shippers or charterers require—or because of other temporary or sudden changes in demand for shipping space in the market sectors where the owner participates or intends to enter. This means that any owner who runs a fleet of ships will operate owned vessels as a more or less permanent base, plus an additional quantity of time-chartered tonnage to suit the market requirements over a period of time. He will also operate supplementary tonnage hired on a spot basis to meet temporary increases in cargo offerings and to fill unexpected gaps in liner or contract schedules. Obviously the shipowning side is involved in buying and selling activity which proceeds parallel to the chartering side of shipping.

The way in which a shipowner operates the vessels under his control will vary according to trading intentions, economy, current market conditions

18

and to an increasing extent according to political regulations enforced by governments. This description of the shipowner's world will enable us to list the activities going on in the day-to-day work on the shipping market as initiated by owners and operators:

—Securing employment for owned vessels from the open market by fixing full or part-cargoes on either a voyage-by-voyage basis or by long range contract engagements.

—Securing bookings of so-called parcels—mostly smaller consignments of various commodities—with a view to filling vessels employed in a liner service with fixed calls for loading and discharging and following a timetable with a pre-fixed and advertised geographical rotation ("itinerary").

—Time-chartering tonnage for "period" (anything from three months to five years or even longer) to supplement the owned fleet of vessels to match the expected market requirements, the contract commitments and the standards of a liner service engagement and generally to obtain maximum efficiency and economy over a period of time.

—Time-chartering tonnage on a voyage-by-voyage basis ("trip charter") or for short periods to meet sudden market developments and temporary increases in volumes to be shipped under a contract or liner engagement.

—To let ("time charter out") owned or time-chartered tonnage to other owners or operators for longer or shorter periods against a fixed daily hire, for those parties to operate the vessels in the open market or in the liner trades.

—Ordering newbuildings or buying second-hand tonnage and selling vessels to other owners or scrapping in accordance with the company's replacement programme and in line with current market developments and conditions.

CHAPTER 4

INFORMATION CHANNELS

INFORMATION NETWORK AND EXCHANGE

Those who are engaged in chartering are important consumers and distributors of information. The exchange of information is a basic prerequisite for chartering and shipping departments, brokers, and agents in order that they get to know the prevailing supply and demand of sea transport services. The continuous flow of information and the treatment and evaluation of the material is necessary for judgement of the situation and the trends of the freight markets. The various means of information exchange and sources of information will be described in detail below.

Order

This is the common denominator for every request for transportation of a specific cargo from one port to another. An order may also concern a requirement from an owner or a shipper or cargo to time charter a ship for short or long duration. Between charterers and their brokers and between owners and their brokers and between the firms of brokers such orders are circulated one by one or by lists covering a number of orders. The party requesting chartering service is said to "place an order on the market" and will then await reactions from the tonnage that may be interested in the order.

OPEN A/C NEW ZEALAND CHARTERERS WITH FOLLOWING CONTRACT:

LYTTLETON/VANCOUVER

1 MILLION TONS P.A.
BULK LIMESTONE
MONTHLY SHIPMENTS COMMENCING JUNE
FIRM INDICATIONS FIOT

20

2000/5000
GENCON C/P
3.75 PCT PASTUS

REQUIRE GEARED TONNAGE

ORDER: *A charterer from New Zealand seeks owners for a contract of affreightment covering one million tons of limestone.*

OUR DIRECT CHRTRS SAGUENAY/ALCAN OPEN FOR T/D 350.000 BALE WITH MIN 25 T H/L DEL HAMBURG 15/16 APRIL FOR TRIP TO WESTINDIES

ORDER: *Saguenay/Alcan seeks a 'tweendecker for a voyage from Hamburg to the West Indies.*

13:58	SEATWN	LEAVING OFFICE NOW STEVE AVAIL ON MOB - G NGT
14:01	CLTNK	TORMSO SPIRIT AUGUST SPOT PLS PROPOSE
14:03	MJL	WE EXPECT EXXON LATER FOR VL AG/OPTS
14:04	FERRO	ISAB COVERED BURAK M ON P.T.
14:07	BRAVO	WE COVERED ISAB - THANKS SUPPORT
14:10	GALTNK	PLS LOOK AT OUR PAGES FOR BP TONNAGE POS
14:11	POTEN	EXXON VLCC AG/OPTS 20-22
14:15	DIETZ	EXXON VLCC AG/OPTIONS MAY 20-22
14:15	MJL	EXXON NOW OFFICIAL AG/USG 20-22 MAY PLS OFF
14:16	WEBER	EXXON VLCC AG/STATES 20-22
14:17	MJL	EXXON IS 1,5 AHEAVY AND BAL A.LIGHT
14:18	MJL	EXXON INTENTION DISCHPOR LOOP
14:20	DIETZ	WE HAVE OFFERS FOR EXXON FOR INFO CALL

ORDER: *Tanker orders and information as it would come out in the Reuter system one early afternoon for alert subscribers to react upon.*

COOK OPEN FIRM 20/22000 HSS GULF/EC MEXICO
MAR 24/2 APRIL 6.75 FIO 5/1000
WHAT CAN U OFFER

ORDER: *Cook asking for offers on a grain cargo from U.S. Gulf to Mexico.*

ACCT COBELFRET OPEN FOR FOLL T/C TRIP

25/30.000 TONNER GRD/GLESS
DELY PERU OR W.C. CENTRAL AMERICA PPT/20
MARCH CANCLNG
TRIP REDEL DOP NCSA
MAX LOA600/MAX BEAM 78'
MAX DIST WL/TOP HC 26'
NYPE 2,5 ADDRESS PASTUS

ORDER: *Cobelfret open for time chartering of a vessel with certain restrictions regarding type and size.*

Positions

This means, information mentioning where and when vessels are expected to become available (open) for new employment is circulated by owners and operators as a guide to brokers and charterers. The intention is that these position lists will generate suggestions for employment of the ships mentioned.

HAVE INTERESTED UPTO 24 MOS T/C PERIOD:
THERMAICOS GULF—DEL EX YARD 6/87
T/D, FLUSH TWEENS ABT 16000 MT DW ON 8.90 M ABT 770.000
CUFT GR IN HOLDS+ABT 40000 CUFT IN BLEEDING UPPER
SIDE TANKS, 4 HO/HA (12, 16, 17.60, 16 ALL BY 11.20 M)—DERR
8×15 TS UP 5 TONS 1×60 TS (SERVING HOLDS 3,4) ABT
15 KNTS ON ABT 25 TS FO+1.5 DO GRAIN FITTED/SELF
TRIMMER/COTTON FITTED/CO2 FITTED/LAKES FITTED

OWS CAN FIX AROUND USDLR 7,500 DELY SOUTH JAPAN
LAYCAN 25 JUNE/20 JULY

PSE PROPOSE+

POSITION: *A newbuilding is looking for employment for her first voyage and a fairly comprehensive description is given of the vessel, supplemented by the owners' "idea" (intended hire level).*

NORDIC WASA
———————— 26.000 T CARGO CAPACITY

OPEN BLSEA END MARCH. WHAT CAN YOU PROPOSE?

POSITION: *An owner informs his brokers when and where a vessel (details about vessel already known to the brokers) will be open next time.*

Market reports

These are circulated by the big shipbroking companies to owners, charterers, other brokers and agents, giving a concentrated picture of the prevailing situation for the day or the week. By comparing the conclusions made in the various reports with one's own judgement of the situation it is possible to form a fairly accurate picture of the state of the market in the sectors of particular interest. A comprehensive market report (see page 116ff.) contains comments on (primarily) the largest markets, i.e. dry cargo and tanker, but also, for example on the sale and purchase of ships. Often the market development within the different areas is commented on separately, for example for the Atlantic or the Pacific, or for different commodities, for example grain, coal, ore, etc. Generally the different tonnage sizes are also dealt with separately. The comments are illustrated by examples of recently made representative fixtures.

Freight negotiations

The most important pieces of information are exchanged during current negotiations between the parties involved. In these the parties participate in influencing the state of the market themselves and the information which they gather relating to the business in question is as important as the description of the agreement reached. For a judgement of the state of the market and the influence on the market development this type of information is of equal importance whether a fixture is concluded or not. The various elements of a chartering negotiation, i.e. general discussions, indications, offers and counter offers, etc., will be dealt with more extensively in the chapter covering chartering routines.

General information

Other necessary information concerns costs for the operation and despatch of vessels, for example costs for the handling of certain cargoes in various ports, port dues and charges associated with the ship's call, costs for canal passages, notes about bunker prices, etc. Information about congestion, formation of ice, opening and closing of canals and other important passages, notes on maximum draught allowed in ports, ships' cargo handling equipment and capacity for different commodities, and availability of labour constitute other valuable pieces of information. Various sudden occurrences and general economic circumstances have a decisive effect on the development of the international shipping market.

Information centres

London, New York and Toyko are of primary interest as information centres but also Oslo, Hamburg, Paris and Piraeus play an important role in the distribution of shipping information. Shipowners who operate their ships world-wide are in daily contact also with shipping centres in many other countries.

The Baltic Exchange

This is a unique and very old institution in London for the exchange of shipping information. Brokers and charterers' representatives meet there regularly for a few hours around noon to distribute cargo circulars and to exchange information in confidence. The prevailing state of the market is discussed—formal freight negotiations may take place and fixtures be concluded on "the floor".

The "Baltic" developed a new and important role as an international freight exchange centre when, in 1985, the Baltic International Freight Futures Exchange (BIFFEX) was inaugurated. On this exchange there are two daily sessions for trading freight contracts which are to be performed at some later date (up to two years) against a weighted freight index. This index, the Baltic Freight Index (BFI), reflects the present market and expectations for the market's development in the future. By BIFFEX trading owners, charterers and other parties on the shipping scene, including, of course, speculators, may protect themselves ("hedge") against the risk of and play on the volatility of freight rates and time charter hires. (See page 117.)

BIMCO

BIMCO (The Baltic and International Maritime Council) in Copenhagen is an organization dealing with various matters of interest to international shipping. There is one important department dealing with the design and development of shipping documents. Many of the common printed charter-party forms have in one way or the other been approved by BIMCO. BIMCO may also at any time be asked to provide information on, for example, congestion in a certain port, port dues and charges, port regulations and practice (Rules of the Trade), etc. If somebody in shipping circles has been repeatedly and deliberately violating the rules of the trade or otherwise has been acting improperly he may be officially reported to BIMCO.

Shipping Market Indicators

DRYCARGO – VOYAGE CHARTER RATES

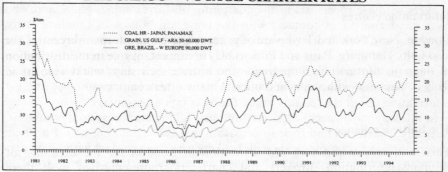

DRYCARGO – TIMECHARTER RATES

LAID UP TONNAGE

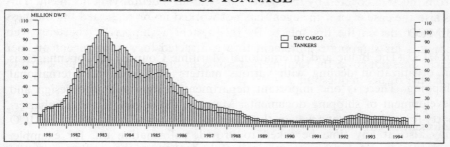

These graphs are good examples of information available to the parties operating in the shipping world. The indicators showing the ups and downs of the dry-cargo market over a period of time are issued monthly by a well-known shipbroking company in London.

Information network

It is of great importance for shipowners, charterers, brokers and agents to establish a network of contacts which catches all interesting opportunities and by which adequate information is quickly transmitted. Different brokers specialize in different markets or market sectors. By communicating with those brokers who are specialists in the chartering of, for example, grain, and who have good and direct contacts with the big grain houses in London, Paris, Hamburg and New York respectively, an owner can keep well abreast of the availability of grain cargoes world-wide. He can also get current information through the brokers about the freight levels that may at any time be interesting to the potential charterer and—which is no less important—he can get information about the freights asked for by competing tonnage.

In this way the owners follow continuously all the market sectors of interest. Basically, charterers find their information in a corresponding way. For them it is important to communicate with brokers who have contact with all owners operating suitable ships and who have an interest in the cargo or trade in question.

What has been said above is valid primarily for tonnage operated in the open market. The information network for liner trading has a somewhat different set-up. The individual owner, the pool or the liner conference maintaining a traffic in a certain trade, have a number of liner agents as part of the service. These agents divide the areas generating cargoes for booking into geographical areas of interest within which the individual agent keeps in contact with the customers, either directly or through sub-agents and/or forwarding agents. The agents and the shipowner normally enter into a formal agreement, by which the agents are guaranteed certain rights and benefits but the agents at the same time agree not to book any cargo or otherwise work for the account of competing lines or outsiders (a so-called exclusivity agreement). Similar agreements are usually made between liner agents and forwarding agents. In principle, the liner owner cannot himself fix his tonnage with cargo from the area covered by the agreement without indemnifying his agent. This is also the case even if the agent has not worked up or suggested the business or the order in the first place. By this system a shipper or charterer who presents his shipping requirement to a contracted forwarding agent or liner agent does not cover the total market, since his order will only be presented to the liner owner in question.

Information coverage

Before we take a closer look at the role of the broker and the agent in chartering activities it may be useful to mention the importance of information coverage. From the owner's point of view one might perhaps think that it would be convenient not to use an intermediary, but instead keep a direct contact with interested charterers. Such contacts do exist but then it is often a question of a very limited market where a reasonably good view can be maintained through a small number of contacts. In the dry cargo market this is not possible since owners would then miss important and, on certain occasions, maybe crucial market information.

In order to keep the chartering staff as small as possible, and to reduce his business inquiry expenses, the owner may even decide to channel all information through one or two brokers only. These brokers will then act as more or less exclusive agents for this owner and will be responsible for the necessary information, i.e. collecting, treating and evaluating material to present to the owner. The disadvantage with such an arrangement is that the owner gets information which is trimmed and important judgements are then made by the middle-man instead of by the owner himself.

The other extreme is the owner working through a very large number of broker contacts without especially favouring any of them. Possibly one would thereby get most of the orders circulating in the market and the same order may be received from a number of different sources. Such an arrangement may, however, result in the work in the owner's office becoming slow and laborious. Another disadvantage is that the owner may also find that none of the brokers will put in the amount of effort which an exclusively appointed broker is supposed to.

In principle, the same approach is applicable from the charterer's point of view, but at the same time the charterer's position is somewhat different. Especially with respect to the important commodities, the charterers do keep a fairly careful check on tonnage available and freight levels through contacts between themselves. For various administrative reasons they may also decide to separate their shipping department from the original body of the company and name it their exclusive agent with authority to seek tonnage for and to fix the company's cargoes. A charterer or shipper of general cargoes must communicate both with liner agents working in the trade concerned and with brokers who are dealing with suitable tonnage in the open market.

Means of communication

People engaged in day-to-day chartering work have to use various technical means of communication. Very often quick-acting push-button gadgets are connected to the telephones which have the most frequent telephone numbers programmed to international contacts, and these may be put through automatically by means of a country-to-country code system. By just pressing a key a line will be opened automatically to the person or company wanted.

In the shipowner's marketing departments, at the brokers and in the shipping departments, working business opportunities, the new chartering opportunities for the day, the present state of the market and the market development are currently discussed on the basis of the inflow of information. This face-to-face contact is so important that persons working the same or adjacent market sectors often prefer to be seated in the same room, although the environment may be very noisy from time to time. The telephone is the most frequently used medium for the daily discussions with intermediaries and principles and negotiations are frequently carried out over this instrument. Information about orders, position lists, market reports and various other matters are primarily received by telex, which is also generally used during the negotiations.

Details for comprehensive negotiations and important printed material which the parties in a negotiation have to study, for example contract forms and *pro forma* charter-parties are frequently transmitted from one place to another by telefax. This is principally a copying machine which is connected to another similar copier through the telephone network. This medium is more and more used as a comparatively cheap and efficient supplement to telex communication. Letters, signed charter-parties, circulars and pieces of information of a less urgent nature are, of course, distributed by mail.

COMPUTERS

The computer is now in use almost everywhere in the shipping world. Besides common usage computers are also serving marketing and ship operations/traffic departments. In ship operations work the computer is used especially for storing information and it is currently updated with regard to ships' positions, cargoes carried and bunkers, etc.

The shipowners' technical departments—in close liaison with the traffic departments—use computers for calculations of optimal speed under variable conditions and for drawing up tables and graphs, for example on speed and consumption. Some shipowners operating big fleets of vessels use computers to calculate the optimum usage of the entire fleet on the basis of inputs of currently updated information on ships' positions and cargo/contract requirements, thus facilitating the scheduling and rescheduling work.

In marketing departments various computer systems are used for calculations related to chartering work. The small table calculators equipped with memories and interchangeable programme units are fed with current data on distances, vessels' particulars, various costs, freight rates, etc., and such information, stored on magnetic tapes or discs, may be run together with a standard voyage programme, and thereby within less than a minute produce a reading or a print-out of the pre-calculated voyage result.

The capacity of table computers is sufficient for individual brokers or shipping managers to have day-to-day calculations based on a limited number of ships in standard type trades, but for more extensive data storage and elaborate data processing shipowners and shipbrokers are now investing in computer terminals with high capacity storage and programming facilities.

A common type of terminal may consist of the programming and memory units built in together with a scanner where inputs and results are read, plus a built-in or separate keyboard—the whole package is of about the size of a medium size television set. This is normally fed with information and operated by the individual broker or by a small group of brokers working together within the same market sector. In such computer terminals a large amount of data on positions, cargoes, particulars of vessels and ports and general market information may be stored. Whenever required, information can be obtained quickly against various parameters. In this case each terminal is individual and operated independently from each other. However, information displayed on the scanner can normally be punched out on a tape or be processed as a normal print-out on paper and may also be sent directly by telex or telefax.

The big shipowning companies sometimes have a special computer or calculations department, where the company's big central computer unit is operated by data professionals. In the marketing, scheduling, operations and technical departments there are scanners and keyboards through which relevant information for each department can be obtained and new information can be fed into the central storage unit. The computer specialist can assist in making sophisticated programs for various sorts of employment calculations, for optimizing the scheduling of the fleet, for optimizing fuel economy for individual vessels and voyages, for calculating cargo intake (considering restrictions in ports and properties of cargoes) with a view to obtaining maximum efficiency and economy. When a voyage is finished the actual result may be run together with the pre-voyage calculations to find differentials which will again be stored to be used in future calculations on similar employments.

There are also world-wide information systems in use that provide useful information, like world-wide coverage of various types of important cargoes, positions of all vessels registered with, for example, Lloyd's Register of Shipping, so that a shipbroker who is a subscriber to the system can easily get a reading on his scanner of the actual state of matters he is immediately concerned with. He can himself feed the system with new inputs by using the keyboard, so that this new or amended information may immediately be read all over the world.

The usage of computer systems as described above is rapidly increasing and makes work more efficient in many areas. Being programmed and fed with relevant information the computer certainly works and distributes information very quickly. However, there are certain difficulties in keeping the systems completely updated with relevant information at all times. Brokers and shipowners are avoiding too laborious and costly programming by using computers mainly for basic standard voyage calculations and basic fleet scheduling on the processing side, while the high capacity computer systems for data storage and distribution of information is extensively in use.

THE TIME FACTOR

Let us look at some of the ways in which time is relevant:

In a shipping company which operates world-wide the chartering work may continue day and night because of the time difference between many countries. It is also important to remember that competition implies that both owners and charterers can normally choose among a number of alternative business partners. These may also be domiciled at diametrically opposite places on earth.

During negotiations every offer and counter-offer is submitted with a time limit for reply within which the party offering or countering is committed. If no reply from the counter party is received within the time allowed then the first party is free to start firm negotiations with any other party. The time for reply is often short, i.e. anything from immediate reply up to a couple of hours. Normally, the parties try to avoid staying firmly committed overnight or over a week-end. In a business opportunity where firm negotiations have started the parties would normally try to conclude without interruptions, at least where the main terms are concerned.

Depending on the uncertainty when judging the state of the market at longer range there are seldom any fixtures made on a spot basis for shipments to be performed later than in two or three months' time. Among other things it is difficult to judge the tonnage position and quite impossible to foresee the alternative chartering opportunities during a narrow period of time that lies a couple of months ahead. Liner companies do not normally alter their tariffs without a pre-notice. It is not unusual to work with notice times as long as six months. Even the liner companies, however, make reservations when giving freight quotations a long time ahead of shipment for price changes that have to be inaugurated at short notice because of unforeseen circumstances.

THE ROLE OF THE BROKER AND THE AGENT

Again, the basic difference between liner operation and tramp traffic must be remembered. In liner traffic *forwarding agents* and *liner agents* play an important role in creating the contract of carriage between the shipowner and the cargo owner. The changing structure of modern liner traffic has brought about increasing co-operation among the various carriers involved in transportation from the seller to the buyer. Thus large freight forwarders often offer "through carriage", performing as carriers throughout the whole transit. In tramp traffic the shipowner and the charterer will often be brought together by *brokers*.

Brokers and agents have informative, intermediary and co-ordinating functions along the transportation chain. Due to their different work areas one may distinguish between *shipbrokers* in general and those concerned with *sale and purchase, port agency* and *liner* or *loading agency*.

Legally, a distinction may be made between different types of representation. Thus, an agent will normally represent one principal and act for him, whereas a broker should bring together two parties and act for both of them. In shipping, the terminology is not very clearly defined and does not seem to be fully in line with the legal theory.

Certain features should be distinguished. Basically, an intermediary will act on behalf of, in the name of and for the account of, the principal. Normally, a shipbroker does not have the authority to conclude an agreement for the principal, but only to negotiate. The situation is quite different where a broker makes a contract in his own name but for the account of someone else. In such cases we face an "undisclosed principal" situation.

In a fairly recent English case the House of Lords found that one broker involved had no "usual or apparent authority" and that a person acting for one of the parties lacked "actual as well as ostensible authority". (See *Armagas Ltd.* v. *Mundogas S.A.* (*The Ocean Frost*) [1986] 2 Lloyd's Rep. 109 (H.L.).)

SHIPBROKERS

As mentioned above, a shipbroker ordinarily specializes in a certain market or in a sector of a market. In chartering, an owner and a charterer have an interest in the broker's sources of information, his particular knowledge, as well as his skill at negotiation. Normally, both parties will have their own broker—the *owner's broker* and the *charterer's broker*. Thus, both parties negotiate through their representatives, who should do their best to preserve their respective principal's interests and intentions. Sometimes the broker will have a certain authority to bind his principal but normally the negotiations will be carried out in close co-operation between the principal and the broker. When the agreement has been concluded the broker will often obtain specific authority to sign the agreement, which he does sometimes "as agent only", without mentioning the party or parties and sometimes "as agent for X". In the former case, certain legal problems may arise as to who has really entered into the agreement. An owner may choose to do his business through one sole *confidential* or *exclusive* broker, or he may prefer to work through a large number of brokers, who will then have equal possibilities to do the business.

Sometimes the broker introduces a "first-class charterer" or a "first-class carrier" without mentioning a name. Should it appear later that the carrier or charterer is not first class, the broker may become liable for the consequences of his wrong description. Both parties may have good reasons to check on their counterparts. Some years ago a carrier entered into a charter-party with, as he believed, an entity named "Indian Shippers". When, after the voyage, the owner claimed dead-freight he discovered that there was no entity called "Indian Shippers", but that this was only a collective description for a number of shippers.

In a market with such widely differing sectors as the bulk market and 'tweendeck market one broker cannot possibly cover all parts with his direct connections. He will then leave his order with other brokers who in their turn may have good connections with colleagues representing an interested counter party. A broker thus engaged in efforts to bring together an owner's confidential broker with the broker of a suitable charterer is engaged in *competitive chartering* and is called a *competitive* broker. *Cable brokers* are those brokers who mainly list orders circulated in shipping centres such as for example New York, and then distribute the lists to brokers in other shipping centres, for example London, Tokyo, Oslo or Hamburg. These brokers may be described as tying together America and Europe and in this capacity their work is mainly that of a competitive broker.

All brokers endeavour to tie to themselves a number of principals (owners or charterers) for whom they may work as one of some few confidential brokers. As broker it is, of course, an advantage to work on such a confidential basis, since thereby the broker may have a fairly secure employment, and a certain continuity in his activities.

The function of the broker is to represent his principal in charter negotiations and he has to work for and protect his principal's interests in the following ways:

(1) The broker should keep both the owner and the charterer continuously informed about the market situation and the market development, about available cargo proposals and shipment possibilities, and should in the best possible way cover the market for given positions and orders respectively.

(2) The broker should act strictly within given authorities in connection with the negotiations. Sometimes the broker will have a fairly wide framework—a wide discretion—within which to work when carrying out the negotiations, with an absolute limit which must not be exceeded.

(3) The broker should in all respects work loyally for his principal and should carry out the negotiations and other work connected with the charter scrupulously and skilfully.

(4) The broker may not withhold any information from his principal nor give him wrong information. Nor may he reveal his principal's business "secrets" and may not act to the advantage of the counter party in the negotiations in order to reach an agreement.

A first-class broker should not advance shipment or vessel proposals to his principal if the business is not seriously founded or if there may be doubts about the counter party's honesty or solvency. The broker should also protect his principal's interests by preventing orders which have been worded wrongfully or incompletely from being sent until they have been corrected or completed. The broker also has a duty to preserve his principal's reputation.

Furthermore, the broker has a duty to take an active part in the negotiations giving advice and recommendations with respect to appropriate offers, proposals and compromises. He should also try to find out as much as possible about the activities of competitors in order to secure as many advantages as possible for his principal. A "mailbox" broker who only furthers information, offers, and counter offers without judging and processing them can hardly—and rightly so—count on a high degree of appreciation from the owner or the charterer.

The broker's personality and temper play a certain role, and somewhat jokingly a distinction is often made between *freight brokers* and *charter-party brokers*. The former is the broker who is always successful in contracting somewhat above the market level, but who will never risk the loss of business due to the details of a particular charter-party clause. The latter will contract at the actual market level, but he will always try to phrase every single charter-party clause so that it will be as advantageous as possible to his principal. It must be stressed that a charter-party that has not been carefully drafted may cause one of the parties considerable losses, and a business's result can only really be determined after the post-calculation.

A broker will hardly ever have full liberty to "go out on the market" with an order to *fix best possible*. Instead, he will normally have an *authority* to go out with certain specified terms and conditions, and if they are not accepted by the counter party the broker must get new instructions. This will be repeated until both parties are in total agreement.

When an owner or a charterer, having received an order or a position, demands additional information or wishes to look more carefully into the possibility of a charter agreement, he is regarded as being *committed* to this broker. If the owner wants to open up negotiations to have his vessel employed for the cargo mentioned in the order it is regarded as good practice to work through the broker to whom the owner is already "committed". Sometimes brokers try to commit a principal by advancing the order by telephone and trying at the same time to discuss the possibility of the order. Such a way of procedure is not regarded as a first-class method.

Normally, the privilege of choosing a broker channel is considered to belong to the owner. But then again regard should be given to factors such as: Who first presented the order or position? Who has the most "direct" connection? Is the broker "taking a chance" or does he make a reference to an actual need or a particular position? Which of the brokers seems to have the best and most complete information and background with respect to the business in question? Consideration is also normally given to whether a previous connection with the same customer has been made through a certain broker with respect to similar charters. Further personal relations naturally play an important role.

In order to entice an owner to work "his way" the charterer's broker may draw up the order in such a way that it indicates, more or less, that he has a close or particularly good relationship with the charterer. In this connection *exclusive* means that a broker will work alone on the order thus instructed directly by the charterer. *Direct* means that there is no intermediary link via an *exclusive agent* or via another broker. The order may in such a case be worked on in parallel by several brokers in the same position. The expression *local charterers* similarly indicates a geographically close connection with charterers. The word *friends* may also be used under different circumstances by brokers to indicate a *special crack* (a special connection).

Such expressions may, when used judiciously, contain useful information. "Scampering"—which may exist—will normally be discovered rather quickly and brokers (and for that matter owners and charterers) who have become known as less serious or skilful may have certain difficulties in ridding themselves of such a reputation.

Sometimes the owner and charterer, after having concluded one agreement through a broker, may do subsequent business directly with each other. Such direct business may be a consequence of a wish to avoid paying commission. Sometimes it happens that, for example, a *competitive broker* has presented an order which for some reason the owner's confidential broker has not received via his direct channel or which he has not observed. The owner may then be tempted to inform his direct channel about the order thereby "committing himself" through this channel instead of giving the other broker a chance. Such methods, too, are considered improper and not quite acceptable from an ethical point of view.

The shipbroker working for a charterer will also have as one of his duties, immediately after the charter negotiations have been concluded, to make out the original charter-party in accordance with the agreed terms and conditions. Another important duty of both brokers is to follow up how the transport undertaking is performed so that the parties receive continuous information, that notices are given correctly, that freight and hire is duly paid, etc.

Sale and purchase broker

Corresponding standards and commercial ethics also apply to the *sale and purchase broker* as to his behaviour during the negotiations and how these are carried out. The final *memorandum of agreement* and the follow-up of this type of commercial transaction differs, however, from the corresponding activities in connection with chartering.

Port agents

The task of the port agent is to represent the owner and assist the vessel for the owner's account in order that she will have the best possible despatch. The port agent should in all respects assist the master in his contacts with all local authorities, including harbour authorities, and he also has to procure provisions and other necessities, communicate orders and messages to and from the owners, etc. It is important that the owner employs a reliable and energetic agent. In tramp traffic, as mentioned, loading and discharging will often be for the charterer's account. The charterer may then prefer to be entitled to nominate the *port agent* in order to further his interests. The question of appointing an agent may therefore be an important detail in the charter negotiations, since the parties have to establish whether the charter-party shall stipulate *owner's agents* or *charterer's agents*. If the charterer's agent is to be appointed it may be an advantage from the owner's point of view that the actual clause states, for example, "charterer's agent to be nominated, but if actually appointed by the owner, the latter will do so only by authority of and for the account of the charterer". If the owner has to accept the charterer's agent he may protect his interests to a certain extent by appointing a *husbandry agent*, who will then assist the master and look after the owner's interests in order that the charterer's agent will not act to the disadvantage of the owner.

Liner agents

Liner agents form an important group of intermediaries in liner shipping. Whereas brokers and port agents seldom enter into written contracts with their principals, liner agents have often entered into such written contracts. There are even some different "standard liner agency contracts". A liner agent functions as a kind of general agent for the line within a geographical area. Liner agents represent the owners in many different ways. Liner agents will have contact with possible shippers and forwarding agents within the area, they procure advertising about departures and arrivals, and normally they will also do all the work for the line otherwise carried out by a port agent. The booking will normally be made without special negotiations through a quotation in accordance with the tariff in force, and as soon as the booking has been noted and confirmed by the agent there is an agreement on the carriage of goods and a booking note is normally issued. The agent will normally have, before every loading occasion, an allocation of space from the owner which he may book up without any further authorization from the owner. Certain cargoes of a dangerous type or unusual goods, heavy lifts, etc., are, however, often excepted, meaning that for such cargoes approval must be obtained from the owner or the line in every single case.

Brokers and agents connected with owners

Though some brokers are wholly independent it is common for at least the large shipping companies to have within their own organizations separate departments working as agents (chartering as well as sale and purchase), brokers, and even forwarding agents. Similarly, as previously mentioned, freight forwarders nowadays frequently go beyond their traditional field and engage themselves in offering ocean carriage. Large brokers are also directly involved in owning or operating fleets, etc. Having a liner agent and a broker in the same company is not always a guarantee that an order given to the liner agent will also be brought out into the open market, or vice versa. When the owner and broker are in the same company certain orders may be prevented from going out into the open market and instead they will be reserved for the "house" tonnage, if the broker is not fully *independent*.

BROKERAGE

The broker will often have very limited instructions and often hardly any express or clear instructions at all. A number of charter-parties of standard type contain a printed text on brokerage but leave it to the parties to fill in the percentage, for instance, Gencon, cl. 15:

"A brokerage commission at the rate stated in Box 20 on the freight earned is due to the party mentioned in Box 20.

In case of non-execution at least 1/3 of the brokerage on the estimated amount of freight and dead freight to be paid by the Owners to the Brokers as indemnity for the latter's expenses and work. In case of more voyages the amount of indemnity to be mutually agreed."

Except for particular agency fees, agents and brokers will receive remuneration calculated as a certain percentage of the gross freight figure, and the intermediaries involved will normally be entitled to remuneration only when the charter agreement, the sale and purchase agreement or the booking has been concluded and/or connected contracts have been signed. The broker's and the agent's income is thus totally dependent on the freight market and the size of the deal involved. Such size may be measured in terms of the cargo quantity, the length of the charter period or the price of the vessel. Normally every broker involved in a charter deal will get an amount corresponding to $1\frac{1}{4}\%$ of the gross freight. In sale and purchase deals the figure varies but is often 1–2%. The liner agent will normally get 3–5%. Port agents will, however, as indicated above, be remunerated by a fixed agency fee which varies considerably between different ports and also depends on the tonnage of the vessel.

Unless otherwise agreed (which is very rare in practice) such remuneration— generally referred to as the "commission"—is paid by the owner and the total actual percentage for a certain deal, the total commission, should be specified in every order presented to the owner.

The commission paid to a broker is called the "brokerage". This is the broker's remuneration for his work and costs in connection with his activities. The brokerage will cover his expenses and give him a net profit. As mentioned, the commission or brokerage is always calculated on a percentage of the gross freight and, depending on what is agreed during the negotiations, sometimes a so-called ballast bonus and demurrage (which will be dealt with later on) may also be the basis of commission, in addition to the gross freight or the charter hire. Thus it is common in the dry cargo sector that every broker gets $1\frac{1}{4}$% and the relevant freight calculations will normally be based on $2\frac{1}{2}$% or $3\frac{3}{4}$% depending on the number of brokers involved. It is, however, not uncommon for the total commission to be higher, but in those cases a so-called address commission will almost invariably be involved. In many trades and with time charters it is usual that part of the commission is "returning to the house" (address) which thus in practice reduces the freight or hire to be paid. Such address commissions may be up to 5% (heavy address). The reason for this system is sometimes said to be that the charterers' shipping department for book-keeping purposes must show some kind of income from their activities. State trading countries regularly include a 5% address commission in their orders. It is also quite common to find that a charterer's broker, who is working on an exclusive basis for his principal, will be entitled to $2\frac{1}{2}$% brokerage. As mentioned, the owners will pay all commissions and will therefore try to cover such costs by a corresponding freight increase.

A great number of cases illustrate how the brokerage fee should be determined and how it should be paid. Thus, at random, *Howard Houlder & Partners* v. *Manx Isles Steamship Co.* (1922) 12 Ll.L.Rep. 93, 137, illustrates a case where the broker was not entitled to any brokerage fee, when a charterer used his option to purchase a vessel. The broker had not contributed to the separate purchase agreement reached, since the purchase involved a different price to that which had been originally agreed. On the other hand, in another case, the broker was entitled to a commission although the buyer was not the same one that had been introduced by the broker. The broker's work was regarded as having been decisive for the purchase.

Several legal problems may arise in connection with the activities of agents, as well as those of brokers.

INSURANCE FOR INTERMEDIARIES

Continuing structural change in the shipping industry has led also to changes for brokers, port agents and other intermediaries in shipping. There is a tendency for intermediaries to be more often involved in disputes. A consequence of this is that need for insurance for intermediaries has increased. P. & I. clubs for shipbrokers, port agents, managers and other intermediaries in shipping have been founded and these clubs seem to be well established as a necessary complement to the traditional P. & I. clubs.

CHAPTER 5

MARKETING

ATTITUDES IN NEGOTIATION

In essence, the purpose of marketing shipping services is to inform the business community of one's presence and ability. In this connection it is important to recognize the difference between a liner company's competitive situation and the situation for an owner working in the open market.

Ships operated in the spot market, for example, must comply with the demands of size and type and must also be suitable in other respects for the intended cargo. Furthermore, the vessel must be available in the right position at the right time and ask for a freight level which is competitive in comparison with what other interested parties may offer. If the employment in question is for a longer duration on time charter or contract basis then the importance of an owner's solvency, reliability and reputation for good performance will increase correspondingly.

For the liner owner who is working with the same freight tariff in the same trade and maybe even with the same frequency of sailings as his competitors, regularity and reliability are the most important marketing features, i.e. he must keep to the advertised schedules without sudden changes and delays. Other features are short transit times, good care of the cargo, efficient handling of cargo bookings, documentation and settlement of cargo claims. Further means of strengthening the competitive position can be by offering package solutions to transport problems, such as the arrangement of door-to-door transport.

The owners, like the charterers, will create for themselves a reputation in shipping circles which is very quickly spread internationally. In the day-to-day exchange of information certain expressive wordings are used like "first-class people", "unprofessional operators", "hard traders", "difficult" or "tricky negotiators", "good performers", etc. No one can count on being referred to as first class without having earned such a classification in the first place. Being labelled "difficult" or even "tricky" indicates that the party in question is difficult to deal with, by lack of flexibility or even lack of knowledge of the trade and for the latter denomination even a touch of dishonesty. The same bad impression is given by the label "unserious", while a reputation as a hard trader should not at all be a disadvantage if it is connected with an otherwise good reputation where performance is concerned. On the other hand, it is less advantageous to be known as one who squeezes his counter party on every occasion whenever possible.

MARKETING AND RELATION TO THE CUSTOMER

For the owners working in the open market it is important first of all to secure such broker contacts which can cover jointly, as completely as possible, the market sector of interest. It is not only a question of finding brokers who can supply relevant and complete information, but the brokers must also provide the ability to present and offer the ships operated by the owner and his services in a serious manner and in such a way that the ships will be preferable to the charterers.

Whenever an owner is discussing an order with a charterer it is in fact a new opportunity to present to the company the services that are offered, and the type of engagement the owner is interested in. These measures are supplemented by personal visits to charterers and organizations who might be interested in services that the owners can offer. Of course it is also important to maintain and to deepen the contacts with old customers, for example through visits. This is being done both regularly as a matter of routine, and in connection with current business deals, and it is customary on those latter occasions for the owners to be accompanied by the broker who assisted in working up the business or originally made the contact. Advertising material such as folders, etc., have so far been rather sparingly used by owners working in the open market. This material is usually sent to already existing contacts and has been used comparatively little in order to obtain new business. It seems, however, that the trend is to work more fully with such direct marketing aids in the future.

Returning to the question of showing one's abilities, the charterers will get to know the owners during discussions and negotiations but, above all, during the performance of the charter. Then the owner's management, employees and representatives under different circumstances will be put under stress to prove their ability to carry out the transport undertaking. It is of equal importance to solve all problems arising in the spirit of good co-operation and flexibility and in an efficient way to the satisfaction of both parties. The standard of the ships and their equipment is, of course, also of great importance in this connection. Breakdowns of machinery due to faulty material or bad maintenance are not good marketing features.

From the early 1990s we see an increasing number of first-class owners who endeavour to obtain a so-called "Quality Class" with the classification societies. This is a certificate of high standard for both ships and management (Quality Assurance and Quality Management). Both charterers and owners

Two in One!

The BOC Fleet of Combined Tanker/Dry Cargo Vessels:

**Identical sisters; delivered by Van der Giessen-de Noord B.V. 1991.
Classed Lloyd´s Register of Shipping +100 A1; Ice Class 1A; UMS
Double bottom and double sides throughout;**

SPECIAL DRY CARGO PARTICULARS
4 stainless steel box-shaped cargo holds. Dimensions: l x b x h = 13,6 x 13,0 x 9,7 m.
4 steel hatchcovers, hydraulically operated. Dimensions: 13,6 x 13,0 m.
Bale capacity holds 1+2+3+4 = 1680+1732+1732+1732 = 6876 cbm.
Container capacity holds 120 TEU, on deck 107 TEU, total 227 TEU.

Hot/ambient mechanical ventilation by fans up to 70 ºC.
About 11,6 airchanges per hour.

2 Hägglund deckcranes positioned on starboard side.
Each 20 mtons SWL. Min. outreach 3 m,
max. outreach 20 m. Cargo spotter fitted.

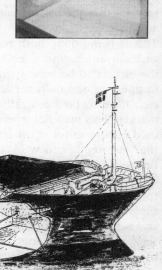

Using ship´s own cranes for
loading of woodpulp into the
boxed stainless-steel covered
cargo holds.

*MARKETING: Owners issue brochures and pamphlets in which they give features and details about
their vessels.*

M/S TALCOR
M/S TALHENA   M/S TALNATI

MAIN PARTICULARS:

Deadweight Summer	6.209 Mtons	Cargo tank capacity no:s 1,2,3,4,5 total	7,351 cbm
Draught Summer S.W.	6,53 m	Cargo (bale) capacity total	6,876 cbm
Length over all	99,55 m	Bunkers capacity heavy oil/diesel oil	402,7 / 38,9 Mtons
Length between p.p.	93,30 m	Service speed	12 knots
Breadth moulded	17,00 m	Consumption:	
Depth moulded	8,50 m	Main Engine, fuel IFO 180	about 13 t/day
Tanks-Holds/Hatches	4+1 tanks,	Auxiliaries,(in port only)	average 0.8 t/day
	4/4 holds/hatches		

SPECIAL TANK PARTICULARS

Tanks No 1, 2, 3 and 4 of stainless steel.
Tank hatch covers with cellular splashwalls coated
with Intershield epoxy. Tank No 5, slop tanks and cargo pipes coated with Intergard epoxy.

Tank cargo capacity, tanks No 1+2+3+4+5 at 98% = 1674+1724+1724+1724+357 = 7.203 cbm.

Vessel capable of 2-grade segregation. Closed loading, Cargo heating via heater changers.

2 Framo SD-200 deepwell centrifugal pumps, 600 cbm/h 9 bar.
1 Framo SD-100 deepwell centrifugal slop pump, 100 cbm/h, 9 bar.

Manifolds on port and starboard sides. Cargo hose derrick on port/starboard side (1 mton).
Manifold sizes: 12" or 8" one grade, 8" two grades.

Toftejorg tankcleaning equipment in tanks and hatchcoamings.
Wash distance 20 m. Wash water tanks 231 cbm, slop tanks 163 cbm.
Hot/ambient mechanical tank ventilation/drying by fans up to 70°C.

Fully segregated ballast tanks.

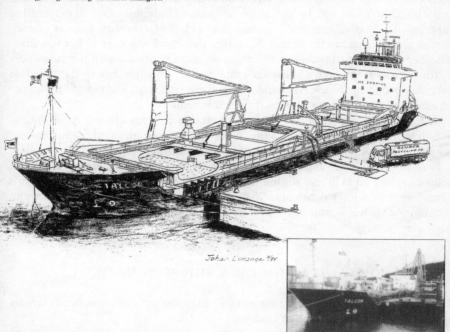

MARKETING: This owner is introducing a new type of combination carrier to the market.

now recognize such improved standards to enhance also the economy. In fact, major tanker charterers now keep lists of owners and ships which have a reputation for quality and good performance. Such owners, when marketing their vessels for chartering, will not forget to state: "Approved by major oil companies".

As mentioned previously, the liner owner has a permanent organization of contracted agents. This agency organization deals with the day-to-day contacts with the customers and is always trying to create new contacts. Also, in this case, it is routine to travel and to visit customers, but there is also a great emphasis put on advertising, such as printed "Sailing Cards" and advertisements in trade magazines and daily newspapers. Very often there is an advertisement appearing in the same space day by day in all papers read by prospective customers within the agency's working area. Additional advertising may be carried out from time to time through big advertising campaigns, especially when a new service is being inaugurated or a new special feature is being introduced. The liner owner must put in great efforts on all matters related to good service. An owner may work on a contact for a long time before he gets the first booking for account of this new customer and he might well lose the same customer overnight if carriage is not considered to have been carried out satisfactorily. Great demands are made with regard to skill and efficiency exercised by the ship's command in cargo care and handling supervision. Also, agents and superintendents have to do their utmost in each port of call to expedite the despatch, so that the vessel will keep to her schedule. Another factor contributing to maintaining good relations with the customers is, for example, that extra ships are employed to fill vacancies in the schedule that may occur due to the permanent ships being delayed, instead of "jumping" an advertised loading position in the fixed schedule.

The regular acceptance not only of profitable cargoes offered for booking, but all varieties of general cargo that are available for shipment from the area, is another factor in the maintenance of good relationships.

It is impossible to avoid cargo claims completely and there is a special demand made on skill and diplomacy exercised by the personnel of the claims department in a liner company. Such matters must be dealt with correctly in accordance with law and good practice—so that the owner does not lose the customer.

ORGANIZATION OF A SHIPPING OFFICE

The organization of the chartering work in a shipowner's office depends largely on the company's main line of trading.

In the liner organization there are two working areas. One includes the activities concerned with the liner operation as such, for example scheduling and operational matters, allocation of space for booking, follow-up of bookings for the individual voyages, control of the ship's despatch during the current voyages and follow-up of voyage results. The other area covers work with chartering-in of extra tonnage, chartering-out for longer or shorter periods of vessels that are taken out from the liner activities for various reasons, and also fixing spot cargoes or certain basic parcels on the open market to be carried by the lines on charter-party terms. This latter activity may be linked to a permanent agency or brokering activity. The personnel dealing with chartering may divide the work between themselves, for example with regard to ship's size and types or by commodities. The working system will be such as to suit the liner operation (being regarded as the main line of business) in the best possible way. The claims department plays an important role in the office organization of the shipowner involved in liner trade.

It is more difficult to present a standard organization for chartering work concerning vessels that are mainly engaged in trading in the open market. Nevertheless, it is possible to recognize different systems of organization. In one system the fleet of ships is divided into classes according to type or size and the personnel doing the chartering work specialize in an individual class or group of ships. Another system divides the work according to commodities or commodity groups. A third way of working is to split the world into geographical areas of operation, i.e. Atlantic, Pacific, Mediterranean and Black Sea, etc. In such cases each person or group in the chartering department will work on all those vessels open within their specific area. Yet another way of dividing the chartering work is to separate between spot market orders and orders concerning longer engagements, like contracts or long period time charters. The personnel will then be divided into one group for contracts and one for spot chartering.

Irrespective of the main line of interest for the shipowning activity and the organization of the chartering work, the main intention is to organize and carry out the carriage of goods or persons as efficiently as possible in co-operation with the charterers and shippers on terms that are advantageous to both parties. Thereby we have also defined the objective of chartering in general from the business point of view.

CHAPTER 6

SALES CONTRACT, CARRIAGE AND BILL OF LADING

SALES CONTRACT—FINANCING—CARRIAGE

Suppose a buyer in Holland wishes to buy some pieces of machinery from a Singapore manufacturer. When making their contract the parties will meet with a number of problems. Who will arrange the transportation, the insurance and the financing of the sale? By what date should the goods be delivered or actually reach the buyer? When and how will payment be made? The above illustrates that the sales contract is the legal vehicle for a set of legal relations. The sales contract is thus decisive for a number of ancillary relations: it sets out rules for price and payment, affecting payment methods, e.g. documentary letters of credit, and it sets out principles for delivery and risk affecting transportation and insurance issues, etc. Several parties may be involved in such international transactions and, depending on the agreed distribution of risks and costs in the sales contract, a number of duties will be put on the seller and buyer who will then enter into different ancillary agreements, e.g. charter agreement, insurance contract, letter of credit.

There is thus need for co-ordination of the different relations and the obligations and rights respectively of the various parties involved in the transaction.

The sales contract is the basic agreement in the export transaction

The sales contract stipulates the object of the agreement (the goods), the price, payment and the means of delivery (payment and transport clauses), the risk distribution between the parties—something that affects the insurance—the financing of the sale, etc. The sales contract then contains the framework of the subsequent contracts, the agreements on financing, insurance and transport. Some of the principal questions of the sales contract are dealt with in the so-called *transport* or *delivery clause*, in which the parties agree on the apportionment between themselves of the risks and expenses involved in the transportation of the goods, e.g. an f.o.b. or c.i.f. clause. Such clauses do not directly regulate security and payment terms and conditions, i.e. when, where and how payment is going to be effected. In English law a c.i.f. clause means that the buyer has to pay against documents, and similar rules have evolved in other legal systems.

Many difficulties and disputes that arise may be explained by disharmony between sales contracts, financing contracts, contracts of carriage and insurance conditions. It is therefore essential that all the parties involved make sure from the beginning that the contracts are designed in such a way that the delivery from the seller to the buyer can be performed without too many problems occurring.

Incoterms

Most legal systems contain legislation dealing with sales of goods or provisions concerning the relationship between seller and buyer, although in practice the parties normally regulate their relationship by agreement. Different legal systems may deal with similar questions in slightly different ways. This has led to certain difficulties in international trade, requiring special efforts to harmonize the sales law provisions of different countries. In the field of sales law a certain amount of harmonization has been achieved, particularly through *Incoterms*, which determine the meaning and effects of certain transport clauses used in international trade (such as f.o.b., c.i.f., ex warehouse, delivered, etc.). Incoterms have recently been revised (1990) and amended in order to bring them in line with modern transportation methods. The revised Incoterms mean, among other things, that some new supplementary clauses have been introduced. These aim at overcoming the tensions which have occurred when applying the traditional f.o.b. and c.i.f. concepts to the modern cargo equipment traffic—above all the container and ro/ro traffic—where the ship's rail no longer serves any practical purpose as a demarcation line for the distribution of costs and risks between the seller and the buyer. Such a new clause is, for example, "free carrier . . . named destination". The revised Incoterms have now been restructured so as to embrace C-, D-, E- and F-clauses.

Risk, cost and liability distribution between the different parties

Every *export transaction* thus gives rise to several relationships:

> between seller and buyer,
> between seller/buyer and carrier,
> between seller/buyer and underwriter, and
> between seller/buyer and financer.

The risk of damage to or loss of goods or their delay may thus pass through several levels. Basically, there is a risk distribution between *seller and buyer*, but then also the other relationships contain a risk distribution. Even if, under the contract of sale and in relation to the seller, the buyer is liable for the goods sold, he may claim damages from the *carrier* or the *underwriter* in case of delay, loss or damage to the goods, depending on the risk distribution formula applied and following applicable contractual provisions.

If the above-mentioned transaction between the Singapore manu-facturer/seller and the Dutch buyer is used as a basis, the parties may interpret their relationship in different ways. Normally, the seller is not willing to grant credit to the buyer unless he has good security. When goods are sold within a country a seller will often regard the goods he sells as the best available security for the price. He will not wish to lose possession of them until the price is paid. If this is not possible he will seek to retain some interest in the goods he sells which he might then realize if payment fails—hence he may examine the options offered by hire purchase and similar transactions. In international sales the seller is in this respect in a less favourable position. Security interests in title are of little value to a seller who might have to try to enforce a right over property several thousands of miles away in another jurisdiction. He often feels that he must have rights which are more predictable and more accessible. Thus a purchase on terms, such as cash on delivery (C.O.D.) prevents the buyer from getting delivery of the goods before he has paid—often through a bank—but it does not protect the seller from expenses for sending the goods, etc., unless such payment is secured.

The buyer, in his turn, is not in a very much better position if he is asked to pay before the goods have even been sent, and when—and if—they have been sent they may not even conform with the terms and conditions of the sales contract. The buyer, therefore, is often not willing to effect payment before delivery has taken place.

International commerce has over the years worked out a number of measures to counteract the consequences mentioned. An important role is played by the use of documents, which represent the goods and record the nature of the transaction which affects them. Even if the differences between the various transport clauses are considerable it will probably suffice to use, for example, the c.i.f. contract as a basis to illustrate these measures.

Under a c.i.f. contract the seller agrees to sell the goods to a buyer and to have them delivered at the buyer's named port of destination. Thus the Singapore seller may sell goods to the Dutch buyer "c.i.f." (cost, insurance, freight) Rotterdam. This means that the seller arranges and pays for insurance and freight as well as certain other costs which are then included in the price. The clause only spells out that the seller shall pay freight, insurance and other costs to Rotterdam, and does not mention the point of shipment (Singapore), where the risk passes from the seller to the buyer. The new Incoterms may in this respect provide the parties with a clearer description through the somewhat revised clauses.

When the seller has arranged the fulfilment of his duty he is entitled to be paid upon the presentation of the documents involved. At this point the buyer, in his turn, should have made financial arrangements so that he can meet this requirement. The procedure may vary, but in international trade payment by letter of credit (see below, page 50ff.) is important to create a balance of security interest for the seller and the buyer.

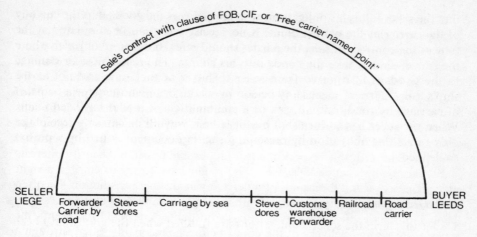

The sales contract may involve several underlying contractual relations.

The Incoterms 1990

The revised Incoterms clauses have new abbreviations and have been restructured into C-, D-, E-, and F-clauses. The C-clauses are CFR (cost and freight), CIF (cost, insurance and freight), CPT (carriage paid to) and CIP (carriage and insurance paid to), the D-clauses are DAF (delivered at frontier), DES (delivered ex ship), DEQ (delivered ex quay), and DDP/DDU (delivered duty paid/unpaid), the E-clauses are EXW (ex works—ex factory, ex warehouse etc.) and the F-clauses FCA (free carrier—named point), FAS (free alongside ship) and FOB (free on board). The meaning and application of the clauses have not been changed.

EXW (ex works)

"Ex works" means that the seller's only responsibility is to make the goods available at his premises (i.e. works or factory). In particular, he is not responsible for loading the goods onto the vehicle provided by the buyer, unless otherwise agreed. The buyer bears the full cost and risk involved in bringing the goods from there to the desired destination. This term thus represents the minimum obligation for the seller.

FCA (free carrier—named point)

This term has been designed to meet the requirements of modern transport, particularly such "multimodal" transport as container or roll-on/roll-off traffic by trailers and ferries. It is based on the same main principle as f.o.b. except that the seller fulfils his obligations when he delivers the goods into the custody of the carrier at the named point. If no precise *point* can be stipulated at the time of the contract of sale, the parties should refer to the *place* or *range* where the carrier should take the goods into his charge. The risk of loss or damage to the goods is transferred from seller to buyer at that time and not at the ship's rail. "Carrier" means any person by whom or in whose name a contract of carriage by road, rail, air, sea or a combination of modes has been made. When the seller has to furnish a bill of lading, waybill or carrier's receipt, he duly fulfils this obligation by presenting such a document issued by a person so defined.

FAS (free alongside ship)

Under this term the seller's obligations are fulfilled when the goods have been placed alongside the ship on the quay or in lighters. This means that the buyer has to bear all costs and risks of loss or damage to the goods from that moment. It should be noted that, unlike f.o.b., the present term requires the buyer to clear the goods for export.

FOB (free on board)

The goods are placed on board a ship by the seller at a port of shipment named in the sales contract. The risk of loss or damage to the goods is transferred from the seller to the buyer when the goods pass the ship's rail.

A particular variation is f.o.b. Airport based on the same main principle as the ordinary f.o.b. term. The seller fulfils his obligations by delivering the goods to the air carrier at the airport of departure. The risk of loss or damage to the goods is transferred from the seller to the buyer when the goods have been so delivered.

CFR (cost and freight)

The seller must pay the costs and freight necessary to bring the goods to the named destination, but the risk of loss or damage to the goods, as well as of any cost increases, is transferred from the seller to the buyer when the goods pass the ship's rail in the port of shipment.

CIF (cost, insurance and freight)

This term is basically the same as CFR but with the *addition* that the seller has to procure marine insurance against the risk of loss or damage to the goods during the carriage. The seller contracts with the insurer and pays the insurance premium.

CPT (freight or carriage paid to—named place)

Like CFR "freight or carriage paid to" means that the seller pays the freight for the carriage of the goods to the named destination. However, the risk of loss or damage to the goods, as well as of any cost increases, is transferred from the seller to the buyer when the goods have been delivered into the custody of the first carrier and not at the ship's rail. It can be used for all modes of transport including multimodal operations and container or roll-on/roll-off traffic by trailers and ferries. When the seller has to furnish a bill of lading, waybill or carrier's receipt, he duly fulfils this obligation by presenting such a document issued by the person with whom he has contracted for carriage to the named destination.

CIP (freight or carriage and insurance paid to—named place)

This term is the same as "freight or carriage paid to" but with the addition that the seller has to procure transport insurance against the risk of loss or damage to the goods during the carriage. The seller contracts with the insurer and pays the insurance premium.

DES (delivered ex ship)

This means that the seller shall make the goods available to the buyer on board the ship at the destination named in the sales contract. The seller has to bear the full cost and risk involved in bringing the goods there.

DEQ (delivered ex quay)

This means that the seller makes the goods available to the buyer on the quay (wharf) at the destination named in the sales contract. The seller has to bear the full cost and risk involved in bringing the goods there.

There are two "ex quay" contracts in use, namely "ex quay (duty paid)", and "ex quay (duties on buyer's account)", in which the liability to clear the goods for import are to be met by the buyer instead of by the seller. Parties are recommended always to use the full descriptions of these terms, namely "ex quay (duty paid)" or "ex quay (duties on buyer's account)", or else there may be uncertainty as to who is to be responsible for the liability to clear the goods for import.

DAF (delivered at frontier)

"Delivered at frontier" means that the seller's obligations are fulfilled when the goods have arrived at the frontier—but before "the customs border" of the country named in the sales contract. The term is primarily intended to be used when goods are to be carried by rail or road but it may be used irrespective of the mode of transport.

DDU (delivered duty unpaid) and DDP (delivered duty paid)

While the term "ex works" signifies the seller's minimum obligation, the term "delivered duty paid" (or unpaid), when followed by words naming the buyer's premises, denotes the other extreme—the seller's maximum obligation. The term "delivered duty paid" may be used irrespective of the mode of transport. If the parties wish that the seller should clear the goods for import but that some of the costs payable upon the import of the goods should be excluded—such as value added tax (VAT) and/or other similar taxes—this should be made clear by adding words to this effect (e.g. "exclusive of VAT and/or taxes").

The new clauses introduced already in the 1980 revision have been designed with regard being given to modern forms of carriage, such as multimodal transports with containers, or ro/ro traffic with trailers. The new clause is based on the same principles as the old f.o.b. clause, but there is an important distinction in that the risk passes from the seller to the buyer at the place where the goods have been delivered to the contracting carrier. Thus the vessel's rail will no longer play a decisive role in this respect when the new clause is used. Similarly "Freight or carriage paid to" or "Freight or carriage and insurance paid to" may be substituted for the old c. & f. and c.i.f. clauses respectively in cases where container or trailer traffic is involved.

There are also alternative clauses, such as FOR/FOT (free on rail/free on truck) which are not Incoterms clauses. These clauses relate to the carriage of goods by rail.

Documentary credit

Except for cash in advance, the export letter of credit gives the seller the highest degree of protection among all the commonly used methods of payment for exports. A letter of credit is essentially an undertaking by a bank upon the instructions of the buyer that it will make certain payments to the seller (beneficiary) under specified conditions. When a letter of credit is used in connection with international transactions more than one bank is normally involved—usually one in the buyer's country and one in the seller's.

The value of the letter of credit to the exporter is that, when presenting the prescribed supporting documents, he is entitled to draw drafts on a bank or to be paid in cash by the bank.

The basis for the whole transaction is the sales agreement. The goods have to be moved from the seller to the buyer and have to be insured in accordance with the terms and conditions of the purchase agreement (c.i.f., f.o.b., etc.). The seller or the buyer will arrange insurance and carriage. If the parties have agreed on payment by letter of credit, a basic precondition of the seller's obligation to deliver

Fields of application of the terms with regard to types of goods and modes of transport

The table below shows broadly the fields of application of the terms with regard to types of goods and modes of transportation. Under special conditions other terms may be used than those enumerated in the table. This is particularly true of multimodal transport systems in which the choice of trade terms may be related to the means in actual operation when passing the respective critical points. To a great majority of exporters/importers the table is directive.

Type of goods	Mode of conveyance via/to destination				
	Forwarder Transporter terminal	Air Rail Road transport	Sea transport	Multimodal transport	Post parcel
General cargo	EXW CPT DDU FCA DDP	EXW CPT DAF DDP FCA CIP DDU	EXW FAS CFR CPT DES DDU FCA FOB CIF CIP DEQ DDP	EXW FAS CIP DES DDU FCA CPT DAF DEQ DDP	FCA CIP DDP CPT DDU
Groupage traffic	EXW CPT DDU FCA CIP DDP	EXW CPT DDU FCA CIP DDU	EXW FAS CPT DAF DEQ DDP FCA FOB CIP DES DDU		
Full container load	FCA	EXW CPT DAF DDP FCA CIP DDU	EXW CPT DES DDU FCA CIP DEQ DDP	EXW FAS CIP DEQ DDP FCA CPT DES DDU	
Bulk cargo		EXW CIP DDP CPT DDU	EXW FAS CFR CPT DDU DDP FCA FOB CIF CIP DDP	EXW CIP DDP CPT DDU	

N.B. In applying FCA the contract should specify the well-defined location of the critical point.

the cargo is then that the buyer has arranged with a bank to open the documentary credit. The buyer's protection lies in the fact that the bank will only pay under the documentary credit if the seller presents documents which contain information and particulars in conformity with the documentary credit provisions. The general idea is that all documentation will be synchronized (sales agreement, letter of credit, bill of lading and insurance documents).

The purchase agreement is thus the source of several obligations. The buyer will have to arrange an agreed or customary type of documentary credit at the agreed time and with a first-class bank, and the provisions of the documentary credit must correspond with those agreed in the purchase agreement. The purchase agreement should thus contain an explicit provision in respect of the letter of credit.

Very often the payment clause is not very elaborate and may give rise to a number of problems. It is therefore necessary for the beneficiary, immediately upon receipt of the documentary credit, to make a thorough check of its provisions and reject it if it is not in conformity with the purchase agreement or with his understanding of it. The carrier's demand for freight may sometimes be secured by the use of a *transferable* credit, whereby part of the original transferable letter of credit will be available for the carrier under a separate credit.

Under an irrevocable letter of credit the buyer's bank undertakes to pay the seller when he has performed his part of the deal, which he will do by presenting the documents prescribed in the letter of credit, normally at least an invoice, an insurance policy and a bill of lading. From the seller's point of view the bill of lading is essential. From the other side, the bill of lading is what is received for payment—the documentary evidence of the goods bought. This, together with the insurance policy, is what the buyer pays for. The bank will take up the documents from the seller, on behalf of the buyer, and they can be used as the basis for further transactions.

It is thus evident that the documents used in international sales contracts play a significant role both in the relationship between the seller and buyer and between the carrier and the shipper/consignee. This is particularly true of the bill of lading. The bill of lading is a *document of title* which is used to enable consignor and consignee to deal in the property which is being carried. The carrier is lawfully in possession of the goods of another, and he is sometimes described in legal terms as a *bailee*. This important role of the bill of lading also means that far-reaching and unpredictable liability exclusions on the part of the carrier will result in the rights which the bill of lading represents varying considerably and consignees or purchasers from them might be prejudiced by contracts made on unfavourable terms by the original shipper of the goods (the bill of lading will be discussed further below). It should be emphasized at this stage that the bill of lading is no longer the predominant document in ocean transportation, but is to a growing extent (and particularly in liner shipping) being substituted by other documents, such as way bills, data freight receipts and also with electronics.

The perspective here employed thus involves several different parameters, and these have their bearings in all those different relationships mentioned. It is therefore essential that the inter-relationships are observed.

How the documentary credit works

The principal advantages of documentary credit, covering transactions in merchandise, are the following:

—The buyer is not called upon to make payment until and unless the goods are shipped and evidence to this effect is produced by means of the documents which are to be surrendered.

—The seller is in a position to proceed with the execution of the order and the shipment of the goods as soon as he is in possession of the advice that the documentary credit has been established by the buyer's bank. On the strength of an irrevocable documentary credit, he is assured of payment by the bank, upon due presentation of the documents.

The handling of a documentary credit involves a minimum of three, but in most cases four parties, as the diagram below illustrates.

When the parties to a business transaction agree to payment terms involving a documentary credit, the buyer instructs his bank to open a credit in favour of the seller and to advise the latter to this effect either directly, or through a correspondent bank in the country of the seller:

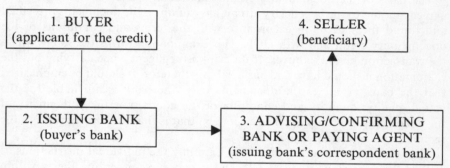

When the terms and conditions of the purchase contract provide that payment shall be made by irrevocable documentary credit the buyer arranges with his bank for the issuance, or "opening", of the required credit. The buyer tells his bank the nature of the transaction and the amount to be paid, gives a brief description of the merchandise to be shipped, specifies the documents required as evidence of shipment, and sets an expiration date for the credit. On the basis of this information the bank issues the letter in a form that meets the requirements of the sales contract.

The bank normally uses a correspondent bank, in the exporter's country, and the next step will thus be that the opening bank instructs its correspondent bank to inform the beneficiary—that is, the exporter—that the letter of credit has been established. The importer's bank may request its correspondent also to *confirm* the letter of credit; such confirmation binds the correspondent bank as well as the importer's bank to honour the credit. Or the importer's bank may request the correspondent bank itself to open the letter of credit, in which case only the correspondent bank is bound.

Documentary credits are regulated by Uniform Customs and Practice (UCP) related to documentary credits last revised in 1993 (UCP 500). The UCP have been drafted by the International Chamber of Commerce (ICC).

THE DOCUMENTS

The payment clause in the sales contract and the document provision in the letter of credit may prescribe, for example, that the following documents shall be presented:

"(a) Invoice; (b) Marine and War Risk Insurance Policy (Certificate) covering 10% above the c.i.f. value of the goods; (c) Full set of clean 'on board' (or received for shipment) Bills of Lading to order, evidencing shipment from Tokyo to Gothenburg latest 30th June 1994, and marked 'Freight paid'; (d) Certificate of Origin in duplicate; (e) Weight Note in duplicate."

The basis of the documentary credit transaction is that the bank pays the agreed amount to the beneficiary after it has examined the documents presented and found them to be in accordance with the terms and conditions of the documentary credit and with UCP. This examination forms the safety which the transaction gives the buyer. If the bank is negligent when carrying out the examination it should have and has a liability therefor. It should be emphasized that the bank examines the documents only; the bank is not liable for the actual quality, quantity and condition of the goods, nor the authenticity of the documents, but only for their accuracy, that is that they correspond to the requirements of the letter of credit.

Thus the bank has a duty to follow carefully the individual instructions as well as the provisions of the UCP, and it may have a certain liberty within strict limits to make the examination at its own discretion in order to avoid problems. In cases of fraud the bank will have no liability for having paid the beneficiary unless it is aware of such fraud. Under such circumstances the bank may be relieved from its duty to pay under the documentary credit. During recent years the number of documentary credit frauds has increased (see below).

The bill of lading

The charter-party is the written charter agreement. It contains all the terms and conditions governing the relationship between the shipowner and the charterer. The bill of lading will be issued upon the goods being received for shipment or, traditionally, upon their shipment.

The bill of lading, sometimes filled in by the shipper or by a forwarding agent, is signed by a representative of the owner, for instance the master of the vessel or, in practice, more often by the owner's agent. The charter-party may sometimes prescribe that the charterer's agent will sign the bill of lading. From the owner's point of view it is then important that it will be in conformity with the mate's receipts. In liner traffic, where numerous bills of lading are issued, the traditional signature may be substituted by a perforation scheme.

The bill of lading performs different important functions. It may constitute—

(a) a receipt for the goods which have been received for shipment or shipped;
(b) a contract for the carriage of the goods and the delivery thereof and thus contain the terms and conditions of carriage.

But the transport documents must also have a certain legal quality in order for the above-mentioned requirements to be met. Some of them give the holder the right to take delivery of the goods and in one way or another such documents entitle the holder of the documents to dispose of the goods while in transit. They are often referred to as "documents of title" and some of them are "negotiable documents" or at least "quasi-negotiable". This is the case with the bill of lading. It should again be mentioned that, to an ever growing extent, the traditional bill of lading in modern cargo transportation is being substituted by a "sea waybill" or by other documents which do not have the same legal qualities as the bill of lading, or by electronic methods.

In liner traffic, the bill of lading is the main document for the regulation of the relationship between the customer (frequently the shipper), the carrier and the consignee. Here the contract of carriage is normally based on a booking note whereby the agent of the carrier promises the customer space in a particular vessel or within a certain period of time. The bill of lading will thereafter be issued upon the shipment of the cargo (*shipped bill of lading*) or upon receipt thereof (*received for shipment bill of lading*).

In tramp shipping, the charter relationship is regulated in a charter-party signed by the charterer and the owner, and the bill of lading will then firstly be a receipt for the goods shipped, but it also retains its other functions to a large degree, particularly in relation to the person who, in good faith, acquires the bill of lading. The bill of lading then sometimes makes a reference to the charter-party.

The bill of lading may be made out to a named person, to a named person or order, to the holder, or to a named person "not to order". In the first three cases the bills of lading are regarded as "negotiable" or "quasi-negotiable" documents of title (except in the United States where in some cases the first one is not). Consignment notes and waybills have only certain of the functions and characteristics and are usually made out to a named person. The named person, not the holder of the document, is here entitled to claim delivery of the goods.

That a document is clothed with the characteristics of being a "negotiable document of title" is connected with the functions of the bill of lading in the sales transaction:

"The bill of lading, as such, is generally a negotiable instrument, entailing the right to demand the goods described therein and to take possession of them . . ."

It has already been mentioned that a sale and purchase of goods will normally form the basis of, *inter alia*, the contract of carriage. In the sale and purchase contract the parties have normally agreed on whether the seller or the buyer will arrange and/or pay for the transportation. The so-called transport clauses are also, therefore, of importance in the transportation relationship, particularly since the carrier will in one way or another have to deal with the shipper, the charterer and the consignee as well.

Schematically the relationship between a transport clause, the charter relationship and the transport document may be illustrated in the following way:

Transport clause: Seller–Buyer	Charter relationship/document Seller–Carrier	Document: Carrier–Buyer
CIF (Voyage charter)	Charter-party	Bill of lading
FOB (Voyage charter)	Shipper relation	Charter-party (and bill of lading)
CIF (Liner traffic)	Booking note, Bill of lading	Bill of lading
FOB (Liner traffic)	Shipper relation, Booking note	Bill of lading

It is important that the terms and conditions of the bill of lading and the charter-party are in accordance with each other as far as possible. Otherwise the result may be that the carrier may become liable for damage to cargo under the bill of lading without being able to invoke agreed exemptions under the charter-party or to seek redress from the charterer. Correspondingly, imbalances may appear in the relationship if laws of different countries apply to the different agreements, etc.

Bills of lading are printed forms normally produced by shipowners or operators. BIMCO has designed various model forms of bills of lading, such as the Conelinebill and Combiconbill which have been used as a basis for a large number of bills of lading. The carrier or the shipper demanding carriage of his goods on board a vessel will usually through agents have three or more copies of such documents filled in. The details required are, generally, the name of the shipper of the goods, the name of the consignee, if known (or quite frequently if a bank has financed the purchase it will be made out "to order", since the document will be pledged as security to the bank), the port of loading, the port of discharge, the name of the ship and a description of the cargo (in terms of loading marks, description of packages, weight or measurement and contents), amount, and place of, and time for, payment of freight.

A large number of bill of lading clauses will govern the carrier's relationship with the shipper and the consignee. Furthermore, the bill of lading is a receipt, wherein the carrier acknowledges that he has received the goods, type, quality and quantity as stated (either on board the ship or for shipment) and that they will be delivered to the consignee. The bill of lading is also a document of title and the holder of it is entitled at the destination to demand delivery of the goods carried.

Usually the carrier in the bill of lading tries to make the terms and conditions of the charter-party applicable to the bill of lading by reference to the charter, for example, by stamping on the bill of lading a clause of the type:

"This bill of lading shall be subject to the terms and conditions of charter-party between . . . and . . . dated . . .".

Frequently, the seller is not prepared to accept such a clause because, when payment is to be made under a documentary credit, the paying bank may, following the provisions of UCP, refuse to accept a bill of lading making reference to a charter-party unless it has been expressly instructed to accept such a bill of lading.

Due to this relationship between the seller and the carrier there has been a strong demand that the holder of the bill of lading—if in good faith and unless he is also the shipper and/or charterer, i.e. a negotiated bill of lading—will be protected by *mandatory* rules to avoid the carrier exempting himself from all of his responsibilities with regard to the cargo. Such legislation based on international conventions (with regard to the Hague Rules, the Hague-Visby Rules and the Hamburg Rules see more below) aims at putting on the carrier as against the cargo owner a minimum liability for damage to or loss of the cargo. In such a situation the carrier may be vested with a more far-reaching liability than he would have had under the charter-party.

"Clean" bills of lading

Bills of lading and other transport documents thus play an important role in international trade.

The basis of the documentary credit transaction is that the bank pays the agreed amount to the beneficiary after it has examined the documents presented and found them to be in accordance with the terms and conditions of the documentary credit. This examination forms the security which the transaction gives the buyer. As already emphasized the bank examines the documents only;

the bank has no liability for the actual quality, quantity and condition of the goods, but only for ensuring that the documents are in accordance with the instructions given to the bank. Thus, most legal problems arising under a documentary credit transaction emanate from the documents tendered and examined.

From the buyer's point of view, it is important for the transport document to give him some information about the type of goods and their quality and quantity, since he may only have the bill of lading and the seller's invoice to rely on when asked to pay. It is also important that the buyer gets an indication of when the goods have been shipped on board or, at least, when they have been received for shipment. On the basis of the terms and conditions of the purchase agreement it may also be necessary that the bill of lading shows whether the freight has been paid in advance. Such evidence is important in, e.g., c.i.f. transactions where the seller is required to pay the freight.

It is also of great importance for the seller/shipper to have a clean bill of lading issued by the carrier, since otherwise the buyer will refuse to pay for the documents or, under a documentary credit, the paying banks will refuse to pay against such a document when tendered, since such qualification is an indication that the goods do not conform with the requirements of the sales agreement.

As mentioned, the ocean carrier has a duty to enter such particulars into the bill of lading, and under the Hague-Visby Rules the carrier is not entitled to produce evidence which conflicts with particulars entered into the bill of lading against a person who has acquired the bill of lading in good faith. The carrier's liability for wrong statements in the bill of lading is then basically governed in the same way as his liability for damage to goods, but other provisions may under certain circumstances complete the picture, and may make the carrier's liability more far reaching.

From the seller's point of view it is then important that a *clean* bill of lading is issued, i.e. a bill of lading not containing any remarks with respect to the condition of the goods. Due to the terms and conditions of the purchase agreement, the buyer is generally under no duty to pay for an unclean bill of lading, at least in cases where a remark gives reason to presume that the goods are not in customary or agreed condition. Under payment by documentary credit the UCP (article 32 in the 500 revision) also prescribe that the bill of lading must be clean. The seller's interest in clean bills of lading has thus, in some instances, caused pressure on the carrier to issue clean bills of lading, although remarks should be entered. In exchange for the clean bill of lading the seller/shipper then issues a "letter of indemnity" in favour of the carrier, whereby he assumes liability for all consequences of the owner issuing a clean bill of lading. Such a back-letter may have a limited value and it should again be underlined that the P. & I. insurance does not give the owner any protection in case of damages due to incorrect statements in a bill of lading.

DOCUMENTATION IN MODERN TRANSPORTATION

Some distinctions may be made between various types of bills of lading. One distinction is made between *shipped bills of lading* and *received for shipment bills of lading*. Traditionally, the shipped bill of lading has been the most common one, a document issued by the master or, in practice, more often by the carrier's agent when the goods have been loaded on board the vessel.

The received for shipment bill of lading is issued when the goods have been received by the carrier for shipment later. The received for shipment bill of lading has come to play a much more important role where unity transports, particularly container transports and ro/ro traffic, dominate the trade.

At a growing rate, carriage of general cargo is now performed in co-operation between different carriers, who each perform one part immediately following upon the preceding part. Either the same means of transportation (*through transport*) or different means (*combined transport*) may then be used to perform the total transport. (Cf. also the concept of *intermodal transport*.) Then combined transport documents (CT documents) or combined transport bills of lading may be issued as well as certain freight forwarder documents (e.g., FCT).

This type of transportation can give rise to problems. Since there is a co-ordination of transport where several different modes of transportation are involved, the document covering the whole transport may be issued either by a non-vessel-owning operator or freight forwarder conducting business *as a carrier* or *as agent only for a carrier* or by one of the carriers, for example the shipowner. Several new types of documents and documentary routines have been introduced involving, to a certain extent, new functions.

Too frequently bills of lading are delayed in the mail with the result that they do not arrive until after the relevant goods have been delivered. This is a problem which can occur particularly when short-sea transits are involved, for example the North Sea. In documentary credit sales, documents can often be delayed in the course of bank handling. From the ocean carrier's point of view this creates problems, since his duty to deliver the goods is based on the duty of the receiver to surrender the bills of lading. This is a legal implication due to the nature and function of the bill of lading. If the carrier delivers the cargo without the bill of lading being surrendered the carrier may be liable for any resulting loss or damage. In such circumstances, as previously mentioned, the carrier is not covered by his P. & I. club. What commonly happens in such a situation is that the consignee may put up a bank guarantee to cover any loss or expenses incurred by the carrier as a result of his delivering the cargo without the bills of lading being surrendered. Such guarantee is not unlawful, but the growing use of such guarantees illustrates the deterioration of the bill of lading system.

For carriage over short distances there is usually less need for financing by documentary credit. In some trades it has become usual practice to issue "destination bills of lading". In these cases, the bill of lading is either issued at the destination in order to avoid loss of time, or else, one bill of lading is carried on board to be signed by the consignee as a receipt when the goods are delivered. Legally this is a questionable custom.

As already mentioned a distinction must be made between *negotiable*—or rather *quasi-negotiable*—and non-negotiable bills of lading. Most bills of lading used in ocean carriage are of the former type. The commercial principle underlying the use of a bill of lading is that it will be exchanged simultaneously for the goods it represents. The carrier is bound to deliver the goods only to the holder of at least one original bill of lading, and by the same token only such holder is entitled to claim delivery of the goods in exchange for surrendering the bill of lading. If two people, each with an original bill of lading, claim delivery at the destination then neither of them is entitled to have the goods. The goods must be stored until a court has decided which is the true owner of the goods. Only a holder of *all* the original bills of lading may dispose of the goods at a place which is not the destination. Thus the carrier can only agree to re-route the goods, for example where all the original bills of lading are produced to him. Similarly, the carrier may only issue a new set of bills of lading in exchange for all the old originals. It must be said, however, that it is now not uncommon in practice for cargoes (especially oil) to be delivered without bills of lading being surrendered, and for new bills of lading to be issued without the old originals being produced. It is also important to keep in mind that, particularly in oil trade, the goods are often sold several times during the trip, and very often the destination may be changed several times. It is obvious that a conflict between the legal rules and the practical requirements will often occur.

THE CARRIER'S LIABILITY

The ocean carrier's liability for damage to or in connection with the goods is regulated in different ways. In a charter relationship the owner and the charterer are basically free to distribute between themselves the liability for cargo damage. In traffic where the bill of lading is the main document governing the relationship between the cargo owner and the carrier, compulsory legislation, based on certain international conventions, has been introduced in many countries. The idea behind these rules is that a minimum liability should be placed on the ocean carriers for damage to cargo, primarily where the bill of lading is the governing document such as, for example, in liner traffic. Under these rules the carrier is vested with a compulsory liability in relation to the shipper as well as to the consignee. Where, on the other hand, a charter-party governs the relationship between the carrier and the shipper, the mandatory rules do not take precedence over the parties' contractual intentions.

A third party holder of the bill of lading in good faith can, however, invoke the mandatory rules.

When making claims for cargo lost or damaged in a carriage by sea, various questions may need to be asked in order to ascertain whether liability can be established against one or more of the parties involved. The main questions are:

—what are the grounds of liability?
—against whom can a claim be made?
—will it be the head owner or the charterer who is held ultimately liable?

In the following pages we are going to discuss the above questions, particularly, of course, the grounds for liability. With respect to the last question let us just briefly mention that even if the charterer and the owner have between themselves agreed on the distribution of cargo liability a cargo receiver may nevertheless, under the bill of lading, have a claim against either of them. In such a situation there may be a question of redress between the owner and the charterer.

Liability for cargo under charter-parties

The questions concerning allocation of liability for cargo under voyage charter-parties and time charter-parties will be dealt with separately under respective chapters (pages 206 and 242). As a bill of lading is usually issued for each parcel of cargo and as the liability for cargo under the bill of lading is governed by international conventions which are not immediately applicable to charter-parties, we shall, in this chapter as a base for following chapters, explain the basic rules of liability for cargo under a bill of lading, which is the document on which cargo receivers usually base their claim.

BILL OF LADING CONVENTIONS

During the 19th century the bills of lading used in different trades were amended with new liability exemption clauses. In the United States, where cargo interests were strong, compulsory legislation was introduced through the Harter Act. Under this Act a minimum liability was put on sea carriers loading or discharging cargo in the United States. Basically this liability covered the period from receipt of the goods until their delivery. This legislation still forms a basis for the carrier's liability in the United States. During the 1920s the time came for an international convention aimed at some protection for the cargo owners and the bill of lading as a negotiable document.

The question of the ocean carrier's liability was also tied to the characteristics of the bill of lading as a document of title and as "representing" the goods and the need for the possibility to transfer the document and thereby basically also the title to the cargo. Those questions were, in English law, dealt with in the

Bill of Lading Act 1855 which was replaced by a new English Carriage of Goods by Sea Act in 1992. The new Act deals with various transport documents, not only the traditional bill of lading.

With respect to the international conventions the basic convention is "The International Convention for the Unification of Certain Rules relating to Bills of Lading, dated Brussels 28th of August 1924", usually called the Hague Rules. This convention was amended by the "Protocol signed at Brussels on the 23rd of February 1968". The amended convention is usually referred to as "the Hague-Visby Rules".

The Hague Rules and the Hague-Visby Rules have been adopted in several countries. In England and the United States the statute based on the Hague Rules is called the "Carriage of Goods by Sea Act" usually referred to as COGSA or United States COGSA. In England the enactment based on the Hague-Visby Rules is known as the Carriage by Sea Act 1971, in force since 1978. In 1978 a new convention, "The Hamburg Rules", was signed and this convention puts on the carrier a more far-reaching liability than the Hague Rules and the Hague-Visby Rules.

Since these conventions are rather complicated, and have not been adopted in the same way in all countries, and since they are interpreted differently in various countries, it is not possible in this book to give detailed information about the carrier's liability for cargo under the bill of lading. We shall, however, try to outline the basic rules and the basic differences between the various conventions.

The compulsory nature of the liability rules

As already mentioned, the different conventions are mandatory—or compulsory—in their nature. This is expressed in the Hague Rules in the following way:

"Any clause, covenant, or agreement in the contract of carriage relieving the carrier or the ship from liability for loss or damage to, or in connection with, goods arising from negligence, fault, or failure in the duties and obligations provided in this article or lessening such liability otherwise than as provided in this Convention shall be null and void and of no effect."

The Hamburg Rules use the following language:

"Any stipulation in a contract of carriage by sea, in a bill of lading, or in any other document evidencing that contract of carriage by sea is null and void to the extent that it derogates, directly or indirectly, from the provisions of this Convention. The nullity of such a stipulation does not affect the validity of the other provisions of the contract or document of which it forms a part. A clause assigning benefit of insurance of the goods in favour of the carrier, or any similar clause, is null and void."

The cargo liability conventions are based on a risk distribution between the carrier and the cargo owner. More risk is placed on the carrier under the

Hamburg Rules than under the Hague Rules. This risk distribution scheme under the Hague Rules exempted the carrier from liability under certain circumstances and limited his liability generally. The Rules impose on the carrier a general duty of care in relation to the goods throughout the applicable period of carriage and provided that the cargo is not exposed to a high degree of risk, for example deck cargo.

Nothing in the conventions prevents the carrier from accepting a more extensive liability than the minimum prescribed. This frequently happens in container and ro/ro traffic. Furthermore, as already mentioned, the Hague Rules' liability is commonly introduced through a so-called *Paramount clause* into bills of lading covering shipments where the Hague Rules would not otherwise apply. Clauses paramount are also commonly inserted into charter-parties, where the Hague Rules are not applicable.

The scope of application of the conventions

The bill of lading conventions may apply automatically, or by agreement. The rules are automatically applicable mainly when the agreement for carriage is included in a bill of lading and when there is a carriage from a country which has signed the bill of lading convention. In some cases the rules are automatically applicable when the carriage is destined to a country which has signed the convention. There are also other supplementary rules which may complicate the picture. Particular legal problems may come to the fore in future if the different conventions all remain in force but operate to various extents in different countries.

It should be noted that in cases where the basic agreement is set out in a charter-party containing provisions as to cargo liability less severe to the carrier than those found in the compulsory regulations, the latter will nevertheless apply in the relationship between the carrier and a consignee in good faith.

The period of liability in the Hague Rules is based on the so-called tackle-to-tackle principle, i.e. from the moment when the cargo is hooked on to the vessel's gear upon loading until it is again hooked off upon discharge. This tackle-to-tackle principle is, however, not applied in the same manner in all countries.

In a number of countries there seems to be some extension of the scope of application of the Hague Rules. There seems to be a trend towards a principle which provides that, even if the goods have in fact been discharged, the carrier may not act so as to cause the purpose of the carriage to fail. There is also a general duty on the master to protect the cargo owner's interest and he may have an obligation to intervene if he becomes aware (or ought to have become aware) of the fact that the goods are not being properly taken care of immediately after discharge. Thus a reefer carrier cannot be sure of relying on the tackle-to-tackle principle if he discharges refrigerated cargo on to a pier where there are no refrigeration facilities. Numerous factors may be relevant in determining the carrier's obligations in such a case, which may depend, for example, on who the actual receiver is; how the port and warehouse system in the harbour functions; what influence the carrier has on the situation, etc. In some countries additional compulsory legislation has been introduced covering the terminal period.

The Hamburg Rules have also adopted the more extensive application, so that they apply from the time the carrier "has taken over the goods from the shipper ... until the time he has delivered the goods ...." Transport documents involving container traffic, ro/ro traffic etc. commonly use this more extensive liability period. It is also used when there is no mandatory legislation to such effect.

The liability system

Before we venture into the liability system it should be mentioned that damage may arise in different ways. There may be physical damage to goods, goods may be short-landed, and goods may be delayed, but there may also be damage due to wrong statements being made in the bill of lading. The liability system is primarily geared towards physical damage and short-landing, but damage due to delay is often covered in some way. At least, if wrong statements have been made intentionally in the bill of lading, the liability system may be supplemented by particular rules relating to liability for wrong statements.

There lies upon the carrier a duty to make the vessel seaworthy. This is expressed in the Hague Rules in the following way:

"The carrier shall be bound before and at the beginning of the voyage to exercise due diligence to:
  (a) Make the ship seaworthy;
  (b) Properly man, equip and supply the ship;
  (c) Make the holds, refrigerating and cool chambers, and all other parts of the ship in which goods are carried, fit and safe for their reception, carriage and preservation."

It must be emphasized that there is no absolute liability on the carrier to make the vessel seaworthy but he shall "exercise due diligence". If he can later prove that he has acted properly in this respect he is relieved from liability for loss of or damage to goods as a result of the vessel's unseaworthiness. In the same provision it is also stated that the carrier shall properly and carefully load, handle, stow, carry, keep, care for, and discharge the goods carried.

The principal rule in the Hague Rules liability system is expressed in the following way:

"Neither the carrier nor the ship shall be responsible for loss or damage arising or resulting from: ...
  (q) Any other cause arising without the actual fault or privity of the carrier, or without the fault or neglect of the agents or servants of the carrier, but a burden of proof shall be on the person claiming the benefit of this exception to show that neither the actual fault or privity of the carrier nor the fault or neglect of the agents or servants of the carrier contributed to the loss or damage."

This rule is fundamental to the liability provisions. The principle is that the carrier is responsible for loss or damage arising or resulting from the fault or privity of himself or his servants or agents. The burden of proof is on the carrier, which means that he has to prove that he, his servants or agents *have not* caused the loss or damage by negligence.

There are a number of specific exceptions which relieve the carrier from responsibility for loss or damage resulting from:

"(c) Perils, dangers and accidents of the sea or other navigable waters.
(d) Act of God.
(e) Act of war.
(f) Act of public enemies.
(g) Arrest or restraint of princes, rulers or people, or seizure under legal process.
(h) Quarantine restrictions.
(i) Act or omission of the shipper or owner of the goods, his agent or representative.
(j) Strikes or lockouts or stoppage or restraint of labour from whatever cause, whether partial or general.
(k) Riots and civil commotions.
(l) Saving or attempting to save life or property at sea.
(m) Wastage in bulk or weight or any other loss or damage arising from inherent defect, quality or vice of the goods.
(n) Insufficiency of packing.
(o) Insufficiency or inadequacy of marks.
(p) Latent defects not discoverable by due diligence."

The above exemptions actually illustrate situations where the carrier is not negligent, but there are also two "true" exceptions from the principal rule. These are "error in navigation" and "fire".

"(2) Neither the carrier nor the ship shall be responsible for loss or damage arising or resulting from:
(a) Act, neglect, or default of the master, mariner, pilot, or the servants of the carrier in the navigation or in the management of the ship.
(b) Fire, unless caused by the actual fault or privity of the carrier."

As regards (a) it should be noted that only negligence, etc., in the navigation or the management *of the ship* relieves the carrier from liability. It is sometimes difficult to draw the borderline between "management of the ship" (error in navigation) and "management and handling of the cargo" (commercial error).

A contractual principle is that a party may not one-sidedly change his fundamental contractual obligations (fundamental breach). In the law of carriage the carrier may thus not "deviate" from the agreed or normal route. The doctrine of deviation may sometimes cause problems when it comes to striking a balance between what is commercially suitable but legally not permitted. If the cargo is lost or damaged in connection with deviation (including consequence of delay), the carrier is not liable provided the deviation was made "in saving or attempting to save life or property at sea" or else provided the deviation was reasonable. If the deviation is not regarded as reasonable considering both the carrier's and the cargo owner's interests the carrier will risk facing liability without any of the defences or limitations in the convention. Most charter-parties and bills of lading contain scope of voyage (or similar) clauses, which allow the carrier to change the route. In bill of lading relations such a scope of voyage clause may, depending on the circumstances, be in conflict with the mandatory rules on deviation.

In this connection particular regard should be given to the common practice of changing tanker crew after minor deviations. Such deviation is necessary for practical purposes since large tankers seldom visit regular ports. Nevertheless such practice from a legal point of view may be regarded as unlawful deviation and the carrier will then have no P. & I. cover unless specifically covered.

There are also some other important exceptions, namely where live animals have been carried and where cargo has been carried on deck, and the bill of lading states so expressly. These exceptions apply unless the carrier has been negligent. If cargo has been carried on deck, but the bill of lading does not state this, it may, in some legal systems, amount to "unlawful deviation" for which the carrier has a strict liability. Furthermore, it should be mentioned that in modern container traffic a number of containers are always placed on what may be described as "deck". To avoid the above-mentioned problems the carrier takes on the same liability for cargo on deck as under deck, a system that seems to have worked.

Cargo claims and time limits

A cargo owner who intends to claim against the carrier for loss of or damage to the goods should do this in writing and enclose the necessary documents and supporting evidence, such as a copy of the bill of lading, survey or tally reports from discharging, invoices stating the value of the cargo, etc.

It is important for the claimant to be aware of the *one-year time limit* which, in the Hague Rules, has the following wording:

"In any event the carrier and the ship shall be discharged from all liability in respect of loss or damage unless suit is brought within one year after delivery of the goods or the date when the goods should have been delivered."

It is not sufficient to make sure that the claim has been sent to the carrier before the year has ended. Unless the claimant gets payment he must either get time extension from the carrier or file a suit before the year has ended as otherwise his claim will be time-barred.

In the Hague-Visby Rules, but not in the Hague Rules, there is a special section dealing with the redress situation by which the claimant gets additional time when the claim is an action for indemnity against a third person. The length of the additional time depends on the relevant law but shall not be

"less than three months, commencing from the day when the person bringing such an action for indemnity has settled the claim or has been served with process in the action against himself."

The Hamburg Rules extend the limitation period to two years.

Limitation of liability

The bill of lading conventions contain rules concerning limitation of the carrier's liability. These rules, which limit the carrier's liability to a certain amount per package or unit, are fairly complicated. It may be difficult to define "package or unit" and it has also been difficult to find an international monetary base for the limitation. As a result of these complications, the final outcome of the claimant's action will vary depending on the law of which country that is applicable.

The Hague-Visby Rules have supplemented the Hague Rules in certain respects. The limitation figure has been increased and the claimant may use either the package/unit limitation or a limitation per kilo of the weight of the goods, whichever is preferable to him. Furthermore, a special rule has been introduced with respect to the carriage of goods in containers. The limitation amounts in the conventions, although previously based on common denominators, such as Poincaré francs—a fictitious monetary standard—now normally fall back on SDR (Special Drawing Rights) which is a "basket" of different major currencies.

Irrespective of the limitation of liability provisions in the cargo liability legislation there is also a system known as the global limitation. This global limitation of maritime liability covers all relationships: the shipowner's liability to cargo owners, to charterers, to other shipowners in case of collision, etc., and to other third parties. A number of conventions have been introduced governing the global limitation, the most recent ones being in 1957 and 1976.

Shipowners' liability as regards inspection and description of the goods

The importance to shippers of getting a clean bill of lading has already been mentioned. According to the bill of lading conventions, the master or the carrier's agents shall, at the request of the shipper, issue a bill of lading after the goods have been received. The bill of lading should contain a statement concerning leading marks for identification of the goods, quantity, and apparent order and condition of the goods. According to the Hague-Visby Rules the carrier is not entitled to bring in counter evidence against particulars entered into the bill of lading, against the person who has acquired the bill of lading in good faith, and it is thus important for the carrier that the master and the ship's officers make proper examination and description of the goods. The goods will be inspected and tallied in connection with the loading but exactly how this inspection and tallying is arranged is dependent on the type of cargo, method of loading, etc., and must be decided from case to case. The usual wording in the bill of lading is that the cargo has been received "in apparent good order and condition" and this wording indicates that the carrier is not strictly liable for the cargo and thus, for instance, not liable for hidden defects.

The master must see to it that remarks about the cargo are inserted into the mate's receipts and that the shippers are made aware of the master's intention to insert corresponding remarks into the bill of lading. If shippers are properly advised, they may have the chance to take back defective cargo and deliver substitute cargo free from defects.

Basically the carrier will in such cases have a liability as if goods were short-shipped or damaged but as mentioned there may be cases where a more far-reaching liability may be imposed on him for wrongful statements.

In this context the use of so-called "back letters" should be kept in mind (see above, page 58).

Some basic features of the Hamburg Rules

As previously mentioned, a new convention, the Hamburg Rules, was signed at a diplomatic conference in Hamburg in 1978. The new convention is intended to supersede the Hague Rules and the Hague-Visby Rules.

Except for the change in layout of the new convention, the major material changes are:

—The new rules will apply to all contracts for carriage of goods by sea between two States, except when the contract is a charter-party.
—The "error in navigation" exception has been abolished and the "fire" exception narrowed.
—The performing and contractual carrier will be jointly and severally liable against the cargo owners.
—The bill of lading will be conclusive evidence against the carrier if the bill of lading has been transferred to a third party who is in good faith.
—The limitation amounts have been increased.

It will still take some time before the Hamburg Rules supersede the old rules.

The date of the bill of lading

The bill of lading is a receipt for the goods which have been received for shipment or loaded on board. In either case the correct method of dating the bill of lading is to insert the date when the last parcel of the lot was received (in the former case) or (in the latter case) when the last parcel of the lot was taken on board. This means that every lot must be regarded separately.

Sometimes the shippers wish to have the bills of lading antedated for various reasons. The master and/or the carrier should not accept such a procedure as this may constitute fraud and, if discovered, may cause serious difficulties with receivers, bankers, authorities, etc. The carrier's liability for incorrect dating of bills of lading is usually not covered by P. & I. insurance. Postdating, particularly in liner traffic, does not seem to be uncommon. This is not unlawful *per se*, but may just mean that all bills of lading are dated and signed some time after all the goods have been received or loaded.

Substitute documents

Above we have given the background of the bill of lading and its functions (page 54ff.). There is thus a tradition of issuing three (or more) *original* bills of lading, one of which is to be surrendered at the port of destination in exchange for the cargo carried. We have also pointed out the difficulties arising from the delay in communication of the documents, having as a consequence that the cargo arrives at the discharging port before the goods. This is true not only in "near traffic" but also in ocean traffic over long distances, in liner traffic, as well as oil transportation and carriage of other bulk cargoes. It has become very common that the carrier demands a bank guarantee or a parent company guarantee indemnifying him for all consequences of his delivering the cargo without the bill of lading being returned to the carrier—basically for the carrier's liability if the cargo cannot be delivered to the correct holder of the bill of lading. Various measures have been taken to avoid these problems; the use of non-negotiable documents, such as waybills, etc. So-called destination bills of lading have been used. In some trades data freight receipts were introduced. In oil transportation a system of registration of the cargoes was contemplated but at the time it was not possible to make it into a workable system. The most ambitious proposal is based on data transmission of all particulars of the cargo and if requested the issuance of a *cargo key receipt*. Such systems work in certain trades and may gradually spread to others.

It is quite common to find in time charter-parties (and for that matter also in voyage charter-parties) a clause explicitly stating that the owner shall "sign bills of lading as presented" and that the owner undertakes to deliver cargo even if bills of lading are not presented in exchange for a guarantee by a charterer's parent or a guarantee by a bank. It needs to be stressed that "as presented" does *not* mean that the carrier shall have a duty to sign a bill of lading that is incorrect. With respect to the delivery of cargo with a bill of lading being presented, a guarantee is not worth more than the guarantor's financial standing.

LIABILITY AGAINST THIRD PARTY

Occasionally there are claims from a third party other than cargo claims. For instance, claims from stevedores injured during loading or discharging, from passengers, claims for pollution of the sea, claims as the result of collision with other vessels, tugs, pilot boats, piers, dolphins, etc.

In most cases the owner is primarily liable against a third party for such damages. Sometimes the primary liability also rests on the charterers. As an example, time charterers in some countries have been held liable for damages caused by oil spillage and for accidents in which passengers have been injured.

When the primary liability rests with the owner, he may sometimes have a chance to claim recovery from the charterers. This is so especially in time chartering when stevedores, tugs, pilots, etc., are employed by the time charterers. When the primary liability rests on the charterer he can, of course, also have the opportunity to seek recovery from the owner.

Although claims from third parties can be very large, they will not be further discussed in this book. Owners who wish additional information are instead referred to their hull and P. & I. underwriters.

Owners' liabilities against third parties are often covered by P. & I. insurance. An important issue regarding shipowner's liability, and one which is ever-growing, concerns oil pollution, and liability rules in this respect have become more and more extensive, with the U.S.A. as the predominant leader with the Oil Pollution Act of 1990. In view of the very high limitation amounts, such liability rules also strain the P. & I. clubs. As regards oil pollution, TOVALOP and Cristal should also be mentioned. TOVALOP is a private organization guaranteeing cover for pollution liability exceeding what is covered by the P. & I. clubs. TOVALOP stands for Tanker Owners Voluntary Liability for Oil Pollution. TOVALOP clauses are found especially in tanker time charter-parties and the intention is in that context to guarantee that any liability should be on the owners and not on the time charterers, and that owners have the extra cover given by TOVALOP. Cristal stands for a Contract Regarding an Interim Supplement to Tanker Liability for Oil Pollution. This is a cargo owner's plan which is a supplementary one to TOVALOP, and which provides compensation in connection with cargoes carried in vessels covered by the TOVALOP scheme.

UCP* AND THE BILL OF LADING

Mention has already been made of the UCP governing the methods of payment for international sales of goods. (See page 50ff.) The bill of lading and other transport documents play a crucial part in the documentary credit system. It is important to bear in mind that a transfer of the bill of lading will normally entitle the holder to claim delivery of the goods. Often the bank demands the right to hold the bill of lading—and goods—as security for payments or advances made, for example under a documentary credit. Several letters of credit prescribe that the bank will have "full ownership", while others, particularly those used in the European continental countries, more often will

* ICC Uniform Customs and Practice for Documentary Credits (UCP 500), ICC Publication No. 500, ISBN 92.842.1155.7(E). Published in its official English version by the International Chamber of Commerce, Paris. Copyright © 1993—International Chamber of Commerce (ICC). Available from: ICC Publishing SA, 38 Cours Albert 1er, 75008 Paris, France. And from: ICC United Kingdom, 14/15 Belgrave Square, London SW1X 8PS.

entitle the bank to a pledge or a lien. From a practical point of view this distinction will make no great difference.

Opinions differ as to the method of describing the cargo in a bill of lading. One view is that the bill of lading should contain a complete description of the cargo. But this is somewhat impractical since the carrier can hardly be expected to break into packages and examine the goods to check their description, quality and quantity. He has neither a right nor a duty to make such a check except possibly where he has reason to suspect that something is not as it should be. The main principle, however, is that the carrier has a duty to inspect the goods externally.

Other problems that may arise and which are closely interrelated are whether the bill of lading must cover the stated voyage and whether the contracting carrier can allow another carrier to perform the carriage and also exempt himself from liability in connection therewith.

One may say that the UCP to a large extent reflect the transportation system. For a long period it was customary that a *shipped* bill of lading was issued and that it was issued by an ocean carrier, that the contemplated cargo transportation was to take place in *one vessel*, that the cargo was not to be carried on deck, etc.

The idea of the UCP is that the parties could agree specifically on any document to be presented to the bank, but that unless something specifically has been said the rules are based on the "normal" course of business. That is why the UCP of 1974 (based on previous versions) in art 19, *inter alia*, prescribed the following:

"a. Unless specifically authorized in the credit, bills of lading of the following nature will be rejected:
If the letter of credit demands one specified type of bill of lading any other type must be rejected by the bank. If a straight bill of lading has been demanded the bank need not accept an order bill of lading or vice versa."

The received for shipment bill of lading has in this connection caused some problems. In English law the principle has developed that under a c.i.f. contract a bill of lading means a shipped bill of lading. Due to particular circumstances received for shipment bills of lading have been recognized as usual in some trades and have in some cases been accepted. If the letter of credit does not contain any particular provision as regards the bill of lading the UCP will govern. Through UCP 500 substantial changes have been made with respect to transport documents in order that the documentary credit provisions shall be synchronized with the handling and practical use of the documents. UCP 500 has been enlarged in this respect and the section on "Documents" now embraces articles 20–38. Efforts have been made in the revision to achieve clarification and precision.

Articles 20–22 contain rules on ambiguity as to the issuer of documents and issuance dates as compared with credit date, articles 23–30 specify different types of documents, such as marine/ocean bill of lading (article 23), non-negotiable sea waybill (article 24), charterparty bill of lading (article 25), multimodal transport document (article 26) and transport documents issued by freight forwarders (article 30). Articles 31–33 contain clarification principles on "on deck", "shipper's load" and name of consignor (article 31), clean transport documents (article 32) and freight payable/prepaid transport documents (article 33).

Article 23 spells out the importance of the dating of transport documents:

"Unless otherwise stipulated in the Credit, banks will accept a document bearing a date of issuance prior to that of the Credit, subject to such document being presented within the time limits set out in the Credit and in these Articles."

UCP 500 thus contains extensive rules on the different transport documents involved and since they are of utmost importance we have chosen to quote articles 23–26 and article 30. Whether the clarifications intended will prove to be sufficient remains to be seen. As is evident the drafters have decided to make every article complete on its own, resulting in very extensive wording.

Article 23 concerns the traditional bill of lading.

"(a)   If a Credit calls for a bill of lading covering a port-to-port shipment, banks will, unless otherwise stipulated in the Credit, accept a document, however named, which:

  (i)   appears on its face to indicate the name of the carrier and to have been signed or otherwise authenticated by:

—the carrier or a named agent for or on behalf of the carrier, or

—the master or a named agent for or on behalf of the master.

Any signature or authentication of the carrier or master must be identified as carrier or master, as the case may be. An agent signing or authenticating for the carrier or master must also indicate the name and the capacity of the party, i.e. carrier or master, on whose behalf that agent is acting,

and

  (ii)   indicates that the goods have been loaded on board, or shipped on a named vessel.

Loading on board or shipment on a named vessel may be indicated by pre-printed wording on the bill of lading that the goods have been loaded on board a named vessel or shipped on a named vessel, in which case the date of issuance of the bill of lading will be deemed to be the date of loading on board and the date of shipment.

In all other cases loading on board a named vessel must be evidenced by a notation on the bill of lading which gives the date on which the goods have been loaded on board, in which case the date of the on board notation will be deemed to be the date of shipment.

If the bill of lading contains the indication 'intended vessel', or similar qualification in relation to the vessel, loading on board a named vessel must be evidenced by an on board notation on the bill of lading which, in addition to the date on which the goods have been loaded on board, also includes the name of the vessel on which the goods have been loaded, even if they have been loaded on the vessel named as the 'intended vessel'.

If the bill of lading indicates a place of receipt or taking in charge different from the port of loading, the on board notation must also include the port of loading stipulated in the Credit and the name of the vessel on which the goods have been loaded, even if they have been loaded on the vessel named in the bill of lading. This provision also applies whenever loading on board the vessel is indicated by pre-printed wording on the bill of lading,

and

(iii)   indicates the port of loading and the port of discharge stipulated in the Credit, notwithstanding that it:

(a) indicates a place of taking in charge different from the port of loading, and/or a place of final destination different from the port of discharge,

and/or

(b) contains the indication 'intended' or similar qualification in relation to the port of loading and/or port of discharge, as long as the document also states the ports of loading and/or discharge stipulated in the Credit,

and

(iv)   consists of a sole original bill of lading or, if issued in more than one original, the full set as so issued,

and

(v)   appears to contain all of the terms and conditions of carriage, or some of such terms and conditions by reference to a source or document other than the bill of lading (short form/blank back bill of lading); banks will not examine the contents of such terms and conditions,

and

(vi)   contains no indication that it is subject to a charter party and/or no indication that the carrying vessel is propelled by sail only,

and

(vii)   in all other respects meets the stipulations of the Credit.

(b) For the purpose of this Article, transhipment means unloading and reloading from one vessel to another vessel during the course of ocean carriage from the port of loading to the port of discharge stipulated in the Credit.

(c) Unless transhipment is prohibited by the terms of the Credit, banks will accept a bill of lading which indicates that the goods will be transhipped, provided that the entire ocean carriage is covered by one and the same bill of lading.

(d) Even if the Credit prohibits transhipment, banks will accept a bill of lading which:

(i)   indicates that transhipment will take place as long as the relevant cargo is shipped in Container(s), Trailer(s) and/or "LASH" barge(s) as evidenced by the bill of lading, provided that the entire ocean carriage is covered by one and the same bill of lading,

and/or

(ii)   incorporates clauses stating that the carrier reserves the right to tranship."

Article 24 is directed at the currently frequent use of sea waybills:

"(a) If a Credit calls for a non-negotiable sea waybill covering a port-to-port shipment, banks will, unless otherwise stipulated in the Credit, accept a document, however named, which:

    (i)   appears on its face to indicate the name of the carrier and to have been signed or otherwise authenticated by:

        —the carrier or a named agent for or on behalf of the carrier, or

        —the master or a named agent for or on behalf of the master.

        Any signature or authentication of the carrier or master must be identified as carrier or master, as the case may be. An agent signing or authenticating for the carrier or master must also indicate the name and the capacity of the party, i.e. carrier or master, on whose behalf that agent is acting,

        and

    (ii)   indicates that the goods have been loaded on board, or shipped on a named vessel.

        Loading on board or shipment on a named vessel may be indicated by pre-printed wording on the non-negotiable sea waybill that the goods have been loaded on board a named vessel or shipped on a named vessel, in which case the date of issuance of the non-negotiable sea waybill will be deemed to be the date of loading on board and the date of shipment.

        In all other cases loading on board a named vessel must be evidenced by a notation on the non-negotiable sea waybill which gives the date on which the goods have been loaded on board, in which case the date of the on board notation will be deemed to be the date of shipment.

        If the non-negotiable sea waybill contains the indication 'intended vessel', or similar qualification in relation to the vessel, loading on board a named vessel must be evidenced by an on board notation on the non-negotiable sea waybill which, in addition to the date on which the goods have been loaded on board, includes the name of the vessel on which the goods have been loaded, even if they have been loaded on the vessel named as the 'intended vessel'.

        If the non-negotiable sea waybill indicates a place of receipt or taking in charge different from the port of loading, the on board notation must also include the port of loading stipulated in the Credit and the name of the vessel on which the goods have been loaded, even if they have been loaded on a vessel named in the non-negotiable sea waybill. This provision also applies whenever loading on board the vessel is indicated by pre-printed wording on the non-negotiable sea waybill,

        and

    (iii)   indicates the port of loading and the port of discharge stipulated in the Credit, notwithstanding that it:

        (a) indicates a place of taking in charge different from the port of loading, and/or a place of final destination different from the port of discharge,

        and/or

        (b) contains the indication 'intended' or similar qualification in relation to the port of loading and/or port of discharge, as long as the document also states the ports of loading and/or discharge stipulated in the Credit,

        and

(iv)   consists of a sole original non-negotiable sea waybill, or if issued in more than one original, the full set as so issued, and

(v)   appears to contain all of the terms and conditions of carriage, or some of such terms and conditions by reference to a source or document other than the non-negotiable sea waybill (short form/blank back non-negotiable sea waybill); banks will not examine the contents of such terms and conditions, and

(vi)   contains no indication that it is subject to a charter party and/or no indication that the carrying vessel is propelled by sail only, and

(vii)   in all other respects meets the stipulations of the Credit.

(b) For the purpose of this Article, transhipment means unloading and reloading from one vessel to another vessel during the course of ocean carriage from the port of loading to the port of discharge stipulated in the Credit.

(c) Unless transhipment is prohibited by the terms of the Credit, banks will accept a non-negotiable sea waybill which indicates that the goods will be transhipped, provided that the entire ocean carriage is covered by one and the same non-negotiable sea waybill.

(d) Even if the Credit prohibits transhipment, banks will accept a non-negotiable sea waybill which:

(i)   indicates that transhipment will take place as long as the relevant cargo is shipped in Container(s), Trailer(s) and/or "LASH" barge(s) as evidenced by the non-negotiable sea waybill, provided that the entire ocean carriage is covered by one and the same non-negotiable sea waybill, and/or

(ii)   incorporates clauses stating that the carrier reserves the right to tranship."

Article 25 deals with bills of lading issued with reference to an underlying charter-party:

"(a) If a Credit calls for or permits a charter party bill of lading, banks will, unless otherwise stipulated in the Credit, accept a document, however named, which:

(i)   contains any indication that it is subject to a charter party, and

(ii)   appears on its face to have been signed or otherwise authenticated by:

—the master or a named agent for or on behalf of the master, or

—the owner or a named agent for or on behalf of the owner.

Any signature or authentication of the master or owner must be identified as master or owner as the case may be. An agent signing or authenticating for the master or owner must also indicate the name and the capacity of the party, i.e. master or owner, on whose behalf that agent is acting, and

(iii)   does or does not indicate the name of the carrier, and

(iv)   indicates that the goods have been loaded on board or shipped on a named vessel.

Loading on board or shipment on a named vessel may be indicated by pre-printed wording on the bill of lading that the goods have been loaded on board a named vessel or shipped on a named vessel, in which case the date of issuance of the bill of lading will be deemed to be the date of loading on board and the date of shipment.

In all other cases loading on board a named vessel must be evidenced by a notation on the bill of lading which gives the date on which the goods have been loaded on board, in which case the date of the on board notation will be deemed to be the date of shipment,

and

(v)   indicates the port of loading and the port of discharge stipulated in the Credit,

and

(vi)   consists of a sole original bill of lading or, if issued in more than one original, the full set as so issued,

and

(vii)   contains no indication that the carrying vessel is propelled by sail only,

and

(viii) in all other respects meets the stipulations of the Credit.

(b) Even if the Credit requires the presentation of a charter party contract in connection with a charter party bill of lading, banks will not examine such charter party contract, but will pass it on without responsibility on their part."

Article 26 is directed at the modern type of multimodal transport documents:

"(a) If a Credit calls for a transport document covering at least two different modes of transport (multimodal transport), banks will, unless otherwise stipulated in the Credit, accept a document, however named, which:

(i)   appears on its face to indicate the name of the carrier or multimodal transport operator and to have been signed or otherwise authenticated by:

—the carrier or multimodal transport operator or a named agent for or on behalf of the carrier or multimodal transport operator, or

—the master or a named agent for or on behalf of the master.

Any signature or authentication of the carrier, multimodal transport operator or master must be identified as carrier, multimodal transport operator or master, as the case may be. An agent signing or authenticating for the carrier, multimodal transport operator or master must also indicate the name and the capacity of the party, i.e. carrier, multimodal transport operator or master, on whose behalf that agent is acting,

and

(ii)   indicates that the goods have been dispatched, taken in charge or loaded on board.

Dispatch, taking in charge or loading on board may be indicated by wording to that effect on the multimodal transport document and the date of issuance will be deemed to be the date of dispatch, taking in charge or loading on board and the date of shipment. However, if the document indicates, by stamp or otherwise, a date of dispatch, taking in charge or loading on board, such date will be deemed to be the date of shipment,

and

(iii)   (a) indicates the place of taking in charge stipulated in the Credit which may be different from the port, airport or place of loading, and the place of final destination stipulated in the Credit which may be different from the port, airport or place of discharge,

and/or

(b) contains the indication 'intended' or similar qualification in relation to the vessel and/or port of loading and/or port of discharge,

and

(iv)   consists of a sole original multimodal transport document or, if issued in more than one original, the full set as so issued,

and

(v)   appears to contain all of the terms and conditions of carriage, or some of such terms and conditions by reference to a source or document other than the multimodal transport document (short form/blank back multimodal transport document); banks will not examine the contents of such terms and conditions,

and

(vi)   contains no indication that it is subject to a charter party and/or no indication that the carrying vessel is propelled by sail only,

and

(vii)   in all other respects meets the stipulations of the Credit.

(b) Even if the Credit prohibits transhipment, banks will accept a multimodal transport document which indicates that transhipment will or may take place, provided that the entire carriage is covered by one and the same multimodal transport document."

Article 30 in its turn concerns those documents which are issued by freight forwarders:

"Unless otherwise authorised in the Credit, banks will only accept a transport document issued by a freight forwarder if it appears on its face to indicate:

(i)   the name of the freight forwarder as a carrier or multimodal transport operator and to have been signed or otherwise authenticated by the freight forwarder as carrier or multimodal transport operator,

or

(ii)   the name of the carrier or multimodal transport operator and to have been signed or otherwise authenticated by the freight forwarder as a named agent for or on behalf of the carrier or multimodal transport operator."

The sketch in Appendix VII illustrates graphically the inter-relationship between the sales contract, the contract of carriage and the documentary credit.

CHAPTER 7

CHARTER FORMS

GENERAL REMARKS ABOUT CHARTERING

Parties generally agree to use a certain type of charter and then add or delete clauses to reflect the circumstances of each individual fixture. The type of charter selected depends on several factors. Some of these have been discussed above and some others will be further discussed below. It is important always to keep certain circumstances in mind.

A charter means that the owner or the disponent owner in one way or another promises to put a vessel or a certain transportation capacity at the disposal of the charterer. The charterer, in his turn, promises to pay the agreed freight or hire.

The use of a ship involves a number of costs. There are capital costs, which always have to be paid. There are costs for the management of the vessel including manning, repairs, maintenance, bunkers, etc. Shipping business is also connected with different risks, which are not the same when the ship is in port or at sea. The costs and risks are always there but they may be divided between the parties in various ways. Judgements of the market development and of the risks involved with regard to the various factors thus influence the choice of the type of charter and level of the rate.

Very few individuals nowadays own ocean tonnage as most shipowners engaged in ocean transportation are companies of various kinds, sometimes large multinational companies. It has also become increasingly common for shipowners to co-operate in many various ways. They may have entered into an agreement to have a common technical inspection of their vessels. This is not a very far-reaching form of co-operation, but there are also several examples of much more important common services, joint ventures and pool agreements. An important feature is also the growing division between ownership, management and operation. One may choose to describe ocean traffic from several angles, but the most important distinction in practice is between *liner service* and *chartering* (tramp shipping, chartering in the open market or free traffic), since these reflect basically different business ideas.

78

LINER SHIPPING AND TRAMP SHIPPING

In liner shipping the shipowner (carrier, operator) runs a regular service between more or less fixed ports and usually on a fixed time schedule. The liner operator acts as a common carrier, accepting all general cargo shipped between the ports covered by his service.

In many instances liner shipping is carried out within liner conferences. These can be characterized as a kind of cartel whereby liner carriers offer their services at fixed rates. Liner traffic not carried out within liner conferences is often referred to as semi-liner. A liner operator who has not yet been admitted into a closed liner conference may compete with the conference members as an "outsider". The shippers are entitled to certain quantity rebates provided they only use the service of the particular line. Liner conferences may be *closed*, which is normal, or *open*, which is a requirement by, *inter alia*, United States authorities. In the latter case anybody who wishes to operate within a liner conference is entitled to do so. There are more than 300 liner conferences operating around the world. Under the auspices of UNCTAD (United Nations Conference on Trade and Development) a code of conduct for liner conferences has been introduced. This has become best known for its cargo sharing schemes 40/40/20, meaning that of the cargo available in a trade 40% shall be reserved for tonnage from the export country and the import country respectively and 20% only for tonnage from a third country. Liner conferences as well as certain types of pool agreements will in the future receive more attention not only from US antitrust authorities but also from the EC competition authorities.

A shipper who wants to book cargo space on board a vessel contacts the agent of a particular line, who then often confirms by a so-called booking note (B/N). When the goods have been received for shipment or shipped on board a bill of lading will be issued on behalf of the carrier.

In tramp shipping, on the other hand, the owner is plying between different ports depending on where he finds suitable cargoes. The basic document here is the charter-party (C/P) and all terms and conditions are negotiated individually, but often based on a previous charter-party. As in liner shipping, bills of lading are issued upon receipt or upon shipment of the goods. There may thus be a conflict between the bill of lading provisions and the charter-party provisions.

A feature of the liner operator's business philosophy is that he will try to remain in his particular trade and develop his tonnage so that it will stay more or less up to date. Sale and purchase of vessels is therefore rather a consequence of a new investment or a non-investment decision with respect to the liner service.

In tramp shipping, by contrast, the sale and purchase of ships plays a much more central role. A tramp owner calculates and decides whether to ride on a favourable high freight level wave or instead sell a vessel at peak price. The second-hand market and the freight market are normally closely related.

In liner traffic the freight is fixed in tariffs and often loyal customers will be granted quantity rebates (a system which may not be looked too favourably upon by EC competition authorities). In some countries rebates, unless applied equally, are unlawful and/or frowned upon by the authorities. The tariffs also often contain currency adjustment factors (CAF) and bunker adjustment factors (BAF), whereby the freight will be adjusted due to certain events. In chartering, on the other hand, the freight is negotiated in the individual case, but the general freight market level plays a decisive role and sets a framework.

Whereas in tramp shipping changes in freight levels are often both very fast and violent, changes are somewhat slower in liner traffic. The liner operator is normally hit at a later stage during a recession than the tramp operator. Also the liner operator, particularly when operating within a conference, will face decreasing cargo quantities which may, by and by, be met by lower tariffs and by fewer ships employed in the trade. Correspondingly the effects of a boom will reach the liner operator later than the tramp operator.

There are no watertight walls between the two sectors. Rather, there may be an exchange between tonnage employed in the two sectors because a liner operator tries to employ his liner vessel on the open market when the cargo quantities available in his liner service decrease. Thereby the freight level in the open market will be forced down even more. On the other hand, there is a tendency for markets to change somewhat and for tonnage to become more specialized—something that may affect "old truths".

CHARTERING DOCUMENTS

The most important documents governing the commercial and legal relationships between the parties are charter-parties and bills of lading, but other documents such as booking notes, delivery orders and mate's receipts also play an important role. On top of these, there are documents such as cargo manifests, invoices, and Customs declarations, etc., which are required by various authorities, that may be involved. In some cases numerous copies of the document are issued as well as the originals, for example as previously mentioned the bill of lading is normally issued in three originals and several copies. An export transaction normally embraces extensive paperwork, although efforts have been made to simplify the documentation and the document routines, for example by the use of computers.

The charter-party

As a matter of principle, oral agreements are generally binding, but due to the necessity of evidence the parties, based on the fixture, regularly make out a written document, a charter-party, particularly in international charter transactions. Charter-parties are almost always made out on standard forms.

BIMCO (Baltic and International Maritime Conference), in Copenhagen, plays an important role in the drafting of standard forms and has produced a large number of so-called *approved documents*. Among such, a distinction is generally made between *agreed, adopted* and *recommended forms*. Large shipping companies and shippers have made their own charter-parties (*private forms*), which they will normally introduce as a basis for the negotiations.

Legal problems may arise if additional terms and conditions are inserted into the standard charter-party, since this may require deletions and adjustments in the printed text, and several amendment clauses are regularly required. It should be mentioned that the parties very seldom use a charter-party form without making amendments.

The purpose of standard charter-parties is to standardize a number of clauses frequently used by varying parties in different trades, and to help the parties, since it will only be necessary to fill in certain items, such as the names of the parties and the vessels, ports, cargo, data about the ship, laytime, notice time, hire, etc. Amendments and modifications in a standard charter-party necessitate careful adjustments in the printed text. This is often forgotten and the charter-party may then become ambiguous and the object of a dispute. *Agreed charter-parties* of the "Scancon" type are intended to be used as is, without any changes or amendments.

Depending on legal cases, changed customs, etc., the parties often have to adjust the old charter-party forms, and new commercial techniques, legislation, practices and circumstances force the parties to make considerable riders. The market situation and the negotiating skills of respective parties may lead to different solutions. Brokers often have a routine to draft a charter-party; among two parties a usage may have grown up to treat certain items in a particular way. Where two parties have already concluded a charter on certain terms and conditions it may often be hard to convince the counter party—or, in practice, more often a broker—that a clause should be drafted differently in a new situation. There may also be difficulties in establishing the borderline between "main terms" and "details" in the charter negotiations. Thus the end product of the charter negotiations reflect not only closely considered commercial realities, but also lack of knowledge and lack of time among brokers, charterers and owners.

The contents and layout of *voyage* charter-parties differ from those of *time* charter-parties. The voyage charter standard forms are numerous, since in voyage charter the trades and the goods show such variations and may require separate solutions. Within time charter the variation is much less and the number of standard forms used is comparatively small.

The forms usually have code names which are often connected with the intended use of the form. Polcoalvoy, for instance, is a voyage form (VOY) intended for coal (COAL) and drafted in co-operation with Polish (POL) shipping interests.

Among the several voyage charter-party forms produced by BIMCO may

"Agreed" – "Adopted" – "Recommended" Documents

The application in practice of the various expressions mentioned above may be explained as follows:

"Agreed". The charter has been agreed between BIMCO (or the Chamber of Shipping of the United Kingdom*) or Comité Central des Armateurs de France or other associations of shipowners) with one or more groups of charterers or other institutions (for instance, the Polish Coal Charter Committee, the Timber Trade Federation of the United Kingdom, the Syndicat National du Commerce Exterieur de Cereales, Paris or CMEA, Moscow).

The printed conditions of an "Agreed" charter must not be altered or deleted without the express approval of all the organisations who have agreed the charter. An "Agreed" document is compulsory for the trade for which it is intended.

"Adopted". If a charter "Agreed" in that way following negotiations between, for instance, BIMCO and one or more groups representing charterers is officially supported by another association of shipowners, for instance, the Chamber of Shipping of the United Kingdom, it is stated that the Chamber of Shipping of the U.K. has "Adopted" the charter; or, on the other hand, if BIMCO wants to support one or the other charter negotiated and "Agreed" between the Chamber of Shipping of the U.K. and one or more groups of charterers, then it is stated that the charter has been "Adopted" by BIMCO.

Moreover, a document issued by an organisation of shipowners, for instance, INTERTANKO, for use in a special trade without having actually been "Agreed" with any particular group of charterers, may be "Adopted" by BIMCO.

An "Adopted" document is compulsory for the members of the organisation who have adopted it if it is an "Agreed" document.

"Recommended". When there has been no proper group or groups of charterers with whom to negotiate a particular charter, for instance, the "Gencon" Charter, it is issued as a "Recommended" charter.

The same is the case if the parties with whom a certain charter has been negotiated will not be able to bind their members to use the charter as a clean document. This is the position, for instance, for the "Norgrain" Charter and the "Nuvoy" Charter.

Whereas BIMCO naturally wishes the printed text of a "Recommended" charter to be followed by charterers and shipowners, there is no compulsion in this respect.

"Approved". This is the expression used for charters – whether "Agreed", "Adopted" or "Recommended".

"Issued". A form of charterparty for the establishment of which it might be said that BIMCO is responsible, is referred to as "Issued" by BIMCO.

"Copyright". In several charterparties printed during recent years it has been shown that the copyright is held by "X", usually the party which has issued the document. This has been done in order to discourage sundry parties from printing copies without having proper authority and possibly in such copies deviating from the "official" wording.

*) (From 1975: the General Council of British Shipping)

BIMCO issue several "approved documents". These are classified in accordance with the above explanation. A booklet with a complete set of the approved documents can be bought from BIMCO.

be mentioned Welcon, Baltcon, Polcoalvoy, Sovcoalvoy, Scancon and Nuvoy. Among the BIMCO forms the Gencon form merits particular mention since it is intended to be used when there is no suitable special voyage charter form available. The Gencon charter-party contains comparatively few standard clauses, since it should be possible to use it in all trades.

In some trades, particularly where United States brokers and charterers are involved, inadequate standard charter-parties are still in use, such as C Ore 7, Amwelsh—frequently used in coal exports from the United States—and Baltimore Berth Grain. (Always make sure that the latest edition is used, unless otherwise agreed.) Although there are several modern much more precise and complete forms it seems to be difficult to work these into certain trades. With respect to the *tanker market*, the charter-party forms are dominated by the large oil companies, which have all drafted their own forms, such as BP-voy, STB-voy, Shellvoy, etc., all of which are regularly revised, such as Beepeevoy 3 and Shellvoy 5. These forms are fairly similar and are—but for the market situation—more or less of a take-it-or-leave-it type. Intertanko, an association of independent tanker owners, has adopted the Intertankvoy, which is used occasionally. This document has been influenced by the charter-party forms introduced by the oil companies. Asbatankvoy corresponds to the previous Exxonvoy.

BIMCO has also produced two time charter-parties, Baltime and Linertime. The former is an old form which has been slightly revised, whereas Linertime is a fairly recent form basically intended for time charter where liner operation is involved. The New York Produce Exchange (NYPE) charter-party was drafted by American broker interests. NYPE has recently been revised into NYPE 93. The new revision has been officially approved by ASBA (Association of Shipbrokers and Agents (USA)) and adopted by BIMCO and FONASBA (Federation of National Associations of Shipbrokers and Agents (USA)). NYPE 93 is a modernization and substantial enlargement compared with NYPE 46. NYPE 93 contains 45 clauses and covers several more elements than the previous 46 version. NYPE 93 to a large extent is based on the revision 81 called Asbatime, but several amendments have also been made in relation to the 1981 version. Furthermore, the International Shipbrokers Federation has, during the 1970s, introduced the Fonasbatime, which has not as yet been frequently used. Baltime is traditionally regarded as the time charter-party most favourable to the owner and NYPE the one most favourable to the charterer. NYPE 93, in spite of the lack of enthusiasm for Asbatime 81, may prove to be regarded as a reasonably balanced document which could be acceptable to both owner and charterer interests. For the *tanker market*, the oil companies have drafted their own forms such as BP-time, Mobil-time, Shelltime, etc., regularly revised. Intertanko has drafted Intertanktime. For the time charter of reefer vessels, Reeftime is a special private form revised in 1978. Cooltime has been introduced in particular types of traffic as a new private form time charter party with a pooling scheme.

It needs to be re-emphasized that there is often not too much left of the printed text when it comes to an individual charter transaction. There are frequent deletions and amendments in the printed text and, on top of that, a large number of additional clauses will be added. It goes without saying that the result is often not a very well thought through legal document, where all the pieces have been carefully put together.

DIFFERENT TYPES OF CHARTERING

Another basis for distinguishing different types of charter agreements from each other is the use of the ship from a capacity point of view. The charterer may have chartered the whole vessel, i.e. all the space in the vessel. The charter-party then spells out that the charterer shall deliver "a full and complete cargo" within the limits of the ship's capacity. If the owner cannot find a charterer for the whole vessel, he may divide the space between several charterers who may each use, for example, certain portions of the vessel or a certain cargo hold. This is known as *space charter*. Space charter is not the same thing as when several charterers together charter the vessel. In the latter case the individual charterers will not have separate rights of control but will have to act jointly or by authority. In the open market these are the most common types of chartering. In liner traffic, on the other hand, the owner normally promises to carry a specified cargo, for instance 10 boxes of machinery, 1,000 bags of coffee, etc. The transportation undertaken is then known as carriage of *general cargo*.

From a functional point of view an important distinction is made between voyage charter, time charter and bareboat charter. The charterer and the owner often agree that the ship will carry a certain cargo from point A to point B (or will make several consecutive voyages between these points). The freight to be paid is calculated for the voyage or the voyages to be performed. This charter is known as *voyage charter*. The voyage charter covering several *consecutive voyages* is a special type of voyage charter.

One type is the so-called *contract of affreightment* where a shipowner may make an agreement with a charterer to carry for the charterer during a specified period a large quantity of goods between certain ports. Depending on the circumstances the concepts of *quantity contract* or *transport contract* may also be used. Furthermore, contracts of affreightment may also be connected with consecutive voyages. In order to perform his obligations under a contract of affreightment the shipowner may employ several of his vessels on an almost continuous basis which in its regularity is similar to liner traffic. The shipowner may, from the basis of contracts of affreightment, fill up his traffic and make a profit on additional cargoes and return cargoes. Contracts of affreightment may imply an efficiently operated, advanced transportation system with a regular flow of cargo. (See further, Chapter 14.)

There may be particular circumstances where a large business enterprise is at the same time cargo owner and shipowner. This is the case in the raw material sector where, for example, the large oil companies own several vessels but are at the same time important charterers.

Several factors have led to a certain specialization in modern shipping. One of these is that ownership, manning and commercial employment of the vessel may be in different hands. Thus, so-called management agreements have become more and more common. A *management agreement* may be characterized as a service and know-how agreement, where the manager may be entrusted with the duty of operating and finding employment for the vessel as if he were the owner and for the account of the actual owner.

Shipping, in common with other industries, has recently undergone a structural change as a result, in particular, of the growing trend towards protectionism and government involvement. Shipowners have consequently looked for ways of co-operating with each other to meet these difficulties.

Various types of co-operative arrangements have been introduced covering the three main functions in the shipping industry, namely (1) ownership; (2) nautical and technical operation; and (3) commercial operation. In some cases, particularly where all three functions are co-ordinated, shipowners and charterers may jointly set up an independent company to carry out those activities. Such joint ventures or pool agreements exist in liner shipping as well as in chartering operations. The objects of such agreements are usually to

— reach a better negotiating position;
— achieve more efficient use of the fleet and the organization;
— achieve a more efficient marketing and chartering position;
— obtain access to otherwise closed markets;
— avoid certain taxes or fees;
— limit competition.

Frequently, the owner puts the ship at the disposal of the charterer for a certain period of time, during which period the charterer, within the limits of the agreement, controls the commercial operation of the vessel. The freight (hire) is determined per time unit (for example per month of 30 days) and is regularly paid in advance. This type of charter is known as *time charter*.

Bareboat charter (demise charter) means that the vessel is put at the disposal of the charterer for a certain period of time, but here the charterer takes over virtually the entire responsibility for the operation of the vessel and all the costs and expenses except the capital costs. A financial lease will often contain the same features although the financing aspect is more dominant here.

The picture is, however, often much more complex, since mixed forms have evolved and also since a charter agreement may sometimes have features of a joint venture, where the co-operation and profit/loss sharing idea comes more to the fore than it does in traditional charter forms. Today it is not uncommon for a second-hand purchase of a vessel to be connected with a joint venture, something which may also be the case in connection with newbuilding contracts. Often a sale and purchase is connected with a "charter-back" arrangement. Furthermore, a bareboat charter or a second-hand purchase may often be combined with a management agreement.

Some examples are given below of the intersection of different forms of traffic and charter and of how the label of different parties involved in a chain of charters varies depending on their relationships. Firstly, however, the different forms of charter will be more closely described, although still in general terms (for a more detailed description, see Chapters 12 and 13).

Voyage charter

Under this type of charter a vessel is employed for a single voyage. The person who charters the ship is known as a voyage charterer, the payment is called freight and the contract a voyage charter-party.

This form of charter is typical within tramp traffic (free traffic). The charterer may be the person owning the cargo but may also charter the vessel for someone else's account. The "owner" of the vessel from whom the actual voyage charterer charters the ship may himself be a time charterer or even a voyage charterer who sub-charters (sub-lets) the ship. In case the owner is not the registered owner of the ship, he is normally described as "time chartered owner" or "disponent owner". Thus there may be a chain of charter-parties which must all be regarded as separate and distinct.

From a practical point of view, a voyage charter means that the owner promises to carry on board a specific ship a particular cargo from one port to another. The vessel shall arrive at the first loading port and be ready to receive the cargo on a certain day or within a certain period of time.

Under a voyage charter the owner retains the operational control of the vessel and is responsible for all the operating expenses such as port charges, bunkers, extra insurances, taxes, etc. The charterer's costs are usually costs and charges relating to the cargo. Loading and discharging costs are divided between the owner and the charterer in accordance with the agreement from case to case, for example, f.i.o (free in and out), in which case the charterer bears the costs involved in connection with loading and discharging. When the charterer controls the cargo handling he also has the responsibility for the efficiency of the loading and discharging operations and for the time which the vessel spends in port. Often, but not always, he may also have a liability with respect to damage occurring to the goods during loading and discharge.

The relationship between the parties is determined in the voyage charter-party. Here, the names of the parties and the ship are stated as well as the size of the vessel, the cargo to be carried, places of loading and discharge, etc. The costs and risks are distributed between the parties. Since the owner bears the operational costs the terms dealing with costs and expenses will only mention explicitly a limited number of items, such as costs and charges with regard to the cargo, perhaps costs for loading and discharging, sometimes certain extra insurance costs, etc., and not least costs due to liability for damage to the cargo and damage to the vessel. The charter-party may also regulate the allocation of costs and risks for unforeseen events.

The discharging port need not be nominated in the voyage charter-party, and if such is the case, the charterer must have the right later to direct the ship within a certain range to a specific port of discharge. A basic feature of the charter is that the nominated vessel shall be put at the disposal of the charterer. It is, however, not uncommon for the actual ship not to be nominated at the time when the charter is concluded but that only the type of ship is described with the actual ship to be nominated later. Furthermore, the owner often reserves the right to substitute the vessel and sometimes this right to substitute may also be a duty to substitute.

The ship must be in the position which the owner specified when the charter was concluded, and the vessel must, without undue delay, be directed to the port of loading. Often a cancelling day has been determined for the latest arrival of the ship at the port of loading, and if she has not arrived at that time the charterer may cancel the charter. The charterer may also be entitled to claim damages when the arrival of the vessel is delayed if this is due to owner's negligence. However, the forthcoming voyage will often take place at a later stage, it being understood/agreed that the vessel will be traded in between. The owner has then a duty to carry out the agreed voyage or voyages without delay and without deviating from the agreed or customary route.

A divergence from the *route* is called *deviation*, and in case deviation is not allowed (by agreement, by custom or by law), the laws of most countries put on the owner a far-reaching liability for damage to the goods, etc. In the port of loading the vessel must proceed to the berth assigned by the charterer provided that this berth is safe. If there are several charterers certain problems may arise, but as a general principle every charterer with a separate charter-party has such a right to assign the berth. If the master does not receive any order to proceed to a certain berth, he has to make the choice himself and should then, if possible, select a customary berth.

In the port of loading the charterer must deliver the agreed cargo. Unless otherwise agreed the cargo must not be of a dangerous nature.

The cargo must be brought alongside the ship at the loading port and must be collected from the ship's side at the port of discharge. Particularly with bulk cargoes the charterer often undertakes to pay for loading and discharge. In this connection one often meets clauses of f.i.o. (free in and out) and f.o.b. (free on board) type—here the latter is used in a somewhat different meaning than the f.o.b. clause in a sales contract. Often the parties agree on f.i.o.s. (free in and out and stowed) or f.i.o.s.t. (free in and out, stowed and trimmed). The f.i.o. clause puts on the charterer an obligation to pay for loading and discharging, and the basis is also that the charterer will be liable for damages to the cargo occurring during loading and discharging operations. Since the master has a duty to supervise the orderly loading and discharge (particularly from a seaworthiness point of view) the owner under a f.i.o. clause may also, under certain circumstances, be liable for damages to the cargo. The f.o.b. clause—when applied in chartering—may have different implications so far as the delivery of the cargo is concerned—from delivery at the moment the cargo is delivered *alongside* the vessel until delivery at the moment the cargo is in the vessel. The phrase *liner terms* is used to express that the owner shall bear the same costs as he would in liner service, in particular, loading and discharging costs. The concept of "liner terms" is not very precise and cannot be recommended unless in the individual case when the parties know the exact consequences of such cost and risk distribution. Reference should also be made in this context to the "gross terms" concept used in Gencon, clause 5(a). (See further below, page 189f.)

Where the charterer carries out the loading and/or discharging the parties generally agree that he will have a certain period of time at his disposal for the loading and discharge of the vessel, the so-called laytime. The laytime is a reflection of the basic idea of voyage charter, that the owner, who is operating the ship, will be liable for all delay in connection with the transit, whereas the charterer may be liable (or partly liable) for delay in connection with loading and discharge. If the charterer fails to load and/or discharge the vessel within the laytime specified he has to pay compensation for the surplus time used (demurrage). To a certain extent the charterer may also be liable for loss of time if there is no berth available for the vessel in the port and also for certain other losses of time that may occur as a consequence of the charterer's acts or omissions. If, on the other hand, the charterer saves time for the ship by carrying out his undertakings more quickly than agreed, he may be entitled to claim compensation (*despatch money*) but generally only if an agreement has been reached to this effect.

A charterer of a whole vessel usually has a duty to deliver a full cargo within the ship's capacity. For that purpose a clause of the type "*a full and complete cargo*" of the agreed goods to be delivered and loaded is used, and correspondingly, the owner has a duty to receive the goods and carry them.

If too little cargo is delivered or the cargo is delivered in such a state that the ship's capacity cannot be utilized (*broken stowage*), a freight compensation, the so-called *deadfreight*, can be claimed by the owner. This compensation is based on the difference between the full freight to which the owner would have been entitled if all cargo were delivered and the freight to be paid according to the intaken quantity, less any expenses saved for short-delivered cargo. If, on the other hand, the vessel cannot load the agreed quantity—she may have been described wrongly or may have taken on board too large a quantity of bunkers—a corresponding freight reduction will be made. In addition, the charterer may eventually claim compensation for additional costs, for example, for other tonnage that has been chartered. Difficult questions of evidence may arise under such circumstances.

The charterer has a duty to deliver cargo and to perform his undertakings and may not, unless there is an express agreement to the contrary, allege that it is difficult to find cargo or to have it made available to the vessel. Some charter-parties, however, do contain exemption clauses to such effect. These clauses are normally understood to mean that the charterer is only exempted from his duty to deliver cargo if the hindrance has had an effect on the loading or discharging work, but in some charter-parties the exemption clauses are more far reaching.

The freight is payable in arrears unless something else has been agreed. Prepayment clauses are, however, common, but freight will be paid only for cargo discharged after the voyage. If the ship is lost or does not reach her destination the Anglo-American principle is that no freight will be paid at all. In some legal systems the owner may be entitled to a proportionate freight under such circumstances, if the cargo has been moved toward its destination. In order to protect the owner's right to freight the freight prepaid clause is often amended with *"freight shall be considered as fully earned upon shipment and nonreturnable in any event whether or not the voyage shall be performed and whether or not the vessel and/or cargo shall be lost or not lost"*.

Unless the freight is earned and has actually been paid upon loading, the owner may need some security for the due freight payment. When the goods have been loaded on board the owner has thus physically taken into charge property belonging to the charterer (if the charterer is the owner of the goods). At least, in this case, the general principle seems to be that the owner has a lien on the goods. If he has such a lien there may also be justification for the charterer to remain responsible for payment, since the owner may, at the destination, refuse to discharge and deliver the cargo unless the receiver pays what is owed. (See further about *lien* and *cesser* below, page 204ff.)

Consecutive voyages

Consecutive voyage charters are a special type of voyage charter where the vessel is contracted for several voyages which follow consecutively upon each other. Sometimes the charter-party states that the ship will make a certain number of consecutive voyages and sometimes that she will make as many voyages as she may perform during a certain period of time. In the latter case, the parties have agreed that, as in time charter, the vessel will be at the disposal of the charterer for a certain period of time. The individual voyages are made on voyage terms and conditions with freight paid per voyage, laytime calculation in ports of loading and discharge respectively, etc. This means that the risk and cost distribution of a time charterer is very different from that of a consecutive voyage charter. Basically the problems arising under agreements for consecutive voyages are those of voyage charters but the time factor causes certain structural differences, for example, with respect to costs and income.

Often these contracts will contain, for example, bunker clauses or other clauses concerning cost variations (see below, page 164ff.).

The owner and the charterer should observe a certain caution when it comes to determining rates of *freight* and *demurrage*, since rates which diverge from the market rate may cause the charterer to abuse the charter-party. If, for example, the freight rate is high and the demurrage rate low, the charterer may be tempted to keep the ship lying idle on demurrage instead of making a new voyage.

Time charter

Under a time charter the crew is employed by the owner, who is also responsible for the nautical operation and maintenance of the vessel and the supervision of the cargo—at least from a seaworthiness point of view. Within the framework of the contract, however, the charterer decides the voyages to be made and the cargoes to be carried. This distribution of functions between owner and charterer puts on the master of the vessel some kind of "in between position" between the owner—his employer and main principal—and the time charterer, and he must take both into consideration.

The time charterer may be a shipowner who for a time needs to enlarge his fleet or a cargo owner (seller or buyer) with a continuous need of transport, who does not want to invest money in a ship but wants to have the control of the commercial operation of the vessel. Sometimes a shipbroker or an agent engages in time chartering in order to speculate on the freight market.

Although differently designed, the time charter, like the voyage charter, determines a time and place for the delivery of the vessel from the owner to the charterer and redelivery from the charterer to the owner. Depending on the place of delivery/redelivery and the length of the charter period one may distinguish between a time chartered trip, a time chartered round voyage and a period time charter. A trip will thus take the vessel from one place to another exactly as under a voyage charter. When there is a time charter on a round trip basis the delivery and redelivery will take place in approximately the same area. Apparently these two hybrid time charters are different from the true, traditional time charter. When the ship is engaged for a period she will be employed within an agreed geographical area or on a *world-wide* basis with delivery/redelivery somewhere within the geographical area, normally within a limited area such as the U.S. East Coast, Jacksonville-Boston range. The time charter period may last from a number of days to a number of years.

It is not uncommon that the parties agree on an option, i.e. the charterer and/or the owner will be entitled to demand a prolongation of the charter for a certain time on the same or revised terms and conditions or on terms and conditions to be mutually agreed. The charter-party then spells out *when* the owner/charterer shall inform his counter party that he wishes to use his option (*option declaration*). This is particularly the situation in cases of time charters over at least one year, and the charter-party may then spell out for example:

"charter period 2 years, 2 months more or less in charterer's option, such option to be declared . . .". The option may, however, also be one for a new two-year charter period with some slight hire adjustment, etc.

The *hire* is payable in advance for a month or other period. If the hire is not paid promptly the owner may be entitled to cancel the charter. This right to cancel, which also may be exercised due to a minor delay in payment, depends on the inadequate legal security the owner enjoys should the hire not be paid. In charter-parties drafted during past years, certain limits have been inserted to prevent the owner from exercising his right of cancellation, at least when caused by technicalities (anti-technicality clauses)—see below, page 229.

The chartered vessel has to be in conformity with the charter-party with respect to cargo carrying capacity, speed, bunker consumption and other agreed terms and conditions. Particularly, the cargo carrying capacity is important to the charterer. If he is planning to transport heavy goods (deadweight cargo) the vessel's deadweight or the weight the vessel can load (*deadweight cargo capacity, d.w.c.c.*) is important to him. If he is planning to transport light and bulky goods (*cubic cargo*) the volume of the ship is more important. Special demands are often made on special tonnage as to particular gear and equipment. With respect to oil tankers, for example, the capacity of the pumps is important. Similarly, reefer vessels must meet certain requirements with respect to refrigerating capacity. The shipowner has normally by contract a duty to keep the vessel seaworthy during the charter period. In Anglo-American law the owner basically has a strict liability for the vessel's seaworthiness and fitness for service at the time of the delivery of the vessel, a liability from which the owner may, however, exempt himself by agreement, at least to a certain extent. On the other hand, it is rather common that the charter-party spells out so "to be maintained throughout the currency of the charter". This principle has also been modified in the Hague Rules.

As under a voyage charter-party the ship must be delivered to the time charterer not later than a certain date, and any delay beyond the *cancelling date* entitles the charterer to cancel the charter. The voyages also have to be carried out without delay. If the vessel is delayed due to a breakdown of machinery or for other specified reasons she may be *off-hire*, and then a reduction of the time may be made so that no hire will be paid during the off-hire period. But under a time charter the owner, basically, is not liable for delay not caused by the ship. Time lost as a result of adverse weather is thus the responsibility of the charterer. This is also in accordance with the basic risk distribution between the charterer and owner in a time charter. It is fairly common that modern tanker time charter-parties state that the owner is entitled to full hire based on an agreed speed from pilot station to pilot station, and thus the owner then bears more of the time risk than he would have according to the time risk distribution under more traditional time charter-parties.

Under a time charter the owner's principal duties are thus aimed at the technical operation and maintenance of the vessel, and the charter-party in that respect puts on him a basic responsibility for the correct performance of the voyages.

The liability for the cargo may be determined in different ways and may rest with the owner or with the charterer or may be divided between them in one way or another. The charterer often has a right to give certain instructions about the signing of bills of lading, whether these are signed by the master or by the agent or the owner or the charterer respectively. If he is not basically liable under the charter-party, the charterer, by express provisions in several charter-parties, has a duty to hold the owner harmless; thus the owner may seek redress from the charterer. Even without such express provision he may have such a right, depending on the particular circumstances of the case.

When giving orders to the vessel the charterer must keep within the trading limits prescribed by the contract, with respect to geographical areas as well as cargoes to be carried (*trading limits* and *cargo exclusions*). Unless the parties have reached an agreement to the contrary, the charterer may only order the vessel to safe ports and berths. He must follow the terms and conditions of the charter-party as to excepted cargoes and, as in a voyage charter, he must not ordinarily have goods carried which may cause damage to the ship, the personnel, or other cargo.

The charterer is liable for costs directly connected with the use of the vessel, for example, bunker costs and port charges, and pays for the loading and discharge. Furthermore, he may be liable for damage (normal wear and tear excepted) caused to the ship in connection with her use. If the charterer fails to employ the ship he must still pay hire since he is principally liable for the commercial use of the vessel.

At the end of the charter period the charterer has to "redeliver" the vessel at the place agreed. It would often be hard for the charterer to use the ship effectively during the last part of the charter period if he had to redeliver her on a particular day. The charter-party therefore usually contains provisions on *overlap*, entitling the charterer to use the vessel for a reasonable time after the expiration of the charter against an agreed hire or on *underlap*, entitling the charterer to redeliver her somewhat earlier than the basic charter provides.

Bareboat charter

As mentioned above, a bareboat charter (demise charter) is a charter of a different type. This contract amounts to a lease of the ship from the owner to the charterer. The bareboat charter usually means that the vessel is put at the disposal of the charterer without any crew. The charterer thus will take over almost all of the owner's functions except for the payment of capital costs. This means that the charterer will have the commercial as well as the technical responsibility for the vessel and will pay for maintenance, crew costs and insurance, etc.

The bareboat charter has been a comparatively unusual type of charter but with changing trading and investment patterns it has become more common.

Sometimes a second-hand sale has been disguised as a bareboat charter with an option to buy in order that taxation can be avoided. Bareboat charter usually covers a certain period of time, sometimes a very long period, and is often hinged to a management agreement. Furthermore, as mentioned, the bareboat charter is often connected with a purchase option after the expiration of the charter or during the charter period. (Cf. BIMCO's Bareboat form Barecon A and Barecon B.)

Bareboat chartering may often be described as a kind of ship financing rather than as a genuine charter agreement, one of the reasons being that the owner has surplus capital to invest, whereas the charterer, lacking such capital, has need for the vessel in his fleet. Such "financing bareboat" is a form of "financial leasing", a modern type of financing based on a three-party relation between seller, financer and "charterer" (buyer), where the charterer ordinarily becomes the owner after the expiration of the charter.

Various reasons, such as maritime policies applied, may lead to a growing use of bareboat in spite of several different problems that may arise with respect to the nationality of the ship, manning rules, etc.

Contract of affreightment

There are also contract forms which have characteristics borrowed from different charter types. One form is known as contract of affreightment. Under a contract of affreightment the owner promises to satisfy the charterer's need for transport capacity over a certain period of time, often one year or several years. It is not unusual that contracts of affreightment are also made up within the framework of liner operation. Under a contract of affreightment the individual vessel has less importance for the charterer, but the important thing is that the owner performs his duty to carry with an agreed type of tonnage, which may very well be a chartered vessel. Frequently, shipping companies without ships of their own undertake as operators to carry out such transportation, and charter in tonnage for the individual voyages. The voyages may then be carried out with tonnage of the owner's choice but within the framework of the contract. The terms and conditions under this contract will not directly affect the head owner, since he is only bound by the agreement with his charterer. (See further, Chapter 14.)

MANAGEMENT AGREEMENTS

Instead of operating ships with owned or chartered vessels a shipping company may instead try to sell "know-how" and services by management agreements. The management agreement is not a chartering agreement in its traditional sense but rather a know-how and service agreement, where the manager in one way or another puts his particular knowledge at the disposal of the principal.

The owner will thus entrust to another person (*the manager*) one or several of his functions.

It may be that the manager will maintain, inspect, man and equip the vessel, keep books, attend to the claims, make calculations and otherwise attend to the commercial operation of the ship. The detailed design varies but principally the manager concludes agreements with respect to the vessel in the name of the owner and for the owner's account. The owner will compensate the "manager" for all his expenses and also pay some compensation, which may be determined in various ways. The idea behind this type of agreement is that the principal shall bear the commercial risk. Obviously there must be a basis of confidence between the parties.

The management agreement has come to play a role of ever growing practical importance for several reasons. Because of the recent shipping depression some owners have gone bankrupt and the receiver normally has no knowledge of shipping, and then the commercial activity may be entrusted to a manager for a period of time. Similarly, several shipyards have become important shipowners, when the buyer under a shipbuilding contract has been unable to or has refused to take delivery of the vessel under construction. Furthermore, investors in some countries have bought second-hand tonnage without sufficient knowledge of the shipping business and for a period they may entrust the ship to a manager waiting for second-hand prices to go up so that she may be sold at a profit.

Also, the management agreement may be used by an investor in shipping lacking sufficient knowledge in the trade but with the intention of becoming a carrier in the longer term. Thus the shipowner's motives for management services may vary.

COST ELEMENTS IN CHARTERING

The commercial operation of a ship always involves certain costs, undertakings and risks irrespective of the type of charter involved. The owners and the charterers have to determine all these different elements before distributing them among themselves when determining the charter form to be used and necessary amendments to be made.

As to the costs involved, regard must first be had to the ship's capital costs, that is, interest with respect to own and external capital (from a cash flow point of view the repayment of external capital must also be brought into the picture). The vessel has to be continuously maintained and repaired. The owner normally has insured the vessel (hull and machinery) as well as his liability. Bunkers, lubricants and other consumption materials have to be paid for. The ship must be manned, involving wages, social costs, sickness costs, travel costs, education costs, etc. Port charges and other fees and charges have to be paid, loading and discharge must be arranged and paid for. Beside this, there are administrative costs which are dependent on the extensiveness of the business generally and the engagement in the individual vessel.

Except for the distribution of these costs there are also risks to be distributed. Who will bear the risk for loss of time arising from weather hindrance during the transit or in port, strikes, or political events, and who will bear the risk for a bad freight market? When the calculation is made it is of course necessary that attention is also paid to the profit or loss arising.

The costs may be divided into fixed costs, costs which are only influenced when the operation ceases during a long period of time, and costs which are directly influenced by the operation. The corresponding standard classes of costs are named: Capital Costs, Daily (Running) Costs and Voyage Costs. The costs may also be influenced by legislation in different countries. The figure and the scheme below show schematically how costs, expenses and risks are distributed among the parties under different types of charter.

		Voyage Charter	Time Charter	Bareboat Charter
Voyage costs	Despatch/demurrage Loading/discharging Stevedoring/trimming Port charges, fees Canal dues Bunkers Other voyage costs	Costs that may be shared in different ways ⋯ 1	Costs of the charterer	Costs of the charterer
Daily (running) costs	Manning costs Insurance (hull, war, P & I) Repairs, maintenance	Costs of the owner	Costs of the owner	2
Capital costs	Interest, own and borrowed capital. Depreciation on invested capital			Costs of the owner

Administrative costs (arrow spanning the categories)

(1) Certain costs arising in connection with port calls are to be paid by charterer.
(2) Costs for insurance, repairs, maintenance, etc., are sometimes shared between the owner and charterer.
Both parties will have administrative costs.

	Bare-boat charter	Time charter	Voyage charter	Liner shipping
Time risk in port	C	C	CO[1]	O
Loading/unloading	C	C[2]	CO[3]	O
Port charges	C	C	O[4]	O
Bunkers	C	C	O	O
Time risk at sea	C	C[5]	O	O
Soliciting for cargo	C	C	O	O
Manning	C[6]	O	O	O
Repairs/maintenance	CO[7]	O	O	O
Insurance	CO[7]	O[8]	O[8]	O
Capital costs	O	O	O	O

C=Charterer   O=Owner

[1] Under a voyage charter the risk of time in port is distributed through provisions dealing with, and rules on, demurrage.

[2] Under time charter the costs of loading and discharge lie with the charterer. The work will normally be carried out under the supervision of the ship's officers and the ship will give so-called Customary assistance with the vessel's crew.

[3] Liability and costs for loading and discharging under voyage charter will be distributed differently from case to case. Sometimes all costs will lie with the owner (liner terms) and sometimes they will rest with the charterer.

[4] The owner will pay for normal port charges, which rest with and are levied on the vessel, as well as tugs, moorings, etc. Certain costs, above all costs resting with and calculated on the cargo, will, according to the main principle, be paid by the charterer.

[5] Some charter-parties, above all charter-parties used in oil transportation, provide that some risks of time, in accordance with the basic concept, at sea will lie with the owner.

[6] Sometimes the master and even some of the senior officers are employed by the owner.

[7] As to repairs, maintenance and insurance there are different solutions in the bareboat charter-parties, but frequently these costs lie with the charterer.

[8] Even if hull, as well as P. & I. and war risk, insurance will normally be provided for and paid for by the owner, it is usual that the time charterer buys a limited P. & I. insurance, and that he will also, under certain circumstances, contribute to extra hull and war risk premiums. Under time charter and sometimes also under voyage charter the charterer may insure his liability towards the owner through a so-called *charterer's liability insurance*.

"CHARTER CHAINS"

As mentioned above, a vessel may at the same time be involved in several different contracts. The following example illustrates such a chain:

A is the registered or "real" owner of the vessel. Since he is only interested in *investing* money in shipping, he has made a management agreement with B, whereby B will be responsible for different tasks in connection with the operation of the vessel, such as maintenance, repairs, manning, insurance, etc. B will also have a duty to operate the ship commercially, but the commercial risk is still vested with A, which means that a bad charter market will affect the income of A. If instead A and B have made a bareboat charter, B will appear as the functional owner, and then the commercial risk will be vested with B. Under a management agreement between A and B, B will act as *agent* for A or possibly as *correspondent owner*. In the case of a bareboat charter between A and B the latter will instead act as a *disponent owner* or in some similar capacity.

B, in his turn, has time chartered out or sublet the ship to C. In the relation B/C, B is still agent for the owner, correspondent owner or disponent owner, while C is the time charterer. C in his turn has chartered the vessel to D under a voyage charter. In the relationship C/D, C is the *time chartered owner*, and D is the voyage charterer. From A's point of view one may say that, under a bareboat charter, B is the charterer and C and D are sub-charterers. A has then no direct relation with C or D. From B's point of view C is the charterer and D is the sub-charterer. Conversely, from D's point of view, C is the owner, etc. It is important to observe that those involved in a charter chain have a basic relationship with their contractual party only. That means that they may not even be able to identify the other links in the chain.

It is common that such charter chains exist, and it is important that each party makes clear his respective position when something happens. The action of each party must be based on the contract in which he is involved. It is also important for a charterer negotiating a sub-charter to be careful and take into consideration the framework set by his charter with the owner. In our example, when sub-chartering the vessel to D, C must take into consideration the terms and conditions of his charter with B. If he fails to maintain the balance he may face greater risks and costs in the one relationship than he will be able to recover in the other. He may also face situations which are impossible to solve because the charter-parties are contradictory. In other words, if C has time chartered the vessel from B, and then sublet the vessel to D, ideally C would prefer to have terms and conditions of the second charter "back-to-back" with the first one.

An important factor from a practical point of view which can lead to complications is the use of bills of lading. The bill of lading is an independent document which, depending on the circumstances, may involve one or several of the parties directly in relation to the cargo consignees.

CHAPTER 8

FREIGHT CALCULATIONS

Companies which export goods will usually have transportation and shipping departments whose job it is to assess comparative costs between the various alternative methods of transportation. The object is to find the most suitable means of transport giving an acceptable total cost "door-to-door". Although it might seem an easy matter to calculate the cost of a voyage from one port to another with a specified cargo, or to calculate the rate of freight which will cover a shipowner's costs, plus a reasonable profit, these calculations can in fact turn out to be somewhat complex.

It is not sufficient for a shipowner to quote just "what is needed and a little bit more". If the prevailing market is low this owner would then be unable to find employment, and if it is a high market situation he would certainly find employment but at an under-marketed price. Since the periods of low market conditions normally last considerably longer than periods with a high freight market, the shipowner applying such a principle when operating in the open market would soon find himself out of business. In liner traffic, however, calculations are largely carried out in accordance with these principles. During a market slump the shippers will then be compensated for above-market prices by a regular and dependable service with fixed schedules. The loyal shippers will also receive compensation during a high market period, when the liner companies will abstain from applying open market freights, maintaining the stable freighting conditions.

Owners have a number of different alternatives when calculating on each individual open-ship position, and it is normally fairly easy to calculate what employment for a specific ship will give the best revenue, for example, per day. On the other hand, it may not be clear whether this is the voyage which puts the ship in the best position for her next employment. If a number of alternative voyage calculations for one ship would show the same result per day, consideration must also be taken of the duration of the voyage or time charter engagement for each specific case. The freight market may change during this time and if the market goes up the owner will, of course, wish to negotiate and start the next employment (which hopefully will give a better result) as soon as possible. It is also natural that the owner will aim at fixing on a level which reflects the upward trend and gives a well balanced result throughout the

98

duration of the charter. Obviously, under falling market conditions, the owner would try to secure longer employments at rate levels reflecting the spot-market conditions ruling on the date of fixing.

A voyage calculation is not an exact science and the work is normally done under pressure of time. There is no time to make very thorough investigations into and assessments of every item. Unfortunately, it also happens that there is usually insufficient time to investigate the counterpart's financial standing. The final voyage result will also be influenced by a number of external circumstances, which, although foreseeable, can only be put into figures by rough estimation at the time when the calculation is made. It is also a question of trying to transfer various terms and clauses in the charter-party form or *pro forma* contract suggested by the charterers into figures and costs for the owner's account. Thereby the owner may, if he is successful, reach a satisfactory combination of the various clauses and charter terms and conditions.

The tools used in the calculation work are—except for easily accessible and complete details of the ships—registers covering port dues and charges, stevedoring tariffs, productivity in various ports for handling of different commodities, information about draught restrictions and other limitations, etc. It is also necessary to have registers naming reliable and efficient port agents all over the world who may assist in supplying necessary information. Owners also keep a library of handbooks on cargo handling and other matters. It is useful and necessary at the stage of precalculation to work in close contact with those persons who are in direct contact with the vessel and are supervising the running of the ship, who are arranging bunkering and giving instructions to the master and who are generally responsible for the ship's performance in fulfilling the undertakings as per the current charter-party. This operational staff, which has accumulated great experience of ports, ships and cargoes, may provide useful information and may foresee the practical consequences and estimate the costs for most of the chartering alternatives and charter-party clauses.

VOYAGE CALCULATION

Income

The practical layout of a voyage calculation as well as the presentation of the result may, of course, vary. Shipping companies often have their own printed calculation forms in order to simplify the work and to facilitate the evaluation of calculation results. Some companies have abandoned manual calculation with table calculators and introduced computer operation, having stored the registers, the ship's details and various tabular information in the computer's memory. One may even keep complete calculations for the most frequent employment alternatives stored in the computer so that the result—after having fed the computer with a ship's position and the main details of an order—can

Saudi Arabia, Kingdom of

GENERAL HOLIDAYS

March	11–16 *)	....	Eid-ul-Fitre (Ramadan) (6 days)
May	18–23 *)	....	Eid-ul-Adha (Eid-el-Haj) (6 days)
September	23	....	National Day

*) Approximate dates as they depend on the visibility of the new moon.

Friday: Weekly day of rest but worked round the clock.

Ramadan: Thirty days' fast and how it affects labour: See page 7.

LOCAL HOLIDAYS
Dammam and Ras Tanura

March	7–17 *)	....	Eid-al-Fitr (End of Ramadan)
May	15–25 *)	....	Eid-al-Adha (Eid-ul-Haj) (Pilgrimage)
September	23	....	National Day

*) Dates approximate, subject to sighting of the new moon. Work round the clock without break.

Working hours Saturday/Thursday: Work round the clock 7 days a week without break. 1st shift 07.00–18.00, 2nd 19.00–06.00. Meals 12.00–13.00, 00.00–01.00.

Friday: Weekly day of rest but work round the clock at normal rates.

Holidays: Work round the clock at normal rates.

During Ramadan month working hours are: 1st shift 07.00–14.00, 2nd 14.00–20.00, 3rd 20.00–02.00, 4th 02.00–07.00.

Jeddah and Yenbo

Working hours Saturday/Friday: Work round the clock 7 days a week in two shifts. First shift 07.00–19.00, second 19.00–07.00. No overtime or shift differential premiums. Meals 12.00–13.00, 00.00–01.00. Reefer cargoes worked 07.00–12.00, 16.00–24.00.

Friday: Weekly day of rest but worked round the clock. No overtime or shift differential premiums. Also see above.

Holidays: Work round the clock at ordinary rates. Cargo clearance only for Reefer cargoes.

During Ramadan month, working hours are: 07.00–13.00, (overtime) 19.00–23.00.

BIMCO issue every year a Holiday Calendar which gives information about working hours, holidays, etc., in ports all over the world.

be presented immediately on a screen or in print. An example of a calculation form is shown on page 105f. and taking that form as a basis for the discussion the following items should be mentioned:

The ship's name

This defines the individual vessel or special class of ships of interest in the calculation and thereby also specifies the cargo capacity, speed and bunker consumption on which the calculation will be based. Generally, this defines at the same time the average type of ship and ship's size for which the result of the calculation will be applicable on a similar voyage under the same market conditions.

Period of time

The period of time for which the figures used in the calculation are valid also has to be noted since the freight market level and the cost levels vary all the time.

Intended voyage

The intended voyage is specified via loading and discharging ports and up to the position where the ship is expected to start her next employment, i.e. so that a possible passage in ballast should also be included. The voyage plan for calculation purposes has to be determined from case to case. For trades and engagements that invariably cover a "ballast leg" it may be made a rule to always begin or alternatively end the voyage with the ballast leg. Passages through canals and other fairways which prolong the duration of the voyage and incur special extra costs also have to be included in the calculation.

Commodity and stowage factor

The name and description of the *commodity* is entered, together with the *stowage factor* (if applicable) used for calculation on cargo intake (quantity to be loaded).

Cargo quantity

The cargo quantity is noted by volume or weight measurement, depending on the measurement on which the freight will be calculated. In this connection some restricting factors must be observed. The weight of the cargo given in the order multiplied by the stowage factor gives the volume or space, including broken stowage, which this cargo would normally occupy in the ship's holds. This figure must, of course, equal or be less than the actual available space on

DEADWEIGHT SCALE

DRAUGHT IN DM	TPCI (M.TONS)	SALTWATER DISPL'T (M.TONS)	SALTWATER DEADW. (M.TONS)	FRESHWATER DISPL'T (M.TONS)	FRESHWATER DEADW. (M.TONS)	DRAUGHT IN DM
70						70
	14,80	9000	6500	9000	6500	
	14,70					
65	14,60			8500	6000	65
	14,50	8500	6000			
	14,40	8000	5500	8000	5500	
60	14,30					60
	14,20	7500	5000	7500	5000	
55	14,10			7000	4500	55
		7000	4500			
	14,00					
50	13,90	6500	4000	6500	4000	50
	13,80	6000	3500	6000	3500	
45						45
	13,70	5500	3000	5500	3000	
40		5000	2500	5000	2500	40
	13,60					
		4500	2000	4500	2000	
35						35
	13,50	4000	1500	4000	1500	
30	13,40					30
		3500	1000	3500	1000	
25	13,30	3000	500	3000	500	25
	13,20					
	13,10					
20	13,00	2500		2500	0	20

LIGHTSHIP WEIGHT = 2448 TONS OF 1000 KG.

MARK	DRAUGHT METERS	DISPLACEMENT SALTWATER	DISPLACEMENT FRESHWATER	DEADWEIGHT SALTWATER	DEADWEIGHT FRESHWATER
		METRIC TONS OF 1000 KG.			
TF	6.814	–	8856	–	6408
F	6.678	–	8657	–	6209
T	6.666	8857	–	6409	–
S	6.530	8657	–	6209	–
W	6.394	8461	–	6013	–
WNA	6.344	8388	–	5940	–

board. For cargoes other than bulk commodities—and especially cargoes with a large volume in relation to their weight—it may happen that the margin for broken stowage included in the stowage factor given by the charterers or shippers is too narrow. Furthermore, the volume given may be "net on quay" and in such a case the owners have to determine what has to be added to cover broken stowage in the ship's holds. Consideration has also to be given to the fact that the vessel's deadweight (deadweight all told) does not equal the cargo weight the ship may load, but gives the total weight the ship can carry, including bunkers, stores, fresh water and ballast. For each calculation it is therefore necessary to determine by what tonnage the deadweight figure has to be reduced, in order to get the deadweight available for cargo (deadweight cargo capacity).

In this connection one of the most important questions is where, when and how much the vessel will bunker for the intended voyage. D.w.a.t. (deadweight all told) as per the ship's specification is given for the summer loadline (SF=Summer Freeboard) in salt water (SW). The ship must under no circumstances be loaded deeper than the relevant loadline and it is therefore of great importance to check on trading areas, season of the year and the salinity in the ports of call throughout the voyage, to be able to determine correctly the figure stating the maximum cargo intake on full deadweight. Obviously another limitation on cargo intake is the maximum draught on which the vessel will be able to transit canals and enter ports included in the voyage plan. This may also be a decisive factor when determining the rotation of loading and discharging ports. Finally, a notation must also be made stating whether the calculations are based on weights in long tons or metric tonnes, or based on volume, for example, per cubic metre (cu.m.) or "per ton of 40 cubic feet (cu.ft.)" or other cubic units.

Generally *the freight* is assessed per metric tonne or per long ton. Most of the fixtures made in the open market concern homogeneous cargoes and it is often the available deadweight for cargo which is the limiting factor. For especially bulky cargoes and for general cargoes there are a number of alternatives for the assessment of freight, for example, per cu.m. or per cu.ft. which are the most common in use, but the freight rate may also be quoted to be applied either per unit weight or per unit cube (W/M). The basic unit for assessment of the freight in this case is the one which gives the highest total freight amount for the parcel or the commodity in question (whichever yields the more). This manner of calculation is commonly used in liner trades and is then referred to as "freight per revenue ton (R/T)". Freight may also be quoted on a lump sum basis which in fact means that the owner puts a specified cargo space at the charterer's disposal. This space may then be filléd in the best possible way in return for payment of the agreed lump sum freight amount.

The items in the voyage calculation mentioned so far can be regarded as being part of the income side. In addition to these regard must also be given to whether *ballast bonus* or *demurrage* or *despatch* will be involved.

Costs

On the costs side in the voyage calculation a lump sum covering port dues and charges (port costs) is noted as well as estimated costs for cargo handling. For every port these two cost items constitute the largest part of the so-called disbursements account, which the port agent will present to the owner after the call.

The *port costs* might be very difficult to determine in advance even if there is sufficient time to get an estimate (*pro forma* account) from the agents. The item of port costs in the calculation does not normally include costs that are related to the cargo itself (cf. page 202f.), although there are exceptions, for example, part of the quay dues might be on the basis of the quantity of cargo which the vessel will handle during the call (quay and tonnage dues). All the different costs which the ship will incur from taking her inward pilot until dropping her outward pilot have, however, to be estimated and pre-calculated in the best possible way and very often information of this nature is available from BIMCO. If the ship, during the current voyage, is required to load or discharge at more than one berth within the same port area, then the owner may also have to take shifting expenses into account. Special port costs that also need to be taken into account are canal transit costs and costs of a similar nature such as the costs for transit of the Kiel, Suez and Panama Canals and for passage through the Bosporus and St. Lawrence Seaway. There may also be

Ship:	WORLD ACADEMY		Period:	Year:	Voy. Nr:
			Jan–Mar	1994	1 A – 94
Voyage/(TC–employment):		Alex – Odessa – Suez – Shanghai			

Currency: $	Exch. Rate:				
Cargo/Employm.	Quantity/Time	Rate	Income	Comm. %	Adj. Income
			0		
Blk urea	27000	28	756000	6,25	
			0		
			0		
			0		
			0		
Desp. / Demurr.:			0	– / + :	0
				INC. TTL: *	756000

Port	Port charges	Port days	C/P–Terms	L/D price	Load/Disch. costs
Odessa	25000	7+1,5+1	4000 shex		
Suez	60000	–			
Shanghai	25000	13,5+3+1	2000 shex		

			Canal		
Distance:	Speed:	Sea days:	(Days on TC)	Port days:	Total days:
10000	14	31,25	1	27	59,25

Fuel/day (ME):	Quantity:	Price:	Cost:	TOTALS:	
22	710	90	63855	Bunkers	84000
Diesel/day (AE):	Quantity:	Price:	Cost:	Port	110000
2	119	170	20145	L/D	0
				Comm.	47250
Notes:				Ex.ins.	
	Freight +/– 1 $ = $ 427 per day			Extras	10000
				COST TTL: *	251250
				GR. REV: */*	504750
				REV/DAY:	8519
					8519
				Date:	Sign:
				94-01-20	JAS

Illustration showing a printed form for voyage calculations which can be PC-based or manual. These are voyage estimates on two employment alternatives available at the same time for a vessel. The form can be used both for voyage charter and time charter. In these calculations the owners only include the costs related directly to the employment in question.

costs for piloting through the English Channel, for instance, or for coastal or offshore pilotage that may be required for some part of the voyage.

When the charter-party stipulates that the *loading and discharging costs* are for the charterers' account (f.i.o.) in the case of break bulk cargo, then the costs for stowage on board are nearly always also to be paid by the charterers

Ship:	WORLD ACADEMY		Period: Jan–Mar	Year: 1994	Voy. Nr: 1 B – 94
(Voyage)/TC–employment:		Alex – Gib – Spore			

Currency: $	Exch. Rate:				
Cargo/Employm.	Quantity/Time	Rate	Income	Comm. %	Adj. Income
			0		
T/C–trip out	70	10500	735000	3,75	
			0		
			0		
			0		
			0		
Desp. / Demurr.:			0	– / + :	0
				INC. TTL: *	735000

Port	Port charges	Port days	C/P–Terms	L/D price	Load/Disch. costs

Distance: (Ball) 2000	Speed: 14 (In ballast)	Sea days: 6,25	Days on TC: 70	Port days: 0	Total days: 76,25

Fuel/day (ME): 22	Quantity: 138	Price: 90	Cost: 12375	TOTALS: Bunkers	14500
Diesel/day (AE): 2	Quantity: 13	Price: 170	Cost: 2125	Port	0
				L/D	0
				Comm.	27563
Notes:				Ex.ins.	
	Hire/day +/– 500 $ = $ 442 per day			Extras	10000
				COST TTL: *	52063
				GR. REV: */*	682938
				REV/DAY:	8957
					8957
				Date: 94–01–20	Sign: JAS

The result under "Revenue per Day" for the various employment alternatives is used for the comparison and evaluation of suitability and will guide the owners on deciding which alternative to go for at that time. The vessels must be fixed "best possible" in whatever status of the freight market, but considering the company's long term survival the "Rev/Day" should give a contribution to, or preferably cover, the vessel's daily (running) costs and capital costs per day for the business to be considered profitable both in the long run and taking a shorter view.

(f.i.o.s.). In the case of bulk cargoes, on the other hand, quite often the owners will have to pay for the trimming of the cargo (trimming for owner's account, f.i.o. ex trimming). If the cargo consists of vehicles, or other types of unitized cargoes, the parties may agree specially on which of them shall pay for lashing

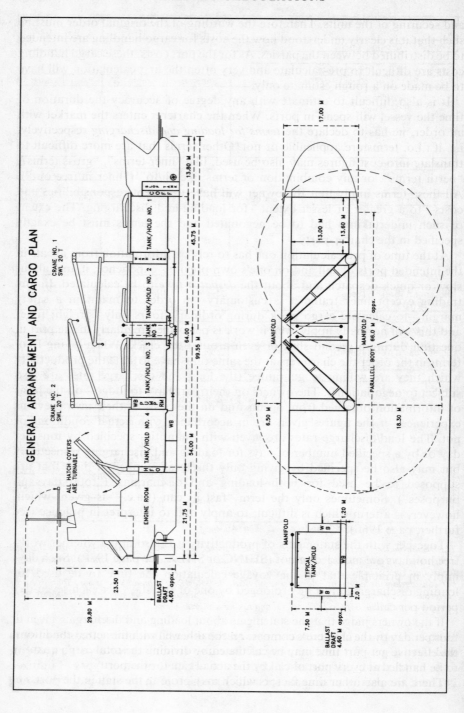

GENERAL ARRANGEMENT AND CARGO PLAN

and securing of the units. Therefore the wording of the original order must be such that it is clearly understood how the costs for cargo handling are intended to be distributed between the parties. As for the port costs, these cargo handling costs are difficult to pre-calculate and very often the first calculation will have to be made on a rough estimate only.

It is also difficult to estimate with any degree of accuracy the duration of time the vessel will spend in ports. When the charterer enters the market with an order, he has to declare the *terms for loading and discharging* respectively, i.e. if f.i.o. terms are applicable or not. Other terms that are more difficult to translate into cost figures may also be used, like "liner terms", "gross terms", "berth terms", or any combination of terms like "li/fo" ("liner in/free out"). All these terms imply that the owner will have to accept responsibilities and costs—to a greater or lesser extent—for loading and discharging. The extent of such undertakings had to be negotiated and the terms must be exactly specified in the charter-party.

At the time of pre-calculation one has to rely on information from agents in the intended ports of call and on one's own previous experience, if any, about slow or quick despatch and about the *despatch time* to be calculated. In any trading except liner traffic it is customary—in order to maintain a safety margin—to calculate cargo work during ordinary hours only (straight time) and this will normally apply even if work is performed regularly in the port in question during a second shift or even around the clock. When giving f.i.o. terms in the order the charterers at the same time have to state the productivity which they are willing to guarantee (the load and discharge rates are also subject to negotiations). The owners on their part have to judge—on the basis of information obtained from agents and on the basis of their own previous experience—if the figures given are in accordance with actual conditions or not. The load/discharge rates are given with quantities specified by tons per day or by a specified number of days for loading and discharging respectively but may also be specified by giving only the total number of days that are supposed to be used for both loading and discharging ("total days all purposes"). Sometimes only the term "fast as can (f.a.c.)" is given, which, however, is a term which is difficult to apply and to interpret in practice (see further, page 196f.).

Together with the statements of productivity it is also noted whether work-free holidays are included or not (SHINC or SHEX, see page 198f.). Such days imply in principle that in the voyage calculation the time to be used for loading/discharging must be prolonged by one or two days per each seven-day period per call.

If the owners judge that the statements about loading and discharging given in tons per day by the charterers compare reasonably well with the actual conditions, the effective net port time may be calculated by dividing the total cargo quantity to be handled at every port of call by the actual rate for the port.

There are also other time factors which may prolong the stay in the port, i.e.

the elapse of time that may occur from when the notice of readiness to receive or deliver cargo has been given until the time when the charterers start the cargo work on board. Owners normally cover such "*notice days*" by increasing the port time used in the voyage calculation by one day per port of call. This is applicable for all f.i.o. chartering. The ship may also encounter delays in *waiting* if it is impossible to obtain cargo stem and laydays that fit in exactly with the ship's position and the ship arrives too early. Finally, delays may be caused by *shifting* between berths, and the ship may be kept waiting for a berth for a number of unforeseeable reasons.

If the loading/discharge rate which the charterers agree to in the charter-party is lower than the actual rate, then the ship will get a turn-round time in port which is shorter than the duration of time corresponding to agreed charter-party terms. In such event the charterers may profit by reimbursement from the owners for time saved (despatch money). It is common in these cases to talk about despatch cargoes and there are charterers and groups of shippers who systematically wish to have such charter-party terms so that they will make a profit on the despatch. It is, however, more common that ships are kept in port for a longer duration of time than provided for in the charter-party. In such cases the charterers will normally reimburse the owners for the extra costs incurred by paying demurrage. Both despatch and demurrage terms have to be considered, i.e. when negotiating f.i.o. terms and very often the amount of despatch money to be paid per day is fixed at half the demurrage amount ("... demurrage/half despatch"). It is important that the calculation conforms as closely as possible with actual circumstances where the number of days in port is concerned, but it is also important for the owners to fix a demurrage amount which covers all costs and extras that may be incurred. The *demurrage*, or *despatch*, amounts, are entered into the calculation by notation, for example, on the income side as a plus or minus item.

It is now necessary to consider the *voyage costs* incurred during the intended voyage and any extras related to this specific employment. The most important of these items and generally the largest single item of the voyage calculation is *bunker costs*.

The main engine in modern ships uses fuel oil of a heavier grade than the auxiliary engines, which require light and more expensive fuel. Therefore the costs for fuel oil (FO)—which is related to the sailing distance—and the costs for diesel oil (DO)—which is consumed each day of the voyage whether at sea or in port—are calculated separately. In the so-called "ship's particulars", or the description of the vessel in the charter-party, the performance speed is given. This is the average speed for which the ship has been built and which she is able to maintain during normal conditions and normally also the speed used in the voyage calculation as a basic figure. It has to be noted, however, that even a small change of the average speed will cause a considerable difference in fuel consumption during the voyage. Under certain conditions it may be economical to reduce the speed and prolong the duration of the voyage for a number of days in order to reduce the bunker costs. The fuel consumption when the vessel is fully loaded is also far larger than when she is proceeding in ballast at the same speed, something that also has to be considered in the calculation.

Ships built during the last decade and ships to be delivered in the future will normally have a shaft generator, which for voyage calculation purposes means that DO consumption is considered only for the time in port. It must also be noted that the main engines of modern ships have a considerably lower consumption than engines of their older sisters.

The theoretical distance covered during a cargo voyage, including connecting ballast legs, is normally increased by use of certain rules of thumb. This may be done by, for example, increasing the total distance by a fixed percentage, by adding one day per each canal transit, etc. This is done in order to allow for practical matters such as weather conditions, streams and currents, passages requiring speed reductions, etc., and it is the *sea voyage time* pre-calculated in this way that determines the *FO consumption* and thereby the cost calculated for fuel oil during the intended voyage.

The *DO consumption* varies from day to day within certain limits depending on which auxiliary engines are running. Nevertheless, for calculation purposes and also in the vessel's official particulars, an average figure is used for the consumption per day which is determined from statistics of previous voyages of the ship in question.

The sum of port days and days at sea gives the *total voyage time* which is used for calculating the DO consumption (except for vessels with shaft generator) and this number of total voyage days is the same number that will be used when arriving at the final calculation for finding the voyage revenue per day.

The *bunker prices* for FO and for DO vary considerably both from time to time and between the different places for bunker replenishment. All ports do not have bunkering facilities and some ports that may supply bunkers might not be able to supply all the different grades.

There are a number of various other cost items that also have to be considered with respect to the intended voyage, such as extra war risk insurance premiums, ice trading, cargo carried on deck at owners' risk, etc. These are not normally included in the ship's regular insurance cover. There may also be a question of war risk bonuses or other occasional additions to the regular costs for the ship's crew depending on the intended trading. Political and labour unions' regulations in certain ports may cause considerable extra costs for the shipowners. Out of other extra cost items the cost of cleaning is the more frequent one, but considerable amounts may also be incurred due to the necessary purchase of dunnage and other material, for example for lashing and securing purposes. Finally, it has also become common for the exporting or the importing country to require a special tax, a so-called freight tax, calculated on the gross freight amount, to be paid by the owners.

The various items discussed above are the ones normally appearing in a pre-calculation for a voyage charter. Using the calculation form with the various boxes to be filled in, the calculation procedure may be summed up as follows:

Notations

—Note in the preamble the name of the ship in question, the time period during which the voyage will be performed and note also the geographical route, including any connecting ballast leg.

—Note on the income side in what currency and at what rate of exchange the freight will be paid. Note the cargo quantity and also the total commission applicable.

—Note ports of call in geographical rotation and also any canal transits or other passages that will incur costs and add to the voyage time.

—Note loading and discharging rates and corresponding time according to the order and whether the basis for time counting will be SHINC or SHEX.

—Note the total voyage distance in Miles (M) including ballast and also the ship's speed in knots or distance per day. Note the bunker consumption (FO respectively DO) in tons per day and further note also the bunker prices per ton applicable for the two kinds.

—Note amounts of any additional extras. These cost items may be specified in detail in the "Remarks" box.

Calculations

—Note the number of whole days which the ship will require for the handling of cargo in each port. Add holidays and notice day and if necessary also enter waiting time and sum up total days for every port. In this connection the weather conditions in the ship's areas of call also have to be considered, for example, rainy seasons.

—Determine any difference between actual time to be used according to "official" view and the shipowner's estimate thereof and enter the amount (for demurrage/despatch calculations).

—Add port days and enter the total sum.

—Increase the total distance in accordance with the company's standard, for example, by 5% and calculate the total number of days at sea (part of a day is normally not considered, it is common to use the nearest number of full days). Add also to this sum any additional time to be used for canal transits and note the total time at sea.

—Add port time and sea voyage time and enter the total voyage time.

—Use the total time at sea for calculating the FO consumption during the voyage and use the total voyage time to calculate the DO consumption (see "shaft generator" above). Thereafter, calculate and enter the respective costs for FO and DO during the voyage.

—Note the rate of freight which owners deem obtainable for the cargo voyage and calculate the gross freight amount in the currency to apply. Thereafter recalculate this amount into the currency that generally will be used in the voyage calculation and enter the gross freight revenue.

—Reduce or increase the gross freight revenue with any despatch or demurrage amount that will be applicable.

—Use the gross freight amount for calculating the costs of commissions and enter the amount of commission.

Summing up and conclusions

—Add the totals of bunker, port, cargo handling, commissions, insurance and other extra costs. This sum is then subtracted from the adjusted amount of gross freight revenue and the result is the amount which represents the income of the voyage after payment of the costs for performance of the voyage.

—Divide this amount by the number of voyage days to get the surplus per day earned by the ship in question during the duration of the intended voyage.

—The daily revenue is a figure used for comparison, and it shows if the voyage is profitable in absolute numbers when compared with the vessel's fixed costs element, and if the voyage gives a better revenue than alternative employments available at the same time. Thirdly it also shows if the revenue per day ("the Time Charter equivalent") conforms with the current spot-market level or not. As mentioned previously, the judgement must also include considerations of the expected freight market development throughout the duration of the voyage. It is also of importance to consider whether the ship will be open again after performance of the voyage in a good or bad position with regard to the then expected possibilities of getting a new employment.

Profitability in the short perspective may be deemed obtained if the revenue per day covers the daily costs for the ship, for example, costs for personnel, running and maintenance of the vessel, provisions and spare parts, insurance and administration. In order to be profitable in the long run, however, the daily revenue must also cover the capital costs (interest and depreciation). The demand for return on the trading activity of a vessel may therefore be put at different levels and the different corresponding amounts are used when evaluating various pre-calculated daily revenue figures representing the alternative possible employments.

In order to facilitate the comparison of results from different calculations and also in view of the function of the voyage calculation as a basis and instrument for negotiations it is practical to pre-calculate and note the variation of the daily revenue figure due to a smaller variation of the freight rate, and also the variation corresponding to an increase or decrease of the voyage time by one day.

SPECIAL CALCULATIONS

Particular factors in connection with consecutive voyages and marginal calculations

The same principles for calculations are also applicable to consecutive voyages or to contracts of affreightment. Such engagements often last for a longer period of time and it might be difficult to estimate, for example, the development of costs during the period. It is also necessary at the stage of pre-calculation to determine how the ship should be traded in the best way in order to minimize the time in ballast. Are cargoes to be carried under the contract to be used for return voyages in a trade where the owners can always count on well-paying cargoes in the opposite direction or where a similar contractual engagement is already secured? Is the intention to execute the contract shipments as round voyages with the return leg in ballast? Or are the contract voyages to be carried out as intermediary voyages and, if required, fill a gap between two other engagements?

Calculations do not necessarily have to cover complete voyages but it may be more appropriate to make a so-called marginal calculation. This can occur, for example, when a ship is definitely fixed for a specific voyage—either in ballast or with only a part of the cargo space occupied. There may also be a cargo which requires some deviation in time and distance from the immediately intended route but which nevertheless would take the ship in the right direction. It is characteristic for such a "way-cargo" that the freight revenue from this cargo alone does not justify fixing the ship for this voyage. The fact, however, that the ship will be directed along largely the same route anyway makes the freight for the way-cargo a positive supplement to the overall voyage result, or at least helps in reducing the loss in the case of a ballast trip. In such marginal calculations only the bunker costs for the extra distance (deviation) and the additional costs related to the prolongation of the voyage time are considered. Of course, the expected costs for extra ports of call, cargo handling, etc., caused by the shipment of the way-cargo also have to be taken into account. The extra freight revenue, minus all extra costs related to the way-cargo, is the supplementary freight for making the deviation and when dividing this supplement by the number of extra days a surplus per day is obtained which can be compared with the general required trading revenue per day for the ship during the period in question and this comparison will show if it is profitable or not to take the cargo.

Liner calculations

In liner traffic there is often a need to make marginal calculations for transports within or in the vicinities of the ordinary trading area which, for various reasons, cannot be regarded as regular cargo bookings. Frequently the additional cargo may involve loading or discharging at a port which is not regarded as a basic port according to the tariff, but which may be reached through a minor deviation. It may also be a question of loading and discharging at ports along the normal route but besides the normally scheduled stops. If a liner vessel has got the time within the framework of the schedule and has also got open space which is not intended to be filled by ordinary bookings, then it may be possible for the owners to calculate a freight for a way-cargo which, in principle, should cover the costs for the extra port calls, extra bunkers, cargo handling and possibly extra material and to give some profit.

If the prevailing freight level is high the owners may, by fixing at market level, get a substantial addition to the voyage net result, but during low market conditions the owners might well have to abstain from taking the cargo. If the ship has no time to spare, however, the calculation has also to take into account not only the required daily trading surplus, but also a possible cost for the chartering of extra tonnage that might have to fill the gap in the schedule caused by the deviation made by the ordinary scheduled ship. If the vessel has not got any free space for the way-cargo, the owners, of course, must find out if the marginal calculation shows an interesting surplus should the ordinary—but low-paying—parcel be replaced by the way-cargo offered. Even if the marginal calculation shows surplus it may nevertheless be impossible for the owner to accept the extra cargo available because of his relationship with regular customers and because of other market implications.

Reefer calculations

In reefer trades the calculations are mainly the same as in the dry cargo trades and the marginal calculations are very similar to those in liner traffic. It is also characteristic that reefer ships have open space on the ballast voyages, but that those ships nevertheless, because of tight scheduling for their contractual undertakings, do not often have time left even for a short deviation.

Calculation and time charter

It is seldom necessary for a shipowner to make regular calculations of the type and pattern discussed so far where time chartering is concerned. The hire normally includes everything except what has to be paid for by the charterer or the owner for bunkers on board on delivery or redelivery. In some cases, however, the owners have to take into account that the intended trading incurs higher daily costs than normal because of overtime work for the crew, expensive travelling when crews are exchanged, higher average costs for maintenance and spare parts, extra insurance premiums and maybe also costs for certain cargo handling material and equipment. The ballast leg to the point of delivery and from the point of redelivery to an employment area is normally for owners' account. Naturally this is a cost which the owner will try to cover by adjustment of the hire level of the time charter. He may also succeed in negotiating a special ballast bonus. In this connection it is also useful to note some different ways of stating the time charter hire.

In the dry cargo market when talking of the smaller tonnage up to and including the so-called handy sizes it is common to note a daily hire rate, e.g., $4,750 *per day*. For longer periods and with regard to larger ships, the hire is more often expressed as a certain amount per ton deadweight per month, e.g., $4.75 *per tdw* (implied: per 30 days).

In reefer trading, however, it is common practice to fix the hire at a certain amount per cubic feet bale, e.g., 75 *cents per cu.ft.* (implied: per 30 days).

Tanker calculations

A complete voyage calculation concerning tanker trading should contain largely the same items which we have already discussed. The practical manner of calculating and, above all, the freight fixing system differs, however, to a great extent. For all tanker cargoes (except for shipping quantities below about 10,000 tons deadweight) freight rates are quoted with reference to an international scale now called the New World-wide Tanker Nominal Freight Scale, or (New) Worldscale for short. By using such an internationally well known standard scale as a reference the parties in the tanker market easily compare and evaluate freight rates for all the different voyages and market levels.

Briefly the basis of Worldscale is that the particulars of a certain standard tanker of 75,000 tons d.w. have been chosen for making round voyage calculations for practically all conceivable tanker trades—which are in fact comparatively few. In these calculations specified standard figures have been used for all items involved, for example, distances (which for owners' information have been printed in the NWS table), port costs, port time (four days), bunker costs, etc., and an additional fictional cost element of $12,000 per day. In this way the freight per metric tonne required by the standard ship in each trade has been calculated, and these freight figures are found in the Worldscale tables given as a certain dollar amount per ton. These values are called WS 100 or WS Flat. In practice, reference is only made to (New) Worldscale in orders, freight negotiations and market reports. The prevailing market level, the actual ship's size, the loading area and also the type and quality of the product to be shipped will then determine how far above or below the reference level of WS 100 the fixture will be concluded—in other words what percentage of the tabulated freight figures will be used for calculating the freight to be paid.

Consequently a fixture covering 150,000 tons deadweight from the Gulf to Western Europe made at WS 75 means that the owners will be paid a freight equal to 75% of the freight per ton enumerated in the Worldscale table for the trade in question. One cannot, however, directly state that another shipowner who has fixed at the same time a cargo of the same size in another trade at WS 80 has obtained a higher freight, since the various cost elements (bunkers, port costs and daily costs) in practice have a different impact on the different voyages.

It must be stressed that the assumed daily cost of $12,000 used for the calculations based on the standard ship is only a fictional figure which does not take into account, for example, the varying cost levels between the different countries. WS 100 is therefore not the rate at which all ships of the world of the same size as the standard ship will cover the daily and voyage costs but WS 100 should be regarded as a mathematically convenient mean level.

Efforts are made to try to keep the basis for the calculations fairly closely in line with actual conditions and the basic items are updated once a year when the tables are revised. The changes affecting the tables are related to port costs and bunker prices, while the fixed hire element of $12,000 is maintained. Since the WS rates may be translated into daily results, the tanker owners can produce a series of voyage calculations for their different sizes of ships for the most frequent trades and tabulate the results. They have then available a number of different WS rates for each trade and can judge and evaluate the various alternative employments offered.

REPORTING

Finally, we shall add some comments on how fixtures made in the open market are reported and interpreted. It is important that our points on the reporting, investigating and negotiation phases are studied together with Chapter 10, below. Legal problems may arise in connection with the negotiation and the making of a contract and we illustrate some of these problems in Chapter 10. The information that will be given about every single fixture is normally sparse. Nevertheless it will contain the minimum of detail that is required to supply an interested party with sufficient information about the prevailing freight level in a certain trade, for example. The information also shows how a specific fixture will compare with other fixtures made, the general activity in the market (many or only a few fixtures), the rate of freight and in this case also the chartering conditions for competing ships. Further, the reports give information about the development of the market over-all or in certain sectors. Thereupon the details given may be used by those who are interested in making a rough calculation or estimation of the expected voyage result for a reported vessel.

We show at page 116ff. some typical examples of market reports covering representative fixtures per a certain day. Largely both the dry cargo

Fix where you can

OCTOBER has started with competition between the ulcc and vlcc sectors. With the current position lists showing 68 vlccs and ulccs available, the 300,000 tonners have had to compete with vlccs and take part-cargoes. One such fixture saw a 350,000 tonner agreeing to carry 250,000 tons of crude oil on the basis of a ship-to-ship transfer from the Middle East to Japan at WS49.5. Voyages to the east are still in the majority, with the Middle East OPEC oil exporters shipping oil eastward for thirty/fifty-day voyages instead of sixty/eighty days as before. Rates have shown little change, at about WS42.5 for Europe, WS50 to Japan and other eastern destinations at an average of WS43.

——————TANKERS——————

West Africa also shows little change from last week, but owners with vessels of the 130,000 ton size are facing problems because of charterers' continuing tendency to double up on stems and to absorb vlccs. A Spanish charterer received at least thirteen offers for a small cargo of about 100,000 tons loading at Kole, and closed at WS90. Further slippage is predicted in this sector, with a fall to about WS65 for million-barrel vessels.

Business in the Mediterranean was slow towards the end of the week. However, the Caribbean and east coast Mexico trade continues to be very healthy. A 70,000 tonner loading in the Caribbean for the US Gulf and US coast obtained WS130.

A similar size vessel for the same destination from east coast Mexico accepted marginally lower. However, it was not particularly busy for the North Sea crude market, with 80,000 tons closing at between WS97.5/WS100 for cross-UK-Continent movements.

After a slow start, the product tanker market picked up and rates regained a certain degree of firmness. The eastern market remained in owners' favour, with long-range-size vessels enjoying WS170 for 55,000 tonne cargoes to Japan. Medium-range-size liftings from the Middle East Gulf have stayed active, India remaining the most important area of demand, with charterers paying WS230. Despite a lack of tonnage available in the Caribbean, charterers have maintained the rate at around WS205 for 28,500/30,000 ton liftings to the US Atlantic coast.

Better than for many years

IN terms of increasing demand, this must be one of the best autumns the dry cargo shipping market has had for several years. Whichever sector is assessed, rates are firm or improving, prospects are better, and owners are in danger of smiling. Perhaps the capesize market, not known for its long periods of improving rates, is best-placed. Modern vessels have begun to receive rates which justify the newbuilding cost and, where there is strong demand for tonnage, as in the Pacific basin at present, these ships are first in the queue for business.

In the Atlantic, reports Norwegian broker Fearnleys, the supply of capesize tonnage is tight. Delay at several major ports has upset schedules and forced expensive changes to planning. Charterers have found themselves trapped by the tight stems available at Atlantic ore ports, and the build-up of tonnage in the Pacific has worked against many owners. So both sides are winning on one side, but both are losing on another. Rates paid include a high $21,000 per day for a 134,000 dwt vessel to make a trip to the Far East, while similar bulk carriers making transatlantic voyages

—————— DRY CARGO ——————

received only $17,000. A 140,000 dwt ore carrier fixed Brazil to South Korea at $12.04 - which reflects the $24,000 per day paid by a local operator to book the ship. In the Pacific, slow business included $7.90 for 120,000 tons coal from Newcastle to Kaohsiung.

Shortage of panamax tonnage in specific areas has pushed rates higher. US Gulf to Continent rose $1 to $14, and Gulf to Japan by $0.50 to $25.50, a fraction short of the point at which charterers take tonnage on time charter to control their costs. Modern tonnage offering trips to the Far East accepted $15,500, while transatlantic round voyages found rates of $10,500-$12,000 per day. South African coal business was very active, but panamax trips from the Far East to the Continent were low, at $9,000. For period business, four to six months was on offer, but charterers shied away from twelve months on the grounds that current rates are too high.

As a result of the strength of panamax demand, the Baltic Freight Index leapt another fifty-six points. September settlement was ninety points above the previous record, in 1991. Among

the causes were weather-related congestion in China, grain demand in Egypt, the Philippines, Yemen and Pakistan, and the strength of the capesize market.

There were even positive signs from the handysize market, although the strength and enthusiasm were somewhat missing. Economical handymax tonnage obtained $10,000 per day for Pacific round voyages, up on previous business, while modern 38,000 tonners agreed $8,000-$9,000 for similar voyages. In the Great Lakes, vessels sought - and found - improved rates, which augurs well for the close of the season in that region.

Better rates dampen any need to scrap tonnage, and this is as much the case today as ever. There have been few capesize vessels scrapped recently, so breakers have had to turn to aged tankers. However, there have been few dry cargo deliveries so far this year, which means a balance in terms of number, and a younger fleet at the end of the year than at its opening. Nevertheless, good rates encourage newbuilding orders, so it is unhealthy to cease scrapping completely. This is an important time for the fleet profile. Unless the oldest vessels leave the fleet, rates can only become hampered by weight of numbers.

Reproduced by kind permission of Fairplay.

A weekly market commentary.

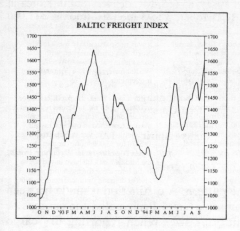

BALTIC FREIGHT INDEX

Biffex

The market started relatively quietly in early September with the spot index (BFI) dropping ten points to 1436, however it soon started to rise again, putting on about 8 points a day until mid September, reaching 1537 on 16th September. For the last ten days it has soared up about 15 points a day to reach 1605 on 26th September. Futures, after a little hesitation have responded in kind with October and November both reaching 1692. However the market still refuses to be very bullish for the Spring and January stands at 1610 as also does April, whereas a conventional view would put them 50 points above October 94.

Date	spot BFI	1994 July	Oct	1995 Apr	July
24 Jan 94	1236	1140	1303	1375	—
24 March	1190	1145	1290	1360	—
25 April	1354	1183	1295	1396	—
25 May	1496	1222	1298	1348	—
23 June	1316	1300	1340	1390	1183
25 July	1437	1443	1425	1445	1270
25 Aug	1473	—	1400	1410	1265
26 Sept	1605	—	1692	1610	1460

A monthly diagram and commentary on BFI and Biffex developments.

The day-to-day reporting on fixtures made may be illustrated as follows:

REPRESENTATIVE FIXTURES

DRYCARGO:

*Grain
US Gulf to Japan, *Sea Yalikoy*, 52,000 tons, grain, October 1/10, $24.50 no combi ports, $25 with combi ports, 11 days all purposes (Cargill)

Kohschiang to Lisbon, Rotterdam or Amsterdam, *Argolis*, 50,000 tons, tapioca, October 15/17, $11.50 via Suez, $11.75 via Cape, fio, 10,000 per day load/8,000 per day discharge (Matco)

*Coal
Puerto Bolivar to Wilhelmshaven, *Permeke*, 100,000 tons, coal, October $9.50, fio, 45,000 per day load, SHinc/20,000 per day discharge SHex (Preag)

*Iron ore
Brazil to Japan, *Chou Shan*, 140,000 tons, iron ore, November 1/15, $12, fio, scale load/30,000 per day discharge SHinc (NSC)

*Time charters
Bunga Saga Satu (built 1993), 73,503 dwt, delivery Cigading, September/October, trip via Richards Bay, redelivery Skaw-Cape Passero range, $10,000 per day (IMC)

Mike K (built 1971), 32,280 dwt, delivery Bosporus, prompt, trip via Black Sea, redelivery India, $9,100 per day (Geepee)

Anangel Argonaut (built 1981), 65,668 dwt, delivery South Korea in direct continuation, early October, 3 to 5 months' trading, $11,000 daily (Halla Maritime)

TANKER

*Western Hemisphere

From	To	Date	Tons	Cargo	Vessel	Rate	Charterers
North Sea	USG	Oct 9	250	d	Pacific Leader	46	Scanports
Indonesia	USG	Oct 20	80	d	MOC tonnage	1 mls	Astra Oil
West Africa	USG	Oct 11	265	d	Stena Concordia	45.25	Sohio
PG	EC Can	Oct 3	50	c	Flaminia	190	Vitol
EC Mexico	USG	Oct 3	75	d	Seraya Spirit	122.5	Coastal

Note: in 000s of tonnes; rates in Worldscale except ls = lump-sum payment in USD 000s; d = dirty (crude), c = clean (products).

and the tanker reports follow the same pattern. A distinction is made between engagements on voyage and on time charter basis. Principally, the cargoes or the ships are listed by order of quantity or size. When reporting dry cargo fixtures there is also often a subdivision into commodities, for example, grain, coal, ore cargoes, etc., and when tanker fixtures are concerned there is a similar separation between crude and product charters.

From the "Vessel Fixtures" we can deduce, for instance, that the panamax vessel "Sea Yalikoy" is fixed for 52,000 tons of grain, from US Gulf to Japan, to present for loading within 1–10 October, total time allowed for loading/discharging is 11 days, different freight rates depending on ports involved, and charterers are Cargill.

"Permeke" is fixed for a coal cargo, 100,000 tons, loading October dates, obtained $9.50 f.i.o. with 45,000 tons daily load at SHINC terms and 20,000 SHEX discharge, voyage from Puerto Bolivar to Wilhelmshaven.

Pacific Time Charter market for panamax vessels is illustrated by "Anangel Argonaut" obtaining $11,000 daily for a continuation of charter with Halla Maritime for 3 to 5 months' further trading.

On the tanker side we note the VLCC "Stena Concordia" obtained WS 45.25 for a cargo of 265,000 tons crude West Africa to US Gulf for loading 11 October.

One products cargo of 50,000 tons was fixed for "Flaminia" at WS 190 for 3 October loading PG for East Coast Canada account charterers Vitol.

Although the fixture reports immediately give some pieces of information there is no direct information given about the real voyage result. To arrive at this a calculation has to be made in the normal way based on the details supplied. Neither can it be found out from details of one single fixture if this is good or bad or if the market level is rising or falling. To make such judgements a comparison has to be made with previous events and with one's own general knowledge about the current market and also with the shipowners' own calculations and fixtures. In other words, it is the continuous and daily follow-up of the fixture reports that makes it possible to make use of the information to its full extent.

CHAPTER 9

CHARTERING ROUTINES

Seen from the practical point of view the chartering procedure can be divided into three stages, namely the stage of investigation, the stage of negotiation and the follow-up stage. We shall describe here the routines as they are practised internationally by persons and institutions who are doing chartering work professionally and in accordance with, for example, Chartering Conditions laid down by BIMCO (The Baltic and International Maritime Conference).

THE PERIOD OF INVESTIGATION

The investigation stage commences when a charterer directly or through a broker enters the market with an order. Circumstances may then vary somewhat depending on whether the purchase transaction generating the transport is finally concluded or not, and this should be evident from the wording of the order. The manner of expressing this may be varied but a business is considered to be complete from the point of view of chartering technicalities only when the purchase deal is fully in order and signed, when the documentary letter of credit is obtained (if required), when shippers and receivers are prepared respectively to sell and buy the goods and when the cargo is ready and available for shipment or can be made available for loading at a certain specified time. Before the charterer enters the market with the order he has to decide if he is prepared to commence immediately firm freight negotiations with a suitable counterpart or if he wishes primarily to collect suggestions for different shipping opportunities and intends to start negotiations only after the material gathered has been sorted out and evaluated.

If the business deal is concluded in accordance with the above-mentioned definition and the charterer is prepared to enter immediately into firm negotiations then the order may open with the wording FIRM ORDER, CHARTERERS ARE NOW FIRM AS FOLLOWS . . . , DEFINITE, FIRM AND READY TO GO or FIRM WITH LETTER OF CREDIT (L/C) IN ORDER. Principally, one may also abstain from applying such "trade expressions" since an order which is circulated on the market by first-class charterers and brokers will normally be regarded as FIRM if nothing to the contrary is said in the order. In such cases there are nevertheless reasons for making the intentions clearer by the wording, for example, FIRM OFFERS INVITED or PLEASE OFFER FIRM.

When the business is concluded but the charterer does not want to enter into immediately firm negotiations, this may be indicated by marking the order FIRM or DEFINITE but at the same time with INDICATIONS ONLY or PLEASE INDICATE or PLEASE PROPOSE.

The expression FIRM WITH XX DAYS' NOTICE indicates that the cargo is ready to be negotiated but loading can take place only XX days after the fixture has been concluded. There may also be from time to time other reservations on orders which are actually ready for negotiations and we shall look into these in more detail.

If, on the other hand, the purchase negotiations have not yet been concluded, but the charterer nevertheless requires a freight quotation or at least an idea of the prevailing freight market level, this should be shown in the order by opening it with PROSPECTIVE ORDER, ORDER EXPECTED TO BECOME DEFINITE, ORDER NOT YET DEFINITE or similar expressions. If the charterers do not have any definite plans but only wish to make a general investigation of the shipping possibilities, this may be indicated by POSSIBILITY ONLY or CHARTERERS HAVE A POSSIBILITY TO WORK UP FOLLOWING BUSINESS.

Voyage charter

The contents of the order will then cover those items which the shipowner requires to make his calculations and evaluations, namely:

- —The charterer's name (full style) and domicile.
- —Cargo quantity and description of the commodity.
- —Loading and discharging ports.
- —The period within which the vessel is to be presented for loading (Lay/Can).
- —Loading and discharging rates and terms.
- —Any restrictions or preferences regarding type or size of ship.
- —Charter-party form on which the charterer wishes to base the terms and conditions.
- —Commissions to be paid by the owner.

In addition to this the charterer may also mention the approximate freight level which he wants to have as a starting point for the discussions or the negotiations (the charterer's freight idea), but such information is often omitted from the original order for reasons of negotiation tactics.

It is not unusual for charterers to put out an anonymous order and request the broker to keep the origin of the order secret until proposals of tonnage have been submitted from serious owners. The broker then denominates the origin and shows that the charterer is well known to him by FIRST CLASS CHARTERERS, A1 CHARTERERS or maybe DIRECT FIRST CLASS CHARTERERS, expressions that, of course, cannot be used by other brokers who receive and further the order to their contacts in turn.

Time charter

An order concerning a time charter engagement is presented on the market in largely the same way as that with respect to voyage chartering, with the exception that details about cargo, ports, loading and discharging rates and terms are exchanged for details about the intended trade, required time charter period and places for delivery and redelivery.

Liner booking

Liner booking procedure is normally much more simple as the traffic is performed in accordance with previously established terms, both as to the freight and as to other conditions that are found in the line's printed tariff. The sailing schedule gives dates for loading and discharging, a description of the vessel, shipping documentation and a statement that the carriage conditions will be in accordance with the standard terms of the Line or the Conference (Liner Booking Note).

The reaction of the shipowner

When the owner deems the received order to be worth considering he reverts to the broker or, in case the order was received direct, to the charterer. As mentioned previously the owner will normally contact the broker who first brought the order. If a number of brokers have presented the order at about the same time the one who is "closest" to the charterer is contacted or, in any case, the one who is supposed to be in the best position to negotiate with the charterer in question for the owner's account. The latter can express his interest in various ways.

If an order is FIRM AND READY TO TRADE the owner may choose to put forward a firm offer right away. This can be done when the trade is well known and the freight level is more or less established and when the ship's size and position fits in well with the conditions given in the order. A firm offer may also be the most suitable when the owner expects keen competition, especially in a declining freight market. Another way more often practised is that the owner presents his ship and his abilities to meet with the intentions according to the order and submits a freight indication. He is then uncommitted with regard to the figures and terms mentioned but such an indication will anyway advise the charterer about the owner's starting point for a possible negotiation. Furthermore, the charterer can compare the freight quoted with his own opinion about the proper freight level and can also compare it with suggestions made by other owners. An indication is often given without any time limit since it will not commit the parties. Still the owner is supposed to present—if and when submitting a firm offer later on—freight and terms that are no worse for the charterer than those indicated.

Alternatively, the owner can give the charterer a fairly rough suggestion just in order to "sound out" the basis for a possible negotiation and let this proposal be accompanied by a so-called freight idea. This will certainly indicate a freight level which the owner considers to be suitable as a basis for further discussions, but which may be adjusted upwards or downwards in an eventual offer, when the owner has made more careful calculations.

A proposal, a freight idea or an indication form part of the negotiation stage and form a basis for the charterer's calculations and evaluations of chartering possibilities. The charterer may go on discussing with a number of owners their own proposals, ideas and indications until he finds a suitable counterpart for negotiations. The charterer will then revert to this owner asking for a firm offer on the basis of the conditions given in the order or in accordance with the previous discussions.

THE PERIOD OF NEGOTIATION

Main terms

The negotiation stage can be divided into two parts. Firstly, negotiation of the so-called main terms will be conducted and secondly, when the parties are in agreement, further negotiations will take place about the details and the wording of the clauses which have not been taken up during the negotiations of the main terms.

In voyage chartering the first offer that starts the firm negotiations will contain the following details:

—The shipowner's name (full style).
—The ship's name and particulars.
—Cargo quantity and description of the commodity.
—Loading and discharging ports and berths.
—Laydays/cancelling day.
—Loading and discharging rates and terms.
—Demurrage and despatch rates.
—Freight amount and conditions for payment of freight.
—Clauses covering time counting, Ice clause, War Risk clause, Bunker clause, clauses covering extra insurance premiums, taxes and dues, etc., which the owner considers to be of prime importance.
—Charter-party form.
—Commissions.

There are certain differences from the details enumerated above when tanker chartering on voyage basis is concerned, where:

—Loading and discharging rates are not given separately but as a number of total days for loading and discharge (laytime allowance all purposes).
—The freight rate is given by reference to Worldscale (above or below WS Flat).

In time chartering the offer will contain the following details:

—The shipowner's name (full style).
—The ship's name and particulars.
—Description of the time charter engagement.
—Place of delivery and redelivery.
—Laydays/cancelling day for the delivery.
—Intended trade with geographical limits and other trading limits from the owner's side.
—Quantity and price for bunkers on board on delivery and redelivery.
—Hire and conditions for hire payment.
—Other clauses which the owner wishes to negotiate as main terms.
—Charter-party form.
—Commissions.

The details of the vessel that are included in the particulars given in the main terms negotiations are:

—Vessel's name.
—Year built.
—Flag.
—Deadweight (may be given in different ways).
—Cargo space cubic (in most cases both Grain and Bale cubic).
—Number of hatches and holds.
—Cargo gear.
—Speed.
—Bunker consumption (FO respectively DO—only applicable on time charter engagement).
—Other details of importance for the intended cargo and trade.

In practice, the particulars cannot be given with great exactness and it is customary that the description of the ship is followed by the words ALL DETAILS ABOUT. (The shipowner's official description of a ship in tonnage lists and pamphlets is often concluded by the sentence ALL DETAILS GIVEN WITHOUT GUARANTEE BUT GIVEN IN GOOD FAITH AND

BELIEVED TO BE CORRECT and that is exactly the meaning of the word ABOUT in the particulars of the ship given when submitting the offer. It may be emphasized that the precise legal effect of these words is not always easy to foresee, but the individual circumstances may differ and thereby also the legal consequences.)

Since the parties start by negotiating the main terms and save the details for a later stage, both parties have to make allowance for this for the duration of the main terms negotiations. Therefore every offer or counter offer submitted by either party during the negotiations is ended by the words SUBJECT TO DETAILS (normally SUB DETAILS for short).

The offer commences with "OWNERS' OFFER FIRM . . ." and in this part or at the very end of the offer a time limit for reply is given. The owners are now committed in accordance with the terms offered until the time limit has been passed or until the charterers have given a reply which on any point differs from the offer made by the owners. In practice it never happens that one party replies to a first offer by a "clean accept", but instead the reply will be one of the following:

—"CHARTERERS ACCEPT OWNERS' OFFER, EXCEPT . . ." followed by the terms that charterers want to change (this is if the owners' offer is acceptable in parts, but some terms must be subject to further negotiations).

—"CHARTERERS DECLINE OWNERS' OFFER AND OFFER FIRM AS FOLLOWS . . .". (If the charterers find most of the terms offered unacceptable, but nevertheless will try to negotiate. The charterers will in this case go back to the owners with a full firm offer of their own.)

—"CHARTERERS DECLINE OWNERS' OFFER WITHOUT COUNTER". (If the charterers find the owners' offer to be completely unacceptable and they find it pointless to continue the negotiations.)

Charterers' reply is firm and is given with a time limit within which the owner has to revert. In the first of the above examples the charterers' reply is called a "counter" and the parties have already agreed on a number of terms. In the second example the charterers submit a "counter offer" and technically the parties have not yet agreed on any point. In the last example the negotiations will be terminated.

Like the owner, the charterers can make provisions or "subjects" in their counters or counter offers, i.e.

—"SUBJECT TO CHARTERERS' BOARD'S APPROVAL".

—"SUBJECT TO RECEIVERS' APPROVAL". (If the receiver of the cargo in question has to give its approval to the transportation arrangements and terms.)

—"SUBJECT TO STEM". (If the charterers have to obtain confirmation from the shippers or suppliers of the cargo that the negotiated quantities will be ready for loading at the time for loading agreed between owner and charterers during the negotiations.)

—"SUBJECT TO CHARTERERS' APPROVAL OF PLAN AND SUBJECT TO INSPECTION". (If the charterers have to ensure that the vessel is technically fully suitable for the intended trade—this refers especially to time charters.)

The owner in his turn can now choose to reply either by "ACCEPT . . . EXCEPT . . ." or advise the counterpart that he turns down the counter and discontinues the negotiations. It is not considered to conform with good ethics for one party to cut off firm negotiations one-sidedly by just not replying to or commenting on offers or counters, which are considered unsuitable as a basis for continued negotiations. If finding only a few points acceptable in a reply given by a counterpart, then the following counter can be given by reference to the last own counter or offer given, together with amendments to points where it is possible to meet with the other party's intentions in order that negotiations be continued. Thus such a reply from the owner's side would be: "OWNER COUNTERS BY REPEATING HIS LAST, EXCEPT . . .".

The negotiations will continue in this way by "taking and giving" from both sides until the parties have reached a compromise regarding terms that are acceptable to both of them. This agreement on "main terms", always "SUBJECT TO DETAILS" and possibly other outstanding subjects, is concluded by a "confirm". The last reply from the owner's side can be expressed as: "OWNER ACCEPTS CHARTERERS' LAST IN FULL AND CONFIRMS HEREBY THE FIXTURE SUBJECT TO DETAILS", or from the charterers' side: "CHARTERERS CONFIRM THE FIXTURE SUBJECT TO DETAILS AND SUBJECT TO STEM". Technically, the parties are now regarded as committed to the charter (even if a party formally may still have the right to "jump off" during the following discussions regarding the details of the charter-party—or if insurmountable obstacles appear relating to other subjects) but for good order's sake it is customary for the party who has received a "confirm" to respond by saying "reconfirm".

At this stage the charterers or their brokers will immediately compile a full recapitulation of all terms and details so far agreed. This "recap" is given to the owner or to the broker representing the owner in the negotiations and this recap should be carefully checked by both parties without delay.

As mentioned previously the parties are working within narrow time limits and the offers and counters are given for reply within a number of hours down to immediate reply ("THIS IS FIRM FOR REPLY HERE XX HOURS OUR TIME TODAY/THIS IS FIRM FOR IMMEDIATE REPLY"), and the time allowance tends to become shorter as the parties are coming closer to a "confirm". It is not unusual that the last round takes place with the owners' and charterers' brokers in direct telephonic contact with each other and both brokers also in direct contact with their respective principals over another line. Alternatively, each broker has at the same time two connections open over telex, i.e. one to the counterpart's broker and one to his principal. The advantage of the latter system is that the parties can obtain confirmation and reconfirmation simultaneously and in print.

It must also be stressed how important it is for the parties participating in negotiations to make careful notes and to keep all the paperwork in good chronological order, keeping records of all notes, telexes and other documents used in any way during the discussions and the firm negotiations from the very beginning until the end. The negotiations may have been a mixture of "Accept ... except" and "Repeat last ..." and may have been carried out both over telephone and over telex. In other words, it must be a prerequisite that the documentation should clearly show what has been said and agreed. It is an advantage if at least the first full round is fully and completely documented on telex and recapitulation is practically always submitted over telex immediately after the parties are "fixed sub details".

Details

The second phase of the negotiating stage is concerned with details, that is all the additional points and terms which have to be fully clarified before the charter is complete (a clean fixture). These discussions might be both laborious and long lasting. As a matter of principle those conditions which are of vital importance for the engagement should be already agreed as main terms. On some occasions the negotiations might be cut off if the parties cannot agree on one or more of the details which could be of importance. One should not, however, use details of the charter-party as an excuse to break off the negotiations if the real reason is something else.

During the negotiations involving the main terms it is sufficient to refer to a charter-party form, which can be one of the following kinds: A standard form adopted or approved by BIMCO, some other well known standard form recognized by both parties or the charterers' or the owners' own *pro forma* charter. Throughout the main terms negotiations the reservation SUBJECT TO DETAILS is maintained by both parties but for the discussion of details the charterers now have to present all suggestions and preferences on amendments, deletions and additions to the printed text relative to the business in question. If the additional clauses and the amendments are numerous it might be necessary to send the full suggested wording by letter or by telecopier, but otherwise the owners will receive the AMENDMENTS TO PRINTED FORM or PROFORMA per telex. Normally this is not regarded as a regular negotiation with offers and counter offers but rather as a discussion. Therefore no time limits are used and the parties instead use phrases like CHARTERERS

SUGGEST THE FOLLOWING AMENDMENTS TO . . . , and the discussions will go on with suggestions and amendments to suggestions until the parties are fully in accord.

When both parties have agreed on every detail, there will follow a confirmation of the deal: . . . HEREBY CONFIRM/RECONFIRM THE FIXTURE. If at the same time all the reservations are removed (the points being waived) a clean fixture has been obtained and there only remains for the parties to fulfil their undertakings according to the charter-party. The ship can immediately start loading where a prompt spot position is concerned and the fact that the parties have not yet had time to sign or even type the formal document—the charter-party original—has no practical influence on the agreement at this stage. The charterers' broker will now draw up and distribute a new complete RECAP which also covers the details.

Sometimes a FIXTURE CONFIRMATION is required before a SUBJECT regarding, for example, STEM can be waived and RECEIVERS' APPROVAL can be obtained. The owners may then protect themselves during the negotiations by requesting SUBJECT TO STEM/RECEIVERS' APPROVAL TO BE WAIVED WITHIN XX HOURS AFTER CONFIRMATION OF FIXTURE. Under such conditions the fixture is still not clean and may fall. The charterers might not succeed in calling forward the cargo for the agreed time of loading or the receivers may refuse to approve the ship or the chartering terms. Should the party who has introduced a subject fail to waive it within an agreed time limit the counterpart is no longer committed to the business.

In all cases of time limits, whether it is a question of time limits for a counter, for declaring STEM/RECEIVERS' APPROVAL IN ORDER or for waiving other subjects, it is of course possible for the parties to make a mutual agreement for a new and extended time limit.

The date of the charter-party will be the last day on which the parties reached a clean fixture, which means the date when the last remaining subject was waived.

THE PERIOD OF FOLLOW-UP

During the follow-up stage there remain some additional matters to be dealt with which form part of the chartering work. The charterers, or the broker who has negotiated on their behalf, has to draw up, copy and distribute the charter-party and to see to it that the documents are duly signed. Thereafter, it is also necessary for all parties involved to follow up notices, payments of freight and hire and all other matters that contribute to good performance from both sides. Mutually acceptable solutions to all problems that may arise in connection with the performance should also be worked out since there will often be matters which could not reasonably have been foreseen or which the parties for various reasons have not protected themselves against during the negotiations.

Normally, the broker acts on behalf of his principal and in most cases a charterer's broker will negotiate with an owner's broker, each of them in accordance with authority given by their respective principals. It is unusual for a broker to have *carte blanche* to fix BEST POSSIBLE. Normally the broker will discuss each offer and counter in detail as well as the negotiation tactics with his principal, and it is the broker's task to do his best to find out the counterpart's position and possibilities. The broker should advise and give recommendations to his principal based on his own judgement of the best way to obtain advantages and to pursue the negotiations. In principle, the broker gets new instructions and authority for each new round of negotiations, which he must not exceed. Sometimes the principal leaves some DISCRETION with the broker, for example, by stating HIRE $4,000 BUT YOUR DISCRETION TO FIX AT $3,800 or in clear words: "I want $4,000 as time charter hire for my ship, but because of urgent need to conclude the fixture you may accept down to $3,800". Then it is up to the broker to decide whether he should try to stick to the offer of $4,000 and run the risk of losing the business or to make a concession in order to come to terms with the counterpart's representative. Consequently, both skill in negotiating and good judgement are required from a first-class broker. Among his duties he must also recommend his principal to break off negotiations whenever the broker deems this to be to the advantage of his principal, and it is also the broker's duty to collect and distribute such information as may lead his principal to terminate the negotiations. The fact that the broker thereby loses—maybe a considerable—income in commissions must not affect his behaviour in such cases.

SPECIAL CHARTERING ROUTINES

Tender business is negotiated in a somewhat different way from normal routines. In the terminology of chartering there are two forms of tenders.

In one case there are no real negotiations but charterers who are very often a governmental or semi-governmental organization will enter the market with an order in the normal way, but with all terms and conditions on a "take it or leave it" basis. The order is marked TENDER or TENDER BUSINESS and states the latest date and time at which offers should be in the hands of the charterers. Often a time will be mentioned at which the charterers will reply. The owner who wishes to submit offers has to state his lowest freight quotation and otherwise declare agreement to all terms and conditions stipulated by the charterers (often given in the order by referring to a familiar official *pro forma* charter).

When the time limit for tendering is reached the charterers will compare the offers received and they will pick out the owner who, in addition to accepting the terms, has also submitted the most favourable freight quotation. This owner will be advised that he has won the tender and thereby the fixture is concluded. The charter-party terms for a business done in this way, sometimes called a FREIGHT TENDER, are often hard and costly as seen from the owner's point of view and sometimes the owner may succeed in compensating himself by quoting somewhat higher freights than would otherwise have been relevant in the market.

The other case of tenders concerns so-called CARGO TENDER. In this case it is the exporter or supplier of goods who has to offer on a tender for sale and transport of the goods to a buyer. The exporter will then act as charterer and has to include complete and fixed chartering conditions in his sales offer. The charterer then enters the market with an order in the usual way, and, of course, in this case it must be mentioned in the order what type of business is concerned. Thereafter, normal routine chartering negotiations will be carried out with the exception that the charterer will maintain a reservation like SUBJECT TO TENDER BEING AWARDED. If the charterer wins this tender, then automatically the owner will get the charter in accordance with the terms agreed.

Offers on such a cargo tender are usually submitted by a number of different charterers-exporters. There is nothing preventing an owner from concluding fixtures with more than one of the exporters since only one of them will obtain the business.

SALE/PURCHASE ROUTINES

Sale/purchase events and market practices

There are three different events in a ship's life when she may be subject to a sale/purchase procedure. The first is when the newbuilding is ordered from the shipyard, the second when she is sold second-hand—and she may indeed be sold several times during her active life—and the third event is, finally, when the ship is sold for scrapping.

The markets for newbuildings, for second-hand vessels and for scrap are interrelated and more or less move along with the variations in the related shipping markets. Practices and procedures for doing business in any of these three sale/purchase market sectors may differ to a great extent from the daily routines in any one of the other sectors.

For practical purposes one can say that the newbuilding business is to a very large extent a matter of arranging finance—besides finding a yard willing and able to build a ship of the required type and standard, at a competitive price and for delivery within reasonable time. The yard to be awarded the contract will be found by a tendering procedure and selected on the basis of all the above-mentioned criteria, including finance, since the yard may well offer credit terms. Even if this is similar to any large technical-economic business deal, and not much like normal shipping market trading, the parties normally have the assistance of sale/purchase brokers, and there are indeed brokers who are especially equipped for and concentrate on newbuilding business and who also act as ship financing consultants.

Looking then at the last sale/purchase event, the sale for scrapping, we find that the scrap market is actually not a shipping market, even if there are obvious connections. In principle it would seem to be part of a sale/purchase broker's job to be involved in selling ships for scrapping but, in practice, it is not necessarily regarded as a normal part of usual shipbroking business, albeit that the well-informed shipbroker may give advice at any time on current scrap prices for various types of ships (which are, by the way, calculated per light deadweight ton) obtainable from scrapping yards worldwide, and this information is also printed in the periodical shipping market reports.

A second-hand sale resembles normal chartering work to a much greater extent. Intending buyers will place an order for purchase of a ship of certain specifications on the market, mostly via a broker or a selected number of brokers, and will expect to receive from these sources proposals for sale. Like owners who are restrictive in giving information on the positions of their open vessels, the possible sellers are not always keen to admit or broadcast their interest in a sale, as this may affect the price discussion and the owner's market position in general. The buyer's broker may therefore mention in the order that the principals are "serious buyers" and that "sellers who want to remain private will be treated so", in order to find those ships which are not openly found on everybody's sale/purchase menu. Generally the "private and confidential" (PC) restrictions are very much apparent in sale/purchase activities. Of course the deal will be officially known when a ship is registered for the new owners and frequently also a change of name and flag takes place, but the price and the terms are not necessarily or often disclosed (reported sold at "unknown/undisclosed terms" or "price believed to be in region of . . .").

Some routines in negotiations

The negotiations and contract forms for the three mentioned sale/purchase events are all different in the following way: that, for negotiating a newbuilding contract, the standard design of the form used by the individual shipyard will often be followed, whilst in a second-hand sale the well-known Norwegian Sale Form (NSF) will normally be used as a basis. NSF has been revised into a new version for 1993/94. Lastly for the scrap sale the individual forms or proformas preferred by the various scrap dealers are mostly used. In 1987, BIMCO adopted a standard form for scrapping, the so-called Sale-scrap 87.

Concentrating now on the routines for a second-hand sale, the basic principle is that the ship is sold "as is/where is" with "payment cash on delivery", but all the terms and details are, of course, subject to negotiations in the same manner as for chartering, viz. starting with a firm offer, followed by counters, etc., on main terms and details, and with relevant subjects attached and to be waived for concluding the deal. One difference from chartering is that in sale/purchase it is normally the buyer who makes the first offer, and the buyer will always make the deal subject to a physical inspection of the ship and of her written records with the relevant class society.

A full firm offer from an intended buyer may include the following points:

—The named ship, with ex-names, and subject to full particulars/details, general arrangement and capacity plans, statement on last/next special survey (SS), last/next drydocking (Dd), etc.
—The price and currency preferred with the specified commission percentage to the sale/purchase broker(s) (payable by the sellers).
—Payment cash on delivery/instalments, named bankers and special terms.
—Subject to inspection of the ship afloat and/or in drydock, with buyer's right to open up engine cylinders, take measurements on engines and crankshaft, open up tanks, sighting logbooks and certificates, etc.
—Subject to inspection of the ship's class records.
—Delivery time and place.
—Delivery terms: "As is/Where is"/other specified terms, in seaworthy condition, with class maintained free of recommendations, notations and free of Average damages.
—All certificates to be clean and valid for a fixed time from delivery date.
—Delivery with clean/swept holds/bilges/gas-free tanks and cargo gear/pumps in good working order and with spare parts minimum as per class requirements.
—Terms regarding bunkers, lubricating oils, stores, equipment, etc., onboard/ashore to be included in the sale.
—Any other terms/details to be mutually agreed.
—Details as per Memorandum of Agreement (M.O.A.), i.e. Norwegian Sale Form (NSF) latest edition.

Sale/purchase with employment

Naturally the sale/purchase of a ship is strongly connected to an employment. A newbuilding may be ordered against a special deal with a charterer, or as a replacement to be used in an existing trade or under a running contract, and in some cases of course also on speculation, but in that last case the owners taking delivery of the new ship will be sure to secure a charterer starting from the day of take-over from the yard. The same reasoning applies to a second-hand purchase, and the owners of the old ship will try to secure her last employment to take her as near the scrapping yard or beach as possible.

Coming back to the financing aspects there are practices whereby the sale/purchase and the chartering may be done as one complete package with the built-in facility to provide financing as an inducement or assistance to the buyers. The sale/purchase procedures discussed above are related to so-called "straight sale/purchase", but there are mainly three types of combination business arrangements as follows:

"Bareboat charter with purchase option"

In practice this means that the financing party will place the hull and machinery—or in other words only the ship, without technical and personnel management—at the disposal of a charterer, who is to take care of the management and commercial operation, and this party has an option to purchase the ship at some agreed time at a mutually pre-fixed price. The revenue from the trading will be used for payment of the bareboat hire and the purchase price to the formal owners as lessors and financing party. This type of deal is not favoured by owners, since they have no real control of the running and maintenance of the ship, and her condition at the end of the bareboat charter period, should the charterers for some reason not exercise their option to purchase, is not expected to be up to standard (judging from experience in too many cases). Besides this, the market may in the meantime have gone bad from the owners' point of view, so they may be left with a non-employed ship which is in great and costly need of upkeep and overhaul.

"Hire-Purchase agreement"

This is in practice a firm sale/purchase agreement where the buyers hire a ship on time charter or bareboat charter, and the hire payments are arranged in such a way that after a fixed period of time the full purchase price has been paid, and the charterers/buyers become owners. It goes without saying that in this type of deal the daily or monthly hire figures according to the charter-party terms may differ substantially from the current market figures, and it is again a business agreement where the owners/sellers are providing financing for a purchase, but in this case with a more reasonable risk factor.

"Sale with charter-back"

This means that a time charter agreement is made in parallel with the sale/purchase agreement, where the sellers will be acting as charterers of the ship for an agreed period of time at a fixed time charter hire. In this case the hire amount payable per day/month is market related, and the time charter period is not normally or necessarily long enough for the buyers to be able to write off the full price from the total hire amount obtainable from this charter. In practice this is more like a straight sale, with the additional feature that sellers are guaranteeing the vessel's employment under the new ownership for a period of time at a fixed income from the buyers. Financially, this method may be considered a benefit for the sellers, since at least in the short term this deal will improve their liquidity situation. Finally this is a rather popular way for owners of high-cost nationalities to shift the flag to a more convenient/cheaper one, while maintaining the ship in their ordinary trade.

It can be seen from the above discussions and examples that sale/purchase of ships is an innovative business—as indeed is chartering—so it only stresses the point that shipping work demands whatever know-how, skill, experience and entrepreneurial abilities and other human resources one can possibly supply.

CHAPTER 10

GENERAL LEGAL POINTS OF VIEW

SOME GENERAL REMARKS ON CONTRACT LAW

Normally, an oral agreement is binding on both parties. Some agreements must be in writing to be effective and this requirement may vary from one legal system to another. Furthermore, the basis is (though not in all legal systems and not under all circumstances) that an oral offer is binding upon the offeror for a certain period unless it is expressly stated or evident that the offer shall not be binding. How long the offer is binding depends on the circumstances, particularly if this is spelt out in the offer, e.g., "this offer is binding until the close of business on November 25".

In practice, it may be very hard to determine exactly when an agreement has been concluded, since the negotiations may be both lengthy and complex. Under such circumstances it is not always easy to determine the exact moment when the parties have come to the final and all-embracing agreement. A dispute may arise on whether an agreement has been concluded or whether it was just a common understanding, whether certain points have been agreed on or have been deliberately left open, etc. It is fairly common that some points have been left open "subject to . . ." (approval of board of directors, approval of central bank, etc.). (See pages 124ff., 142ff.)

The reason why commercial contracts are frequently in writing is the need for evidence as between the parties and also the administration need for documentation in a large organization. Charter agreements are probably very seldom oral—bills of lading, being documents, are, of course, always written—another thing is that the functions and information in the bill of lading may be transferred into other means of communication. When a written contract is used the agreement is, for practical purposes, often regarded as concluded upon the signing of the contract. Legally, the agreement may very well be binding at an earlier stage, unless the agreement states that it shall be binding upon its signing only, which is occasionally expressly stated or commonly understood.

Charter negotiations are normally carried out by telex, telephone and telefax, and the agreement may thus legally be binding when the telex and telephone negotiations have been ended. As mentioned above, charter negotiations are often carried out step by step. The "main terms" may first be agreed "subject details".

134

Often the negotiations are also brought up to a point where the charter agreement will be concluded as soon as specified "subjects" have been waived.

Normally a *recap* (recapitulation of the terms and conditions agreed) will be made out to be accepted by the parties. The accepted recap may then be the legally binding agreement, even if the charter-party is signed later. As also mentioned above, charter agreements are almost always concluded in written form. Sometimes time is too short to fix the terms and conditions in a written document; sometimes a charter-party is not signed as a result of a mistake, or because of the refusal of one of the parties, etc. The voyage may nevertheless take place and in some cases this may give rise to problems.

It goes without saying that a dispute arising after a voyage has been performed, without a charter having been signed and without a recap having been transmitted, may be very hard to resolve. There may then be a situation where the parties may be in disagreement as to cargo quantities, demurrage, laytime and even the freight level. It may also be a problem to determine whether a dispute shall be referred to arbitration in accordance with an intended charter-party or whether it will have to be brought before a competent court—this in itself may be a very costly and lengthy item of dispute.

Since parties normally use a standard form of charter-party and then make deletions, modifications and amendments (the charter-party will often contain more rider clauses and amendments than printed base texts), several ambiguities may arise unless the parties are very careful when making alterations. Since charter negotiations are carried out under pressure of time the final charter-parties may often be easily criticized from a formal legal viewpoint.

If a dispute arises between the parties concerning the interpretation of the charter-party or the way it has been performed, the matter is decided either by arbitrators or by a court of law. In most cases the parties choose to settle their disputes by arbitration rather than by court proceedings. In either case, however, certain rules and principles of law will be applied to decide the particular matter in dispute, although it must be said that it is often difficult to predict the result with any degree of certainty.

THE PARTIES

As mentioned above, the sales contract is the mechanism which, to a large extent, gears the charter agreement. Seller and buyer thereby have a central importance for the contents of the charter agreement. Depending on the transport clause the seller or the buyer will be the carrier's counter-party and either the seller or the buyer will appear as charterer. At the same time, the seller is often the shipper and the buyer the consignee. Depending on the circumstances the carrier may be a shipowner, a time chartered "owner", but he may also be a freight forwarder.

Basically only the person who makes an agreement is bound by it. Charter-parties are, however, often signed by an agent or a broker ("for the owner", "for the charterer" or "as agent only"). The owner and the charterer are naturally bound by the measures taken by and the signature of their agent if these are made within the limits of his authority. If the broker does not disclose his principal he may himself be bound by the contract. These problems have been illustrated above at page 31ff.

The following is an illustration of the practical problems that may arise: It is common that a brokerage firm or an agent in London or New York is owned by a person who is also the owner of one or several one-ship companies, often registered in Panama or Liberia. In accordance with general legal principles only the principal is bound by the agreement entered into for his account by his agent. Furthermore, a company is a legal entity and liable only for its own debts. Therefore, if the agent mentioned above signs a charter-party *as agent* for the owner, the shipping company only (at least as a general principle) is bound by the contract, even if the same person owns the agency and the shipping company and is personally rich. There are, however, limitations to this principle. Such limitations may be referred to as the doctrine of "piercing the corporate veil".

MARITIME LAW AND LEGISLATION

It is sometimes difficult to decide which country's law should apply to a dispute. The choice of the applicable law may depend on several individual factors: the nationality of the parties, the place where the contract has been concluded, the place of the contractual performance, the language of the agreement, etc. This choice is important since legal principles vary between different legal systems. It may thus be difficult to determine the law applicable in a case where, for example, the shipowner is Swedish, the time charterer (time chartered owner) is French, the sub-charterer English, the shipper Dutch, and the cargo consignee American. These several relationships are, however, governed by different agreements and different laws may be applicable under the different contracts. The contracts often contain a forum and a jurisdiction clause, explicitly referring a dispute to be decided by arbitration in London and in accordance with English law. In ocean charter-parties disputes are often referred to arbitration in London or New York, English or American law to apply. Very few disputes reach the point of arbitration proceedings, and most are settled more or less amicably.

Every country thus has its own law, which differs to a greater or a lesser degree from that of another country. In certain fields the differences are much smaller than in other fields. In parts of the commercial law, such as international contracts of sale and purchase, chartering, bills of lading, etc., there is a much higher degree of international harmonization than there is in many other fields of law, but the law is still basically national. Also, in this context, it is important to spell out that there are certain groups of legal systems linked to each other. Very roughly one may thus distinguish a number of legal families, such as the Anglo-American common law system, from the European continental civil law system, or a socialist system, etc. The most important legal families have had great impact on the development of legal systems in several countries. The common law system is based on case law, whereas the civil law system is basically codified. These basics are no longer very true in practice, since there is much legislation in common law systems and much case law in "civil law" countries.

French law and German law, for example, have a maritime codification covering, *inter alia*, chartering through non-mandatory regulation. That means that it will prevail only if the parties have not specifically contracted on a particular point or there is not a custom to another effect. In English or American law there is, on the other hand, no codification with respect to chartering but case law prevails. The standard charter-parties used have, although differently designed, contributed to a harmonization of the law of charter-parties. Furthermore, charter-parties often make English law applicable, so in that respect English law has had a harmonizing effect.

As to bills of lading, the situation is very different, since legislation has been introduced with respect both to the carrier's liability for damage to goods carried and to the particular characteristics of the bill of lading. (See above at page 54ff.)

COURT AND ARBITRATION PROCEEDINGS*

Should a dispute arising between the parties be referred to court proceedings, the first problem may be to find out whether the court is competent. The procedural rules vary from country to country. The most frequent pattern is that court proceedings may be channelled through three layers of courts. This means that a judgment at first instance may be appealed to a Court of Appeal and then to a Supreme Court (in England, the House of Lords). The possibilities of appealing from a judgment may vary considerably in different legal systems. Court proceedings are public and may take a long time due to appeals.

The costs may be considerable, covering certain court charges, counsel's fees, interest losses, losses due to inflation, costs for and in connection with witnesses, etc. Often the winning party may be awarded counsel's fees, or part thereof, from the losing party. In some countries the winning party may have interest (at varying rates) and possibly compensation for loss due to currency exchange rate changes, etc. In the United States the prospects of a winning party being compensated for counsel's fees are not good. English rules allow cost compensation to the winning party but they are rather restrictive as to interest awarded, since the discretion allowed to the courts is used rather cautiously.

* See also page 168.

Arbitration

Unless the charter-party expressly states that a dispute under the agreement shall be settled by arbitration it will be referred to court proceedings. It is thus necessary that the parties agree on arbitration as the means of resolving a dispute. Certain types of disputes may not be referred to arbitration. National legal systems usually contain legislation stating how arbitrations should be conducted. Such legislation may contain provisions as to the procedure for the nomination of arbitrators, the possibility of appealing from an arbitration award, the public character of the arbitration award, etc. A common principle seems to be that each party nominates one arbitrator, and the arbitrators thus appointed in their turn jointly appoint an *umpire*. If the arbitrators cannot agree on a solution the umpire will have the casting vote. A losing party may not normally appeal from the award. In many countries an arbitration award may be appealed only on formal grounds, for example, if the arbitrators have wrongfully refused to hear a witness, or if they have been bribed, etc.

Prior to the Arbitration Act 1979 English courts maintained their power to guide the development of the legal system and thus, even under arbitration proceedings, one party could demand that a legal question be referred to court procedure before the arbitration was finished (*to state a special case*). The advantage of a relatively faster proceeding was thereby lost. Particularly in times of inflation, the opportunities of stating a special case were sometimes utilized by parties with "bad cases" to make certain pecuniary gains. This unsatisfactory situation has been remedied to some extent by the Arbitration Act 1979 which now only allows judicial review in certain cases. In shipping, the new Act seems to have made less difference, and there are some English solicitors and barristers who favour court proceedings instead of arbitration. It is very likely that more and more restrictions will be put on too extravagant use of a review of an arbitration award.

The International Chamber of Commerce has drawn up a special procedure for the appointment of arbitrators which is, however, rather circumstantial and not generally favoured in shipping. The Comité Maritime International (CMI) has suggested an arbitration system where the parties choose arbitrators from a CMI list covering a number of well qualified persons. This system should be completed with an agreement on the law to be applied and the place where the arbitrators should meet.

Arbitration or court procedure

It is not possible to state in general terms whether arbitration or court procedure is preferable. In commercial contracts arbitration is often preferred due to the costs, the time aspect and secrecy. By tradition, arbitration procedure has been regarded as faster and less expensive than court procedure, and the parties, for different reasons, generally prefer that the procedure is not public.

In countries where the courts have little commercial experience the parties may also prefer to have a dispute decided by persons who, in their view, have such knowledge.

The most popular arbitrators are, however, frequently very busy and as to the time factor it should be underlined that a long time may elapse before three busy arbitrators and two busy counsellors find sufficient time available for meeting. Certain parties may also consider it to be an advantage to have a dispute decided by ordinary courts.

Arbitration awards may have another advantage due to an international convention on the enforcement of arbitration awards, whereby arbitration awards given in one country are recognized in another country which is a party to that convention. A winning party may otherwise meet with difficulties when trying to enforce an arbitration award in the losing party's country. The authorities of that country may request a new trial or at least an affirmation of the decision before it can be enforced. Only a limited number of countries are parties to the convention.

It should also be mentioned that in practice a winning party may find that a favourable decision will not bring him any money since there is no money to be had. When a party has reason to suspect that the other party has no money he will try to arrest some property belonging to the latter to be used to cover the amount to which he may be entitled. The provisions as to such arrest differ between the various legal systems.

Both New York and London are popular centres for arbitration in charter-party disputes, but, depending on the parties involved, arbitration proceedings are also conducted in Moscow, Paris, Peking, etc. New York has previously been less well thought of as a place of arbitration than London. It should be mentioned that a dispute may be determined differently by English arbitrators than by American arbitrators and differently again if the arbitrators are "commercial men" rather than lawyers.

It is important to bear in mind that a charterer, having in his charter-party with the owner an arbitration clause referring a dispute to arbitration in London and according to English law and when chartering the vessel out, he should, if possible, at the same time arrange that any dispute is referred to the same court or the same arbitrators. It may also be an advantage to refer general average proceedings and a charter-party arbitration to the same place.

Furthermore, it should also be emphasized that it is rather common that the parties, instead of a traditional arbitration clause, make a special agreement to refer a certain question of principle or the whole dispute to BIMCO or to a qualified and neutral person, for example, a lawyer or a university Fellow.

EVIDENCE

It does not matter how the material rules governing a relationship are designed unless the party invoking the rules can convince the arbitrators or the court that his version of the facts and his suggestions are correct. It is therefore of the utmost importance that the party who relies on a certain provision produces evidence of the facts supporting his view. Thus, for example, a basic legal idea seems to be that an injured party will have to prove that damage has occurred, who has caused the damage, and the extent of the damage, and in many legal systems he may also have to prove that his counterpart has been negligent. In some instances the burden of proof will change from one party to the other; in other cases the court or the arbitrators prefer to have an overall picture of the facts brought in, etc. Sometimes there will be a presumption which a tortfeasor (wrongdoer) has to overcome in order to avoid liability.

Legal principles concerning evidence and the burden of proof are highly complex, and it is impossible to give a broad outline, but suffice it here to mention that they exist, and that the parties, in their contracting, may dispose of them to some extent. Thus a certain clause may prescribe that the burden of proof shall rest with one party. The parties may have agreed that a common independent surveyor shall be appointed, etc. For practical purposes it may, however, be of considerable benefit that those involved have a basic knowledge of the material rules in order that they can obtain relevant evidence according to the circumstances. This means that these persons, when something occurs, may try to get a written statement from a reliable person, find witnesses, make careful notes and observations about the facts, etc.

CONSTRUCTION AND INTERPRETATION OF CHARTER AGREEMENTS

The design of the charter-party

A charter relationship will normally be covered by a charter-party, and the basis will then normally be a standard charter-party which is modified and amended by *riders* and *addenda* in accordance with the individual agreement. As mentioned above, a charter-party must be correct as to its material contents and should reflect precisely what the parties have agreed. Its language should be unambiguous so that it expresses the intention of the parties.

Above all, English court decisions have had an important impact on the meaning given to certain expressions and contractual clauses used in chartering. The effect of court decisions which change or modify the established under-standing of a principle may cause confusion and may result in certain counter-measures being taken by BIMCO, the Chamber of Shipping, or other organizations such as Nordisk Skibsrederforening and the P. & I. clubs. New clauses and/or wordings will probably be introduced to meet the demands of the courts or to avoid or restrict the effects of the courts' decisions. It is thus important to follow closely new court decisions in order to have an up-to-date knowledge of the meaning of certain expressions and clauses.

When comparing charter-parties one will find that they differ considerably with regard to their material contents as well as to their layout. Such differences depend on varying customs and demands in different branches and trades, and naturally revision of the documents is constantly going on in order that they will meet such demands. Several charter-parties have a code name, often printed at the top of the form. The clauses are numbered and sometimes every line is numbered—this is the case with, for example, Gencon. In the margin of the form there is often a heading giving a general idea of the contents of the clause. BIMCO now seems to have adopted a system with a box layout (a system where individual particulars will be entered into the boxes on the first page while the general clauses are found on a separate sheet (see further, page 151). This is, however, by no means a generally accepted method: tanker charter-parties, NYPE 93 and many other forms do not use this practice.

The offer and the making of the contract

When a shipowner is informed that a charterer needs tonnage of a type that the owner may provide he makes a calculation based on the actual vessel. If the calculation seems reasonable the owner may make an offer. This process has been described above, pages 108ff., 134.

Although the agreement is binding as soon as the parties have agreed on all terms and conditions a charter-party is usually made out in order that the provisions shall be precisely fixed. Basically, one may say that the charter-party is decisive to show what has been contracted between the parties unless one of them proves that something else has been agreed. English law is regarded as more restrictive than many other legal systems with respect to the parties' contentions that the contract does not express what has been agreed, unless of course such contention has been made immediately upon receipt of the written contract. English courts still seem to be less inclined to allow other evidence than what is found *in* the contract than are, for example, German or Scandinavian courts and also, for that matter, American courts. This so-called *parol evidence rule* means that English courts will only reluctantly allow circumstances in connection with the negotiations as evidence contrary to what the contract stipulates.

We have described above schematically how the charter negotiations may be carried out. The general contract principle is that an offer is binding. Then a counter-offer will be regarded as a rejection of the original offer in conjunction with a new offer binding upon the person who has given the counter-offer. In order that there shall be a binding agreement, offer and acceptance must be identical. Then both parties will be bound.

An offer is not binding for any length of time. If the offer prescribes a certain time before which it must be accepted, the expiration of this time means that the offeror is no longer bound. If no time has been expressly stated the basis is that the offeree shall have reasonable or customary time at his disposal to reply. This time is determined with regard to the importance of the business, the circumstances under which the offer has been given, the speed of the transactions in the trade, etc. If, for example, the offer is given by telex the acceptance must be given by telex, cable or telephone. The parties may, however, prescribe the terms and conditions in connection with the offer and acceptance.

The above describes the basic general principles of contract law. Details differ among various legal systems. In English law the doctrine of *consideration* is prevailing, which means that the offeror is not bound by his offer unless the offeree has given some value, *consideration*. The consideration given may have very little value. Indeed, the doctrine of consideration means that there is no binding contract, unless consideration has been given. English law and American law, though to a lesser extent—and other law systems influenced by them—thereby differ from the general basic pattern that an offer is binding. It is hard today to foresee whether an English court would really apply this doctrine of consideration to an international contract, but it is clear that many business transactions are made without regard being given to this doctrine. This is the situation in connection with shipping contracts. It is apparent that when these principles are applied practical problems may arise when determining if and when an agreement is binding, if a certain offer is binding, etc. Particularly, various "subjects" employed may cause problems.

"Subject" problems

A "subject" provision may give rise to various legal problems. Apparently "subject to government approval" gives a much narrower frame to act within than "subject to the board's approval" or "subject details". Unless the parties have agreed on the specific reason why the board's approval has to be obtained, any refusal by the board to accept the contract may be invoked to avoid the binding force of the contract.

"Subject" provisions are very common in contracting in shipping. The "subjects" involved vary largely: "subject stem", "subject board's approval", "subject approval of relevant authority", "subject financing", "subject details", etc. A "subject" may sometimes be regarded as a "condition precedent" sometimes not. To some extent, at least, this must depend on the quality of the "subject": does it have any substance or only minor importance?

Naturally, the general idea of a "subject" provision is that it shall be used in a loyal way in relation to the counter-party. For reasons of evidence it may be hard to establish a case of disloyalty, and whether such disloyalty will have any legal effects. If a party has accepted such wide "subject" provisions as "subject board's approval" he has given a wide discretion to his counter-party, and it will be hard for him to establish that there will nevertheless be a binding agreement or that he is entitled to damages. He may possibly have a claim in damages if he can establish that the counter-party made a contract with him—although "subject board's approval"—only to prevent him from making a contract with somebody else, and that the counter-party has declared to him that the "subject" provision is only a "formality", i.e. there is a case of good faith with one party and bad faith, in some cases amounting to fraud, with the other.

Another question may be raised in connection with "subject details". Where do we stand in the contracting process when the parties have agreed on the "main terms" but "subject details". Are they then bound at all? Could either of them use disagreement on any minor detail to correctly allege that he is not bound? Could there in some instances be a claim for damages?

The basic rules of contract law will apply, but regard must be given to the peculiar practices of shipping. The basic idea in English as well as in American law—and as a general remark this should be true for most legal systems—is that there can be no contract until the parties have reached clear agreement on at least all essential terms.

As we have seen, chartering negotiations are carried out in two steps; that part where the "main terms" are covered and that where the "details" are determined. When the parties have fixed the "main terms" they have made a fixture "sub details", but as mentioned several other "subjects" may also be involved. The practice of chartering negotiations may bring some legal problems. The basic legal questions are: Is a "sub" a condition precedent? Is "sub details" always/sometimes a condition precedent, when the parties have fixed the main terms? If fixing the main terms would imply the conclusion of a contract what happens then if the parties cannot agree on the details?

Different types of "subjects" may have different implications but the individual circumstances of the negotiations and the individual design of the "subject" will have a decisive role. There are basically three possibilities: either there is no binding contract at all, or there is a contract that will, however, not bind fully until the subject has been waived, or there is a contract which binds immediately but will cease to do so if the subject is not waived. As mentioned "subject to contract" in English law has been held to show an intention not to be bound until a formal contract is subsequently entered into. Generally the expression "subject to contract" seems to indicate clearly that there is not yet any binding contract and presumably most legal systems would come to the same conclusion under similar circumstances.

In an American case *A/S Custodia* v. *Lessin International, Inc.*, 503 F.2d. 318 (2 CCA) the issue was whether there was a binding charter-party.

Early in June 1973 Haakon Steckmest, of the brokerage firm of J. H. Winchester & Co., received a quotation from Lessin's broker, Ocean Freighting & Brokerage Corp., to transport a cargo of scrap. This quotation was circulated by cable to various correspondents of Winchester. About two weeks later, on 20 June, Steckmest received an offer on this business from Custodia's broker in Norway. The offer was conveyed on 20 June to Ocean Freighting which, on the same day, made a counter-offer on the vessel on behalf of Lessin. After the terms of the contract allegedly were agreed upon between Custodia and Lessin, Ocean Freighting prepared a form of charter-party and forwarded it under cover of a letter dated 25 June to Steckmest with the request that he have it signed by Custodia. After obtaining authority from Custodia, Winchester signed the document on behalf of the owner and returned it to Ocean Freighting for execution by Lessin. Later, Steckmest was advised by Ocean Freighting that, since Lessin was unable to obtain the scrap cargo, it refused to sign the document.

Custodia claimed $76,000 in damages as a result of Lessin's failure to perform the alleged charter-party. The unsigned contract which had been forwarded under cover of the letter of 25 June contained a standard arbitration provision. Pursuant thereto, Custodia named an arbitrator and demanded that Lessin do likewise so that the controversy could be submitted to arbitration. Upon Lessin's failure to comply with the arbitration request, Custodia filed its petition in the district court to compel arbitration. A week later, Custodia filed its motion to compel arbitration. The court held *inter alia*: "The critical issue is not whether the charter-party was signed by the party sought to be charged (Lessin), but whether there was a meeting of the minds of the parties as to the essential terms of the agreement, even though unsigned by one party."

When considering the phrase "sub details" it must not be overlooked that the parties may to some extent themselves characterize what are "main terms" and "details", respectively. By agreeing on a fixture "sub details" the parties have actually made an agreement at least to some degree, and they may thereby also have agreed to come to terms with respect to the details. It may on the other hand be maintained that the parties have only come to a conclusion regarding the main terms and that the details remain to be agreed on. The details would then be regarded as conditions precedent.

A number of American cases have determined the question. We have chosen one at random as an illustration. *In the matter of the arbitration between Pollux Marine Agencies, Inc. and Louis Dreyfus Corp.*, 455 F.Supp. 211 (1978):

On or about 27 July 1976 Sagus Marine quoted a time charter to Dillon's officer (the charterer's broker) for a vessel of the size of the *Captain Demosthenes* for a period of two or three years. Dillon then quoted the order to a Mr O'Reilly at Pollux, agents for the *Captain Demosthenes*. O'Reilly communicated a firm offer of the vessel to Dillon on 27 July. Dillon then relayed the offer to Robert Spaulding Jr. at Sagus who talked to his principals and about half an hour to an hour later made a counter-offer providing in part that the vessel must be "Greek Flag with ITF in order ... (S)ub details pro forma."

Dillon testified that "ITF in order" means that the vessel's crew is employed under a trade union agreement which is acceptable to the International Transport Workers Federation. "Sub details pro forma" meant that what they were negotiating were the "main terms" and that further details were to be based on the Dreyfus *pro forma* (Eldece Time) charter.

This counter-offer was communicated to O'Reilly at Pollux on 27 July. Later that day O'Reilly made a counter-offer repeating the owner's last offer, but agreeing to provide a Greek flag vessel and suggesting that the use of a Greek flag vessel obviated the need for ITF.

Some time later, between 1.00 p.m. and 1.30 p.m. on 27 July, Spaulding made a counter-offer calling in part for Greek flag, Greek Collective Agreement and "otherwise per Dreyfus last". Dillon communicated this to O'Reilly who, about 3.30 or 4.00 p.m., repeated the owner's last offer, except changing the rate, for a reply by 10.00 a.m. on 28 July. Dillon communicated this to Spaulding.

"For reply by 10.00 a.m. next day" means, Dillon testified, that the vessel is "out firm" to those prospective charterers until 10.00 a.m. the next day.

On the morning of 28 July, Dreyfus advised that it would not take a time charter without a boycott clause. Dillon explained that a boycott clause meant that if the vessel were boycotted because of unacceptability to ITF then the vessel would be off-hire during the boycott. Clause 15A pt (ii) of Eldece Time contained such a boycott clause and Clause 15A pt (iii) provided for ITF. O'Reilly told Dillon that he would discuss this with the owners, but did not think they would fix the vessel with a boycott clause. There were several discussions that day on the boycott clause. In the meantime, negotiations regarding the charter period, delivery and re-delivery areas, rate, commissions and overtime—the terms on which there was still no agreement—were suspended because neither side would negotiate unless they could agree on a boycott clause.

On 29 July, Dreyfus made a bid which included a provision for a Greek Collective Agreement and a boycott clause. Dillon telephoned and telexed the boycott clause to O'Reilly that same day. Later that day, O'Reilly declined the bid, did not make a counter-offer, and would not proceed with the negotiations so long as Dreyfus insisted on a boycott clause. There were no further negotiations on 29 July.

During the afternoon of 30 July, Sagus, through David Robin Masters, rather than Spaulding, stated that Dreyfus would go ahead without the boycott clause. On that basis, O'Reilly made a fresh offer about 6.00 p.m. on 30 July. Dillon telexed this offer to Sagus, which proposed a counter-offer. Negotiations continued for a couple of hours by telephone, with Dillon eventually speaking with both sides simultaneously on two telephones. The culmination of this was a fixture on all the main terms reached at about 8.00 p.m. on that Friday evening 30 July, and memorialized in a fixture recap sent from Dillon to Sagus that same evening.

This fixture recap of 30 July provided in part:

"We confirm having fixed the foll with you today subject details of Eldece Time, and provided that the Owners warrant that on delivery vessel will be Greek Flag Vessel, crew will be of Greek Nationality and vessel's crew will be members of the Greek Collective Agreement and to be so maintained throughout the term of this Charter."

On Monday morning, 2 August, O'Reilly telephoned his exceptions to the *pro forma* details. Sagus agreed to some, but not to others. The parties continued to negotiate the details and by 3 August all of them had been agreed upon, except *pro forma* Clause 15A pts (ii) and (iii).

As to Clause 15A pts (ii) and (iii), the Eldece Time boycott and ITF clauses, respectively, when O'Reilly telephoned in his objections on the morning of 2 August, he stated that this clause should be deleted on 30 July. Dreyfus, however, stated around noontime on 2 August, that it wanted to retain Clause 15A pts (ii) and (iii). Later that day, O'Reilly reiterated that these matters had already been agreed to and therefore the clause should be deleted. Subsequently, on 2 August, Dreyfus again commented on details and said it would "revert" in the morning regarding Clause 15A pts (ii) and (iii). Nothing further was said about the boycott clause on 2 August.

On the morning of 3 August, Dreyfus commented on details and as to the boycott clause stated that it would be willing to make minor alterations to it but would prefer that the owner made a proposal. In response, O'Reilly reluctantly proposed a modification to Clause 15A pts (ii) and (iii). Dreyfus then added a clause to O'Reilly's proposal and O'Reilly added a clause to Dreyfus. Dreyfus then stated that it wanted Clause 15A pt (ii) as printed on Eldece. O'Reilly would not agree and so the negotiations on this point ceased on 3 August.

On 5 August, O'Reilly made a proposal with respect to a boycott clause without prejudice to his position that there had already been a fixture which covered this matter. Dillon communicated this proposal to Dreyfus on 5 August.

Dreyfus responded on 6 August that the proposal would have been acceptable with minor alterations while negotiations were still going on, but it was too late now inasmuch as Dreyfus was already trading other tonnage. All negotiations then ceased.

Dillon further testified that he had no recollection of Dreyfus' imposing a deadline of 1500 hours on 2 August as the time by which all *pro forma* details must have been agreed upon.

Taking into consideration a number of cases the court found that "contrary to the agreement originally advanced by Dreyfus, a binding fixture occurs when there is an agreement on all essential ("main") terms. The "subject details" does not create a condition precedent . . . Thus a party is not entitled to renege on a main term just because *pro forma* details still remain open.

We are thus facing some difficult problems. Firstly the borderline between "main terms" and "details" must be determined. To what extent do they operate by custom and trade practice? How do they operate in various trades? To what degree may the parties dispose of the significance of the terms respectively.

Undoubtedly the parties have the disposal of what is included in "main terms" and "details" and if they have explicitly characterized as a "main term" an item that would normally be referred to as a "detail" it must be recognized as a "main term". There may also be a distinction between the understanding of "main terms" and "details" in various trades, and it is impossible to determine with any degree of accuracy an exact overall significance of "main terms" and "details". Furthermore, it may very well be that a certain detail may have more significance in one trade than in another.

From the cases here referred to, the following general principles could be extracted, although such conclusions can be made only with great caution. If the parties have agreed on most main terms, but there are still some outstanding points, at least an American court may find that there is already a binding contract if the outstanding items do not have major significance. From the last case it seems, however, to be in the court's discretion to decide if an item should be characterized as "main" or not and we agree with the arbitrators' conclusions, and maybe the arbitrators have expressed in other words the principle that a clear and precise clause made for the particular case will take over a contrary provision, if this has not been negotiated. When the Court of Appeal in the *Great Circle Lines* case describes "details" as including, *inter alia*, fuel to be used, speed of the vessel, cargo capacity, demurrage etc., we are convinced that the court has misunderstood what is generally regarded as a "main term" and a "detail" respectively. Several of the items described as "details" are indeed important features in the characteristics of the vessel and are clearly to be referred to as the "main terms". Another thing is that the parties may expressly use another terminology.

We are also inclined to believe that an English and maybe also a Scandinavian court or arbitration panel would be more cautious in allowing a contract binding force in spite of outstanding points, unless these could be regarded to have only insignificant importance. The basic understanding of the shipping industry also seems to be that there is normally no contract until all terms have been fixed, or at least the great bulk of them. The individual situation and the circumstances may undoubtedly have a major impact.

In the case of the common phrase "sub details" we also feel that American courts have gone far in establishing that there is a binding contract if the parties have made a fixture "sub details". The impression one gets is that US courts hold that the parties "fixing sub details" have thereby declared that there is a meeting of minds between them and that the details will not mean any change in this. One may, of course, ask why the parties are then fixing "sub details". Did they by that intend to leave to the court or arbitration panel to fill in what they cannot themselves agree on? Cases seem to indicate that a particular item may by a US court very well be regarded as a "detail" in one case and a "main term" in another one. This is not a very satisfactory situation.

Problems of interpretation

Charter-parties are the result of negotiations. It is important to keep this fact in mind when a charter-party is interpreted. A charter-party is ordinarily based on the fixture made by a broker covering what the parties have agreed. Sometimes particular fixture notes are used. If it is alleged that a clause does not express the parties' will, the oral agreement behind it may be regarded as decisive if its content can be established. If legislation is applicable it may give some guidance. Sometimes the exchange of messages during the preceding negotiations may be used to cast some light on the meaning of a clause which the parties dispute. Even circumstances which have been used in previous negotiations and agreements between the parties or otherwise may be taken into consideration in interpretation. In general, however, the written provisions in the charter-party will be given priority. Sometimes reference is made to the discussions during the negotiations in order that the meaning of a certain phrase can be explained. Basically, the clauses used should be interpreted as they are worded in the charter-party. Courts and arbitrators may apply various principles or methods in their interpretation and, as mentioned, the basic idea under English law has been that the court has to find the meaning of the contract in the contract. This principle nowadays seems to be applied less rigidly than before.

It is, however, necessary to bear in mind that several of the charter-party clauses have not been individually negotiated between the parties but were drafted collectively in the printed text of the charter-party. The parties may not even have been aware of many clauses, and it is then hardly possible to trace any individual intentions.

It is typical, particularly in voyage chartering, that the freight agreements are negotiated under great pressure of time. The parties have no time to weigh and balance their words carefully. Separate clauses are sometimes hinged to or stamped on the contract without regard being given to the printed wording.

New provisions are brought into the printed form between the narrow lines without regard being given to their effects on the charter-party as a whole. One interpretation principle is generally considered to be that clauses hinged to, stamped on or typewritten into the charter-party will apply before the printed original text.

The riders are often less well phrased than the original provisions of the form. It is not unusual that they are intended for situations other than those actually regulated in the charter-party and it may then be difficult to give them an unambiguous meaning. Another principle that may be applied is that imprecise and ambiguous wording will be construed against the party who furnished the provision. When interpreting a charter-party it may be necessary to disregard details and try to determine the intentions of the parties. If then no intention can be unambiguously determined it may be necessary to reconstrue the charter-party to give it a sensible meaning. "Subject details" may cause certain difficulties, since it is not always very clear what is a "main term" and a "detail". Maybe one cannot always rely on a minor detail to avoid a contract. But maybe also a detail may be regarded as a main term.

In long term agreements it is necessary to observe that the parties will later often introduce more or less formal adjustments and modifications in their relationship, and it is very common for them to find an informal *modus vivendi* in which case it may be difficult to establish what really applies.

Standard charter-parties often contain a provision that a dispute shall be decided at a certain place in accordance with the law there governing. Several standard charter-parties state that a dispute shall be decided by arbitrators in London, whereas others refer disputes to be settled by arbitration in New York. The parties may agree on another solution and may also decide the law to apply in case a dispute arises. In charter-parties with East European, Russian or Chinese charterers it is not uncommon to find that a dispute shall be settled in Moscow or Peking. Some charterers seem to prefer arbitration in Paris, etc.

As mentioned, English or American law dominates in ocean charter practice. There is in English or American law no particular legislation specifically dealing with charter-parties, and if the parties disagree on the understanding of the contract the dispute will be decided in the light of previous court judgments. The importance of English and American law in ocean chartering has led to a certain importance and great interest being attached to English and American court and arbitration decisions. Even very old decisions may thus still have great fundamental importance, if no later case has changed their effect. The growth of the number of decisions has caused charter-parties to become more and more extensive, since the parties may wish to clarify certain principles or avoid the effects of a decision. Additional clauses may be introduced which govern new problems arising.

Certain general principles may be discussed. English courts or arbitrators will make their decision taking into account, first, the wording of the charter-party, then using previous decisions, and commercial customs as a basis to determine the applicable legal principles. There is no general principle preventing the parties from trying by agreement to avoid the effect of court decisions. Furthermore, English courts still seem generally to feel more or less bound by a decision made by a higher court.

On the other hand, the courts, in practice, in order to avoid the consequences of Court of Appeal and House of Lords' decisions, distinguish the case in point from the one previously decided. This means that the court finds that the facts of the actual case differ from the earlier one. This may lead to a situation whereby a court which does not approve of a principle may distinguish the facts from those relevant in a case where a higher court adopted a legal principle which the lower court does not like. One of the reasons why English and American cases appear so hard to review seems to be that several court decisions which differ in minor details and nuances may cover a narrow point, and it may be hard to extract the precise underlying principle.

Even if the parties are supposed to have comprehensively regulated their relationship in the charter-party, there are circumstances which may not have been clearly expressed but are implied. Such *implied terms* have the same effect as express provisions and may be used by the courts to determine the agreement of the parties (for example, reference to commercial customs or the conduct of the parties) and the meaning of certain legal principles.

CHAPTER 11

COMMON CLAUSES AND CONCEPTS

Before we discuss the typical Voyage and Time Chartering clauses we shall in this chapter deal with some questions and problems common to the two types of chartering.

PREAMBLE

Written contracts often start with a preamble, in which the parties and the main contents of the agreement are presented. A preamble can be formulated in the following way:

GENCON

1. It is agreed between the party mentioned in Box 3 as Owners of the steamer or motor-vessel named in Box 5, of the gross/nett Register tons indicated in Box 6 and carrying about the number of tons of deadweight cargo stated in Box 7, now in position as stated in Box 8 and expected ready to load under this Charter about the date indicated in Box 9, and the party mentioned as Charterers in Box 4 that:
The said vessel shall proceed to the loading port or place stated in Box 10 or so near thereto as she may safely get the lie always afloat, and there load a full and complete cargo (if shipment of deck cargo agreed same to be at Charterers' risk) as stated in Box 12 (Charterers to provide all mats and/or wood for dunnage and any separations required, the Owners allowing the use of any dunnage wood on board if required) which the Charterers bind themselves to ship, and being so loaded the vessel shall proceed to the discharging port or place stated in Box 11 as ordered on signing Bills of Lading or so near thereto as she may safely get and lie always afloat and there deliver the cargo on being paid freight on delivered or intaken quantity as indicated in Box 13 at the rate stated in Box 13.

In a preamble of this design the various parts of the agreement are tied up with each other. In the Gencon form of 1976 (a revised version is expected in 1995) and in many other modern charter-party forms the Box Layout system is used, which means that the written agreement is divided into two main parts (the *box part* with all specifications for the relevant vessel and voyage, and the *text part* with all the printed clauses) with cross-references between the parts.

150

SECTION OF GENCON'S BOX PART (NOT FULL SIZE)

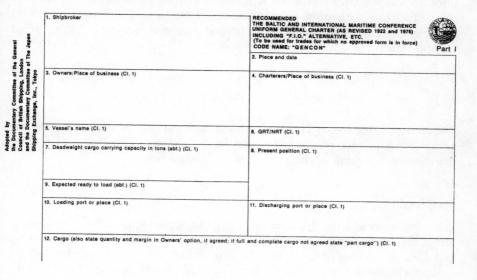

In forms with a traditional layout the details of the specific fixture are inserted directly into the open space of the printed clauses, as for instance:

Code word for this Charter Party
"SHELLVOY 5"

Voyage Charter Party

LONDON,   19

PREAMBLE   1

IT IS THIS DAY AGREED between   2

of   (hereinafter referred to as "Owners") being owners/disponent [   ]

owners of the motor/steam tank vessel called   [   ]

(hereinafter referred to as "the vessel")   5

and   of   6

(hereinafter referred to as "Charterers")   7

that the services for which provision is herein made shall be subject to the terms [   ]
and conditions of this charter which includes Part I and Part II. In the event of [   ]
any conflict between the provisions of Part I and Part II hereof, the provisions of [   ]
Part I shall prevail.   [   ]

In most cases the charter-party also has a third part, the *rider*, where additional, photocopied standard clauses or typewritten clauses are inserted. This rider is often much longer than the printed form used and so many changes have been made in the basic standard document that one may question if it is still a standard form.

THE PARTIES TO THE CONTRACT

The charterer, the owner and other persons and parties involved in the charter agreement have been mentioned above. In this section we shall deal with some questions in connection with the identity of the parties.

The identity

Both the owner and the charterer must have an opportunity to form an opinion about the other party before they are bound to the agreement. Both during and after the charter period it may be important for one of the parties to have an opportunity to force the other party to fulfil his obligations. It is therefore essential in the first place to know the identity, and if possible also the full style, telephone and telex numbers, etc., of the other party. It is not unusual for the charterer to be represented by an agent and known to the other party only by expressions like "Messrs. NN as agents for charterers". It is important not to make any commitments and always to have a chance to terminate the negotiations if the other party turns out to be unacceptable owing to insolvency, bad reputation, etc. As various kinds of notices must be given to shippers, receivers, etc., it is important also to know the identity, telex number, etc., of those persons.

Substitution of owner or charterer

Sometimes the owners or the charterers wish to replace themselves with other owners or charterers. It is, for instance, not unusual that the owner in a long period time charter agreement wishes to sell his vessel and let the new owner of the vessel enter as owner into the time charter-party. It also happens that the charterer wishes to sub-charter the vessel to another charterer. Basically, the owner may not sell the vessel during the time charter period and let the new owner enter into his place as party to the agreement unless a particular agreement has been made to such effect. If the owner who is selling is solvent and reliable a practical solution and compromise is that the charterer accepts the new owner as party to the agreement in combination with a guarantee from the selling owner that he agrees to guarantee the fulfilment of the obligations of the new owner.

The charterer's right to sub-let the vessel is usually confirmed in the charter-party. This can be done in the following way:

LINERTIME
22. Sublet
The Charterers to have the option of subletting the Vessel, giving due notice to the Owners, but the original Charterers always to remain responsible to the Owner for due performance of the Charter.

The agreement is, in other words, that the time charterer remains responsible to the owner although he has handed over his rights to "order and direct" the vessel to another time charterer. Unless it is expressly agreed in the charter-party, the time charterer cannot transfer his obligations against the owner to another time charterer. In voyage chartering it is not unusual that the charterer exempts himself from certain obligations or from all his obligations as charterer. This is usually done in a so-called Cesser clause, which will be dealt with in connection with the voyage charter-party.

The current trend is that instead of a shipowner undertaking performance with one particular vessel the undertaking is a more general one, i.e. the particular named vessel does not play the same decisive role. In liner shipping a corresponding and even more pronounced development is illustrated by through transportation where the contracting carrier performs only part of the whole carriage. Such through transportation (or in modern terminology—at least where carriers with different modes of transportation are involved—combined transport, intermodal or multimodal transportation) has become more and more common. Also in conventional bills of lading this development is from a contracting point of view well established. By *transhipment* and/or *scope of voyage* clauses of varying width and scope the carrier can reserve his right to arrange the performance as it suits him. Such far-reaching clauses may, however, be in conflict with the compulsory provisions of the cargo liability conventions and may therefore be unenforceable.

THE VESSEL

Nomination, identity and substitution

Depending on the type of contract, the ship may have a more or less central position in the charter agreement. The basic idea in shipping has been that it is important for the customer to know the vessel to be used for the carriage. It is also important for him that a particular vessel is nominated at an early stage. This basic concept nowadays seems to be less predominant, but it applies with varying force depending on the circumstances.

In conventional liner shipping the bill of lading is normally of the type known as a shipped bill of lading, i.e. the bill of lading is issued when the goods have been loaded on board the vessel. Obviously, this particular vessel then plays a central role. In modern liner traffic, where the received for shipment bill of lading plays a much more dominant role, the particular vessel has less importance, but the customer trusts the carrier to perform well, irrespective of which vessel is going to be used.

In time charter and bareboat agreements, which can both be classified as a kind of leasing agreement, the vessel is a central factor. In the voyage charter agreement, which can be classified as a transportation agreement for a certain cargo between certain ports, the description of the vessel herself does not have the same central position as in the time charter and bareboat agreements. It is, for instance, not unusual that time and bareboat charter agreements are concluded before it is known what ship will be used. In such cases the ship in the charter-party is mentioned as "Vessel to be nominated" or similar. The owner has in such a case an obligation to nominate a vessel suitable for the intended cargo, ports, etc. In contracts of affreightment (definition on pages 93, 247ff.), where the basic task under the contract is to move goods, the normal procedure is that the ship is not named in the agreement. In those cases where the vessel is not nominated at the time of the fixture it is advisable to agree as to when the owner shall make his nomination. If the nomination is made too close to the loading the shippers may have difficulties in supplying the goods, preparing the shipping documents, etc.

When a certain ship is fixed for a charter the existence of the agreement is also dependent on the existence of the vessel. If the vessel is lost or declared a "constructive total loss" the charter agreement is "frustrated", which means that it is terminated automatically and no longer exists. The charter agreement can be frustrated for other reasons, for instance if the ship is delayed for an extensively long period.

The English "doctrine of frustration" is sometimes referred to by charterers or owners when they wish to cancel a charter agreement for economic reasons. We cannot here deal with all the difficult questions in connection with the doctrine. It should be noted, however, that it is usually very difficult to judge in advance whether the court or the arbitrators will consider an agreement frustrated or not. One should therefore be careful and always take legal advice before informing the counter-party that the agreement is considered to be terminated on the ground of "doctrine of frustration".

In voyage chartering, especially, it is often agreed that the vessel may be substituted by another vessel. Sometimes the charter-party prescribes "MS Eugen or substitute", sometimes "MS Eugen, owner's option to substitute vessel of same class and similar size and position". It is essential to specify how far this right to substitute goes. Is there only a right for the owner to nominate another ship, or is there also an obligation for him to nominate another ship if the one already nominated is lost, or not available? Can the vessel be substituted several times? Should the right to substitute cease a certain number of days before the planned commencement of loading? Should it be possible to substitute only with certain vessels or should it be possible to substitute with any vessel that can carry the cargo?

Not only the name but also the nationality, call sign, year of build, type (motor tanker, reefer, passenger ferry, etc.) is usually specified in the agreement. The owner cannot, without the permission of the charterer, alter any of the vessel's essential characteristics. If, for instance, the owner wishes to change the nationality of the vessel, he has to get permission from the charterer as the nationality of the vessel in many cases is essential to the charterer for various reasons. The technical description of the ship will be dealt with separately in connection with the voyage charter-party and the time charter-party. It should be mentioned that oil companies often have far reaching demands on the quality of the vessel in their charter-parties.

Vessel's trading limits

The hull underwriters maintain geographical limits in connection with the insurance of vessels. The limits are slightly different between various underwriters. Some areas are always accepted, others are always excluded (mainly the Arctic areas) and others are accepted only between certain dates and excluded for the remaining part of the year. Owners often have to pay additional insurance premiums for the last mentioned areas. Common rules are the so-called Institute Warranties Limits (IWL).

The hull underwriters' rules concerning accepted and excluded areas are based on the average ice and weather conditions and these rules are therefore normally the same year after year. The restrictions drawn up in connection with war insurance for the vessel are based on the risk of damage caused by war, hostilities, etc., and as these risks vary the underwriters often issue new rules about restricted areas and additional war premiums.

The ship's trading limits can be based on the manning and construction of the vessel and of the technical equipment on board. It may be, for instance, that the ship to be used in world-wide ocean trading must have more officers and crew members than if the same vessel is used for coastal traffic only. In some countries, and for the transiting of some canals and seaways, it is necessary to have special technical equipment. Such equipment is required, for example, when passing through the Suez Canal and the St. Lawrence Seaway.

Note that only the *vessel's* trading limits are mentioned here. Additional limits, mainly based on political relations between various countries, are often expressly inserted into the charter-party. This will be explained further in Chapter 13.

The concept of seaworthiness

It is usually stated in the charter-party that the owner shall keep the vessel in a seaworthy condition. Also, when no such clauses are inserted, the owners usually by law or by an "implied warranty" have an obligation to keep the vessel in a seaworthy condition. According to English law, the owners, basically, have a strict liability for the ship's seaworthiness but as it is possible to insert exception clauses concerning seaworthiness, the owners are seldom liable for all consequences caused by unseaworthiness. Note also that if, as a general rule, it is possible for the owners to insert a valid exception clause concerning the liability for seaworthiness, the clause may, in specific cases, not be valid. The most obvious example is perhaps when owners try to exempt themselves from liability under the Carriage of Goods by Sea Act and other laws based on the Hague Rules or similar rules (see further, page 64ff.).

The concept of seaworthiness can be described as having three aspects:

—seaworthiness from the technical point of view;
—cargoworthiness;
—seaworthiness for the intended voyage.

Technical seaworthiness includes the ship's design and condition in hull and machinery and also her stability. *Cargoworthiness* means that the vessel shall be suitable for the intended cargo and properly cleaned and *seaworthiness with respect to the intended voyage* means that she will be satisfactorily equipped, bunkered, etc., for the intended voyage.

When judging whether the vessel is seaworthy or not the circumstances at each stage and in each situation must be considered (seaworthiness by stages). A ship that is seaworthy for traffic on the River Thames may not be seaworthy for a voyage from England to New York, and a ship that is seaworthy during loading may not be seaworthy for the intended voyage unless additional fuel, charts, etc., are taken on board.

A special question connected with seaworthiness for the intended voyage is to what extent the vessel must be technically equipped and furnished with certificates necessary for her to be able to call at a certain port or a certain country without risk of delay.

So far as the usual certificates and documents are concerned, the owner and the master must, both in time and voyage chartering, keep all necessary certificates up to date. An exception may be the situation when the vessel is, for instance, on time charter trading world-wide. If in such a case the ship's schedule is changed at very short notice and the vessel is destined for a port or country normally not called at by the charterer, the owner should be entitled to some extra time to get the necessary documents.

Concerning documents requested by persons other than national authorities—for instance by the ITF (International Transport Workers' Federation)—the situation is not clear. In those cases where it is generally known that labour unions, etc., claim a certain document or certificate the owner has, most probably, an obligation to keep such documents or certificates on board, but when the request from a union or other body could hardly be expected, the situation is more difficult. Quite often special clauses dealing with this problem are found in the charter-parties. As regards restrictions and rules issued by authorities at very short notice, the problem must be solved from case to case. A general trend in shipping seems to be an increasing demand for a careful description of the ship and the certificates to be on board or available and a more extensive liability on the shipowner as to his warranty in this respect.

A particular aspect of making the ship seaworthy, in the sense of being fit for the reception of cargo, is cleaning. This goes for all vessel types but the extent of cleaning depends on the trade. As to dry cargo trades it goes without saying that a cargo of grain cannot follow upon certain types of cargoes without very careful cleaning. A tanker regularly lifting crude oil (Dirty cargo) cannot carry a clean cargo without a considerable amount of cleaning. Tanks, pipelines and pumps must be cleaned between each voyage. Several types of cleaning devices have been developed in tanker trades, such as the Butterworth and Gunclean systems.

Frequently one finds in charter-parties provisions such as "cleaned to the Charterer's inspector's satisfaction". Such a clause can be dangerous for the owner. In certain trades the cleaning has to be to the satisfaction of a certain authority. This clause is usually less risky from the owner's point of view.

Shellvoy 5 may be used as an example of a description clause which is rather far reaching.

"

		PART I	11
(A) Description of vessel		Owners guarantee that at the date hereof the vessel:—	12
			13
	(i)	Is classed	14
	(ii)	Has a deadweight of tonnes (1000 kg.) on a salt-water draft on assigned summer freeboard of m.	[ ] [ ]
	(iii)	Has a capacity available for the cargo of tonnes (1000 kg.) 5% more or less in Owners' option.	[ ] [ ]
	(iv)	Is fully fitted with heating systems for all cargo tanks capable of maintaining cargo at a temperature of up to degrees Celsius.	[ ] [ ] [ ]
	(v)	Has tanks coated as follows:—	[ ]
	(vi)	Is equipped with cranes/derricks capable of lifting to and supporting at the vessel's port and starboard manifolds submarine hoses of up to tonnes (1000 kg.) in weight.	[ ] [ ] [ ] [ ]
	(vii)	Has cargo pumps capable of discharging a full cargo within hours or maintaining a back pressure of at the vessel's manifold (provided shore facilities permit and the cargo does not have a kinematic viscosity exceeding 600 centistokes at the discharge temperature required by Charterers).	[ ] [ ] [ ] [ ] [ ] [ ]

(viii) Has or will have carried the following three cargoes [ ]
        immediately prior to loading under this charter:—   [ ]

        Last   29

        2.   30

        3.   31

(ix)   Has a crude oil washing system complying with the [ ]
        requirements of the International Convention for the [ ]
        Prevention of Pollution from Ships 1973 as modified by [ ]
        the Protocol of 1978 ("MARPOL 73/78").   [ ]

(x)   Has an operational inert gas system.   34

(xi)   Has on board all papers and certificates required by any [ ]
        applicable law, in force as at the date of this charter, to [ ]
        enable the vessel to perform the charter service without [ ]
        any delay.   [ ]

(xii)   Is entered in   P&I Club." 37

LAY/CAN

Both in voyage charter and time charter it must be agreed when the vessel
should be ready to load at the first port or delivered to the charterer. Usually
a so-called Lay/Can is agreed, for instance "Lay/Can March 1–15".

"Lay"

"Lay" is a short form of "Laytime not to commence before". If the ship, under
a voyage charter-party, is ready at the first loading port before the agreed
"layday" the owner cannot claim that the charterer should start to load the
vessel or that the time should commence to count. This situation will be
discussed further in Chapter 12, on voyage chartering ("Laytime" section page
191ff.).

If a vessel chartered under a time charter-party arrives at the port or place
of delivery before the layday, the charterers have no obligation to take delivery
of her and, unless the charterers agree to an earlier delivery, the ship has to
wait without earning anything for the owners. Sometimes the charterers wish
to commence the loading of the vessel before the first layday but without
taking delivery of her and thus also without paying for her. The owner has no
obligation to accept such a procedure and if the charterers wish to commence
the loading before the first layday the owner and the charterer must be in
agreement concerning the payment of hire, allocation of risks, etc., during the
period up to the agreed layday.

The layday is not always exactly stated. For instance, in the preamble to the Gencon form the expression "expected ready to load under this Charter about the date indicated in Box 9" is used. To find out the meaning of the word "about", the circumstances in the relevant case must be taken into consideration. The longer the period between the fixture and the first layday, the wider the period covered by the expression "about".

"Can"

If the vessel has not arrived at the loading port, or port or place of delivery, on the cancelling day most charter-parties give the charterer an absolute right to cancel the charter agreement. The ordinary Cancelling clauses, as for instance in Gencon and Baltime, are, in other words, applicable also when the ship has been delayed for reasons which cannot be controlled by the owner and when the owner and the master have done their utmost to speed up the vessel.

When it is obvious to the owner that he has no chance of arriving at the first loading port or place of delivery before the cancelling date, it is important for him to get the charterer's declaration whether or not he will cancel. Under English law the charterer is not obliged to give such a declaration unless this is expressly stated in the charter-party.

Both the Gencon and the Baltime Cancelling clauses deal with this question:

GENCON
10. Cancelling Clause
Should the vessel not be ready to load (whether in berth or not) on or before the date indicated in Box 19, Charterers have the option of cancelling this contract, such option to be declared, if demanded, at least 48 hours before vessel's expected arrival at port of loading. Should the vessel be delayed on account of average or otherwise, Charterers to be informed as soon as possible, and if the vessel is delayed for more than 10 days after the day she is stated to be expected ready to load, Charterers have the option of cancelling this contract, unless a cancelling date has been agreed upon.

BALTIME
22. Cancelling
Should the Vessel not be delivered by the date indicated in Box 23, the Charterers to have the option of cancelling.
    If the Vessel cannot be delivered by the cancelling date, the Charterers, if required, to declare within 48 hours after receiving notice thereof whether they will cancel or take delivery of the Vessel.

According to the Gencon form the charterer must on demand declare his option to cancel at least 48 hours before the vessel's expected arrival at the port of loading. This means that where the owner, a couple of weeks before the cancelling date, knows that the ship has no chance of arriving before the cancelling date, he has no right to demand the charterer's declaration and, if the charterer is not co-operative, the owner may have to start the ballast voyage towards the first loading port, or place of delivery, in order to avoid a claim for breach of contract from the charterer.

The solution in the Baltime cancelling clause is better for the owner because the charterer, according to this clause, has to declare whether he intends to cancel or not "within 48 hours after receiving notice" that the ship cannot be delivered by the cancelling date. Other, more modern, charter-party forms, sometimes contain a clause to the effect that the owner cannot require a declaration from the charterer before, for instance, the ship has reached the last port before the voyage to the loading port or delivery port (place). Usually, the vessel's position at the time of the fixture is stated in the charter-party. The statement of the position must be corrected and the estimated day for readiness for loading realistic.

The owner and the master have an obligation to do their utmost to ensure that the vessel reaches the first loading port or the place of delivery at or before the day stated for the expected or estimated readiness for loading. If the owner or master intentionally or by negligence delays the vessel and causes her to be late, the owner may be liable in damages for breach of contract.

With respect to the relation between shipowner and charterer under charter-parties there are no compulsory (mandatory) rules concerning cargo liability. Some charter-parties tend to relieve the owner from much of his cargo liability, whereas others have provisions more or less in line with the mandatory cargo liability rules. Although the parties in charter-parties are thus basically free to determine the extent of the owner's cargo liability it is not uncommon to find a separate provision, a so-called *Paramount clause*, concerning the liability for damage to or loss of the goods. A Paramount clause may be drafted in different ways; but the basic idea is that the Hague Rules and/or Hague-Visby Rules or local legislation based on these conventions shall be applicable in case of cargo damage.

The Paramount clause may prescribe that it shall be inserted only into all *bills of lading* issued in connection with the charter-party, that it shall cover the *cargo liability* under the charter-party, or that it shall apply to the charter-party entirely. In the latter case, various legal problems may arise, since the Hague Rules and amendments are geared to cargo liability and not to chartering in its entirety (cf. above, page 64ff.).

THE WAR CLAUSE

In time of war, revolution or other similar disturbances the crew, the vessel and the cargo may be exposed to certain risks. The personnel on board may be injured or killed and cargo and ship damaged or lost. Furthermore, there is a risk of delay and extra costs, for instance, extra insurance premiums for cargo and vessel and extra payment to the crew. In order to make sure of the rights and the obligations of the parties when crew, ship and cargo are exposed to such risks, it is usual to have a special War clause in the charter-parties. War clauses can be divided into two groups, War Cancellation clauses and War Risk clauses.

War Cancellation clauses

A War Cancellation clause may have the following wording (part of Clause 23 in Barecon A):

BARECON A

(c) In the event of the outbreak of war (whether there be a declaration of war or not) between any two or more of the following countries: the United Kingdom, the United States of America, France, the Union of Soviet Socialist Republics, the People's Republic of China or in the event of the nation under whose flag the Vessel sails becoming involved in war (whether there be a declaration of war or not), hostilities, warlike operations, revolution, or civil commotion preventing the Vessel's normal trading, either the Owners or the Charterers may cancel this Charter, whereupon the Charterers shall re-deliver the Vessel to the Owners in accordance with Clause 13, if she has cargo on board after discharge thereof at destination or if debarred under this Clause from reaching or entering it at a near open and safe port as directed by the Owners, or if she has no cargo on board, at the port at which she then is or if at sea at a near open and safe port as directed by the Owners. In all cases hire shall continue to be paid in accordance with Clause 9 and except as aforesaid all other provisions of this Charter shall apply until re-delivery.

The intention of the War Cancellation clause is usually to give both parties a chance to cancel the charter agreement when the freight market has totally changed as a result of war between certain countries or when further trading with the vessel is prevented as a result of requisition or similar action from the vessel's home country. The War Cancellation clauses are found mainly in long term charter-parties and contracts of affreightment, but they are to a growing extent also found in time charter-parties, e.g. NYPE 93 cl. 32, and even voyage charter-parties.

War Risk clauses

While the War Cancellation clauses at first hand are found in long term charter agreements or contracts of affreightment, the War Risk clauses are found, or at least should be found, in all charter agreements.

The War Risk clause must have a definition of "war risk". The following example is from BIMCO's clause Voywar 1993 (found, for instance, in Gencon):

(b) "War Risks" shall include any war (whether actual or threatened), act of war, civil war, hostilities, revolution, rebellion, civil commotion, warlike operations, the laying of mines (whether actual or reported), acts of piracy, acts of terrorists, acts of hostility or malicious damage, blockades (whether imposed against all vessels or imposed selectively against vessels of certain flags or ownership, or against certain cargoes or crews or otherwise howsoever), by any person, body, terrorist or political group, or the Government of any state whatsoever, which, in the reasonable judgement of the Master and/or the Owners, may be dangerous or are likely to be or to become dangerous to the Vessel, her cargo, crew or other persons on board the Vessel.

According to this definition, war risks include not only actual war and warlike operations but also the threat of war and warlike operations. In many War Risk clauses the definition is narrower. Sometimes the War Risk clause is applicable only when the port is "declared blockaded by reason of war" or similar. Sometimes the War Risk clauses also state that the decision as to whether a war risk exists or not lies exclusively with the owner.

It is also important to establish the respective parties' rights and obligations when crew, vessel and cargo are exposed to a war risk. Can the owner only or both the charterer and the owner cancel the charter agreement without compensation or is it an obligation on the charterer to arrange other cargo or to pay deadfreight? Is the owner obliged to go to another port or another area where the war risk does not exist? Who will pay for delay when the loading, the sea voyage or the discharging is hindered and who will pay for the extra insurance and extra wages for the crew? Sometimes the hull and war risk underwriters or the authorities give instructions to the ship that certain areas, owing to war risks, must be avoided and a War Risk clause must state that the owners are entitled to follow such instructions.

War clauses in voyage charters and time charters

Usually the standard charter-party forms have a printed War Risk clause. In time chartering the Conwartime clause is often used. The new Conwartime 1993 has also been introduced into the NYPE 93 and its full text is as follows:

BIMCO Standard War Risks Clause for Time Charters, 1993
Code Name: "Conwartime 1993"

(1) For the purpose of this Clause, the words:

   (a) "Owners" shall include the shipowners, bareboat charterers, disponent owners, managers or other operators who are charged with the management of the Vessel, and the Master; and

   (b) "War Risks" shall include any war (whether actual or threatened), act of war, civil war, hostilities, revolution, rebellion, civil commotion, warlike operations, the laying of mines (whether actual or reported), acts of piracy, acts of terrorists, acts of hostility or malicious damage, blockades (whether imposed against all vessels or imposed selectively against vessels of certain flags or ownership, or against certain cargoes or crews or otherwise howsoever), by any person, body, terrorist or political group, or the Government of any state whatsoever, which, in the reasonable judgement of the Master and/or the Owners, may be dangerous or are likely to be or to become dangerous to the Vessel, her cargo, crew or other persons on board the Vessel.

(2) The Vessel, unless the written consent of the Owners be first obtained, shall not be ordered to or required to continue to or through, any port, place, area or zone (whether of land or sea), or any waterway or canal, where it appears that the Vessel, her cargo, crew or other persons on board the Vessel, in the reasonable judgement of the Master and/or the Owners, may be, or are likely to be, exposed to War Risks. Should the Vessel be within any such place as aforesaid, which only becomes dangerous, or is likely to be or to become dangerous, after her entry into it, she shall be at liberty to leave it.

(3) The Vessel shall not be required to load contraband cargo, or to pass through any blockade, whether such blockade be imposed on all vessels, or is imposed selectively in any way whatsoever against vessels of certain flags or ownership, or against certain cargoes or crews or otherwise howsoever, or to proceed to an area where she shall be subject, or is likely to be subject to a belligerent's right of search and/or confiscation.

(4) (a) The Owners may effect war risks insurance in respect of the Hull and Machinery of the Vessel and their other interests (including, but not limited to, loss of earnings and detention, the crew and their Protection and Indemnity Risks), and the premiums and/or calls therefor shall be for their account.

  (b) If the Underwriters of such insurance should require payment of premiums and/or calls because, pursuant to the Charterers' orders, the Vessel is within, or is due to enter and remain within, any area or areas which are specified by such Underwriters as being subject to additional premiums because of War Risks, then such premiums and/or calls shall be reimbursed by the Charterers to the Owners at the same time as the next payment of hire is due.

(5) If the Owners become liable under the terms of employment to pay to the crew any bonus or additional wages in respect of sailing into an area which is dangerous in the manner defined by the said terms, then such bonus or additional wages shall be reimbursed to the Owners by the Charterers at the same time as the next payment of hire is due.

(6) The Vessel shall have liberty:

  (a) to comply with all orders, directions, recommendations or advice as to departure, arrival, routes, sailing in convoy, ports of call, stoppages, destinations, discharge of cargo, delivery, or in any other way whatsoever, which are given by the Government of the Nation under whose flag the Vessel sails, or other Government to whose laws the Owners are subject, or any other Government, body or group whatsoever acting with the power to compel compliance with their orders or directions;

  (b) to comply with the order, directions or recommendations of any war risks underwriters who have the authority to give the same under the terms of the war risks insurance;

  (c) to comply with the terms of any resolution of the Security Council of the United Nations, any directives of the European Community, the effective orders of any other Supranational body which has the right to issue and give the same, and with national laws aimed at enforcing the same to which the Owners are subject, and to obey the orders and directions of those who are charged with their enforcement;

   (d) to divert and discharge at any other port any cargo or part thereof which may render the Vessel liable to confiscation as a contraband carrier;

   (e) to divert and call at any other port to change the crew or any part thereof or other persons on board the Vessel when there is reason to believe that they may be subject to internment, imprisonment or other sanctions.

(7) If in accordance with their rights under the foregoing provisions of this Clause, the Owners shall refuse to proceed to the loading or discharging ports, or any one or more of them, they shall immediately inform the Charterers.

No cargo shall be discharged at any alternative port without first giving the Charterers notice of the Owners' intention to do so and requesting them to nominate a safe port for such discharge. Failing such nomination by the Charterers within 48 hours of the receipt of such notice and request, the Owners may discharge the cargo at any safe port of their own choice.

(8) If in compliance with any of the provisions of sub-clauses (2) to (7) of this Clause anything is done or not done, such shall not be deemed a deviation, but shall be considered as due fulfilment of this Charterparty.

Other War Risk clauses, such as the Chamber of Shipping War Risk clauses 1 and 2, are also used. These are *not* sufficient for a modern charter agreement; nor for a voyage charter and much less so for a time charter. These clauses have been withdrawn but they are still in frequent use. We must warn against the use of these clauses and particularly they should be banned in time charter-parties.

An operator should not mix War Risk clauses designed for voyage chartering with those designed for time chartering and vice versa and must also remember that when he acts as "Time Chartered Owner", "Disponent Owner" or similar, he must be careful to include in the charter *out* a War Risk clause that is no less favourable to him than the one included in his charter *in*. If the Conwartime clause, as printed in NYPE 93, is used when chartering *in* the vessel, Voywar 1993 should be used if the ship is chartered *out* on a voyage basis. Also, the bill of lading War clauses must give sufficient protection.

EFFECT OF COST VARIATIONS ON THE CONTRACTUAL RELATIONSHIP

The basic idea is that the parties are bound by their agreement, irrespective of any later economic development. This idea is sometimes stressed by a "come hell and high water clause", whereby the parties agree that they will be bound by their contractual rights and obligations, whatever the circumstances. Should there be an unforeseen cost increase this will normally not affect the obligations of the party having to pay unless it amounts to "frustration", which is not often the case. Thus the parties will have to regulate contractually connected questions if they want the economic development to have any effect on their rights and duties. Such clauses are sometimes found, particularly in contrasts covering a long period of time. They may be described as "Hardship clauses", "Bunker clauses", "Currency clauses", "Escalation clauses", etc., and their aims and constructions vary a great deal.

A "Hardship clause" may aim at the renegotiation of the contract if the economic conditions change substantially, and if the parties cannot agree the suffering party may possibly cancel the agreement. Such clauses may be drafted in many different ways and are often said to be "toothless". "Bunker clauses" may be of a type whereby the owner will be compensated when bunker prices are increased or where he is relieved from his obligations in case of bunker shortage. "Currency clauses" and "Escalation clauses" are generally designed as "Compensation clauses".

When the charter agreement covers a long period (particularly time chartering, contract of affreightment and consecutive voyages) the parties must consider the risks arising from changed economic conditions, especially rising costs and variations in the exchange rate. It is often hard to draft a Currency clause, an Escalation clause, or a Bunker Cost clause, etc., which will cover all occurrences, and such clauses may in some cases appear to have an effect adverse to what was intended. It may therefore be advisable to consult financial experts and lawyers when it comes to the drafting of such a clause. Standard clauses drafted by BIMCO, for example, may be used as a base but, as in every case when a standard clause is used, the circumstances in connection with the specific agreement should be taken into consideration. Let us here just give a few examples to explain the situation and the difficulties.

Currency clauses

The following examples may explain the problems which may arise due to variations in the relative exchange rate:

A shipowner, who has all his costs in pounds sterling, estimates the costs for a certain voyage at £12,000. The freight is fixed at U.S.$25,000 which, with a relation between U.S.$ and £ at U.S.$2=£1, gives a contribution of £12,500. The surplus is consequently calculated at £500. If, before the payment of the freight, the relation between U.S.$ and £ is changed to U.S.$2.20=£1, the owner's compensation will only be about £11,364, which means that instead of a surplus of £500 he will have a deficit in the amount of £636. If there was a Currency clause in the charter-party stating that the freight was based on U.S.$2=£1 and that possible changes in this rate would be compensated accordingly, the owner would have been entitled to a freight payment of U.S.$27,500.

When drafting such a clause several problems have to be considered. First, the parties have to decide whether a Currency clause shall be inserted or not. If they so decide they have to draft the clause. This is not always easy. The parties have to decide whether the clause should work two ways or if it will only protect one of them, whether the variations have to reach a certain level before it will be applied, etc.

In liner traffic the tariffs will often be based on a certain currency adjustment factor (CAF).

The following B.P. Parity clause gives a two-way protection:

"The freight and the demurrage rate in this charter party is based on a rate of exchange where U.S.$1.– is equal to Sw. Crs. . . . (the contractual rate of exchange). If at the date of actual payment, the bind rate for U.S. dollars quoted by . . . bank, differs from the contractual rate of exchange, the U.S. dollar shall be adjusted to realize the same amount of Sw. Crs. as if the contractual rate of exchange was used."

Escalation clauses

The object of an Escalation clause is to protect the party suffering from cost increases or rather to compensate him wholly or partly for his cost increases. The idea may then be that the freight shall continuously, or at certain intervals, be changed in accordance with the cost changes. The costs, which are particularly important in this perspective, are the costs for manning, maintenance and insurance.

The basic problem in connection with Escalation clauses is to find a base or a formula for the recalculation of the freight. Sometimes a particular cost factor will be used, sometimes an index (of one kind or another) will be applied and in other cases the actual cost changes will be used. Thus, if the owner's costs have increased by 11% over a period he will also be entitled to an 11% freight increase. Such a clause may, however, be thought to minimize the owner's cost incentive. Another way is that the parties agree beforehand that the freight will be increased by an agreed percentage at certain intervals. One example of an Escalation clause is the following:

"Escalation Clause
The rate of hire agreed in this charter is based upon the level of owners' monthly operating expenses ruling at the date of this charter as shown in the statement for future comparison attached hereto, including provisions, stores, master's and crew's wages, war bonus and other remuneration, maintenance and usual insurance premiums.

By the end of every year of the charter period the average monthly expenses for the preceding year shall be compared with the basic statement attached hereto. Any difference exceeding 5 per cent, to be multiplied by 12 and regulated in connection with the next hire payment. The same principle to apply *pro rata* at the termination of the charter for any part of a year."

Other clauses dealing with change of costs

Currency clauses and Escalation clauses are mainly used in agreements covering a long period of time. It may, however, be advisable to insert into short term agreements clauses covering other cost elements which may vary rapidly, and where neither of the parties may affect the cost. If bunker prices increase considerably during the period between the fixture and the commencement of the voyage, the owner's calculation may turn out to be totally wrong. A particular Bunker clause may be entered specifying that the freight is based on a bunker price at U.S.$X per ton and that any change in the bunker prices shall entitle the owner to a corresponding freight compensation. Liner shipping tariffs are normally based on a bunker adjustment factor (BAF).

Also certain other costs which are unknown or difficult to estimate may be dealt with in special clauses. For instance, the following clause is often found in charter-parties:

"Any additional insurance on vessel and/or cargo levied by reason of the vessel's age, flag, ownership, management, class or condition to be for owner's account."

Another example is:

"Freight tax, if any, to be for Charterers' (or Owners') account."

Many countries levy freight taxes. BIMCO issues a booklet, *Freight Taxes*, which gives information about taxes in various countries like the example below:

USA

Attention!
The U.S. Tax Reform entered into force on 1 January 1987.

It should be noted that at the time of compiling this information some implementing rules particularly related to the enforcement of tax filing procedures still need to be drafted.

Summary
The U.S. Tax Reform Act 1986 provides that 50 per cent of all transportation income attributable to transport which begins or ends in the U.S.A. will be considered U.S. income and subject to a 4 per cent gross basis tax.

Transportation income includes bareboat, voyage and time charter hire.

Tax on transportation income will be levied retroactively for the year 1987.

The 4 per cent tax will be applied annually. Corporations that do not maintain an office or place of business in the U.S. have until the 15th day of the 6th month after the end of their tax year to file a tax return Form 1120F. Corporations which maintain an office or place of business in the U.S. have until the 15th day of the 3rd month after the end of their tax year to file a tax return Form 1120F.

Exemption Agreements
Exemption is possible subject to reciprocity.

It should be noted that the following countries have signed individual exemption agreements with the U.S.A.: . . .

The general principles for allocation of costs between charterers and owners are explained in more detail both above and below in connection with the voyage charter-party and the time charter-party.

THE ARBITRATION CLAUSE

We have dealt with questions in connection with choice of law, arbitration, etc. (page 137ff.). To avoid discussions and disputes about what law is applicable to the charter agreement, all charter-party forms should contain a clause dealing with the law applicable to and the procedure for the handling of disputes between the parties. The charter-parties usually have reference to arbitration while bills of lading more often refer to procedure in the courts.

An Arbitration clause should not only have a reference to the applicable law but also rules about the procedure when arbitrators are nominated, etc. When English law is applicable the Arbitration clause sometimes has a reference to the Arbitration Act 1950, which deals with the procedure; reference should now instead be made to the Arbitration Act 1979 (cf. above, at page 138).

NYPE 93 contains a "split" arbitration clause where the parties choose whether an arbitration shall be referred to New York or London. Also note that this clause makes special reference to "small amounts disputes".

"45. Arbitration   497

*(a) NEW YORK   498
    All disputes arising out of this contract shall be arbitrated at New York in the [   ]
following manner, and subject to U.S. Law: [   ]

    One Arbitrator is to be appointed by each of the parties hereto and a third by   [   ]
the two so chosen. Their decision or that of any two of them shall be final, and   [   ]
for the purpose of enforcing any award, this agreement may be made a rule of   [   ]
the court. The Arbitrators shall be commercial men, conversant with shipping   [   ]
matters. Such Arbitration is to be conducted in accordance with the rules of the   [   ]
Society of Maritime Arbitrators Inc.   [   ]
    For disputes where the total amount claimed by either party does not exceed   [   ]
US$............** the arbitration shall be conducted in accordance with the Shortened [   ]
Arbitration Procedure of the Society of Maritime Arbitrators Inc.   [   ]

*(b) LONDON   509
    All disputes arising out of this contract shall be arbitrated at London and,   [   ]
unless the parties agree forthwith on a single Arbitrator, be referred to the final   [   ]
arbitrament of two Arbitrators carrying on business in London who shall be   [   ]
members of the Baltic Mercantile & Shipping Exchange and engaged in Shipping,   [   ]
one to be appointed by each of the parties, with power to such Arbitrators to   [   ]
appoint an Umpire. No award shall be questioned or invalidated on the ground   [   ]
that any of the Arbitrators is not qualified as above, unless objection to his action [   ]
be taken before the award is made. Any dispute arising hereunder shall be   [   ]
governed by English Law.   [   ]
    For disputes where the total amount claimed by either party does not exceed   [   ]
US$............** the arbitration shall be conducted in accordance with the Small   [   ]
Claims Procedure of the London Maritime Arbitrators Association.   [   ]

*Delete para (a) or (b) as appropriate   520

**Where no figure is supplied in the blank space this provision only shall be void   [   ]
but the other provisions of this clause shall have full force and remain in effect.   [   ]"

TIME LIMITS

Most countries have general time limits for claims and usually also the charter-parties have such limitations. We have already mentioned (page 66) the one-year limit in connection with cargo claims under the bill of lading conventions. As regards time limitations in charter-parties a general recommendation is to avoid limits shorter than a year.

The time limits under the general contract law differ from country to country and both parties in the charter agreement must find out what limitations for bringing suit are applicable in the relevant case. The general limitation applicable to most charter-parties under English law is six years. Other countries have shorter limits, for example, France, which has a one-year limit, and Spain, which has a six-month limit. It must also be noted that if the charter agreement is governed by English law, and the limitation is thus six years, the laws and the rules of the country where the defendant has his place of business may be relevant. If, for example, the charterers are Spanish, the owners must be aware of the Spanish six-month limit and not rely on the English six-year limit which is applicable to the charter-party if it is governed by English law. It is also important to find out from what day or from what event the time should count. Sometimes time in this respect starts to run from the time of final discharge and sometimes it starts to run from different points.

EXCEPTION CLAUSES

Charter-parties usually contain clauses which exempt the owners or both owners and charterers from liabilities. These clauses are sometimes related only to specified loss or damage (for instance, loss or damage to cargo) but sometimes they are of a more general nature. We have already mentioned the bill of lading conventions (above, at page 61ff.), which in some cases exempt owners from loss or damage to cargo. Another example is the Cesser clause (see below, at page 204ff.).

The following two clauses are of a general nature:

GENCON
2. Owners' Responsibility Clause
Owners are to be responsible for loss of or damage to the goods or for delay in delivery of the goods only in case the loss, damage or delay has been caused by the improper or negligent stowage of the goods (unless stowage performed by shippers/Charterers or their stevedores or servants) or by personal want of due diligence on the part of the Owners or their Manager to make the vessel in all respects seaworthy and to secure that she is properly manned, equipped and supplied or by the personal act or default of the Owners or their Manager.
And the Owners are responsible for no loss or damage or delay arising from any other cause whatsoever, even from the neglect or default of the Captain or crew or some

other person employed by the Owners on board or ashore for whose acts they would, but for this clause, be responsible, or from unseaworthiness of the vessel on loading or commencement of the voyage or at any time whatsoever. Damage caused by contact with or leakage, smell or evaporation from other goods or by the inflammable or explosive nature or insufficient package of other goods not to be considered as caused by improper or negligent stowage, even if in fact so caused.

BALTIME

13. Responsibility and Exemption

The Owners only to be responsible for delay in delivery of the Vessel or for delay during the currency of the Charter and for loss or damage to goods onboard, if such delay or loss has been caused by want of due diligence on the part of the Owners or their Manager in making the Vessel seaworthy and fitted for the voyage or any other personal act or omission or default of the Owners or their Manager. The Owners not to be responsible in any other case nor for damage or delay whatsoever and howsoever caused even if caused by the neglect or default of their servants. The Owners not to be liable for loss or damage arising or resulting from strikes, lock-outs or stoppage or restraint of labour (including the Master, Officers or Crew) whether partial or general. The Charterers to be responsible for loss or damage caused to the Vessel or to the Owners by goods being loaded contrary to the terms of the Charter or by improper or careless bunkering or loading, stowing or discharging of goods or any other improper or negligent act on their part or that of their servants.

Both the Gencon and the Baltime clauses seem to be very favourable to the owner. It should be noted, however, that courts and arbitrators are restrictive in their interpretation of such clauses and the owner cannot therefore rely fully on the text.

Another kind of Exception clause is this:

Force Majeure

Charterers and Owners exempt each other from responsibility for non-performance of this agreement when same is caused by Acts of God, Governmental, Institutional Restrictions or any other cause beyond control of either party.

This clause can be referred to both by charterers and owners, which is not the case with the above-cited Gencon and Baltime clauses.

Sometimes the clauses are drafted as "Limitation of Liability" clauses, for instance:

GENCON

12. Indemnity

Indemnity for non-performance of this Charterparty, proved damages, not exceeding estimated amount of freight.

As indicated, many different kinds of Exception clauses are found in the charter-parties and it is often difficult to find out to what extent they are applicable to a relevant situation. The main problem with the Exception clauses is, however, that they are very often disregarded during the negotiations. The printed clauses in standard forms easily "slip in" more or less unnoticed by the parties. The explanation for this is probably that they are not often referred to by the parties and therefore considered as harmless. This, however, is not correct. The existence and wording of an Exception clause may be decisive and, particularly when large amounts of money are involved, the parties refer to the Exception clause to try to win the case. The parties are recommended to read the clauses and consider their contents before they accept them (this is also, of course, a recommendation which applies to other clauses in the charter-party).

SIGNING OF THE AGREEMENT

A charter-party can be signed either by the parties or by someone authorized by them, usually a broker (concerning the identity of the parties, see above, at pages 30f., 128, 135f.). By whom and where the charter-party is signed can be important in some situations. If United States law is applicable, the charter-party should not be signed by the owner himself or by any of his directors or servants as this may prevent the owner from limiting his liability. Another example is that taxes will sometimes be debited to owners and/or charterers by the country in which the charter-party is signed. This is the case, for instance, in Australia.

It is important to check that the charter-party has been written out in accordance with the fixture and the "recap" made at the time of the fixture (see pages 127 and 135). If an incorrect charter-party is signed and sent to the other party, or if a party fails to protest when he gets an incorrect charter-party signed by a broker, the incorrect charter-party may be binding for the parties. The chances of rectifying afterwards are limited under English law unless a protest is made "within reasonable time" (and unless, of course, the parties are in agreement about the rectification).

Sometimes no written charter-party is drawn up. The parties instead base their relationship on the telex exchange or on a "recap", perhaps with an additional reference like "otherwise as per Gencon form", "otherwise as per C/P dated . . . for M/V XYZ" or similar. Such methods easily give rise to confusion and disputes. If the parties charter vessels to and from each other frequently they had better work out a *pro forma* charter-party and a fixture note form, which can be issued for each individual fixture.

MARITIME LIENS

A shipowner may have a lien on goods carried on board the vessel for charges like freight, deadfreight, demurrage, expenses for the cargo, general average contribution, etc. Liens on goods can be based on the general law, on express agreement in the charter-party or bill of lading or on both the general law and express agreement. Sometimes a claim against the owner will be connected with a lien on the vessel. Such a lien *may* remain on the ship if she is sold to another shipowner. In time and bareboat chartering owners, by agreement, often have a lien on the freight due under any underlying bill of lading or sub-charter-party. In order to find out the chances of exercising a lien in a relevant situation, not only the contracts (charter-party and bill of lading) but also the applicable laws (the law of the contract and the law in the relevant country) must be considered. For additional comments about liens we refer to the various sections where the question is discussed (see Index under "Lien").

ARREST OF VESSELS

Persons or companies who have claims against a shipowner sometimes arrest one of the shipowner's vessels in order to get payment or security for payment. The rules about arrest of vessels are very different, depending on applicable law (usually the law in the country where the arrestor intends to arrest the vessel). It is therefore essential both for the arrestor and the shipowner to appoint a local lawyer for legal advice and the handling of formalities.

As an example of the variations between countries a ship in some countries can be arrested only for claims secured by a maritime lien or a mortgage on the vessel. In other countries the ship can be arrested for any type of monetary claim. Sometimes the arrestor must produce evidence and security for his claim and in other cases a vessel can be arrested on very loose grounds and without security. Considering this, it goes without saying that we cannot give detailed recommendations to the parties in this respect. Generally we can, however, recommend a shipowner to act immediately when there is risk of arrest. He should consult his legal advisers, P. & I. club, bankers, etc., and prepare defence, arguments, securities, etc., to avoid delay to the vessel. The person or company who intends to arrest a vessel should also note that if it is sometimes very easy to do so and thereby get security, they risk a claim for the delay of the vessel if she has been arrested without justification.

GENERAL AVERAGE

The principle of general average can be described in the following way:

"There is a general average act, where any extraordinary sacrifice or expenditure is voluntarily and reasonably made or incurred in time of peril for the purpose of preserving the property imperilled in the common adventure."

As an example of general average we can mention the situation when deck cargo is jettisoned in order to correct a vessel's list and thereby save her,

her other cargo and freight. Another example is when a vessel in distress is saved.

Nearly all general averages are adjusted in accordance with the York-Antwerp Rules (last revised in 1990) and most charter-parties and bills of lading have a reference to these rules. Before the cargo is discharged from a vessel when general average is declared the cargo owners, other interests or their underwriters usually have to give "bonds", which guarantee their contribution to the forthcoming general average adjustment.

We cannot deal here with the complicated questions which arise in connection with a general average situation, but want to draw attention to the "Jason clause" ("New Jason clause" or "Amended Jason clause"), which is often found in contracts of carriage. This clause was drafted to avoid the consequences of a court case in the United States which held that a shipowner could not recover the cargo's proportion of general average arising out of negligent navigation or errors in management. It is, however, doubtful to what extent a Jason clause is valid.

The clause can have the following wording:

New Jason Clause.

In the event of accident, danger, damage or disaster before or after the commencement of the voyage, resulting from any cause whatsoever, whether due to negligence or not, for which, or for the consequence of which, the Carrier is not responsible, by statute, contract or otherwise, the goods, Shippers, Consignees or owners of the goods shall contribute with the Carrier in general average to the payment of any sacrifices, losses or expenses of a general average nature that may be made or incurred and shall pay salvage and special charges incurred in respect of the goods.

If a salving ship is owned or operated by the Carrier, salvage shall be paid for as fully as if the said salving ship or ships belonged to strangers. Such deposit as the Carrier or his agents may deem sufficient to cover the estimated contribution of the goods and any salvage and special charges thereon shall, if required, be made by the goods, Shippers, Consignees or owners of the goods to the Carrier before delivery.

COLLISION

Collision between ships or between a vessel and a quay, dolphin, shore crane or similar object can give rise to considerable loss or damage to the vessel, goods and other property. Very often delay is also caused and in some cases people are injured or killed. The rules about liabilities in connection with collisions are complicated and will not be discussed in this book. As many contracts of carriage contain a "Both to Blame Collision clause" we will, however, explain its background.

In the Collision Convention of 1910 it is stated that when two ships are to blame for a collision, the cargo in vessel A can recover its loss from vessel B in the same proportion as if B was to blame for the collision. If the contract of carriage exempts the owner of vessel A from liability for loss or damage to cargo when the loss or damage is caused by error in navigation (cf. page 65), the owner of cargo on board vessel A cannot get the remaining part from owner A. The Convention of 1910 has not been ratified by the United States and according to U.S. law the cargo in vessel A can recover the whole of its loss from vessel B, which in turn can get 50% of this loss back from vessel A, notwithstanding the fact that vessel A is exempted from liability for damage caused by nautical error.

The "Both to Blame Collision" clause was designed with the intention of achieving the same result under U.S. law as under the 1910 Convention. The clause has, however, been held by the U.S. Supreme Court to be void and cannot be enforced in the U.S.A. The clause can therefore only be invoked under very special circumstances outside the U.S.A.

The clause may have the following wording:

Both-to-Blame Collision Clause. (This clause to remain in effect even if unenforceable in the Courts of the United States of America.)
If the vessel comes into collision with another vessel as a result of the negligence of the other vessel and any act, negligence or default of the Master, Mariner, Pilot or the servants of the Carrier in the navigation or in the management of the vessel, the Merchant will indemnify the Carrier against all loss or liability to the other or non-carrying vessel or her Owner in so far as such loss or liability represents loss of or damage to or any claim whatsoever of the owner of the said goods paid or payable by the other or non-carrying vessel or her Owner to the owner of said cargo and set-off, or recouped or recovered by the other or non-carrying vessel or her Owner as part of his claim against the carrying vessel or Carrier. The foregoing provisions shall also apply where the Owner, operator or those in charge of any vessel or vessels or objects other than, or in addition to, the colliding vessels or objects are at fault in respect of a collision or contact.

TOWAGE AND SALVAGE

Although towage and salvage are outside the scope of this book, we will give a brief account of the subjects and how owners and charterers can be involved.

Towage

Ocean-going vessels very often have assistance from tugs on arrival and departure from ports. The vessel and the shipowner usually have little chance to influence the terms and conditions for such towage and consequently the terms of the towing contracts are, in the first place, protective of the tug owner and the crew. The owner of the vessel which receives assistance, usually called "the Tow", is, as regards liability in this respect, in most cases covered by the ordinary hull and P. & I. insurance.

In voyage chartering and liner traffic the contract is between the tug company and the owner of the tow. When the tow is on time charter or on bareboat charter, the time charterer or the bareboat charterer is the one who pays for the tug. Sometimes the time and bareboat charter-parties contain a clause saying that although tugs are ordered and paid for by the charterer, the contract with the tug company will be considered as a contract between him and the original owner of the vessel.

If a vessel has a breakdown during her voyage or in any other way is unable to proceed, a tug is sometimes employed for towing her to her final destination or to another port where the cargo can be discharged. It is not possible to give general recommendations on how the owner should act in such a situation. The nature of the cargo, costs and risks of towing, the voyage or time charter-party terms about freight and off-hire, respectively, the intended place for repairs, etc., must be considered. Usually, not only the vessel's owner and charterer but also the underwriters for the ship and cargo, cargo owners, etc., are involved in discussions about whether the ship shall be towed or not.

Many tug companies have their own forms as a base for a towage contract. Such private forms may contain standard conditions, as, for instance, "United Kingdom Standard Conditions for Towage and other Services". Sometimes the tug companies use standard forms, such as Scan-Tow Lump Sum or Scan-Tow Daily Hire, or similar.

As indicated by the code names Scan-Tow Lump Sum and Scan-Tow Daily Hire, the towage can be performed either on a lump sum basis or on the basis of a daily rate. The lump sum contract usually gives the owner of the tow a certain time at each port for connecting and disconnecting the tug. If this time is exceeded, the tug owner is entitled to demurrage. Usually he is also entitled to demurrage if the towage is delayed for necessary deviation. If the towing contract is made on the basis of a daily hire, this hire usually runs from when the tug sails from her station until she is again back on her station. The payment can be divided into several instalments, usually payable or deposited at an early stage of the towage. Brokerage commission, which is negotiated from case to case, is paid by the tug owner. Sometimes the owner of the tug is liable for all harbour dues, pilot costs, etc., and sometimes the tug owner and the shipowner pay their own costs in this respect. The shipowner should arrange a seaworthiness certificate for his vessel and necessary certificates for the towage. From case to case it is agreed whether the tow shall have her ordinary crew, only a skeleton crew, or if she will be towed as a dumb craft. It is also possible that the tug owner supplies a crew for the tow. It is usually expressly agreed that the tug owner cannot claim salvage for the tow but with the additional remark "unless circumstances arise outside the contemplation of this agreement". As regards salvage of other vessels, tug owners in most contracts reserve their rights to "interrupt the towage service and/or deviate for the purpose of saving life and/or property". Although the allocation of liabilities varies from contract to contract, the general solution is that the master and crew of the tug shall be considered as servants of the owner of the tow and that the latter is also liable for damage not only to the tug and the tow but also for claims by a third party. Considering the allocation of liabilities which is very burdensome for the shipowner, he should, in each case when he intends to have his vessel towed, consult his underwriters and arrange the necessary extra insurance.

Salvage

Masters and shipowners are sometimes, in accordance with international conventions, obliged to give assistance in the saving of life and/or property at sea. We have already mentioned (see above, page 65f.) that deviation for the purpose of saving life or property is not unlawful or contrary to the terms of the relevant contracts and that owners are not liable if the cargo is damaged as a result of such lawful deviation.

In the relationship between charterer and owner, the costs for salvage when the vessel is on voyage charter fall on the owner. Salvage money (the remuneration for the salvage operation), if any, goes to the shipowner for division between him and the crew. In time chartering the charter-parties usually contain a clause under which the salvage money is divided between the time charterer and the owner. Such a clause may have the following wording:

LINERTIME

21. Salvage
All salvage and assistance to other vessels to be for the Owners' and the Charterers' equal benefit after deducting the Master's and Crew's proportion and all legal and other expenses including hire paid under the Charter for time lost in the salvage, also repairs of damage and fuel consumed. The Charterers to be bound by all measures taken by the Owners in order to secure payment of salvage and to fix its amounts.

Usually, if no salvage money is payable, the costs for bunkers and for delay to the vessel fall on the time charterers. Damage to the vessel or other extra costs are for the account of the owners.

Nearly all salvage operations are conducted under "Lloyd's Open Form" (Lloyd's Standard Form of Salvage Agreement). This form is based on the principle of "no cure—no pay" which means that the salvor is entitled to salvage remuneration only if the salvage operation is successful (partially or totally). The salvage remuneration is normally agreed afterwards and often by arbitration. The salvors have a lien on the property salved (vessel, cargo, bunkers, freight) and the property must not, without the consent of the salvors, be removed from the place to which the salvors took it before the salvors have obtained sufficient security for their salvage claim. Such security is usually supplied by the respective underwriters.

The intention is that the salvage agreement should be signed by the masters of the salved and the salving vessels but the agreement can very well be signed by their principals and also accepted telegraphically or by telex. The salvage remuneration is finally fixed on the basis of the value of the salved property, the risks and difficulties involved in the salvage operation, and the skill and efforts shown by the salvors.

CHAPTER 12

THE VOYAGE CHARTER-PARTY*

We are now going over to the more specific Voyage Charter-Party clauses. The text in this chapter is to a certain extent based on the previous chapter ("Common Clauses and Concepts").

The most significant parts of the voyage charter-party are the description of the voyage and cargo, the allocation of duties and costs in connection with loading and discharging, the specification of the freight and the payment of the freight, the laytime rules, the allocation of the liability for the cargo and the allocation of other costs and risks. Depending on the circumstances, other questions and clauses can be very important in the negotiations between the owners and the charterers.

THE VESSEL

Description of the vessel

In those cases where the ship is nominated, the vessel's name and call sign, year of build, nationality, deadweight, gross and net tonnage and sometimes speed are stated in the charter-party. The need for the description of the vessel in the voyage charter-party very much depends on the circumstances. The type of cargo and the intended ports and seaways especially determine what details about the ship must be mentioned during the negotiations and in the charter-party.

The ship's draught, length, breadth and sometimes also the height over the waterline can be very important in narrow seaways and ports and in passage under bridges and hanging power-lines. Also, the equipment for cargo handling (winches, cranes, pumps, etc.) and the design and condition of the cargo compartments are often important for the vessel's fitness for the intended cargo. The number of hatches, type of hatch covering and length and breadth of hatch openings are important details when the charterers and the owners estimate the speed and cost for loading and discharging. Some cargoes need special equipment, such as reefer plant and CO_2 equipment.

* For a general introduction, see page 86ff.

178

In oil transportation the pumping capacity of the vessel has particular importance.

Both the owners and the charterers must, as far as possible, try to specify all those details about the cargo and the vessel that are necessary for economic calculation and practical planning of the loading, carrying and discharging of a cargo. If the cargo or the ship have some unusual or unexpected qualities, the other party should be made aware of these.

Specification of cargo capacity

The specification of the vessel's cargo capacity is important, and it can be described in several ways—the deadweight capacity and the cubic capacity are the most common. The deadweight capacity is the ship's weight carrying capacity, usually specified in long tons or metric tons. The deadweight capacity normally includes the vessel's capacity not only for cargo but also for fuel, fresh water and stores. To avoid mistakes and to make clear that fuel, etc., is also included it is common to add the words "all told" to the deadweight capacity figure.

Instead of deadweight capacity the cargo carrying capacity figure is sometimes used (see, for instance, the Gencon form). The difference between deadweight capacity and cargo carrying capacity is that the cargo carrying capacity does not include the capacity necessary for fuel, fresh water and stores. It must be noted that when the deadweight capacity is stated in the charter-party the owners are not free to bunker the vessel as they wish. Bunker quantity, as well as fresh water and stores, must be adjusted to the intended voyage (including, of course, necessary extras). If the vessel has unjustified high quantities on board and the charterers thereby cannot use the ship as intended, the owners might be held liable for damages against the charterers. These damages may include both reduction of freight and compensation for the charterers' extra costs to ship the cargo in another vessel. If the cargo is perishable, as for instance, bananas, the owners also risk liability for damage to the cargo as a result of short shipment. Both the deadweight capacity and the cargo carrying capacity must be related to a certain draught and a certain freeboard mark.

The vessel's cubic capacity is usually stated both in grain and in bale. The bale capacity is the volume available for boxes, cartons, etc. The grain capacity, which is always bigger than the bale capacity, includes also those parts of the cargo holds that can be filled with "floating" cargo, such as grain, phosphates, etc.

Both the deadweight capacity (or cargo carrying capacity) and the cubic capacity are usually stated in connection with the word "about". This word does not relieve the owners from their obligation to state the capacity as correctly as possible.

THE VOYAGE

Nomination of ports—rotation

The place for loading or discharging can be agreed in several ways, for instance:

A fixed berth, e.g., "berth 2 at Lagos".
A fixed port, e.g., "1 safe berth Sydney".
A fixed area, e.g., "1 safe port/1 safe berth Japan".
A port or an area for order, e.g., "US Gulf for order".
Several ports, e.g., "berth 2 at Lagos and 1 safe berth Casablanca".

If a port is to be nominated later, and thus is not fixed in the charter-party, it is advisable to state the latest time at which the charterers can nominate the port. Such a clause may have the following wording:

"Loading ports to be nominated by Charterers latest when the vessel is passing Gibraltar",

or

"Discharging port to be nominated by Charterers latest at commencement of loading".

Also, when no such clause is inserted into the charter-party the charterers should nominate the port or ports in such a good time in advance that no extra cost for waiting time and deviation is caused to the vessel. When the charter agreement contains several loading ports or discharging ports it is common that the owners try to introduce a clause saying that the ports shall be called "in geographical rotation". The intention is to avoid extra steaming time.

Unless otherwise expressly agreed or customary the charterers are entitled and have a duty to appoint a berth for the vessel.

The charterers cannot nominate *any* port or berth and the owners are not strictly obliged to follow the directions from the charterers. Most voyage charter-parties state that ports and berths shall be safe. The voyage charter-parties usually also contain an Ice clause and a Near clause.

Safe port, safe berth, always afloat, etc.

Most charter-parties state that the ports and berths nominated by the charterers shall be safe. The word "safe" in this context refers not only to factors such as high winds, heavy swell, insufficient or bad construction of quays, dolphins, etc., but also to other factors such as warlike operations and political disturbances (these last mentioned factors are often dealt with in special War clauses, cf. page 160).

A stipulation in the charter-party that charterers shall nominate safe ports and safe berths does not mean that the owners and the master can refrain from investigating the safety of the port and the berth. Neither are the charterers strictly liable for its safety. It is difficult to find the borderline between the respective parties' liability and the obligation to investigate and it is in most questionable cases impossible to establish beforehand whether a certain port or berth is safe or not.

As a general rule, it can be said that the earlier the owners and the master are informed about intended ports and berths, the more liability rests on them as regards investigation of the safety. This means that when the owners, during the negotiations, and in the charter-party, have accepted a certain port or a certain berth they have little chance of getting damages from the charterers if the port or the berth turns out to be unsafe. On the other hand, the charterers have little chance of escaping liability for damage to the ship when the port or berth has been nominated after the negotiations and the fixture. In the latter case, the owners and the master have had little or no chance to influence the choice of port or berth.

Another general rule is that where the master has agreed to call at a certain port or to moor at a certain berth it does not mean that the owners' right to claim damages from the charterers has been waived. The charterers' liability for safety remains also when the master has made an excusable wrong decision and called at a port which later turns out to be unsafe.

Disputes about safe ports and safe berths are very complicated, especially as regards production of evidence. The outcome of a dispute very much depends on by what law the charter agreement is governed. Apart from safety it is also common that the charter-parties contain a special statement saying that the ship shall always lie afloat. Sometimes the charterers are entitled to nominate a berth where the vessel can lie safely aground.

The Near clause

There is an obligation on the owners to take the vessel to the agreed loading or discharging place. In order to protect the owners against unforeseeable difficulties, a so-called Near clause is often inserted in the voyage charter-party. In Gencon this clause is part of clause 1, section 2 and reads (*inter alia*):

"The said vessel shall proceed to the loading port . . . or so near thereto as she may safely get and lie always afloat . . .".

There is a similar clause for the discharging port. The intention of the clause is to protect the owners against such hindrances that arise after the negotiation and the fixture. When such a hindrance arises the owners are not obliged to take the ship closer to the agreed place or port than she can safely get and lie always afloat. When judging whether a port is safe or unsafe there is in this situation a difference between those cases where the vessel, according to the charter-party, should go to a certain berth or port and those cases where the vessel is ordered to a certain range. In the first case there is an obligation on the owner to find out beforehand whether the ship can safely go to the port or the berth. In the latter case, it is the charterers' duty to make sure that they nominate ports and berths suitable for her.

The owners cannot usually rely on the Near clause where there is a possibility of reaching the port or the berth via another route even if this means extra costs for the owners (cf. the comment about Frustration on page 154).

The Ice clause

In some trades and at times of the year where there is risk of ice, the charter-party must contain an Ice clause.

Under the subsection "Vessel's trading limits", page 155, we have mentioned that hull underwriters issue special trading limits based on ice and weather conditions in certain areas. It goes without saying that the owners cannot accept ports or trading outside these limits and also when there is a possibility of breaking the trading limits against extra insurance the owners should be careful. Under all circumstances the owners must insist on having a sufficient Ice clause when there is any risk of ice on the intended voyage. The Near clause gives the owners some, but far from sufficient, protection in this respect.

Questions that must be dealt with in the Ice clause are, for instance:

—Are the owners obliged to let the vessel break ice or follow an ice-breaker?
—What possibilities have the owners to refuse a certain port or area, or to order the ship to leave before loading or discharging is completed, when there is a risk of the vessel being frozen in?
—Are the owners entitled to full, or only reduced, freight when the vessel has to leave the loading port with a part cargo only?
—Who shall decide what to do with the cargo on board when it is impossible to reach the originally intended discharging port?
—Who shall pay for delay caused to the ship as a result of ice or ice risk at the loading port, sea voyage or discharging port?
—Who shall pay for extra insurance on the vessel and damage caused to the ship by ice?

All these and other questions are important when there is a risk of ice. It should also be noted that delay of the ship by reason of cold weather can be dealt with in the Laytime clauses and the parties must see to it that these clauses are not contradictory to the Ice clause.

In the Gencon form there is a printed Ice clause called General Ice clause (17). From the owners' point of view BIMCO's clause Nordice is, however, better than the General Ice clause.

The sea voyage

Sometimes the charter-party expressly states what route the vessel shall take, for instance "Sydney to Lisbon via Cape of Good Hope". With such a clause the owners or the master cannot go via the Suez Canal. Without such or a similar clause concerning the route the master will choose the usual route or one of the usual routes. In both cases the master has the right to make such alterations of route or deviations as he deems advisable for the safety of the crew, vessel and cargo. As a general rule it can be said—and this is also an implied term of the contract—that the master shall carry out the voyage with the utmost despatch.

Deviation

The word deviation basically embraces only geographical deviation. It must, however, be remembered that the concept of deviation also contains deviation other than geographical. As examples of non-geographical deviation stoppage, steaming with reduced speed and unusual handling of the cargo may be mentioned. It is difficult to give a precise definition of deviation.

As mentioned in connection with the Hague Rules (page 62ff.) the distinction between lawful deviation and unlawful deviation is important. The borderline between these two concepts is not always so easy to find. Generally, it can be said that deviation for the purpose of avoiding danger to crew, vessel and cargo and deviation for the purpose of saving life or property are lawful deviations. Naturally, the deviation must be reasonable and when judging whether the deviation is reasonable not only the interests of the owners, but also the interests of the charterers, must be considered.

Most voyage charter-party forms contain a printed Deviation clause. Sometimes this clause is called Scope of Voyage clause which is the frequent expression used in bills of lading. The Deviation clause in Gencon has the following wording:

GENCON
Deviation Clause
The vessel has liberty to call at any port or ports in any order, for any purpose, to sail without pilots, to tow and/or assist vessels in all situations, and also to deviate for the purpose of saving life and/or property.

The Deviation clauses are usually interpreted to the benefit of the charterers (or cargo owners) and if an owner really wishes to safeguard his rights to deviate for a certain reason he must specify this, as clearly as possible, during the negotiations and in the charter agreement. During the past few years, when bunker prices have risen and when it has sometimes been difficult to get bunkers, special Bunker Deviation clauses have become common. These clauses give owners the right not only to deviate for the purpose of getting bunkers, but also usually expressly state that the owners have the right to order the ship to proceed at reduced speed in order to get a lower bunker consumption. It should also be noted that re-routing for the changing of crew is often regarded as unlawful deviation (see also page 65f. above).

Unlawful deviation is a breach of contract and the charterers may be entitled to damages as well as to cancel the charter agreement, in some cases. A shipowner should consider arranging *S.C. deviation insurance* if he is not sure that a planned deviation is a lawful deviation.

THE CARGO

Type and specification

The description of the cargo is important for several reasons. Owners who, during the negotiations and in the fixture, accepted a certain cargo are also obliged to carry out the transportation of the cargo. This means that the owners have to get all necessary details of the cargo from the charterers or from someone else, in order to be able to find out whether the cargo is suitable for the vessel and to be able to estimate the costs of handling and transportation.

Exactly what details about the cargo need to be specified during the negotiations and in the written agreement depends on the type of cargo. Some commodities are so well known to the parties that only a very short specification has to be given. In other cases it may be necessary to give a detailed declaration about the physical and chemical specifications of the cargo and also to give specified instructions for its handling and transportation.

If the cargo delivered to the vessel is not in accordance with its description the owners might be entitled to compensation and, in some cases, when the cargo delivered differs on essential points from the previous description, the owners may also be entitled to cancel the agreement and to claim compensation for loss of freight.

It is especially necessary when the cargo is described in terms such as "general cargo" to insert special clauses about dangerous goods. In such a "Dangerous Cargo clause" the owners usually limit their obligations to carry dangerous cargo and also state that the charterers are under an obligation to give all essential details of the cargo to the owners well in advance of loading.

When it comes to the transportation of oil products the carrier must be aware of the difficulties connected with cargo handling, problems occurring in connection with loading/discharging and he must also be familiar with measures which need to be taken to prevent fire and explosion as well as damage to tanks and their coatings, and pipelines. This may be particularly complicated with regard to chemical products, but also to some extent in relation to the crude oil trade. Crude oil may be dangerous when it is *spiked* with naphtha to ease the flow. Some kinds of crude oil are sulphurous and corrosive, others have a waxy deposit. In low ambient temperatures the question may be whether the *heating coils* in the tanks are effective enough and whether a considerable amount of bunker fuel will have to be spent in maintaining or increasing the temperature. This may create problems both as to the ongoing voyage and subsequent trading of the vessel.

A particular problem relates to the heating of cargo, i.e. whether the owner has an obligation to raise the cargo temperature. Shellvoy 5, clause 27, is based on a "best endeavours" principle in this respect. Suffice it here to make the parties aware of the problems that may occur in this connection, particularly cost and time problems.

Cargo quantity

It is important both for the charterers and for the owners that the cargo quantity is specified. The freight is often calculated on the cargo quantity and the owners must therefore make certain that at least a minimum quantity is stated in the charter-party. For the charterers, the specification of the cargo quantity in the charter-party is important as the owners' acceptance of the quantity also means that the charterers have a chance to claim damages if the owners fail to load the accepted quantity.

The cargo quantity can be fixed in several ways. Many charter agreements state that the charterers shall furnish the ship with "a full and complete cargo". This means that the charterers are obliged to load as much cargo as the vessel can carry, i.e. the vessel's deadweight capacity is fully used when it is a heavy cargo and the cubic capacity is fully utilized when it is a light cargo.

Other ways to state the cargo quantity are "x tons", "about x tons", "between x and y tons", "between about x and about y tons", "not less than x tons", etc. The word "about" gives a flexibility that varies depending on the type and quantity of the cargo and the trade (5% is often regarded as a recognized variation figure). If the charter-party prescribes a specific variation it should also state in whose interest there is such flexibility, for instance "in owners' options", "in master's option", "in charterers' option", etc. If, for some reason, it is important that certain limits must not be exceeded or underdrawn this should be clearly stated and a special note should be served to the master and to the agents.

When quantities are stated during the negotiations, in the charter agreement and in instructions, the type of ton referred to should always be explicitly mentioned. It is thus not sufficient to say, for instance, 5,000 tons. It must also be stated what kind of tons are meant ("metric tons, long tons, etc.). This can also be important when the stowage factor (the number of cubic feet a ton will occupy in stowage) is used, as the stowage factor is sometimes based on long tons and sometimes on metric tons.

THE FREIGHT

Definition

In the well-known legal work *Scrutton on Charterparties and Bills of Lading* freight is defined in a very precise way as "the reward payable to the carrier for the carriage and arrival of the goods in a merchantable condition, ready to be delivered to the merchant".

Fixing of the freight

The freight can be fixed in several different ways. One way is to base it on the cargo quantity, for instance "X $/metric ton" or "X $/ctn" (ctn=carton). Another way is to fix the freight at a certain amount independent of the cargo quantity. This is usually called "lump sum freight". A variation on the lump sum freight is to base the freight on the size of the vessel, for instance "X $/deadweight ton". This solution is used especially in connection with contracts of affreightment where the voyages are performed by different ships often not known when the contract is fixed. In oil transportation the particular World Scale (WS) system has already been referred to above at page 114.

When the freight is based on a certain amount "per ton" it is also important to make clear what kind of ton is meant (long ton, metric ton, etc.).

Sometimes there are disputes about the question whether the freight should be based on intaken or delivered quantity or if it should be based on the gross or the net weight of a cargo. Concerning the latter problem, it is usually said that the freight will be based on the gross weight unless otherwise agreed or customary in the trade. As regards the first question, the basic rule under English law is that the freight is payable only on so much cargo as has been both shipped, carried and delivered and this means that the smallest of the two quantities is the base for the calculation of freight. Both these questions are often expressly dealt with in the charter-parties. In this connection reference should again be made to cargo retention clauses (see below at page 208).

When is the freight earned and payable? Freight risk

The principal rule is that the freight is earned when the owners have fulfilled their obligation to carry the cargo and are ready to deliver it to the receiver. Thus the master should, figuratively speaking, deliver the cargo with one hand at the same time as he collects the freight with the other. This means that if, for some reason, the owners cannot deliver the cargo they are not entitled to freight. The freight risk, i.e. the risk that the owners, fully or partly, fail to fulfil their obligation to carry the cargo, and thereby lose their right to collect freight, thus lies with the owners. Should the vessel sink and, together with the cargo, be a total loss, the owner is not entitled to freight even if the vessel has almost reached her destination. In some legal systems the owner will under such circumstances be entitled to a so-called distance freight, proportionate to the distance actually carried as compared with the total distance.

If only part of the cargo is delivered at the port of destination (short delivery, shortage) the owners are, according to this rule, only entitled to proportionate freight for the cargo actually delivered. If the cargo reaches the port or place of destination in a damaged condition the owners are entitled to freight only if the cargo is "in a merchantable condition" and if it is still the same kind of cargo. In connection with a shipment of cars, for instance, the owners are entitled to freight for damaged cars only if the cars can still be considered as cars, and not as scrap metal, and if the damaged cars have some value.

The owners' right to collect freight must not be mixed with their obligation to pay compensation for the damaged cargo (dealt with in separate sections, pages 64ff. and 206f.). Note also that the charterers have basically no right to deduct counterclaims for damaged cargo or other counterclaims from the freight. According to English law freight is normally payable in full even if the charterers have a justified counterclaim against the owner. Tanker voyage charter-parties, however, often allow for deductions against the freight.

If a lump sum freight is agreed the owners are entitled to full freight if some part of the cargo reaches the port or place of destination. If all cargo is lost the owners are not, according to the above-described principle, entitled to freight. If the cargo is delivered at the wrong place the owners are not, according to English law, entitled to freight. In order to collect freight the owners must arrange transportation from the discharging port to the correct port or place of destination agreed.

The rules about when the freight is earned and payable are often modified in charter agreements. Clauses like "Freight Earned and Payable upon Shipment, Ship and/or Cargo Lost or not Lost" (see also page 89) are frequently found in voyage charter-parties and mean that the owners are entitled to freight at the loading port and the freight is not repayable if part of the cargo, or the whole cargo and the vessel, does not reach the destination. When the freight risk lies with the owners they can take out a special freight risk insurance which covers the situation where the cargo is lost during the transportation. Note that this insurance does not protect the owners against insolvent charterers.

Deadfreight

When the charterers fail to deliver the agreed quantity of cargo to the vessel, the owners will normally be entitled to compensation for their loss of freight. This compensation is called "deadfreight" and is calculated by deducting what is saved in costs from the freight that should be paid for that part of the cargo which has not been delivered.

In order to secure the payment for the deadfreight claim the owners (or the master) must arrange the following:

—They must get a declaration from the charterers that no further cargo will be delivered to the vessel. It is not sufficient to get this declaration from the shippers only as the charterers may say later that they could have arranged additional cargo if they had been contacted before the vessel sailed.

—The vessel's additional capacity, both in cubic or in deadweight, must be established before commencement of discharging. This can be done, for instance, by an independent surveyor.

—Finally, in order to safeguard the possibility of exercising a lien over the cargo against the receiver, a remark concerning the short shipment which establishes the owners' claim for deadfreight should be inserted into the bills of lading (cf. security for payment of freight, page 189 below).

Another difficult question is to find out when the owners are entitled to let the vessel sail from the loading port if they fail to get a declaration from the charterers that no more cargo is available, or when the charterers say that additional cargo will come but nothing happens. As long as the owners get sufficient compensation in the form of an acceptable demurrage paid day by day, week by week or on a similar basis, the problem is perhaps not so bad. The situation is worse when the demurrage rate is low, demurrage is not payable until after the voyage and when owners fear that the charterers are insolvent or unwilling to pay. The questions and problems in connection with such situations are difficult and the owners should be careful and take legal advice before they order the vessel to leave the port.

Payment of freight

Payment of the freight may not necessarily take place at the same stage as when the freight is considered earned. It is thus possible and not unusual that the voyage charter-parties contain a clause "Freight earned upon shipment . . ." in combination with "Freight payable before commencement of discharging" (or "before breaking bulk"). Sometimes the charterers and the shippers wish to have the bills of lading marked "Freight prepaid". In such cases the owners must see to it that the freight is payable and that they get the freight before the bills of lading are issued and delivered to the shippers.

The procedure for payment should also be specified in the charter-party. Currency (cf. page 165), mode and place of payment, name of bank and number of bank account, etc., are usually stated in the Payment clause. As the costs of transferring freight are sometimes quite large they should also be allocated in the charter-party. Shellvoy 5 allows for 14 days payment of freight, which in our view is far too long.

A problem which can cause serious trouble is that some countries have restrictions on payment abroad. In some countries, particularly in connection with demurrage, it is practically impossible to arrange a remittance to another country and a careful owner should investigate these questions before he finally accepts the fixture.

In tanker charter-parties regard should also be given to residues and possible freight payable in that connection. For example, Shellvoy 5 contains some reference to this point.

Brokerage

When brokers have been involved they are entitled to commission. The brokerage is usually a certain percentage of the freight (cf. page 36f.). Brokers are not entitled to "commission" on demurrage and damage for detention unless this is expressly stated in the charter-party or otherwise agreed. Usually the brokers try to get "commission" on demurrage and damage for detention and often the printed charter-party forms also entitle the brokers to some compensation if the charter agreement is cancelled or otherwise terminated beforehand. In Gencon the Brokerage clause has the following wording:

GENCON

Brokerage
A brokerage commission at the rate stated in Box 20 on the freight earned is due to the party mentioned in Box 20.
In case of non-execution at least $\frac{1}{3}$ of the brokerage on the estimated amount of freight and dead-freight to be paid by the Owners to the Brokers as indemnity for the latter's expenses and work. In case of more voyages the amount of indemnity to be mutually agreed.

Security for payment of freight

As mentioned in the section on "Maritime Liens" (Chapter 11, page 171) the owners usually have a legal and/or a contractual lien over the cargo as security for the payment of freight. As regards such claims and such freights which are due for payment but not paid before the bills of lading are issued, the owners and the master must see to it that a remark concerning a claim for non-paid freight is made in the bills of lading. Without such a remark the owners have no possibility of exercising a lien over the cargo as security for claims and payments accruing or due for payment before the issuing of bills of lading. Sometimes the owner succeeds in securing freight payment by way of irrevocable letter of credit (cf. above, at page 50), which often gives the owner a fair security but at the same time complicates the negotiations.

LOADING AND DISCHARGING

Allocation of costs

The task of arranging and the costs for loading and discharging may be allocated in different ways. The following clause is from the Gencon form:

GENCON

5. Loading Discharging Costs
(a) Gross Terms
The cargo to be brought alongside in such a manner as to enable vessel to take the

goods with her own tackle. Charterers to procure and pay the necessary men on shore or on board the lighters to do the work there, vessel only heaving the cargo on board. If the loading takes place by elevator, cargo to be put free in vessel's holds. Owners only paying trimming expenses.

Any pieces and/or packages of cargo over two tons weight, shall be loaded, stowed and discharged by Charterers at their risk and expense. The cargo to be received by Merchants at their risk and expense alongside the vessel not beyond the reach of her tackle.

(b) F.i.o. and free stowed/trimmed

The cargo shall be brought into the holds, loaded, stowed and/or trimmed and taken from the holds and discharged by the Charterers or their Agents, free of any risk, liability and expense whatsoever to the Owners.

The Owners shall provide winches, motive power and winchmen from the Crew if requested and permitted; if not, the Charterers shall provide and pay for winchmen from shore and/or cranes, if any. (This provision shall not apply if vessel is gearless and stated as such in Box 15.)

indicate alternative (a) or (b), as agreed, in Box 15.

According to the first alternative, called gross terms in Gencon, the borderline at loading is when the cargo is delivered alongside the vessel at a place where the vessel can reach the goods with her own tackle. At discharging the borderline is when the vessel delivers the cargo alongside but not beyond the reach of her tackle. This alternative can also be described as "from hook to hook" and the intention is that the owners shall arrange and pay for all work within the "hook to hook" period.

The gross term alternative is the one commonly stated in the liner bills of lading and is also sometimes called "Liner terms". The expression "Liner terms" is, however, not very precise and should be avoided. The true definition of "Liner terms" originally was that the cargo should be loaded and discharged on the same terms and conditions as were used by liner vessels for the same kind of cargo in the same ports and berths. As the terms and conditions used by the liner vessels can be difficult to find out and define and as they can also vary within one port, both parties must be sure that they know what the expression means for the intended voyage before they use it in negotiations and in a charter-party. Concerning "Liner terms" compare also the sections on the owners' liability for cargo on page 64ff. and the section about time counting on page 198.

In the other alternatives (f.i.o.s. and f.i.o.s.t.) the main part of the planning and the costs lies on the charterers. They should not only deliver the cargo to the vessel but also load and sometimes stow and trim it. At the discharging port all arrangements are similarly the responsibility of the charterers. According to the cited Gencon clause, the owners should only provide winches and power. It is also said that the owners should provide winchmen, but as this nowadays is quite unusual that part of the clause is often deleted.

As the costs for handling the cargo at loading and discharging ports are often an important part of the total costs for the voyage, both parties should, during the negotiations, carefully investigate what costs will be involved in the intended voyage. It is, of course, also important that the clauses dealing with loading and discharging make sufficiently clear the allocation of costs, duties and liabilities.

Securing and lashing of cargo

The way the stowing, lashing and securing of the cargo is performed is important for the safe carrying of the cargo and for the vessel's seaworthiness. The owners usually have some responsibility for the cargo and they are always to a certain degree liable for the seaworthiness of the vessel. Also, in those cases where the charterers, according to the charter-party, should arrange for and pay everything in connection with loading, stowing, trimming, lashing, securing and discharging of the cargo, the master must see to it that the cargo is properly handled and that the loading, securing, etc., is performed in a way that does not endanger the crew, the vessel and the cargo during the voyage. The master has not only a right, but also an obligation, to intervene when the cargo is loaded, secured, etc., in an unacceptable way with regard to the safety of the crew, vessel and cargo.

LAYTIME

In voyage chartering the financial risk of delay during the sea voyage normally rests with the owners. The risk of delay during a vessel's periods in port can be shared in different ways between the owners and the charterers.

A great many of all the discussions and disputes that arise out of voyage charter agreements are connected with the calculation of laytime. Many of the problems could have been avoided if the laytime clauses had been worded more distinctly. Unfortunately, the printed clauses in the standard forms are also worded in a hazy way and therefore the well-known printed standard forms must often be amended to get a clear picture of how laytime should be calculated.

The fundamental idea is that the charterers, without extra payment to the owners, have a certain time, "allowed time", to spend for the loading and/or discharging of the vessel. If this time is exceeded they must pay compensation—demurrage—at a rate agreed beforehand to the owners for their loss of time. Sometimes it is also agreed that the owners will compensate the charterers if the ship is loaded and/or discharged before the agreed time expires. This situation and this compensation is called "despatch".

The most common mistake when drafting the laytime calculation is to mix the various rules or groups of rules. When the Laytime clauses are worded and when the calculation is made, a step-by-step method must be used as it is important not to mix, for instance, the rules dealing with notice time and the rules dealing with the laytime itself.

Some of the items which are important for the calculation of laytime may be connected with a number of questions, such as:

(1) At what point will time start to count? Will laytime start, or if once started will it be suspended, if the berth is inaccessible? Until when does time run?

(2) How is congestion in the port treated?

(3) How is time lost due to adverse weather, storms or swell to be treated on and off the berth?

(4) Does "all time used for charterers' purposes" count for laytime and demurrage?

(5) How is delay after disconnection of hoses to be handled when tanker operation is involved?

(6) In transhipment at sea are any delays other than those due to owners' or vessel fault excluded?

(7) What is the effect of non-compliance with any of the owner's obligations? Some forms provide that consequential loss of time if the vessel is ordered off the berth, etc., is for owner's account.

(8) Ballasting and deballasting time should logically be excluded from laytime only to the extent that they delay cargo operations.

(9) How is shifting time in a port to be treated? Who pays for delays on port authority orders?

(10) What events give rise to half rate demurrage? Are they, for example, limited to those occurring without fault on either side? Are these exception clauses applicable with respect to laytime and demurrage provisions?

Arrived ship

As the risk of delay during the sea voyage rests with the owners while the risk of delay when the vessel is in port is shared between the owners and charterers, it is important to be able to establish when the sea voyage is at an end and the system of rules applying to the ship's stay in port takes over.

The vessel must reach the agreed destination before she can be considered as an arrived ship. Consequently the more precisely the destination is described the more is needed before the vessel has arrived. It is thus better for the owners to have the destination described as "the said vessel shall proceed to X town" than the destination described as "the said vessel shall proceed to berth 2 at the free port of X town". In the first example it is a so-called "Port Charter-Party" and in the latter a "Berth Charter-Party". The borderline between these two concepts is sometimes difficult to find.

Also in connection with port charter-parties, the owners might very well find difficulties in getting the laytime running because under English law—after several contradictory cases and after many years of discussions—it is still required that the ship must be within the port area before she can be treated as an "arrived ship". It does not make it easier that it is also often difficult to find out what is meant by the port area.

The best way for the owners to protect themselves is to insert a special "waiting for berth" clause or to have the words "whether in berth/port or not" (w.i.b.p.o.n.) inserted in the Laytime clause to make it clear that the time can count when the vessel is at the customary or indicated waiting place. Such clauses also allow time to count when the ship is not an arrived ship with relation to the destination as described in the charter-party.

The question whether the berth is reachable on vessel's arrival has been much discussed in connection with voyage tanker charters for a number of years.

To be "reachable on arrival" a berth must be both available and accessible.

Clause 9 of Asbatankvoy requires the charterer to designate a berth "reachable on arrival". The House of Lords has decided that this is a condition precedent, so that the final sentence of Clause 6 only comes into operation if the charterers have designated a safe place which is reachable on arrival (*The Laura Prima* [1982] 1 Lloyd's Rep. 1). As a consequence, the provision in Clause 6 regarding delay after giving Notice of Readiness will only protect the charterers if they have complied with Clause 9.

The broad protection which charterers often claimed under Clause 6 thus now only applies if a berth nominated is reachable on arrival and delay is then caused by an intervening event outside charterers' control and occurring after the vessel has given Notice of Readiness. Also with respect to causes within owner's areas of risk such as tide or fog, the *Laura Prima* decision seems to apply (*The Fjordaas* [1988] 1 Lloyd's Rep. 336; *The Sea Queen* [1988] 1 Lloyd's Rep. 500).

Notices, notice time and readiness

When the vessel has arrived the master usually gives a Notice of Readiness and quite often the charterers are entitled to notice time (free time, grace time) before the laytime starts to run. The original intention with the notice time was that the charterer, or the shipper/receiver, after they had been made aware of the ship's arrival and readiness, should be allowed a certain time to arrange loading or discharging. Today, when ships are equipped with radio and sometimes also telex and telefax, and when the owners in most cases are in constant contact with the charterers, there is no practical reason for such notice time. Most printed voyage charter-party forms, however, still entitle the charterers to notice time. In the Gencon form the clause is worded (part of Clause 6):

GENCON

(c) Commencement of laytime (loading and discharging)
Laytime for loading and discharging shall commence at 1 p.m. if notice of readiness is given before noon, and at 6 a.m. next working day if notice is given during office hours after noon. Notice at loading port to be given to the Shippers named in Box 17.

Time actually used before commencement of laytime shall count.
Time lost in waiting for berth to count as loading or discharging time, as the case may be.

Although the system providing for notice time is obsolete today there is a situation in which a special solution for the time immediately after the vessel's arrival may be justified. If she arrives during a holiday period or during the night, the charterers perhaps have no practical chance of commencing the loading or the discharging. In other words, there is a risk that she will be idle from the time of arrival until the commencement of ordinary working hours in the relevant port. If the parties agree that this risk shall rest with the owners, they can insert a clause of the following type in the charter-party:

"Laytime to commence at the beginning of next ordinary working shift after vessel's arrival."

It is, of course, also possible to put this risk on the charterers or to have the risk shared between the two parties by saying that only half such time shall count as laytime.

Readiness includes both physical readiness and legal readiness. Physical readiness means that the vessel shall be clean and ready to take on board the intended cargo or to discharge the cargo on board. Legal readiness means that the ship shall be clear of the formalities (Customs clearance, etc.) necessary for the commencement of loading or discharging. The vessel need not necessarily be in all respects physically and legally ready to be able to give a valid notice of readiness. Depending on the circumstances the charterers must accept that the notice time starts to run although some preparations on board remain to be done (for instance, the uncovering of hatches and rigging) or some formalities remain to be dealt with (for instance, "free pratique" as required by the Health Authorities). If tanks are to be inspected by or on behalf of charterers for cleanliness, there is need for provisions related to consequences of time lost (e.g. Exxonvoy 90, lines 48/49).

Unless otherwise expressly agreed, the notice can be delivered orally, telegraphically or by a written message. In order to avoid difficulties and discussions the oral notice should, however, be avoided.

The notice of readiness should be delivered as soon as the ship is ready to commence loading or discharging. This means also that if the vessel is ordered to wait outside the berth or port, notice should be delivered. If the charter-party states that the notice must be given within office hours, a notice given after office hours will not be valid and will not come into force until the next period of office hours. Office hours are generally understood to mean ordinary office hours in the relevant port and the charterers cannot, by closing their office, postpone the notice time and thereby the counting of the laytime.

Notices of readiness and the so-called Statements of Facts usually state both when a notice has been delivered and when it has been accepted. It should be noted that if the notice of readiness is correct the charterers cannot postpone the running of notice time and laytime by refusing to accept it.

Once the notice time has started to run, it runs, unless otherwise expressly agreed, notwithstanding any exceptions in the Laytime clause. The notice time can thus normally be counted during a Sunday or holiday even though these days are excluded from laytime under "the Laytime clause". In many cases the relevant clause will take this problem into consideration.

When the loading or the discharging commences before the notice time expires the owners are, according to English law, not entitled to count time unless this is agreed in the charter-party. Such a clause can have the following wording: "Time actually used before commencement of laytime shall count."

The word "Lay" in the expression "Lay/Can" is, as mentioned above (page 158), a short form of "laytime not to commence before". This does not prevent the master from giving a valid notice of readiness before the layday, and notice time can also run before the layday. Thus if the notice of readiness is given and the notice time expires before the layday, the counting of laytime normally starts at midnight on the layday.

According to English law the notice of readiness must be given at the first loading port even if this is not expressly stated in the charter-party. At the subsequent loading ports and in the discharging ports (also in the first discharging port) a notice of readiness *must* be given only if such has been expressly agreed.

Notwithstanding this, notice of readiness should always be given. This, however, does not mean that the owners should give the charterers notice time simply because a notice of readiness has been given. The charterers are entitled to notice time only if such is agreed or if it follows by custom or by the governing law. English law does not entitle the charterers to notice time. German and Scandinavian law, for example, do.

Time allowed

The time allowed is usually fixed in the charter-party, either by a number of days or hours or by a rate per day. Instead of fixing the time allowed the parties sometimes use clauses like "vessel to be loaded and discharged as fast as vessel can receive and deliver" or similar. Such clauses are sometimes called f.a.c. clauses (fast as can) and problems may often arise when the parties try to determine the precise meaning of such a clause in a particular case.

Fixed time

The length of the time allowed can be agreed as a fixed number of days, for instance:

"Five running days allowed for loading."

Another method is to state a daily rate or a rate per day and hatch, e.g.,

"loading at a rate of 500 metric tons per day",

or,

"loading at a rate of 125 metric tons per day and hatch".

In connection with rate per day and hatch various phrases are used. "Workable hatch" and "available hatch" indicates that only the hatches actually used shall count and the total time allowed is usually calculated by dividing the quantity in the largest hatch with the daily rate per workable or available hatch. This method is less favourable to the owners than the method when only the word "hatch", not connected with the words "available" or "workable", is used. In the latter case the total time allowed is calculated by dividing the total quantity loaded on board a vessel with the product of the number of hatches and the daily rate. In the tanker trade the laytime is often counted until the disconnection of hoses, or until the delivery of the necessary documents.

Especially in contracts of affreightment it is not unusual that the time allowed is connected to a fixed capacity figure for the size of the vessel and that the time allowed varies with larger and smaller ships, for example:

"Five running days allowed for loading based on vessel's cubic capacity 500,000 cb. ft. Time allowed to be adjusted *pro rata* for larger or smaller vessels."

Time not fixed

Clauses like:

"Liner terms with customary quick despatch",

or,

"as fast as the vessel can receive (deliver)"

are not beneficial to the owners. It is difficult to prove that the charterers have loaded or discharged the ship so slowly that the owners are entitled to demurrage.

For the owners it is important to have the f.a.c. clause connected with the capability of *the vessel* as in the second of the two cited clauses. If the f.a.c. clause, like the first clause, is *not* connected with the capability of the vessel, the owners have very little chance to get compensation for delay beyond the control of the charterers (for instance, lack of wagons or traffic problems ashore). Some charter-parties also contain far-reaching *force majeure* clauses.

Also a problem for the owners is the fact that the charterers (shippers and receivers) who have entered into a charter agreement with an f.a.c. clause normally calculate that the owners will claim demurrage. This "psychological "difficulty", together with the judicial difficulties, make it problematical whether the owners will collect the demurrage they are entitled to.

Reversible time

Unless otherwise agreed, the calculations for demurrage/despatch are drawn up separately for loading and discharging. If more than one loading port or discharging port is involved only one calculation is, however, made for the loading ports together and one for the discharging ports together.

The main principle of separate calculations for loading and discharging is often set aside by special agreement in the charter-party. This can be done by using, for instance, the following wording:

"Time allowed for loading and discharging, eight days altogether";

or,

"time allowed, eight days all purposes".

Sometimes also the words "reversible" or "average" are used, as, for instance:

"Three days for loading and five for discharging, loading and discharging times to be reversible";

or,

"three days for loading, five for discharging. Charterers have the right to average loading and discharging times".

In the first case (reversible time) the times are added to a total time for loading and discharging. What is left from the total time after the loading will be "allowed time" for discharging. If all the time is used for loading, the vessel is on demurrage on arrival at the discharging port and the time will then count immediately. (Note that also in this case notice of readiness should be delivered in order to avoid disputes, although a notice of readiness is not necessary.)

In the second example (average) the loading and discharging calculations are drawn up separately. Thereafter, the demurrage and despatch *times* are added or set off (averaged) against each other and finally the demurrage or despatch amount is calculated on the result.

The result will often be the same whether the reversible time system or the average system is used. As, however, the rule "once on demurrage, always on demurrage" (see page 199) may cause considerable financial difference between the two systems, it is important to be aware of the difference. The clauses are often constructed as optional in the charterers' choice, for instance: Laytime for loading and laytime for discharging to be reversible in charterers' option.

In such cases the owners will always lose as the charterers will calculate both separately for loading and discharging and also with the reversible time system and thereafter use the system which gives the best outcome.

Crude oil washing (COW) and disposal of residues

Crude oil washing will normally be required in accordance with Marpol requirements (International Convention for the prevention of pollution from ships, 1973 and its 1978 Protocol (Marpol), and sometimes charterers will have further demands. The COW requirements may also have laytime effect.

To comply with the requirements of Marpol, oil residues must be retained on board and not discharged to the sea. All modern tanker charters contain clauses which, in broad terms, have the effect of giving the charterer the right to dispose of residues, compensating the owner for any loss of freight caused by their segregation and retention. Many charterers are willing to take delivery of residue oil, and to pay freight on it, but incompatible residues are sometimes refused by shore installations. Only Asbatankvoy obliges charterer always to arrange for residues to be pumped ashore.

A disposal of residue clause should take into consideration a number of points, such as how to deal with residues when there are two or more charterers, and how to deal with the situation when the loading port does not have any facility, etc?

Time counting and exceptions

When all the prerequisites which are necessary in order that laytime starts to run have been met it will start to count. The principal rule is that once laytime has started to run, it runs seven days per week, 24 hours per day, notwithstanding hindrances and interruption of the loading or the discharging.

In some ports the loading and discharging take place 24 hours per day seven days a week but more often the vessel is loaded or discharged only in one or two shifts during weekdays with interruption during nights and holidays. Loading and discharging may also be interrupted if cargo is not available, if the receiver cannot take delivery as fast as the ship can deliver, if the weather is too bad, if the loading or the discharging equipment breaks down, or if strikes or go-slows occur, etc.

According to English law these and other disturbances only interrupt the time counting if this is expressly agreed in the charter-party. The most common exceptions in the Laytime clauses are exceptions for holidays and bad weather. Many clauses and wordings are used and it is important both for charterers and owners to be aware of the meaning of the expressions used.

When the parties agree that time shall not count during Sundays and holidays (see above, page 100) the expression "Sundays and holidays excluded" (SHEX) will normally be used. To clarify that Sundays and holidays *shall* count the expression "Sundays and holidays included" (SHINC) is sometimes used. Variations of these expressions are used in countries where Sundays are not the weekly day of rest. For instance SHEX and SHINC will be FHEX and FHINC in those Arabian countries where Friday is the weekly day of rest. It is also common that a so-called "Saturday clause" is linked to the SHEX clause. In a Saturday clause time on Saturday and sometimes also on Friday and Monday is excepted from time counting. The expression "unless used, but only time actually used to count" is often used in conjunction with SHEX. The effect is that if loading or discharging, for instance, takes place from 08 00 hours to 12 00 and from 13 00 hours until 17 00 on a Sunday, these eight hours shall count as laytime.

As regards weather hindrances, the expressions "weather permitting" (w.p.) or "weather working" (w.w.) are used. The meaning of the "weather permitting" exception is that time shall not count if the loading or the discharging is actually prevented. When the "weather working" clause is used all time during which the weather hindered, or would have hindered, loading or discharging, will be excepted. In other words, the latter clause will also prevent laytime from counting when it is raining outside ordinary or planned working hours. Rain is no problem for tankers, but they may have to leave a sea buoy if the swell becomes too violent. In the charter-parties used by the major oil companies demurrage is often reduced to half rate for bad weather and for some other events.

Note that the exceptions are usually linked only to the loading or the discharging work and not to the transportation of cargo to or from the vessel. Unless otherwise expressly agreed, the charterers have a strict liability to furnish the ship with cargo and to remove the cargo from her after discharging. Many other wordings are used in the exception clauses. The above cited expressions are only some of the most common.

Many voyage charter-party forms, among them the Gencon form, have a separate clause dealing with the situation when the vessel is waiting for a berth. In the Gencon form, this clause has the following wording:

"Time lost in waiting for berth to count as loading or discharging time, as the case may be."

This clause is important for the owners as it solves many of the problems that arise when the vessel cannot get to her berth immediately. Also fault on the vessel's or owner's side hindering the loading or the discharging interrupts the time counting (see further below).

Once on demurrage, always on demurrage

The well-known expression "Once on demurrage, always on demurrage" means that Exception clauses (see above) do not apply to demurrage, unless they are clearly worded so as to have that effect. In most cases this means that when the laytime expires and the vessel is on demurrage, all the time thereafter (24 hours per day, seven days per week) shall count notwithstanding weather hindrances, holidays, etc. Time counting may, however, be interrupted where such interruption is caused by the owner or owner's servants or by fault on the vessel's side. It is not clear whether "fault" in this respect means negligence, unseaworthiness or suchlike or if it is the same as inability from the ship's side to provide power to winches. In other words, are the owners, when the ship is on demurrage, strictly liable for hindrance on the vessel's side or are they only liable for hindrance caused by negligence from the owners', master's or crew's side?

This principle is frequently excluded in tanker charter-parties through wording such as ". . . shall not count for laytime or as time on demurrage".

Demurrage and damages for detention

The demurrage rate is the compensation owners are entitled to when loading and/or discharging is not completed before the allowed time expires. The demurrage rate is usually agreed to a certain amount per 24 hours or *pro rata*. Since demurrage is a kind of liquidated damages agreed beforehand between the parties, the owners do not have to prove their loss and also, if they can prove that their loss is higher than the demurrage compensation, they are nevertheless not entitled to more than the agreed rate. On the other hand, they get full demurrage even if their actual loss is lower.

Sometimes the demurrage time is limited. Such a limitation is, for instance, printed in the Gencon form, Clause 7:

GENCON
7. Demurrage
Ten running days on demurrage at the rate stated in Box 18 per day or pro rata for any part of a day, payable day by day, to be allowed Merchants altogether at ports of loading and discharging.

In some countries the demurrage time is limited by law (for instance, in the Scandinavian countries where, according to the Merchant Marine Code, the demurrage time is half the laytime).

When demurrage time is limited by agreement or by law and allowed demurrage time is used, the owners are instead entitled to "damages for detention". When owners claim damages for detention they have to prove their loss. The demurrage rate is sometimes considered as *prima facie* evidence in this respect and quite often neither of the parties think about the changed situation when the allowed demurrage time has expired. It is, however, important to be aware of the difference between demurrage and damages for detention as the economic difference can be considerable.

Instead of limited demurrage time and damages for detention the parties sometimes agree to have an increasing demurrage rate, for instance

"demurrage for the first 10 days is agreed to be U.S. $5,000 per 24 hours, thereafter U.S. $7,000 per 24 hours".

Clauses limiting the demurrage time do not solve the difficult question which arises when shippers fail to deliver the agreed quantity of cargo and the charterers do not declare that they cannot get more cargo. It is in this situation difficult for the owners to decide whether they should order the vessel to sail or wait for the remaining cargo. As long as the demurrage rate is sufficient and as long as the charterers also pay demurrage, the owners in many cases do not suffer but if the rate is low, if the charterers do not pay, or if the owners have other commitments for the vessel, they should take legal advice in order to find out how to act (see also the comments about consecutive voyages on page 89f.).

Payment of demurrage

In most cases the calculation and payment of demurrage is made after final discharge and delivery of the cargo. If the owners wish to have a chance to exercise a lien over the cargo against their claim for demurrage they should ensure that it is clearly stated in the charter-party that the demurrage is "payable day by day". Without such a clause it is not clear when demurrage is payable and it may therefore be difficult for the owners to use the cargo as security by exercising a lien.

Despatch money

Despatch is the reverse of demurrage. Despatch is thus payment by the owners as compensation to the charterers for loading and/or discharging the vessel in a shorter time than the allowed laytime. Despatch is not used as commonly as demurrage and when the charterers are entitled to despatch the rate is often 50% of the demurrage rate.

Despatch can be calculated in different ways. Sometimes charterers are entitled to despatch for "all time saved" and sometimes only for "all working time saved". In the first case, the charterers should have compensation for all time the owners actually saved, which means running time from the moment the ship was actually ready until the moment the allowed laytime theoretically should have expired—all excepted periods not counted as laytime—if she had still been in port at that time. In the latter case, when despatch is counted in accordance with the "all working time saved" clause, the compensation to the charterers is only counted on the basis of the remaining laytime allowed after the ship was finally loaded and/or discharged.

Influence of other clauses—several charterers

The counting of laytime may also be influenced by other clauses and circumstances than those mentioned in the basic Laytime clauses. Both during the negotiations and when the laytime calculation is drawn up, other clauses in the charter-parties must be considered in connection with the Laytime clauses.

An example of a clause which often in a very drastic way influences the time to count is the Strike clause. Some Strike clauses expressly deal with the counting of laytime. Other Strike clauses are worded in less precise terms and it is sometimes difficult to find out whether they influence the time counting or not. The Strike clauses are generally difficult to draw up and to interpret (see further below on page 203).

Another situation which may raise very difficult questions in connection with the counting of laytime is when more than one charter-party is in force for one voyage. Owners will face this situation if they have a voyage charter with two or more charterers, who each have only a part cargo for the vessel. Laytime calculations must be made out for each charterer. Provided the statement of facts is detailed and clearly states during which time and in which holds the various part cargoes have been loaded and discharged, the time counting for actual loading and discharging should not cause too many problems. Time lost in waiting for berth and other idle periods will, however, easily give rise to long discussions between owners and charterers. Owners who intend to voyage charter to several charterers for the same voyage should, even during the negotiations, try to draw up precise clauses in order to solve any problems beforehand.

ROUTINES AND ALLOCATION OF COSTS

ETA notices

The voyage charter-party usually has clauses according to which the owners shall keep charterers, shippers and receivers informed about the vessel's position and estimated time of arrival (ETA) at respective ports. The purpose of these clauses is to give charterers (shippers and receivers) a chance to prepare documents and cargo and also to plan the loading or discharging.

A notice clause may have the following wording:

"Master to give telegraphic ETA-notice to Messrs. X 96, 48 and 24 hours before vessel's estimated arrival to loading port."

Unless this is expressly agreed, owners are not strictly liable for the consequences if the vessel arrives later than indicated in the notices. If, for instance, the shippers or the receivers have to pay waiting costs for stevedores when the ship arrives late due to bad weather or other hindrances outside the owners' control, the owners are not liable for these extra costs. Only if the ETA notices have been unrealistic when given or if the master or the owners have intentionally delayed the ship or failed to inform about delay in relation to given ETA notices, can charterers, shippers or receivers have a chance to get compensation from the owners.

Allocation of costs

Harbour dues

A vessel's call at port gives rise to several costs as, for instance, costs for pilots, tugs, mooring, lights, watchmen and dues for quay and cargo. The principal rule is that dues which fall on the vessel and are calculated on the basis of the ship's size shall be paid by the owners and dues which fall on the cargo and are calculated on the basis of the type and quantity of the cargo shall be paid by the charterers (or shippers/receivers).

During the past few years it has become more and more common that local rules demand payment by the owner of dues that were traditionally connected with the cargo or the cargo handling ashore. In the relationship of port authority/shipowner, the latter usually has no other choice than to pay, but this does not mean that the shipowners are also responsible for the cost under the charter-party. If the owners, under the rules of the port, have been forced to pay for something which under the charter-party falls on the charterers, the owners are entitled to recover from the charterers. To avoid disputes it is advisable to insert, for instance, the following clause in the voyage charter-party:

"If one of the parties to this Charterparty has been forced to pay dues in connection with calls at any port which, as between the parties, would have been the responsibility of the other party under the terms of this Charterparty, the latter shall compensate the former for such payment."

Freight taxes

In many countries the tax system includes special taxes on freight and other taxes connected with the loading or discharging of ships in the country. The parties must agree on whose account such taxes shall be. The best way is to find out exactly what taxes will be debited for the intended voyage. A very useful guide is the book *Freight Taxes*, issued and kept up to date by BIMCO. Taxes known beforehand can be dealt with directly in the charter-party but as new tax laws may be introduced with very short notice it is advisable also to have a clause dealing with the question in a more general way, as for instance:

"Taxes on freight or cargo to be for Charterers' account and taxes on vessel to be for Owners' account."

Strike clauses

Considerable delay and costs may be the result of strikes in loading or discharging ports or in seaways through which the vessel has to pass on her voyage. Voyage charter-parties therefore usually contain a Strike clause where the various problems and costs connected with strikes are dealt with. Strike clauses are often complicated to construe and to interpret. The General Strike clause in the Gencon form is, for instance, interpreted differently by English lawyers and BIMCO, the organisation drafting the clause.

Since Strike clauses are complicated, we will here only indicate what kind of questions and problems must be considered when a Strike clause is drafted.

—To what extent are owners entitled to compensation from charterers for delay of the ship and how shall the compensation be calculated (demurrage rate, daily cost for vessel, market rate, or . . .)?

—Liability for consequential loss?

—The parties' rights to cancel?

—Situation where a part cargo is already on board when a strike starts and prevents further loading?

—Owner's rights to complete with other cargo in the same or other ports?

—Charterers' right to order the vessel to other ports?

Additional questions and examples on how the problems can be solved can be found in the General Strike clause in Gencon.

Agents

Normal practice in voyage chartering is that agents are paid by the owners. Notwithstanding this, it is not unusual that the agents are nominated by the charterers, a situation that may sometimes be very difficult for the owner. When agents are nominated by charterers, the owners sometimes nominate their own agent—usually called husbandry agent—to take care of owners' matters such as repatriation of crew members and contact with shipyards or similar and sometimes also to take care of the owners' interests against the charterers, shippers or receivers.

If the agents are reputable and established as agents it should not be necessary for the owners to have their own husbandry agents, but as it still happens too often that port agents who are closely connected with shippers or receivers disregard their obligations to the owners and take care of shippers' or receivers' interests, the owners should always be careful when the port agents are not known to them.

In some countries and ports only one firm is available as a port agent and this firm often also acts as a representative for shippers or receivers as well as representative for P. & I. clubs, hull underwriters, cargo underwriters, etc. It goes without saying that it is difficult for one firm with all these functions to act in a correct way when there are conflicts between the various interests it represents.

CESSER AND LIEN

We have in this chapter and in other chapters of this book described how various costs, obligations, liabilities, etc., are allocated to the parties. In voyage chartering it is not unusual that the charter-party contains a clause which relieves the charterers from liability from the moment the vessel has been loaded. Such a clause, often given the heading "Cesser clause", may, for instance, have the following wording:

"Charterers' liability to cease when cargo is shipped and Bills of Lading signed, except as regards payment of freight, deadfreight and demurrage (if any) at loading port."

The intention is that the owners shall turn to the cargo owners with any additional claims as, for instance, demurrage at the discharging port. Sometimes the owners are also referred to someone other than the charterers, usually the shippers, for demurrage at the loading port. The Cesser clause is usually combined with a so-called "Lien clause" according to which the owners, as security for their claims, have a lien on the cargo (see above, page 171). A Lien clause may have the following wording:

"It is also agreed that the Owners of the said vessel shall reserve to themselves the right of lien upon the cargo laden on board for the recovery and payment of all freight, deadfreight and demurrage (if any)."

It is not unusual that the Cesser and Lien clauses are combined. This is the case in the Gencon form, Clause 8, which has the heading "Lien Clause". The Cesser clause here is "hidden" at the end of the clause.

GENCON

8. Lien Clause
Owners shall have a lien on the cargo for freight, dead-freight, demurrage and damages for detention. Charterers shall remain responsible for dead-freight and demurrage (including damages for detention) incurred at port of loading. Charterers shall also remain responsible for freight and demurrage (including damages for detention) incurred at port of discharge, but only to such extent as the Owners have been unable to obtain payment thereof by exercising the lien on the cargo.

Is the Cesser clause justified and valid?

The Cesser clause is out of date and should not be proposed by charterers or accepted by owners. Notwithstanding this, it is often found in modern charter-parties. One of the reasons for this may be that the clause is often hidden as in the above-cited Gencon clause. Another reason may be that the parties sometimes are not aware of the seriousness of the clause. Also, if the charterers and owners have made several shipments with a Cesser clause included in the charter-party, the owners should not take it for granted that the charterers will continue to disregard the clause. Charterers may encounter economic difficulties or be in difficulties with the receivers and then, in order to protect their own interests, they perhaps read the charter-party more carefully and find that legally they have an opportunity to avoid some expenses they originally thought they had to bear.

As regards the validity of the Cesser clause, under English law it seems to be an established rule that the Cesser clause is valid only if it is combined with a Lien clause giving a right to lien which is legally valid and which it is practically possible to exercise in the relevant case ("Cesser is co-extensive with Lien").

Exercising of lien

Before the owners place a lien on the cargo they must find out legal and practical possibilities and difficulties in the actual country and port. In some countries it is not at all legally possible to exercise a lien over cargo. If they are legally entitled to exercise a lien over the cargo it may nevertheless be impossible for practical reasons. It may, for instance, be that the only place, shed, tank, etc., where the cargo can be stored ashore is controlled by the same person or company against whom the owners have a claim.

It is often legally doubtful if the owners are entitled to exercise a lien by keeping the cargo in the vessel and under all circumstances they will, by such an action, delay the vessel which will cause additional costs and legal difficulties. In some countries, where legal security is less developed, it also happens that although the owners exercise a lien in a correct way, they are involved in various difficulties which delay the ship and thereby cause extra costs.

Considering all these difficulties owners should take legal advice and if they have reason to fear difficulties they should take advice well in advance of the ship's arrival at the discharging port.

Collecting by owners from receivers

When the owners, by a clause in the charter-party, are obliged to collect demurrage from the receivers, for instance, it should be clearly stated that the charterers remain ultimately responsible and it should also be stated after how long a time the owners may claim payment from the charterers if they are not paid by the receivers, shippers, etc. A clause which may be considered as reasonable and which could be accepted by owners is the following:

"Demurrage at discharging port to be settled directly between Owners and Receivers but Charterers to remain ultimately responsible and in case payment from Receivers is not effected within x days after discharging (or: after invoice date) Charterers to pay demurrage to Owners."

It goes without saying that the owners should only accept such a clause if the charterers are reliable and solvent, as the owners in this situation have no way of using the cargo as security for their claim against the charterers.

CARGO LIABILITY

(Compare the following with the section about the bill of lading conventions at page 61ff.)

The liability for the cargo, in a voyage charter-party, shall be allocated as the owners and charterers agree. There is no minimum liability for owners as there is in the Hague Rules, Hague-Visby Rules and Hamburg Rules.

Some charter-party forms more or less free owners from liability for the cargo and others put a far-reaching liability on owners in this respect. Sometimes the charter-party contains a Paramount clause (cf. above, at page 63) which makes the Hague Rules or Hague-Visby Rules applicable to the liability for cargo under the charter-party or to the whole charter-party as the case may be.

Owners' liability for cargo when both a voyage charter-party and a bill of lading are involved

Owners' responsibility for cargo under many standard forms, as for instance under the Gencon form, is very limited but as the master in most cases issues a bill of lading with a more extensive liability for the owners, the question may arise whether the charter-party or the bill of lading shall be decisive for the owners' liability. The problem may be divided into two questions. The first is to what extent owners are liable against the receivers/bill of lading holder and the second is to what extent owners can recover from the charterers if they are forced to pay something to the receivers/bill of lading holder which they are not liable for under the charter-party.

Liability as against cargo owners

The bills of lading usually contain a Paramount clause, a Jurisdiction clause and some other clauses which are contradictory to the clauses contained in the voyage charter-party. To make clear that the charter-party, and not the bill of lading, is the governing agreement for the shipment, owners often insist on having a clause inserted in the bill of lading with reference to the terms of the charter-party. Such a clause can, for instance, have the following wording:

"All the terms, conditions, clauses and exceptions contained in C/P dated .... between ....) including the Jurisdiction clause, are hereby expressly included in this B/L and are deemed to be incorporated herein. All the terms, conditions, clauses and exceptions contained in this B/L—including the Paramount clause—are null and void to such extent as they are contrary to any provisions in the said C/P but no further."

It is doubtful to what extent owners can rely on such a clause as regards liability for cargo in relation to the consignee (who is not the charterer) as it is contradictory to the rules contained in the Hague Rules, Hague-Visby Rules and Hamburg Rules prescribing a minimum liability for the carrier. The clause may, however, be of some value for other reasons (for instance, in connection with demurrage claims) and when countries are involved which have not signed the bill of lading conventions.

To avoid difficulties with bankers when the payment for the cargo is made by way of a letter of credit, owners should state in the charter-party that bills of lading issued shall contain a clause referring to the charter-party. Unless the bankers are instructed that such an incorporation clause is acceptable, they will not accept the bill of lading.

When the receivers are also the charterers, the bill of lading will not have the same effect as usual and the receivers/charterers cannot claim against the owners under the bill of lading as the charter-party is the main contract between them. Owners must, however, be aware that receivers/charterers may transfer the bill of lading to someone else who is not bound by the charter-party and therefore not prevented from claiming under the bill of lading.

Cargo retention clauses

There has been a growing number of cargo claims during past years because of the peculiarities of cargoes carried by tankers. Some shortage of cargo always occurs due to evaporation and sedimentation. The allowance for such losses should be determined by the custom of the trade. In oil cargoes an allowance of 0.5 to 0.75% to cover evaporation and unpumpable sediment was generally accepted. Increasing oil prices caused charterers to introduce so-called Cargo Retention clauses, which often have the effect of letting the owners bear all the risks in this connection and payment of freight being based on *delivered weight*.

Some of the printed forms do not include a clause dealing with "cargo retention", but in most deals the charter-party will contain such a provision. It is particularly important for an owner to ensure that a right of deduction from freight is without prejudice to defences available to the owner. From the charterer's viewpoint it is important that any requirement that the quantity R.O.B. be "determined" or "established" by an independent surveyor is strictly complied with before any deduction from freight is made. The principles embodied in clause 12 of Tankervoy 87 seem to protect all legitimate interests of both parties.

Redress

If owners have to make payments for cargo claims under the bill of lading to a greater extent than according to their liability under the charter-party, it seems clear that they are under English law entitled to compensation from the charterers. This is, however, more a "legal right" than a "real right" as charterers usually only very reluctantly agree to such compensation. If the owners intend to seek recourse against the charterers it may therefore be advisable to make the charterers aware of this from the beginning by inserting a Redress clause into the charter-party. Such a clause may have the following wording:

Redress Clause 1968. Code Name: "Redress".

"If one of the parties to this Charterparty has been obliged to make payment or institute defence in respect of a claim by a third party, under a Bill of Lading or otherwise, of a nature which, as between the parties, would have been the responsibility of the other party under the terms of this Charterparty, the latter shall indemnify the former for all loss, damage or expenses resulting therefrom. However, the indemnity payable under this Clause in respect of discharge of such claims shall be reduced to the extent the party in question could have limited his liability if he had been held liable directly to the claimant in the jurisdiction in which the claimant proceeded against the other party."

DAMAGE TO THE VESSEL

If the vessel is damaged as a result of bad weather, error in navigation or handling, collision with other ships, buoys, etc., the owners will have little chance of getting compensation from the charterers. Only if agreed, or in some cases if the charterers are in breach of contract, or if they have acted negligently or fraudulently may the owners have a chance of recovering financial compensation from the voyage charterers for such damage. The most common situation is when the damage has been caused by an unsafe port or berth, or by stevedores, or when the cargo has been injurious. The concept of safe and unsafe ports and berths has been discussed above, on page 180.

Concerning damage to the ship caused by the cargo, charterers' description of the cargo during the negotiations and in the charter-party is important. This question has also been dealt with above (page 184ff.). From the owners' point of view, it is important to have a satisfactory description of the cargo in the charter-party and, as it is often difficult to judge beforehand whether the cargo will be injurious or not, it is to the benefit of the owners to have a general statement in the charter-party to the effect that the cargo will be non-injurious to the vessel.

When the damage is caused by stevedores it is essential from the viewpoint of liability to ascertain whether the charter-party provides that the owners or the charterers should arrange and pay for the loading and/or discharging of the vessel (cf. page 189ff.). The fact that the charterers, according to the charter-party, must arrange and pay for the loading and/or discharging of the ship does not, however, automatically mean that the charterers are also liable for damage caused by stevedores. The mere fact that the damage has been caused by charterers, or someone employed by charterers, is in many countries not itself sufficient ground for liability. Very often negligence must also be proved. Another complication is that damage to the vessel in connection with loading or discharging may be discovered only a long time after the damage has occurred and in those cases it may be difficult for the owners to prove on what voyage the damage occurred.

When the damage has been caused totally or partly by bad stowage, the owners face additional difficulties as the master has an obligation to supervise the loading. Compare this with same problems under time chartering (pages 239, 242ff.).

CHAPTER 13

THE TIME CHARTER-PARTY*

As already mentioned (page 90ff.) the time charter agreement may be classified as an agreement for hire of a certain vessel. In this respect the time charter agreement differs from the voyage charter agreement which is rather an agreement for carriage of a certain cargo, with a certain vessel and for a certain voyage. The character of a time charter-party as a hire agreement can be noticed in several ways. The compensation to the owner is called hire instead of freight, and instead of a certain voyage, a certain hire period and trading area will be agreed. Instead of mentioning a certain cargo, the time charter-party, mostly in general terms, states the type of cargo the time charterers are allowed to carry with the ship. Also the owners' position against a third party is not the same in time chartering as in voyage chartering. It is the time charterer who operates the ship commercially and thus also the time charterer who has the closest contact with shippers, receivers, etc.

THE VESSEL

Description of the vessel

Generally, the description of the vessel is more important in the time charter agreement than in the voyage charter agreement and the description is also mostly more detailed and precise. All details about the ship (carrying capacity, construction, speed, fuel consumption, nationality, etc.) must be known by the charterers during the negotiations with the owners. Charterers should form an opinion about the commercial value of the vessel and it is therefore important for them that they have correct and sufficient information about her.

The normal situation in voyage chartering is that both cargo and ports are known beforehand and owners and charterers can therefore pick out only those details about the vessel that are relevant. In time chartering the charterers also sometimes know beforehand what cargo they will carry and what ports will be used for loading and discharging but more often the time charterers do

* For a general introduction, see page 90ff.

210

not know beforehand what cargo they will carry with the ship and which ports and areas she will visit and they cannot, therefore, as in voyage chartering, accept only a few main details about her.

In addition to the general data about the vessel (name, call sign, year of build, nationality, draught, length and depth, number of hatches, etc.) charterers, especially when the ship will be chartered for a long period, need a more detailed description and usually they therefore get copies of the so-called General Arrangement plan (GA-plan) and other plans that give information about the ship and her construction. Sometimes it is also important to know the vessel's ice class and to have information about special certificates.

Cargo capacity

The ship's cargo capacity is described in the same way as in the voyage charter-party (cf. page 179), i.e. in most cases by deadweight and/or cubic capacity. In some cases it is necessary to have additional information about the vessel's cargo capacity, for instance, how many containers she can take on deck and under deck respectively.

The time charterers dispose all compartments which can be used for cargo. In the Linertime form this is expressed in the following way:

LINERTIME
9. Cargo Space
The whole reach and burden of the Vessel, including lawful deck-capacity to be at the Charterers' disposal, reserving proper and sufficient space for the Vessel's Master, Officers, Crew, tackle, apparel, furniture, provisions and stores.

When the ship has accommodation for passengers it is usually also stated whether or not the charterers have the right to use this space and what extra payment per passenger per day owners are entitled to.

As information about the vessel's cargo carrying capacity is very important for the time charterers, the owners must declare these details as correctly as possible. Incorrect information about the cargo carrying capacity may lead to deduction of the hire or, when the difference is big, the charterers may also be entitled to cancel the agreement and claim damages.

Speed and bunker consumption

As the charterers pay hire per time unit, the vessel's speed capability and bunker consumption are essential for judging the operating potential of the vessel. The speed capability and bunker consumption statements in the time charter-parties are usually connected to certain weather conditions and to a certain draught. Also, the type of fuel is important. In the Linertime form (preamble) it is said that the vessel shall be "fully loaded capable of steaming about the number of knots indicated in Box 13 in good weather and smooth water on a consumption of about the number of tons stated in Box 13 per 24 hours".

Considering the fact that vessels often are ordered to proceed with "economical speed" or "low speed" it is recommended that not only consumption on full speed is stated in the charter-party. Also consumption on "economical speed" and "low speed" should be agreed.

This type of clause is, in accordance with English law, not understood to be a warranty of the ship's speed capability and bunker consumption during the time charter period. The Linertime wording and other similar wordings only warrant that the vessel, during the negotiations and at the time of the fixture, is capable of steaming the stated speed on the stated consumption, etc. As the charter period is more important for the time charterers they often try to get the speed described as "average service speed" or similar. In the modern tanker time charter-party forms the technique in construing the Speed clause is usually more like the one used in a voyage charter-party. The weather risk at sea is here put on the owners and the speed is described, sometimes in great detail, like e.g. in Article 24 of Shelltime 4.

"Detailed Description and Performance	**24.** (a) Owners guarantee that the speed and consumption of the vessel shall be as follows:—		302 [ ] [ ]
	Average speed in knots	Maximum average bunker consumption main propulsion – auxiliaries fuel oil/diesel oil fuel oil/diesel oil	303 304 305
	Laden	tonnes tonnes	306
	Ballast		307

The foregoing bunker consumptions are for all purposes except cargo heating and tank cleaning and shall be pro-rated between the speeds shown.   308 [   ] [   ]

The service speed of the vessel is   knots laden and   310 knots in ballast and in the absence of Charterers' orders [   ] to the contrary the vessel shall proceed at the service speed. [   ] However if more than one laden and one ballast speed are [   ] shown in the table above Charterers shall have the right to [   ] order the vessel to steam at any speed within the range set out [   ] in the table (the "ordered speed"). [   ]

If the vessel is ordered to proceed at any speed other than   314 the highest speed shown in the table, and the average speed [   ] actually attained by the vessel during the currency of such order [   ] exceeds such ordered speed plus 0.5 knots (the "maximum [   ]

recognised speed"), then for the purpose of calculating any [　]
increase or decrease of hire under this Clause 24 the maximum [　]
recognised speed shall be used in place of the average speed [　]
actually attained. [　]

For the purposes of this charter the "guaranteed speed" at　319
any time shall be the then-current ordered speed or the service [　]
speed, as the case may be. [　]

The average speeds and bunker consumptions shall for the　321
purposes of this Clause 24 be calculated by reference to the [　]
observed distance from pilot station to pilot station on all sea [　]
passages during each period stipulated in Clause 24(c), but [　]
excluding any time during which the vessel is (or but for Clause [　]
22(b)(i) would be) off-hire and also excluding "Adverse [　]
Weather Periods", being (i) any periods during which reduction [　]
of speed is necessary for safety in congested waters or in poor [　]
visibility (ii) any days, noon to noon, when winds exceed force [　]
8 on the Beaufort Scale for more than 12 hours. [　]

(b) If during any year from the date on which the vessel　327
enters service (anniversary to anniversary) the vessel falls [　]
below or exceeds the performance guaranteed in Clause 24(a) [　]
then if such shortfall or excess results. [　]

    (i) from a reduction or an increase in the average speed of　330
         the vessel, compared to the speed guaranteed in Clause [　]
         24(a), then an amount equal to the value at the hire [　]
         rate of the time so lost or gained, as the case may be, [　]
         shall be deducted from or added to the hire paid; [　]
         [　]

    (ii) from an increase or a decrease in the total bunkers　333
         consumed, compared to the total bunkers which would [　]
         have been consumed had the vessel performed as [　]
         guaranteed in Clause 24(a), an amount equivalent to [　]
         the value of the additional bunkers consumed or the [　]
         bunkers saved, as the case may be, based on the average [　]
         price paid by Charterers for the vessel's bunkers in such [　]
         period, shall be deducted from or added to the hire [　]
         paid. [　]

The addition to or deduction from hire so calculated for　339
laden and ballast mileage respectively shall be adjusted to take [　]
into account the mileage steamed in each such condition [　]
during Adverse Weather Periods, by dividing such addition or [　]
deduction by the number of miles over which the performance [　]
has been calculated and multiplying by the same number of [　]
miles plus the miles steamed during the Adverse Weather [　]
Periods, in order to establish the total addition to or deduction [　]
from hire to be made for such period. [　]

Reduction of hire under the foregoing sub-Clause (b) shall be　342
without prejudice to any other remedy available to Charterers. [　]
[　]

(c) Calculations under this Clause 24 shall be made for the　344
yearly periods terminating on each successive anniversary of [　]
the date on which the vessel enters service, and for the period [　]
between the last such anniversary and the date of termination [　]
of this charter if less than a year. Claims in respect of reduction [　]

of hire arising under this Clause during the final year or part [   ]
year of the charter period shall in the first instance be settled [   ]
in accordance with Charterers' estimate made two months [   ]
before the end of the charter period. Any necessary adjustment [   ]
after this charter terminates shall be made by payment by [   ]
Owners to Charterers or by Charterers to Owners as the case [   ]
may require.   [   ]
  Payments in respect of increase of hire arising under this   351
Clause shall be made promptly after receipt by Charterers of [   ]
all the information necessary to calculate such increase."   [   ]

As already indicated, speed capacity should be connected with bunker consumption and when the charterers scrutinize the log abstract to find out the vessel's performance they must look at both speed and consumption. Speed claims, i.e. claims based on low speed/high bunker consumption, are often complicated and difficult to negotiate. In most cases considerable amounts are involved and the parties should therefore be careful when they draw up the charter-party clauses.

A special problem in connection with speed and bunker consumption is the problem of bottom growth on the vessel. When the vessel has been idle for a long period in tropical areas the speed capacity will be reduced considerably. Some charter-parties have special clauses dealing with this problem. The following example is from the old New York Produce Exchange form:

NYPE 93

That as the Vessel may be from time to time employed in tropical waters during the terms of this Charter, Vessel is to be docked at a convenient place, bottom cleaned and painted whenever Charterers and Captain think necessary, at least once in every six months, reckoning from time of last painting, and payment of the hire to be suspended until she is again in proper state for the service.

Maintenance

The shipowners' obligations as regards the vessel's seaworthiness have been dealt with above on page 155f. In the time charter agreements it is often expressly said that the owners shall deliver her to the charterers in a seaworthy condition. In the Linertime form it is, for instance, said that the ship at delivery shall be "in every way fitted for ordinary cargo service" (Clause 1, line 25/26).

For the charterers it is important not only that the vessel is delivered in accordance with the agreement and in a seaworthy condition, but also that she will be kept in the same good order and condition during the charter period. Usually this is also expressly stated in the charter agreement. In the Linertime form it is thus stated in Clause 4, line 73/74 that the owners shall "maintain her in thoroughly efficient state, in hull and machinery during service". When the charter agreement covers long periods it might be especially advisable to make this clause a little more specific. In this connection clauses dealing with liability for damage to the vessel and other clauses concerning liabilities and exceptions from liabilities must also be considered.

Even without an express agreement to that effect the shipowner basically will have a duty with respect to seaworthiness and maintenance. In English law, for instance, the owners' warranty of seaworthiness is implied unless anything to the contrary is stated in the charter-party.

THE TRADE

Geographical limits

We have already mentioned that the hull and war risk underwriters dictate certain limits for the vessel. Time charter-parties usually contain additional limits for the trading. Basically it is the time charterers who direct the vessel. In the Linertime form this is expressed in the following way (part of Clause 10):

"The charterers to give the necessary sailing instructions, subject to the limit of the charter."

The "limit of the charter" usually includes several kinds of limitations. The owners must, in the first place, see to it that those limits stipulated by the underwriters are included also in the time charter-party. This is usually done by the wording ". . . but always within hull underwriters' trading limits" or similar. Note that a reference to Institute Warranty Limits is not always sufficient as other limits are used by many underwriters.

In the War Risk clause it is also often stated that the owners and the master "have liberty to comply with any orders . . . given by any committee or person having under the terms of the war risk insurance on the vessel the right to give any such orders or directions".

Additional limitations contained in the concept "limits of the charter" are for various reasons usually inserted. One reason may be that the owners do not want to have the ship trading too far from the home country as this will cause extra costs for the crew. Very often there are also political reasons for limitation. Some countries do not accept vessels which have earlier traded with other countries or are owned or controlled by persons or companies from certain other countries. To avoid difficulties the owners must provide exclusions in the charter-party.

A general recommendation when geographical concepts are used is that wordings such as "southern Europe" and "Baltic in season" should be avoided as it is difficult to find out what they really cover. It is better to mention the various countries included or excluded or to give geographical limits. When the wording "in season" is used, the season should be specified.

When the trading limits cover a large area, for instance, "world-wide trading always within IWL and excluding following countries . . .", the owners, for financial reasons, generally wish to have a written undertaking from the charterers' side that they will visit the vessel's home country or countries near the ship's home country once or twice a year for changing of crew, drydocking, etc. Such a clause may have the following wording:

"Vessel to call Europe twice a year evenly spread."

Non-geographical limits

There are also usually limitations of a non-geographical nature for those trades, countries and ports which are within the geographical limits. The following clause is from Linertime:

LINERTIME
3. Trade
The Vessel to be employed in lawful trades for the carriage of lawful merchandise only between good and safe ports or places where she can safely lie
    (a) always afloat*
    (b) always afloat or safely aground where it is customary for vessels of similar size
         and draught to be safe aground*
within the limits as stated in Box 20.
(* *state alternative agreed in Box* 20).

The vessel shall, according to this clause, only be used for lawful cargo in lawful trades. This means that the trade and the cargo must be lawful not only in the countries where the loading and discharging take place but also in the country where the ship is registered and by the law governing the charter-party.

Ports shall be safe (cf. page 180) and the ship shall, as agreed by the parties, either lie "always afloat" or "always afloat or safely aground where it is customary for vessels of similar size or draught to be safe aground".

Besides this clause there is usually also a clause dealing with ice and other difficulties or dangerous situations. Such a clause, often called "Excluded Ports", can have this wording (Linertime):

LINERTIME
17. Excluded Ports
The Vessel not to be ordered to nor bound to enter:
    (a) any place where fever or epidemics are prevalent or to which the Master,
        Officers and Crew by law are not bound to follow the Vessel;

    Ice
    (b) any ice-bound place or any place where lights, lightships, marks and buoys are
        or are likely to be withdrawn by reason of ice on the Vessel's arrival or where
        there is risk that ordinarily the Vessel will not be able on account of ice to
        reach the place or to get out after having completed loading or discharging.

The Vessel not to be obliged to force ice, nor to follow ice-breakers when inward bound. If on account of ice the Master considers it dangerous to remain at the loading or discharging place for fear of the Vessel being frozen in and/or damaged, he has liberty to sail to a convenient open place and await the Charterers' fresh instructions. Detention through any of above causes to be for the Charterers' account.

The intention behind the first section of the clause (a) is to protect the crew against fevers and epidemics. The next section (b) is the Ice clause which is self-explanatory (cf. the section about Ice clauses on page 182).

The War clause also sometimes limits the charterers' rights to use the vessel (see above page 160ff.).

Breaking of trading limits

If the time charterers wish to direct the vessel to ports or places outside the limits of the charter-party they must, of course, first get permission from the owners, who sometimes must get permission from the underwriters.

Sometimes clauses such as "The charterers have the right to break vessel's trading limits provided they pay the extra insurance premiums" are found in the time charter-parties. This clause is not acceptable from the owners' point of view as they cannot generally promise to break the trading limits. Each time the question arises the underwriters must be consulted and a special agreement between the charterers and owners should be drawn up. In such agreement not only the costs for extra insurance premiums should be considered but also the risk of delay and physical damage to the vessel.

Requirements of the trade

As it is important for the charterers that they can use the vessel within the trading limits and without disturbances they often insist on clauses like for instance

"Owners to ensure both that the Vessel is provided with such technical equipment and certificates, and that the terms and conditions on which the Master, Officers and Crew are engaged are such, as are necessary to avoid any delay or hindrance with respect to the use of the Vessel within the trading limits."

Clauses like this may create difficulties for the owners, especially when new regulations are introduced. Another solution is that owners and charterers agree that owners' obligations in this respect are limited to rules and regulations in force when the charter-party is agreed.

Trip time chartering

When the ship is chartered for a specified trip (cf. page 90) clauses like the following are sometimes used instead of usual trading limits:

"One time charter voyage with loading 1 or 2 ports in Sweden and discharging 1 or 2 ports in Brazil. Redelivery on dropping outboard pilot at last discharging port. Total period estimated to 30 days."

As always, when the basic principles are set aside, the parties must look through the other clauses of the charter-party and make necessary amendments. Most standard time charter-party forms have a clause giving the owners an opportunity to claim additional hire for the last voyage under the charter-party if the vessel is not redelivered in due time. The wording of these clauses is not suitable for trip time chartering and should thus be amended, for example, by stating that the charter hire is applicable only for 30 days (in our example) and that the owners thereafter are entitled to the market rate if higher than the charter rate.

Sometimes the charter-party contains both ordinary trading limits and a description of a time charter trip, for instance:

"World-wide trading within IWL"

combined with

"One time charter trip from U.K. to one or two ports Spanish Mediterranean coast".

Are the charterers, for instance, then entitled to send the vessel from the United Kingdom via Norway to the Spanish Mediterranean coast? The answer is difficult to find and such confusing combinations of clauses should be avoided. If the intention in our example is to send the vessel directly from the U.K. to Spain, the words "world-wide trading" should not be inserted and if the intention is that the charterers should have a possibility of sending the ship to other places, the trip to U.K./Spain should not be mentioned in the charter-party or only be mentioned as a non-binding intended voyage.

Ballast bonus

It goes without saying that it is advantageous for the time charterers if the vessel is delivered at a place where she can be loaded immediately. Similarly, it is to the advantage of the owners if the vessel is redelivered at a place where she can easily get a new cargo at a good rate. As a consequence of this, the delivery and redelivery ports or places are often reflected in the economic calculation and in the hire (cf. Chapter 8).

Instead of having the hire influenced by delivery and redelivery positions, the parties sometimes agree about a so-called ballast bonus to be paid. If, for instance, a vessel is planned to be finally discharged under the time charter at port X, the time charterer most probably also wishes to deliver her at port X. If we presume that it is impossible to find a new cargo at port X and the nearest port where cargo is available is town Y, 10 days' steaming from port X, the owner must in his calculation for the time charter consider also the 10 days' steaming and bunker consumption from port X to town Y. This can be done in several ways. One possibility is, of course, that the vessel continues on charter and is not redelivered until her arrival at town Y. Sometimes the parties agree instead that the vessel shall be redelivered at port X and that the owners shall get a lump sum compensation—a ballast bonus—for the theoretical steaming time and bunker consumption from port X to town Y. Such a ballast bonus may also be converted to hire and added to the hire for the actual charter period.

The advantage of a ballast bonus, either paid as a lump sum compensation or added to the ordinary hire, is that the parties are discharged from their obligations and liabilities during the ballast bonus-covered period and voyage. This means, for instance, that the charterers are not liable for the safety of ports and channels and bear no financial risk for the delay of the vessel by bad weather, strikes of pilots or similar occurrences. The owners are free to do what they wish with the vessel and must not, in our example, direct her to town Y. Depending on the circumstances, ballast bonuses can be paid by the owners to the charterers or by the charterers to the owners and at delivery and/or at redelivery.

THE CARGO

Type and specification

Besides the trading limits, the most important restriction as regards the time charterers' freedom to use and direct the ship is the restriction on cargoes to be carried in the vessel. The type of vessel is, in the first place, decisive for the kind of cargo to be carried. Some vessels are specially built and equipped for one kind of cargo only and in such a case this should, of course, also be stated in the charter-party. Other ships can take a limited number of cargo types and also in this case the best way is to specify them in the charter-party. Many ships are, however, intended and suitable for many kinds of cargoes and in those cases time charter-parties usually describe the accepted cargo as, for instance, "lawful merchandise non-injurious to the vessel", "ordinary dry cargo non-injurious to the vessel" or similar. Note the difference compared with the voyage charter-party where the description and specification of the cargo have a more central position (cf. page 184).

Excluded cargo

The general description of cargo accepted for the vessel sometimes by itself excludes some cargoes. If, for instance, the general cargo description is "lawful merchandise non-injurious to the vessel", unlawful and injurious cargo is not allowed. In addition, the printed charter-party forms usually also contain a specification of cargo that is not allowed. In Linertime this clause has the following wording (part of Clause 3):

LINERTIME

No live stock, sulphur and pitch in bulk to be shipped. Injurious, inflammable or dangerous goods (such as acids, explosives, calcium carbide, ferro silicon, naphtha, motor spirit, tar, or any of their products) to be limited to the number of tons stated in Box 21 and same to be packed, loaded, stowed and discharged in accordance with the regulations of the local authorities and Board of Trade as specified in Box 21, and if any special measures have to be taken by reason of having this cargo aboard including cost of erection and dismantling magazines, etc., same to be at Charterers' expense and in Charterers' time.

Nuclear Fuel

Notwithstanding any other provisions contained in this Charter it is agreed that nuclear fuels or radioactive products or waste are specifically excluded from the cargo permitted to be loaded or carried under this Charter. This exclusion does not apply to radio-isotopes used or intended to be used for any industrial, commercial, agricultural, medical or scientific purposes provided the Owners' prior approval has been obtained to loading thereof.

THE PERIOD

The length of the period

Time charter-parties regularly contain a clause stating the length of the charter period. The basic period intended is sometimes called the "flat period". The traditional way to describe the period is to fix a certain period. See, for instance, the first line of Clause 1 in the Linertime form which reads:

"The owners let, and the charterers hire the vessel for a period of the number of calendar months indicated in Box 15 . . .".

Another solution is to agree that the vessel shall perform one or several fixed voyages as described in the sub-section "Trip time chartering" on pages 90, 217f.

As it is difficult to determine beforehand exactly when the ship will be redelivered, the charter-parties usually have a certain built-in flexibility. Both the flat period and the redelivery day are often described together with the word "about". It is also possible to state a certain flat period or a certain redelivery day with the addition "± 15 days in charterers' option" or similar. Combinations of these two methods as well as other methods are also found.

When establishing the meaning of "about" several factors will be considered, but particularly decisive will be the length of the "flat period", or the length of the voyages embraced by the charter period. Sometimes the charterers have an optional right to prolong the charter period. Such options are normally for the benefit solely of the charterers. If the market rate goes down during the charter period, the charterers will probably not use their option and the owners will have to find new employment for the vessel. The charterers may choose another ship, or maybe the same ship, at a lower hire than in the old charter. If the market rate has gone up the charterers will probably use their option as they thereby get the vessel at a rate lower than the market rate.

Especially when there is a big gap between the market hire and the charter-party hire, disputes easily arise concerning the length of the period. If the charter-party hire is higher than the market hire, the charterers try to redeliver the ship as soon as possible, and if the charter hire is lower than the market hire, they try instead to keep her as long as possible.

Overlap/underlap—last voyage

Sometimes the vessel is redelivered before and sometimes after the agreed redelivery date or period. In the first case we have an underlap situation and in the latter an overlap situation.

The owners cannot refuse to take the ship if the charterers redeliver her earlier than they are entitled to in spite of this being a breach of contract on the charterers' side. The owners have an obligation to try to minimize their loss by seeking alternative employment for the vessel but if they fail or if they get lower revenue compared with the previous charter they are entitled to compensation from the charterers. It is, however, not always clear how this compensation should be calculated.

When the charterers are planning the last voyage for the ship under the charter they must take into consideration that she has to be redelivered in accordance with the agreement in the charter-party. As it is often difficult to plan or estimate exactly when the vessel will be redelivered, the charter-party forms usually have a special clause about the last voyage. In the Linertime form this is dealt with in the last section of Clause 8:

LINERTIME
Should the Vessel be ordered on a voyage by which the Charter period may be exceeded the Charterers to have the use of the Vessel to enable them to complete the voyage, provided it could be reasonably calculated that the voyage would allow re-delivery about the time fixed for the termination of the Charter, but for any time exceeding the termination date the Charterers to pay the market rate if higher than the rate stipulated herein.

According to this clause, the owners are entitled to the market rate for the overlap period if the market rate is higher than the rate stipulated in the charter-party. If the market rate is lower than the charter-party rate, the latter rate will apply also for the overlap period. Note that this clause does not mean that the charterers are free to prolong the charter period. The clause only deals with the situation where "it could be reasonably calculated that the voyage would allow re-delivery about the time fixed for the termination of the charter". If, during the planning, it has become obvious that the vessel cannot be redelivered in accordance with the charter-party, there may be a breach of contract and if the charterers decide nevertheless to send the vessel on a new trip then the owners have an opportunity to claim additional damages and not only the market rate. Compare this with the remarks about trip time chartering on pages 90, 217f.

Extension of the flat period due to off-hire periods during the charter

Charterers are not entitled to an extension of the flat period because of off-hire periods which occurred during the charter unless this is expressly stated in the charter agreement. If such a clause is inserted it is advisable also to state the latest time by which the charterers must notify the owners that they intend to use their option to extend the charter period. Furthermore, the hire for the additional period should be determined as well as the question of whether off-hire during the extension period will give the charterer a right to additional extension.

DELIVERY AND REDELIVERY

A charter period is demarcated by the delivery to and redelivery from the time charterers. In connection with delivery and redelivery several questions arise which must be dealt with in the charter-party. The relevant clauses in Linertime are as follows:

LINERTIME

1. Period and Port of Delivery
The Owners let, and the Charterers hire the Vessel for a period of the number of calendar months indicated in Box 15 from the time (not a Sunday or a legal Holiday unless taken over) the Vessel is delivered and placed at the disposal of the Charterers between 7 a.m. and 10 p.m., or between 7 a.m. and noon if on Saturday, at the port stated in Box 16 in such ready berth where she can safely lie
   (a) always afloat*
   (b) always afloat or safely aground where it is customary for vessels of similar size and draught to be safe aground*
as the Charterers may direct, she being in every way fitted for ordinary dry cargo service with cargo holds well swept, cleaned and ready to receive cargo before delivery under this Charter.
(* *state alternative agreed in Box 16*).

Time for Delivery
The vessel to be delivered not before the date indicated in Box 17.
The Owners to give the Charterers not less than the number of days' notice stated in Box 18 of the date on which the Vessel is expected to be ready for delivery.
The Owners to keep the Charterers closely advised of possible changes in Vessel's position.

LINERTIME

8. Re-delivery
The Vessel to be re-delivered on the expiration of the Charter in the same good order as when delivered to the Charterers (fair wear and tear excepted) at a safe and ice-free

port in the Charterers' option in the place or within the range stated in Box 29 between 7 a.m. and 10 p.m., and 7 a.m. and noon on Saturday, but the day of re-delivery shall not be a Sunday or legal Holiday.

Repairs for the Charterers' account as far as possible to be effected simultaneously with dry-docking or annual repairs, respectively; if any further repairs are required, for time occupied in effecting such repairs the Owners always to be properly notified of the time and place when and where repairs for their account will be performed.

Notice
The Charterers to give the Owners not less than the number of days' preliminary and the number of days' final notice as stated in Box 30 of the port of re-delivery and the date on which the Vessel is expected to be ready for re-delivery. The Charterers to keep the Owners closely advised of possible changes in the Vessel's position.

Should the Vessel be ordered on a voyage by which the Charter period may be exceeded the Charterers to have the use of the Vessel to enable them to complete the voyage, provided it could be reasonably calculated that the voyage would allow re-delivery about the time fixed for the termination of the Charter, but for any time exceeding the termination date the Charterers to pay the market rate if higher than the rate stipulated therein.

There are also other clauses connected with the delivery of the vessel, for example, the following:

LINERTIME
2. Cancelling
Should the Vessel not be delivered by the date indicated in Box 19, the Charterers to have the option of cancelling.

If the Vessel cannot be delivered by the cancelling date, the Charterers, if required, to declare within 48 hours (Sundays and Holidays excluded) after receiving notice thereof whether they cancel or will take delivery of the Vessel.

When shall the vessel be delivered?

We have already discussed, in the sections "Lay/Can" (page 158ff.) and "The Period" (page 220ff.), when the vessel shall be delivered to and redelivered from the time charterers. In the section "Lay/Can" we dealt with the consequences when the ship is delivered too early or too late to the time charterers. If she arrives too early, the charterers are not obliged to take delivery before the layday and if she arrives too late they are entitled to cancel the agreement. As mentioned, the charterers are, in some situations, also entitled to damages.

In the section "The Period" it was mentioned that time charter-parties usually accept a certain flexibility as regards the time for redelivery. If the charterers redeliver the ship too late, the owners may be entitled to damages from the charterers. The terms in the charter-party, governing law and the reason for the late redelivery, must be considered. If it becomes evident that at the time the vessel was ordered on her last voyage the charterers realized, or should have realized, that it would not be possible for them to redeliver the vessel in accordance with the contract, the owners usually stand a good chance of getting damages for their loss, if any. The situation is more difficult when the redelivery has been delayed by a reason outside the charterers' control provided that the charterers were not negligent.

Many charter-parties state that the vessel can only be delivered and redelivered during weekdays and during office hours (see the above-cited Clauses 1 and 8 from Linertime). Quite often these limitations are deleted in the individual charter-party. It is recommended to clarify whether GMT or local times should be applied when the exact time for delivery and redelivery is established.

Where shall the vessel be delivered?

The port or place of delivery and redelivery can be more or less specified. Sometimes a certain port is mentioned and sometimes a certain area or range, i.e. "vessel to be delivered and redelivered in the Mediterranean". When only an area or a range is mentioned it is usually the owners who choose the place of delivery and the charterers who decide the port of redelivery.

Delivery and redelivery may not necessarily take place when the ship is in port. It is not unusual that the charter-parties contain a Delivery or a Redelivery Clause of the following type:

"Vessel to be delivered (redelivered) on dropping outward pilot at x-town."

It should be noted that such a clause can cause difficulties in situations where for instance both port pilots and river pilots are available.

In what condition shall the vessel be delivered and redelivered?

The vessel shall, on delivery to the charterers, be seaworthy and conform to the requirements of the contract. This is, for example, stated in clauses such as:

". . . she being in every way fitted for ordinary dry cargo service with cargo holds well swept, cleaned and ready to receive cargo before delivery under this charter".

As regards redelivery, the following or similar clauses are used:

"the vessel to be redelivered on the expiration of the charter in the same good order as when delivered to the charterers (fair wear and tear excepted) . . ."

The meaning of this clause is—if we disregard the problems connected with damage to the vessel which will be dealt with separately (page 244ff.)—that upon delivery the charterers can require the ship to be in the condition specified in the contract and ready to commence commercial trading for them. They are also obliged to redeliver the vessel in a similar condition, enabling the owners to start immediate commercial trading for their own account (or for another time charterer).

A question which quite often causes problems is the cleaning of the cargo holds. At delivery the charterers, who in principle cannot redeliver the vessel before she is swept and cleaned, sometimes wish to have clauses of the following type inserted into the charter-party:

N Y P E 93 (part of clause 36)
"The Charterers shall have the option to re-deliver the vessel with unclean/unswept holds against a lumpsum payment of . . . . in lieu of cleaning."

This and similar clauses can be very burdensome to the owners. They cannot beforehand estimate how many men/hours they will need to clean the ship and if they do not have sufficient time on a ballast voyage before the next charter they may lose expensive time during which she cannot be used commercially. From the owners' point of view it is better to discuss such a lump sum compensation when the vessel is at the redelivery port and when it is known what the next employment will be.

Allocation of costs at delivery and redelivery

When the vessel is delivered under the charter, liability for certain costs, for instance the costs for bunkers, harbour dues, and agency fees, goes over from the owners to the charterers. In the same way liability for these costs goes back to the owners at redelivery.

In order to get a basis for the allocation of costs, special *survey reports*—on-hire and off-hire survey reports—are usually issued in connection with the delivery and the redelivery. In these reports the exact time for delivery and redelivery and quantities of fuel and diesel on board are stated. Usually damage to the vessel and her general condition are also stated. Such *damage reports* often have an important function in discussions about liability for damages which sometimes arise during and after the charter period.

Charterers and owners can make separate surveys but it is also common that they agree to have a joint survey by an independent surveyor. The parties must agree not only for whose account the survey is, but also in whose time. The following clauses show alternative solutions:

"Unless otherwise mutually agreed the Owners and Charterers shall each appoint surveyors for the purpose of determining the condition of the Vessel at the time of delivery and redelivery hereunder. Surveys whenever possible to be done during service, but if impossible any time lost for on-hire survey to be for Owners' account and any time lost for off-hire survey to be for Charterers' account."

"A joint survey at delivery to be arranged by Owners and effected in their time. A joint survey on redelivery to be arranged by Charterers and effected in their time. Costs for both surveys to be shared equally."

As regards fuel the charter-party should state the prices to be applied at delivery and redelivery. The following example is from Linertime:

LINERTIME

6. Bunkers

The Charterers at port of delivery and the Owners at port of re-delivery to take over and pay for all fuel remaining in the Vessel's bunkers at
   (a)   current price, at the respective ports*
   (b)   a fixed price per ton*
(* *state alternative agreed in Box 24*).
The Vessel to be delivered with not less than the number of tons and not exceeding the number of tons stated in Box 25 in the Vessel's bunkers.
The Vessel to be re-delivered with not less than the number of tons and not exceeding the number of tons stated in Box 26 in the Vessel's bunkers.

Alternative (b) should be used only in connection with short charter periods as it is difficult both during the negotiations and at the fixture to estimate what the prices will be at the time of redelivery. Alternative (a) sometimes causes difficulties as there is not always a current price at the respective ports. It is, however, very difficult to draft a clear fuel price clause and alternative (a) is therefore often used. Also, the permissible quantities at the respective ports should be stated.

When the vessel is delivered or redelivered at the quay the liability for harbour dues will change from one party to the other during the ship's call at port, and it may then be difficult to find out how the harbour dues should be shared between them. To avoid this problem the charter-parties usually contain a clause dealing with this question. The Linertime form and also the Baltime form have the following solution (first part of Clause 5):

LINERTIME

The Charterers to pay all dock, harbour, light and tonnage dues at the ports of delivery and re-delivery (unless incurred through cargo carried before delivery or after re-delivery).

THE HIRE AND PAYMENT OF HIRE

The hire is the financial payment to the owners for leasing the manned and equipped vessel to the time charterers. The basic rule is that hire shall be paid from the moment when the ship is delivered to the charterers until she is again redelivered to the owners at the termination of the charter period. Under some circumstances—mainly defined in the Off-hire (or Suspension of hire) clauses— the time charterers are relieved from their obligation to pay hire to the owners.

Fixing of the hire

The hire can be expressed in various ways, for instance "X dollars per 30 days", X DM per day", "X £ per 30 days and deadweight ton", etc. The choice depends mainly on the type of vessel and the trade.

Hire "per month" should be avoided as this expression is understood as a calendar month, for instance, from and including 9 February to and including 8 March. The number of days during such a period will vary between 28 and 31 days and this means that the hire per day will be different from month to month, which may cause difficulties when off-hire is calculated. It may then be better to express the hire in such a way that the daily hire will be the same throughout the charter period, and it is common that the hire is calculated and payable "per month of 30 days".

Payment

The procedure for payment of hire is dealt with in the Linertime form in the following way (part of Clause 7):

LINERTIME

Payment
Payment of hire to be made in cash, in the currency stated in Box 28 without discount, every 30 days, in advance, and in the manner prescribed in Box 28.
In default of payment the Owners to have the right of withdrawing the Vessel from the service of the Charterers, without noting any protest and without interference by any court or any other formality whatsoever and without prejudice to any claim the Owners may otherwise have on the Charterers under the Charter.

In time chartering the financial payment to the owners—the hire—is paid in advance. Note the difference from voyage chartering where the principal rule is that the owners get their payment—the freight—when the sea voyage has terminated and they are ready to deliver the cargo at the port of destination (see page 186ff.). The reason the owners in time chartering are paid in advance is because they do not have the same possibility as in voyage chartering of securing their payment by exercising a lien over the cargo (see, further, the next sub-section "Late payment—owners' security").

Payment periods of 30 days are commonly used but also other routines exist. See, for instance, NYPE 93 where, according to clause 11, the payment shall be made "15 days in advance". This is also rather common in short time charters.

Periods of hire and periods for the purpose of payments must not be mixed. If the hire is to be paid for 30-day periods in advance, the monthly date of payment will differ from period to period. The amount paid will, however, be the same (if we disregard deductions for off-hire and similar reasons). If, on the other hand, the hire is to be paid "monthly in advance" and is fixed at "x dollars per day" or with a similar method where the daily hire all the time is the same, the monthly date for payment will be the same from one period to another. The amount paid will, however, be different as the number of days in the period will vary from 28 to 31.

Late payment—owners' security

As mentioned above, the hire is payable in advance. If the charterers are in default with payment by paying either too late or too little, the owners are entitled, under English law and according to most time charter-party forms, to cancel the charter agreement. In the Baltime form this is expressed in the following way (part of Clause 6):

BALTIME

In default of payment the Owners to have the right of withdrawing the Vessel from the service of the Charterers, without noting any protest and without interference by any court or any other formality whatsoever and without prejudice to any claim the Owners may otherwise have on the Charterers under the Charter.

According to the wording of the Baltime clause and similar clauses in other forms, a small default in payment gives the owners a right to cancel the whole agreement. The explanation for this clause, which must be considered rigorous, is that the right to cancel is one of the few possibilities owners have to protect themselves against insolvent charterers and charterers who are not willing to pay. Unfortunately, these clauses very often do not give owners the protection intended when it comes to the practical situation, at least not when cargo has been taken on board. For, as soon as a bill of lading has been issued, the owner will have a duty to the bill of lading holder to perform the transport. Unless the owner can get a lien over the freight payable to the time charterer under the sub-charter, he may have to deliver the cargo at the bill of lading destination without getting anything from the time charterer.

Over the years there have been several disputes about the owners' right to cancel on the ground of default in payment of hire. It is difficult to extract the principles from these cases but it can be noted that the owners may lose their right to cancel if they have previously, without protest, accepted late payment and that—if charterers have previously made correct payments—the owners may not be entitled to cancel for only a small default in payment. From this we can learn that it is important for owners always to protest when the hire payment is late or when the charterers have made unauthorized deductions from the hire. If the owners fail to protest it may become considered as an accepted procedure for future payments.

Payments of hire are commonly made via banks and in most cases payment is not considered as effected before the money reaches the owners' bank. As the remittance is frequently delayed in the banks, it is nowadays not unusual to have a so-called "Non-technicality clause" or "Anti-technicality clause" in time charter-parties in order to prevent the owner from cancelling due to technical delays in the payment. Such a clause should contain an undertaking by the owners to notify the charterers if and when the payment is late (or if the owners, for other reasons, do not accept the amount) and should also allow the charterers some additional time before the owners are entitled to cancel the charter agreement. The following clause is from NYPE 93:

NYPE 93

(b) Grace Period
Where there is failure to make punctual and regular payment of hire due to oversight, negligence, errors or omissions on the part of the Charterers or their bankers, the Charterers shall be given by the Owners . . . . clear banking days (as recognized at the agreed place of payment) written notice to rectify the failure, and when so rectified within those . . . . days following the Owners' notice, the payment shall stand as regular and punctual.
Failure by the Charterers to pay the hire within . . . . days of their receiving the Owners' notice as provided herein, shall entitle the Owners to withdraw as set forth in Sub-clause 11(a) above.

From the above we learn that both the charterers and the owners must be very careful. Charterers must see to it that remittances of hire are made well in advance before the hire is due as there is always a risk that the owners will take the opportunity to cancel the charter agreement if they can get better terms from another time charterer. On the other hand, it is important that the owner is cautious and takes legal advice before cancelling on the ground of default of payment, as an unjustified cancellation may entitle the charterers to damages from the owners.

The time charter-parties usually also have a Lien clause which can have the following wording (Linertime):

LINERTIME

20. Lien
The Owners to have a lien upon all cargoes and sub-freights belonging to the Time-Charterers and any Bill of Lading freight for all claims under this Charter, and the Charterers to have a lien on the Vessel for all moneys paid in advance and not earned. The Charterers will not suffer, nor permit to be continued any lien or encumbrance incurred by them or their Agents, which might have priority over the title and interest of the Owners in the Vessel.

The intention of this clause is also to protect the owners against insolvent charterers but it looks more helpful than it actually is in practice. The cargo on board the vessel usually belongs to someone other than the time charterers and the owners have, according to the bill of lading, an obligation to deliver the cargo to the bill of lading holder. As the owners are bound by their obligations to the cargo owners (see above in this section) as soon as they have started to load the cargo, they, in most cases, have to fulfil the cargo voyage and their obligations to the cargo owners even if the time charterers fail to pay hire.

Regarding "sub-freights belonging to the time charterers and B/L-freights" it is often difficult for the owners to get the information which they need to notify the bill of lading freight payer that they have a lien over the sub-freight which he is bound to pay. In many cases the sub-freight (bill of lading freight) is prepaid, which means that the owners have no security.

Deductions from hire

When the advance payment of hire is to be made the charterers often wish to make deductions for off-hire during previous periods, for cash paid by agents to the master, for disbursement for owners' account, for planned off-hire (for instance drydocking), and for other monetary claims that the charterers may have against the owners. As default in payment may give the owners a right to cancel the charter (cf. the above sub-section) it is important for charterers either to rely on a clause in the charter-party which gives them a right to make such deductions, or to get the owners' approval before the deduction is made. It is not clear to what extent the charterers are allowed to make deductions without permission from owners and without clauses in the charter-party to such effect.

Payment of last instalment of hire

As the last period of hire in most cases is not as long as the full hire period and as the charterers will usually have a claim against the owners in connection with the redelivery for bunkers remaining on board, the time charter-party forms frequently contain a "Last Hire Payment" clause which may have the following wording (part of Clause 7 in Linertime):

LINERTIME
Last Hire Payment
Should the Vessel be on her voyage towards port of re-delivery at time a payment of hire is due, said payment to be made for such length of time as the Owners or their Agents and the Charterers or their Agents may agree upon as estimated time necessary to complete the voyage, taking into account bunkers to be taken over by the Vessel and estimated disbursements for the Owners' account before re-delivery, and when the Vessel is re-delivered any difference to be refunded by the Owners or paid by the Charterers, as the case may require.

OFF-HIRE

As already mentioned, the principal rule is that the charterers must pay hire from the moment the vessel is delivered until the moment she is redelivered to the owners at the end of the agreed charter period. The financial risk for delay of the vessel due to bad weather, strikes of pilots or stevedores, etc., during the charter period normally rests on the charterers. Under certain conditions, agreed in the charter-party and usually attributable to the crew or other conditions connected with the vessel, the charterers may, however, be entitled to compensation in accordance with a special clause called an "Off-hire clause", "Suspension of hire" clause or similar. In Linertime the clause is worded:

LINERTIME
14. Suspension of Hire, etc.
(A) In the event of dry-docking or other necessary measures to maintain the efficiency of the Vessel, deficiency of men or Owners' stores, strike of Master, Officers and Crew, breakdown of machinery, damage to hull or other accident, either hindering or preventing the working of the Vessel and continuing for more than the number of consecutive hours indicated in Box 31, no hire to be paid in respect of any time lost thereby during the period in which the Vessel is unable to perform the service immediately required.
Should the Vessel deviate or put back during a voyage, contrary to the orders or directions of the Charterers, for any reason other than accident to the Cargo, the hire to be suspended from the time of her deviating or putting back until she is again in the same or equidistant position from the destination and the voyage resumed therefrom.

Winch Breakdown
In the event of a breakdown of a winch or winches, not caused by carelessness of shore labourers, the time lost to be calculated pro rata for the period of such inefficiency in relation to the number of winches required for work. If the Charterers elect to continue work, the Owners are to pay for shore appliances in lieu of the winches, but in such cases the Charterers to pay full hire.
Any hire paid in advance to be adjusted accordingly.

Detention for Charterers' Account
(B) In the event of the Vessel being driven into port or to anchorage through stress of weather, trading to shallow harbours or to rivers or ports with bars or suffering an accident to her cargo, any detention of the Vessel and/or expenses resulting from such detention to be for the Charterers' account even if such detention and/or expenses, or the cause by reason of which either is incurred, be due to, or be contributed to by, the negligence of the Owners' servants.

Dry-docking
Owners to give the Charterers at least four weeks' notice of their intention of dry-docking the ship for bottom painting and normal maintenance work and actual time and place for such dry-docking to be mutually agreed.

This can be compared to the quite extensive off-hire clause of Shelltime 4.

Off-hire   21. (a) On each and every occasion that there is loss of time   205
                   (whether by way of interruption in the vessel's service or, from [   ]
                   reduction in the vessel's performance, or in any other manner)   [   ]

(i) due to deficiency of personnel or stores; repairs; gas-freeing 207
for repairs; time in and waiting to enter dry dock for [ ]
repairs; breakdown (whether partial or total) of machinery, [ ]
boilers or other parts of the vessel or her equipment [ ]
(including without limitation tank coatings); overhaul, [ ]
maintenance or survey; collision, stranding, accident or [ ]
damage to the vessel; or any other similar cause preventing [ ]
the efficient working of the vessel; and such loss continues [ ]
for more than three consecutive hours (if resulting from [ ]
interruption in the vessel's service) or cumulates to more [ ]
than three hours (if resulting from partial loss of service); [ ]
or [ ]

(ii) due to industrial action, refusal to sail, breach of orders or 213
neglect of duty on the part of the master, officers or crew; [ ]
or [ ]

(iii) for the purpose of obtaining medical advice or treatment 215
for or landing any sick or injured person (other than a [ ]
Charterers' representative carried under Clause 17 hereof) [ ]
or for the purpose of landing the body of any person (other [ ]
than a Charterers' representative), and such loss continues [ ]
for more than three consecutive hours; or [ ]

(iv) due to any delay in quarantine arising from the master, 219
officers or crew having had communication with the shore [ ]
at any infected area without the written consent or instruc- [ ]
tions of Charterers or their agents, or to any detention by [ ]
customs or other authorities caused by smuggling or other [ ]
infraction of local law on the part of the master, officers, [ ]
or crew; or [ ]

(v) due to detention of the vessel by authorities at home or 223
abroad attributable to legal action against or breach of [ ]
regulations by the vessel, the vessel's owners, or Owners [ ]
(unless brought about by the act or neglect of Charterers); [ ]
then [ ]

without prejudice to Charterers' rights under Clause 3 or to any 226
other rights of Charterers hereunder or otherwise the vessel shall be [ ]
off-hire from the commencement of such loss of time until she is [ ]
again ready and in an efficient state to resume her service from a [ ]
position not less favourable to Charterers than that at which such [ ]
loss of time commenced; provided, however, that any service given [ ]
or distance made good by the vessel whilst off-hire shall be taken [ ]
into account in assessing the amount to be deducted from hire. [ ]

(b) If the vessel fails to proceed at any guaranteed speed pursuant 231
to Clause 24, and such failure arises wholly or partly from any of the [ ]
causes set out in Clause 21(a) above, then the period for which the [ ]
vessel shall be off-hire under this Clause 21 shall be the difference [ ]
between [ ]

(i) the time the vessel would have required to perform the 234
relevant service at such guaranteed speed, and [ ]

(ii) the time actually taken to perform such service (including 236
any loss of time arising from interruption in the performance [ ]
of such service). [ ]

For the avoidance of doubt, all time included under (ii) above shall   238
be excluded from any computation under Clause 24.   [   ]
    (c) Further and without prejudice to the foregoing, in the event of   240
the vessel deviating (which expression includes without limitation   [   ]
putting back, or putting into any port other than that to which she   [   ]
is bound under the instructions of Charterers) for any cause or   [   ]
purpose mentioned in Clause 21(a), the vessel shall be off-hire from   [   ]
the commencement of such deviation until the time when she is again   [   ]
ready and in an efficient state to resume her service from a position   [   ]
not less favourable to Charterers than that at which the deviation   [   ]
commenced, provided, however, that any service given or distance   [   ]
made good by the vessel whilst so off-hire shall be taken into account   [   ]
in assessing the amount to be deducted from hire. If the vessel, for   [   ]
any cause or purpose mentioned in Clause 21(a), puts into any port   [   ]
other than the port to which she is bound on the instructions of   [   ]
Charterers, the port charges, pilotage and other expenses at such   [   ]
port shall be borne by Owners. Should the vessel be driven into any   [   ]
port or anchorage by stress of weather hire shall continue to be due   [   ]
and payable during any time lost thereby.   [   ]
    (d) If the vessel's flag state becomes engaged in hostilities, and   251
Charterers in consequence of such hostilities find it commercially   [   ]
impracticable to employ the vessel and have given Owners written   [   ]
notice thereof then from the date of receipt by Owners of such notice   [   ]
until the termination of such commercial impracticability the vessel   [   ]
shall be off-hire and Owners shall have the right to employ the vessel   [   ]
on their own account.   [   ]
    (e) Time during which the vessel is off-hire under this charter shall   255
count as part of the charter period.   [   ]

Charterers are entitled to off-hire only if the ship is delayed for a reason which in accordance with the Off-hire clause (or in accordance with the applicable law) is recognized as a ground for off-hire. Off-hire can be compared with *liquidated damages* which means that it is compensation agreed beforehand between the parties. The compensation to charterers is based on the charter hire and charterers do not have to prove their loss. Even if they can prove that their loss is higher than the charter hire, they are not entitled to more than agreed beforehand. On the other hand, they still get compensation based on the charter hire also if their actual loss is less. A characteristic of off-hire is that the charterer may be entitled to make the deduction from hire notwithstanding the absence of any breach of contract or negligence by the owners. If the owners are in breach of contract or if they or the people on board have been negligent, the charterers may, however, be entitled to damages *or* off-hire at their own choice, or both.

    Off-hire clauses sometimes have a special section about "Detention for Charterers' Account". See for instance section (B) of the above-cited Linertime clause. The "Detention for Charterers' Account" clause is not dealing with situations where the vessel is hindered or prevented by charterers' breach of contract. If charterers are in breach of the contract owners shall not suffer. The situation can be handled in different ways. One possibility is that the vessel continues on-hire and another possibility is that the vessel is considered off-hire and the owners are compensated by way of damages. The difference can be important if for instance charterers have an insurance for Charterers' Liability for Damage to Hull. Such an insurance may compensate charterers for payments of damages but not for hire costs payable during a period when the vessel is hindered or prevented in accordance with the "Detention for Charterers' Account" clause.

The off-hire claim

To find out if a vessel is off-hire or not and to prepare the off-hire claim, the following questionnaire can be used:

- —is the reason for the delay included in the list of grounds for off-hire in the Off-hire clause?
- —is there any "threshold rule" and, if so, will this rule be applicable in the relevant situation?
- —the loss of time?
- —the loss of money?
- —the deduction of off-hire?

Before we deal with these questions separately it must be pointed out that if the charterers have caused the delay to the ship they cannot normally get off-hire compensation from the owners even if the delay is covered by the Off-hire clause (see (B) in the above-cited Linertime clause).

The grounds for off-hire

The first step is to find out whether the reason for the delay is covered by the Off-hire clause in the relevant charter-party. In the Linertime form the off-hire reasons are mentioned in the first part of Clause 14:

LINERTIME
14. Suspension of Hire, etc.
(A) In the event of dry-docking or other necessary measures to maintain the efficiency of the Vessel, deficiency of men or Owners' stores, strike of Master, Officers and Crew, breakdown of machinery, damage to hull or other accident, either hindering or preventing the working of the Vessel and continuing for more than the number of consecutive hours indicated in Box 31, no hire to be paid in respect of any time lost thereby during the period in which the Vessel is unable to perform the service immediately required.

Some charter-parties are more and others less extensive in this respect. When the charter-party is governed by English law it seems that the clause is generally interpreted restrictively. Under other legal systems, for instance, the

Scandinavian, the clause is more regarded as a description of a principle and, as it is supplemented by the maritime code, it can generally be said that the charterers have less chance to get off-hire compensation when the charter-party is governed by English law compared with the situation, for instance, under Scandinavian law.

The threshold rule

If it is found that the reason for the delay is covered by the Off-hire clause, the next step will be to find out if there is a threshold in the Off-hire clause and, if so, whether it is applicable.

Many standard time charter-party forms have thresholds like the one above in Linertime Clause 14, where it is stated that the charterers are entitled to off-hire only if the vessel is hindered or prevented more than an agreed number of hours (usually 12 or 24 hours). Baltime has such a threshold (24 hours) but in NYPE 93 no such favour is given to the owners.

As the threshold rule is worded in Linertime and Baltime, the hindrance—and not the loss of time—must continue for a certain number of consecutive hours. This means that if the ship has problems with her main engine and steams at half speed for 30 hours, a threshold of 24 hours does not prevent off-hire, although the time loss is only 15 hours.

Note that the rule as construed in Linertime and Baltime is a threshold and not a deduction. If the vessel has to stop for 35 hours due to engine breakdown, the off-hire deduction will be for 35 hours and not 35 less 24 hours. Some charter-party forms have thresholds for some kinds of delays but no threshold for other delays. See, for instance, the second sub-section of Linertime, Clause 14, above, where no threshold rule is applicable when the reason for the delay is breakdown of winches.

The threshold rule causes many disputes and it is arguable whether it is at all justified. After all, the charterers pay hire to the owners in return for the use of the vessel and it is difficult to understand why the charterers should also pay for periods when they are unable to use her on account of breakdown or other hindrances on the vessel's/owners' side.

The loss of time

The next step is to calculate the loss of time. Charterers are not always entitled to off-hire for all time actually lost. According to Baltime, for instance, the ship is on hire again when she is able "to perform the service immediately required". This means that if she has an engine breakdown in the North Sea and is towed to Hamburg for repairs, she will be on hire again when the main engine is repaired in Hamburg and the charterers are not entitled to off-hire for the time the vessel needs to get back into the position she had when she went off-hire.

To avoid this disadvantage charterers often wish to insert a so-called "Put back" clause. Such a "Put back" clause is included in Linertime's Clause 14 above (latter part of first section).

The NYPE 93 form adopts another approach and its clause states that "the payment of hire and overtime, if any, shall cease for the time thereby lost". This expression is wider than the expression used in Baltime but still it is doubtful to what extent consequential loss of time will be considered as off-hire. As an example of questions which can easily arise in connection with off-hire we can mention the situation when the vessel has been off hire in port awaiting crew members (deficiency of men) and then, when the crew members are on board, has to postpone her departure due to a tug strike which started while the vessel was off hire awaiting the crew members. To find out whether such a consequential delay will entitle the charterers to an off-hire deduction the wording of the off-hire clause in the relevant charter-party and the applicable law must be checked.

NYPE 93 has a special section about the situation when the vessel is steaming with reduced speed. When time is lost as a result of slow steaming caused by defect in the vessel, breakdown etc., the time lost shall be deducted from the hire.

The loss of money

When the loss of time is established, it must be converted into money. This is not very hard when the hire is counted per day, per 30 days or similar. When the hire is counted "per month" the situation is a little more complicated as the hire per day, which may vary during the off-hire period, must first be established (cf. above, on page 228).

Deduction of off-hire

As mentioned above under the section "The Hire and Payment of Hire" (page 226ff.) default in payment of hire may give the owners a right to cancel the charter agreement. The charterers must therefore be careful and investigate their legal position before the off-hire is deducted.

Other obligations during off-hire periods

Especially when the ship is off hire for a long period, the question arises as to what extent the charterers' other obligations under the charter agreement remain during off-hire periods. Do the charterers, for instance, have to pay for bunkers consumed and harbour dues incurred during the off-hire period? Legally, it seems to be clear, at least under English and American law, that unless express provision has been made to the contrary, the charterers' other obligations remain during off-hire periods. For some reason the development in practical life has been to the contrary, i.e. charterers usually do not pay for fuel during off-hire periods, and, in order to establish this legally, the words "whilst on hire" are often inserted at the beginning of the clause "Charterers to Provide" (see Linertime, Clause 5 below, at page 242).

Insurance for loss of hire

Long periods of off-hire can be disastrous especially for shipowners operating only one or a few vessels. These shipowners should therefore consider arranging a "loss of hire" or "loss of earnings" insurance which gives protection when the vessel, as a result of a breakdown or similar emergency, is off hire. The traditional "loss of hire" insurance is based on loss of time resulting from the same kind of casualties as are covered in the vessel's hull insurance. This means that loss of time resulting from strikes is not covered but shipowners have the possibility of arranging strike insurance.

DAMAGES AND PRE-TERMINATION OF THE CHARTER

One situation which really can be difficult for the time charterer is when the vessel he has chartered turns out to be of an unacceptable standard. If the ship runs into various kinds of technical difficulties and breakdowns and for other reasons is often hindered during her service, the charterer can, to a certain degree, get compensation under the Off-hire clause, but consequential damages and costs are usually not covered by the Off-hire clause. If the vessel is unusually bad it may be difficult or impossible for the time charterer to use her in his service.

The best way for time charterers to protect themselves in this respect is to have a performance guarantee in the charter-party. It can, however, be difficult to draft such a clause as a good performance of the vessel includes not only the various technical aspects but also the maintenance and manning aspects as well as the owners', master's, officers' and crew's willingness to give good service.

The main problem with the performance guarantees is, however, that, it is usually very difficult to get the owners to accept such a guarantee. A peformance guarantee which gives the charterers sufficient protection will at the same time give them an option to cancel the charter-party if the vessel turns out to be below the agreed standard. Such option to cancel is not acceptable by owners and their bankers.

The questions and problems which arise for time charterers when they intend to claim damages, and not only off-hire, and when they wish to terminate the charter before the flat period expires, are too difficult to discuss in detail in this book. We shall here only mention some of the different legal bases that may be used by the charterers.

—Misdescription of ship (the vessel is not in accordance with the description given by the owners during negotiations and in the charter-party).

—The vessel is not kept and maintained in accordance with the description.

—The ship is not delivered and maintained in a seaworthy condition as stated or implied in the charter-party.

—The vessel is not manned with master, officers and crew formally and practically competent to handle her, the equipment on board and the cargo.

ROUTINES AND ALLOCATION OF COSTS

We have dealt above in several sections with the charterers' and the owners' respective tasks and costs under a time charter agreement. In this section we shall go a little bit deeper into some of the clauses.

Directions and instructions to the vessel. Log books

All time charter-parties have clauses of the following type (Employment clause):

LINERTIME

10. Master
The Charterers to give the necessary sailing instructions, subject to the limits of the Charter.

The Master to be under the orders of the Charterers as regards employment, agency, or other arrangements. The Master to prosecute all voyages with the utmost despatch and render customary assistance with the Vessel's Crew.

The Master and Engineer to keep full and correct logs including scrap logs accessible to the Charterers or their Agents.

If the Charterers have reason to be dissatisfied with the conduct of the Master, Officers, or Engineers, the Owners on receiving particulars of the complaint, promptly to investigate the matter, and, if necessary and practicable, to make a change in the appointments.

Since it is the time charterers who use the vessel commercially, the master will receive all his instructions and directions concerning the employment from them and not from the owners. The master should keep full and correct logs of the voyage or voyages as requested by the time charterers or their agents. The master should furnish charterers when required to do so with copies of log books, port sheets, weather reports and reports about the ship's speed and bunker consumption, etc. All these documents are important for the time charterers, both for their relationship with sub-charterers, shippers and receivers, and for their relationship with the owners.

Master's position

The master has a difficult position under a time charter since he has to follow the instructions of both the owner and the time charterer. He represents two parties and has to look after the interests of them both.

Although the master receives sailing instructions, etc., from the time charterers and should comply with those instructions he need not necessarily in every situation follow the orders and instructions. The master has a responsibility for the safety of the crew and the vessel and he usually also has responsibilities with regard to the cargo owners and the other third parties. If, according to the master's well-founded opinion, the time charterers' orders and instructions jeopardize the crew, ship, cargo or other persons or property, he has not only a right, but also an obligation, not to obey the orders. The master must, in such a difficult situation, contact not only the time charterers but also the owners and try to deal with the situation without causing too many problems for the parties involved.

If the master does not get clear and acceptable orders from the time charterers and the cargo owners, he should follow the orders he gets from his own owners provided that these are acceptable considering the safety of the crew, vessel, etc. Many time charter-party forms have a special clause about the situation when the time charterers are not satisfied with the master, officers or crew. Such clauses can, for instance, have a wording such as in the one cited above (last part). In other time charter-party forms the corresponding clause is more severe for the owners and obliges them to make changes in the appointments.

Whether it is expressly stated in the charter-party or not, the master must prosecute the voyage with the utmost despatch. The time charterers pay per time unit and delay of the vessel often means less revenue. During the sea voyage the master must choose the fastest route without jeopardizing the safety of the ship. Before arrival in port, all documents must be prepared to avoid delay with formalities and the master must supervise loading and discharging in order to get the quickest possible despatch. He should also co-operate with the time charterers and their agents and give them all necessary information and assistance.

Customary assistance. Overtime

Most time charter-party forms state that the master must give the charterers customary assistance with the vessel's crew. The concept of "customary assistance" is often discussed and argued about between charterers and owners.

The general definition of the customary assistance concept is that the master and the crew should give the same assistance to the time charterers as they would give the owners if they were trading for their account. This means that the crew, without extra charge to the time charterers, should carry out the usual cleaning of cargo holds after discharging. They should also undertake the necessary rigging, opening and closing of hatches before, during and after loading and discharging. The master's and owners' obligation to give customary assistance is not limited to such assistance which can be given without overtime compensation for the crew but the charterers must accept that cleaning, rigging, etc., cannot always be done without delaying the vessel. If the charterers wish to avoid delay by employing extra men from ashore, the cost of doing so will usually be for the charterers' account. Also, when local rules or customs will not allow the crew to carry out those duties, the cost of stevedores or extra labour will be for the charterers' account.

During the voyage the master and the crew should, without extra cost to the charterers, keep control over the cargo and, if necessary, make additional lashing or securing. The charterers cannot normally claim, however, that the crew, without additional payment, should arrange for the shifting and restowing of large quantities of cargo.

In time chartering, owners and charterers, for practical reasons, sometimes make more detailed agreements about the cleaning of holds specifying, for instance, that all cleaning of holds should be for charterers' account and carried out by extra men from ashore if the ballast voyage is shorter than X days. On longer ballast voyages the cleaning should be performed by the crew.

Concerning overtime for officers and crew, various methods are used. Sometimes it is stated that the hire includes overtime to officers and crew and sometimes the charterers pay an extra lump sum per month for overtime. Both these ways are, for practical reasons, probably better than the alternative method of keeping a special book for recording overtime for time charterers' account, as this will create additional work both for the people on board and for the owners and time charterers.

Allocation of costs

The owners must place the vessel at the time charterers' disposal and during the charter period provide and pay for manning, insurance and maintenance. The charterers provide and pay for fuel (lubricating oil is, however, usually for the owners' account), harbour dues, pilotage, costs for loading and discharging, and other costs relating to the commercial use of the vessel.

Time charter-parties normally contain clauses in which the parties' respective obligations are specified. These clauses have the following or similar wording:

LINERTIME

4. Owners to Provide

The Owners to provide and pay for all provisions and wages, for insurance of the Vessel, for all deck and engine-room stores and maintain her in a thoroughly efficient state in hull and machinery during service.

The Owners to provide one winchman per working hatch. In lieu of winchmen the

Charterers are entitled to ask for two watchmen. If further winchmen or watchmen are required, or if stevedores refuse or are not permitted to work with the Crew, the Charterers to provide and pay qualified men. The gangway watchman to be provided by the Owners but where compulsory to employ gangway watchmen from shore, the expenses to be for the Charterers' account.

5. Charterers to Provide

The Charterers to pay all dock, harbour, light and tonnage dues at the ports of delivery and re-delivery (unless incurred through cargo carried before delivery or after re-delivery).

Whilst on hire the Charterers to provide and pay for all fuel, water for boilers, port charges, pilotages (whether compulsory or not), canal steersmen, boatage, lights, tug-assistance, consular charges (except those payable to the consulates of the country of the Vessel's flag) canal, dock and other dues and charges, including any foreign general municipality or state taxes, agencies, commissions, also to arrange and pay for loading, trimming, stowing (including dunnage and shifting boards, excepting any already on board), unloading, weighing, tallying and delivery of cargoes, surveys on hatches, any other survey on cargo, meals supplied to officials and men in their service at the rate per man per meal indicated in Boxes 37 and 38, respectively, and all other charges and expenses whatsoever.

Cargo Gear

All ropes, slings and special runners actually used for loading and discharging and any special gear, including special ropes, hawsers and chains required by the custom of the port for mooring to be for the Charterers' account unless already on board. The Vessel is fitted with cargo handling gear as specified in Box 22.

This gear is to be kept in full working order for immediate use, the Charterers however to give sufficient notice of their intention to use heavy lift gear.

The Owners guarantee the Vessel possesses cargo gear register and certificates in compliance with requirement of International Labour Organization Convention No. 32.

Fuel Consumption in Port

The Vessel's normal fuel consumption whilst in port working all cargo gear is about the number of tons stated in Box 23 per 24 hours.

It is not possible to mention in the charter-party all the costs which may arise during the charter period. Discussions and disputes concerning the responsibility for various expenses are common in time chartering. As regards costs not expressly mentioned in the charter-party it may, as a general rule, be said that all costs which are compulsory in a port are for charterers' account as they are a direct consequence of the charterers' directing the vessel to the port and the owners cannot avoid them. Concerning other costs which are not compulsory and not clearly related to one of the parties, the question must be discussed from case to case. As an example of costs which often lead to disputes we can mention the cost of watchmen and garbage disposal.

Agency fees (where the principal rule is that they are for the time charterers' account) can also quite often give rise to disputes. Most charterers accept that they have to provide owners with a certain basic service from agents without extra cost to the owners. If, however, the agency fees can be directly related to something which is for the owners' account, for instance, manning or maintenance, the charterers are not willing to pay to the same degree. To avoid this problem the charterers sometimes wish to insert a remark by way of clarification, such as:

"Whilst on hire the Charterers to pay for . . . agencies (unless attributable to maintenance and manning of the Vessel or otherwise for the benefit solely of the Vessel, Master, Crew or the Owners), . . .".

Information

In order to achieve better co-operation and planning, the parties in most cases have an obligation to keep each other informed about future schedules for the vessel, etc. The owners need a schedule for the ship in order to be able to better plan the exchange of crew members, the supplying of spare parts, etc., and the charterers need for their planning an owners' schedule for drydocking and other necessary maintenance for the vessel.

CARGO LIABILITY

(Compare the following with the section about the bill of lading conventions, page 61ff.)

In time chartering, as in voyage chartering (cf. above, at page 206ff.), the charterers and owners can allocate the liability for cargo as they wish but as liability under a bill of lading is also involved, the situation is sometimes complex from a legal standpoint. Cargo owners usually claim under the bill of lading and the first question is whether the owners, time charterers, or both, are liable to the cargo owners. A second question is how the liability should ultimately be allocated between the charterers and owners.

Liability to cargo owners

The bills of lading regularly contain a clause named "Identity of Carrier" or "Demise" clause with the following or similar wording:

CONLINEBILL

17. Identity of Carrier.
The Contract evidenced by this Bill of Lading is between the Merchant and the Owner of the vessel named herein (or substitute) and it is therefore agreed that said Shipowner only shall be liable for any damage or loss due to any breach or non-performance of any obligation arising out of the contract of carriage, whether or not relating to the vessel's seaworthiness. If, despite the foregoing, it is adjudged that any other is the Carrier and/or bailee of the goods shipped hereunder, all limitations of, and exonerations from, liability provided for by law or by this Bill of Lading shall be available to such other.
It is further understood and agreed that as the Line, Company or Agent who has

executed this Bill of Lading for and on behalf of the Master is not a principal in the transaction, said Line, Company or Agent shall not be under any liability arising out of the contract of carriage, nor as Carrier nor bailee of the goods.

The liability for cargo under the bill of lading rests, according to this clause, on the owners of the vessel (the performing carrier) and not on the time charterers (the contractual carrier). The clause is, however, considered invalid under many legal systems. Under English law the clause is basically valid.

Although the time charterers may legally be able to reject liability for cargo claims under the bill of lading by reference to the Demise clause, they quite often handle the claims as if they were liable to the cargo owners. Especially when the time charterers are large operators and use their own bill of lading forms in the traffic, they want to maintain good relations with the cargo owners and therefore settle claims as if the time chartered ship was their own.

Allocation of liability between owners and charterers

As already mentioned, charterers and owners are free to make what allocation of liability they wish under the charter-party. Some printed forms, as, for instance, the Baltime form, more or less relieve owners from liability. According to Baltime, the owners are liable for loss or damage to cargo on board only if the loss or damage (part of Clause 13)

"has been caused by want of due diligence on the part of the owners or their manager in making the vessel seaworthy and fitted for the voyage or any other personal act or omission or default of the owners or their manager".

Sometimes the charter-parties contain a Paramount clause which brings in the Hague Rules or the Hague-Visby Rules (cf. above, at page 63).

The problem is made even more complicated when the Paramount clause is inserted in the time charter-party, and in order to avoid endless discussions between owners and charterers, several P. & I. clubs have agreed a special procedure for the apportionment of liability for cargo under a time charter agreement based on the NYPE form. This agreement, officially named "The Inter-Club New York Produce Exchange Agreement", but usually called "The Interclub Agreement" or "The Produce Formula", has the following allocation:

Claims for loss of or damage to cargo due to unseaworthiness	100% Owners
Claims for damage due to bad stowage or handling, including slackage/ullage	100% Charterers
Claims for short delivery, including pilferage, and overcarriage	50% Owners
	50% Charterers

NYPE 93 has in clause 27 a reference to The Produce Formula "of February 1970, as amended May, 1984, or any subsequent modifications or replacement thereof".

Depending on what amendments to the printed text the parties have agreed, the basic Produce Formula as cited above is sometimes varied. The Produce Formula is often used between the parties when a Paramount clause has been inserted in the Baltime form. The apportionment of liability for cargo is important and, especially when the time charter agreement is for a long period, the parties should be careful and take legal advice from their P. & I. clubs.

DAMAGE TO THE VESSEL

The vessel, during the charter period, is exposed to wear and tear and certain risks of damage. Both wear and tear and damage may cause considerable maintenance and repair expenditure and it is therefore important to make the allocation of liability in this respect as clear as possible. As mentioned above (page 214) the owners should insure the ship and maintain her in a thoroughly efficient state in hull and machinery during the charter period. In the redelivery clause it is usually stated that the charterers have to redeliver the ship in the same good order and condition as when delivered under the charter (fair wear and tear excepted). Sometimes the charter-party also has a clause expressly stating under what conditions the charterers shall be liable for damage to the ship but in most cases the answer must be found in other clauses and by reference to the applicable law.

Damage caused by bad weather, collision and grounding

Owners normally have little chance of obtaining compensation from the charterers for damage caused to the vessel by bad weather, collision, grounding, etc. Only if the owners can prove that the charterers' breach of contract or negligence has caused the damage may they have a chance of obtaining compensation. The most practical example is where time charterers have directed the vessel to an unsafe place or port. For additional comment about this, see above, at page 180.

Damage caused by fuel oil

Increases in fuel oil prices have created a market for fuel oil of poorer quality. Traditionally, charter-parties have described with only a few words what kind of fuel oil should be supplied to the vessel. As a result of difficulties with bad fuel oil many charter-parties today have a more precise description of the fuel oil to be used. We can for instance mention NYPE 93, Clause 9(b) including the reference to Appendix A. Section (b) of Clause 9 reads:

(b) The Charterers shall supply bunkers of a quality suitable for burning in the Vessel's engines and auxiliaries and which conform to the specification(s) as set out in Appendix A.
The Owners reserve their right to make a claim against the Charterers for any damage

to the main engines or the auxiliaries caused by the use of unsuitable fuels or fuels not complying with the agreed specification(s). Additionally if bunker fuels supplied do not conform with the mutually agreed specification(s) or otherwise prove unsuitable for burning in the Vessel's engines or auxiliaries, the Owners shall not be held responsible for any reduction in the Vessel's speed, performance and/or increased bunker consumption nor for any time lost and any other consequences.

Damage caused by cargo

If the ship has been damaged by cargo, the owners can seek compensation from the charterers in two ways. Firstly, the charterers may be held responsible if they have shipped a cargo which is not permitted under the charter agreement. As mentioned above (page 219) time charter-parties usually have a clause which excludes a number of specified cargo types and all cargo likely to be injurious to the ship.

Secondly, the owner may seek compensation from charterers when the cargo has been loaded, stowed or secured insufficiently and the vessel is damaged thereby. This situation is usually more complicated as the master and officers normally supervise the loading and securing of the cargo. It is difficult to find the borderline between the charterers' and owners' liability in this respect. The tendency, however, seems to be for charterers to be held liable unless there is obvious negligence on the part of the master or officers.

Other damage

The most common type of damage to the ship is damage caused by stevedores. The extent of the charterers' liability should be defined in the charter-party and the applicable law will, of course, supply additional rules. Time charter-parties quite often contain special clauses stating under what circumstances the charterers are liable for damage caused by stevedores and these clauses are usually very harsh for owners. It is, for instance, not unusual to find clauses which say that the charterers are liable for stevedore damage only if the master informs the charterers immediately, when the damage occurs, and also obtains a statement in writing from the stevedores that they accept liability for the damage. Stevedore damage is sometimes found weeks or perhaps months after it occurred and as it is more or less impossible to get an acceptance of responsibility from stevedoring companies, such a clause is hard for the owners to accept.

The master must, however, assist the charterers and help them to get evidence to support their claim against the stevedores, and a requirement for some kind of activity on the part of the master should be included in the charter-party. The following is taken from NYPE 93 (part of Clause 35):

35. Stevedore Damage
Notwithstanding anything contained herein to the contrary, the Charterers shall pay for any and all damage to the Vessel caused by stevedores provided the Master has

notified the Charterers and/or their agents in writing as soon as practical but not later than 48 hours after any damage is discovered. Such notice to specify the damage in detail and to invite Charterers to appoint a surveyor to assess the extent of such damage.

The Master and the officers on board must, of course, also supervise the loading, stowing, trimming and discharging and see to it that damaging material and methods are avoided. If the stevedores do not follow the instructions they get from the master or the officers, both the owners and the time charterers should be informed. In many cases, also, the local representatives for underwriters and P. & I. clubs can assist.

The vessel may also be damaged by pilots, tugs, etc. Although pilots and tugs are employed and paid for by the charterers, such damage will only under special circumstances be considered the charterers' responsibility.

Repair of damage

As mentioned above, the vessel should, under many charter-party forms, be redelivered in the same good order and condition as when delivered. This does not mean that the charterers are prevented from redelivering her before any damage has been repaired for their account. Under normal circumstances the owners cannot refuse to take redelivery of a damaged vessel. If the charterers are liable for the damage, and the repairs delay the ship, the owners can instead include the loss of time in their claim against the charterers.

CHAPTER 14

THE CONTRACT OF AFFREIGHTMENT

The traditional voyage charter agreements as drawn up in standard forms for chartering are designed for the situation

One Agreement—One Voyage

There is, however, very often a need for a contract which covers several shipments. This is sometimes arranged by time chartering and sometimes by voyage chartering for consecutive voyages (see page 89). In both cases the voyages are normally performed with the same vessel and in direct continuation. Another solution is to enter into a so-called Contract of Affreightment (CoA).

Agreements covering more than one shipment or voyage give rise to several questions in addition to the questions arising in contracts covering one voyage only. We have already dealt with time chartering and consecutive voyages and will under this chapter deal with some of the questions arising under the Contract of Affreightment.

DEFINITION OF CONTRACT OF AFFREIGHTMENT

Although it is not necessary, and not even important, to have a precise definition of the CoA, the concept and the terminology need some clarification.

Examples

A CoA can have different bases. The following examples illustrate some of the situations.

- —The owner undertakes to carry between X and Y tons of grain from A to B during 1993.
- —The owner undertakes to carry all cargo shipped by the charterer from loading port A to the destination B during the period 1992–1995.
- —The owner to have the right to carry all crude oil imported by the charterer during 1993 and 1994.

—The owner to have the right and obligation to carry all vehicles exported by the charterer during the period 1993–1995, and the charterer to guarantee that he will have at least five shipments per year, each consisting of X-Y vehicles.

Characteristics and definition of the Contract of Affreightment

The CoA is usually a contract

—for the carriage of a specified type and quantity of cargo
—covering two or several shipments
—running over a long period.

In the CoA it is the cargo—and not the vessel—that has the central position. The CoA is thereby different from other contracts of carriage, which are built up with a specified ship as a base. This difference is important as a traditional charter-party is usually abandoned if the vessel is lost, while a CoA is normally still in force if the ship intended for the voyage is lost or is otherwise not available for the shipment. This does not mean that the identity and characteristics of the ship are unimportant—they may be some of the most important parts of the CoA—but the main obligation on the owner is to carry the cargo and he is not normally relieved of this obligation if the vessel is lost. The explanation for this is that the owner is usually free to choose tonnage and therefore he can rarely claim that he is exempted from his duty to nominate a ship due to difficulties in arranging tonnage. The idea is that, even if the vessel which the owner has intended to use for the voyage has become a loss, he still has the opportunity to arrange another ship of similar type.

The number of voyages is another important characteristic of CoA. Although a CoA can be fixed for one voyage only, one would hardly recognize such a contract as a CoA. As a general rule, a CoA covers at least two shipments. On the other hand, a contract can cover several shipments without actually being a CoA. This situation arises, for instance, when a voyage charter-party is drawn up for consecutive voyages. Such a contract differs from the CoA in two ways. First, the contract for consecutive voyages is linked to a certain vessel, with or without the right or obligation of the owner to substitute. Secondly, the voyages covered by a contract for consecutive voyages are *consecutive*, i.e. coming immediately after each other. Another difference between a contract for consecutive voyages and a CoA is that the former, but not necessarily the latter, is based on voyage charter conditions.

The third of the characteristics mentioned at the beginning of this section is that the CoA usually runs over a long period. This is not an important characteristic as the period covered by a CoA can be shorter than other contracts of carriage.

Terminology

As the most important characteristic of a CoA compared with other contracts of carriage is that it is more linked to the cargo and less to the vessel, it would perhaps be better to use terms like Cargo Contract of Affreightment, Cargo Contracts, Quantity Contracts, Volume Contracts, etc., but as the term Contract of Affreightment now seems to be generally used and accepted, we will use it here.

The documents

A number of standard documents are in use for voyage chartering, time chartering and bareboat chartering (see page 80ff.). This is, however, not the situation for contracts of affreightment and the explanation is probably that a CoA in most cases needs a design which is tailor-made and adapted for the specific circumstances. The CoA must also include a number of clauses dealing with questions which are specific for this type of contract.

Quite often the parties use a standard form as a part of the CoA. One construction is to have an overruling CoA dealing with cargo quantities, periods, owner's remuneration, type of vessel, etc., and then use an ordinary standard charter-party for the specific voyages and for the daily operation. Another solution is to have a standard charter-party with additional clauses dealing with the specific CoA questions. A third possibility is to use a tailor-made contract where all parts are negotiated and designed solely for the parties, cargo and carriage involved. The circumstances around the specific negotiation must be foremost in the choice of documentary construction.

Sometimes the individual vessels are nominated only by telex, but in other cases the parties prefer to draw up a formal *fixture note* for each vessel. Such a fixture note refers to the CoA and gives necessary details about the vessel. It should be mentioned that *fixture notes* are also commonly used in spot chartering. The system here is that the fixture note covers the facts individual to the planned voyage and that other terms are included in the agreement by a reference to some standard form (for instance "otherwise as per Gencon Charter-party form 1976").

Intercoa 80

A standard CoA, intended to be an overruling, steering, contract is Intercoa 80 which has been dealt with in Chapter 5 of *Gram on Chartering Documents* (2nd edition by S. Bonnick, Lloyd's of London Press Ltd., 1988). Intercoa 80 is designed as a steering contract for shipments of oil under Intertankvoy 76. It is, however, also possible to amend the contract for use in combination with other voyage forms. For further comments on Intercoa 80, we refer the reader to *Chartering Documents*, page 85ff.

Volcoa

Another standard CoA is the Volcoa, which is intended for bulk cargo. Volcoa (Volume Contract of Affreightment) has been presented in BIMCO Bulletin V-1982.

GENERAL

It goes without saying that the more extensive the carriage is, the greater is the need for a contract where all parts are specially negotiated and worded. In a contract covering a single voyage it is easier for the parties to accept a standard contract containing solutions which are not perfect than it is in a long-term contract covering many shipments. In the latter case each and every cost, risk, function, etc., must be thoroughly considered and all clauses in the written contract properly worded.

Generally, the parties should try to find a solution whereby the one who can best influence the situation is also the one who profits or loses if a problem is handled in a good or a bad way. With this in mind the parties have to analyse and specially design each component in the contract. The result will not necessarily be a contract which can be considered as a voyage agreement or a time charter agreement. The result can instead be a contract which contains parts from traditional voyage chartering and other parts from a traditional time charter. It is therefore incorrect to say that a CoA is a special form of voyage chartering. A CoA might very well be a contract which cannot be classified as a voyage agreement or a time charter agreement. This may cause difficulties as shipping people usually think in terms of voyage chartering or time chartering (or liner service). When they come into contact with a "*hybrid contract*" they will therefore most probably try to classify it as time or voyage chartering, and this may lead to conclusions which the parties never intended. It is also for this reason important that the contract is properly worded.

It is also important that both parties are as flexible as possible. In connection with the nomination of vessels and cargo it is especially important that both parties do their utmost in order to find the optimal solution (see further under the section "The Nomination Procedure" on page 254ff.).

THE CONTRACT PERIOD

There are no limits as regards the length of the contract period in a CoA. However, the maximum and minimum periods are governed by practical considerations. If it is possible to make a CoA for one trip only, the parties will hardly recognize such a contract as a CoA. If, however, the owners have both the right and the obligation to substitute the vessel, a charter-party is legally more like a CoA than an ordinary voyage or time charter-party.

Practical considerations will limit the contract period to a certain extent. It is difficult for both parties to foresee changes in the market, costs, or in technical developments. Also, the political situation in the world is difficult to foresee and, as all these factors are important for long-term contracts, it is not usual to find complete and finally fixed contracts covering longer periods than, for example, five years. The parts of the contract dealing with the owner's remuneration and currency are difficult to handle. The parties often choose to indicate that they intend to prolong the contract instead of trying to solve all the difficult questions that must be solved if they draft a firm contract covering a very long period.

Some different ways to agree about the period

The contract period can be established in many ways, for instance:

1. A fixed period which automatically (i.e. without notice from any of the parties) terminates.
2. A fixed period which is automatically prolonged with another fixed period unless one of the parties gives notice of termination.
3. A fixed period with an option for one of the parties (or both) to get prolongation with another fixed period.
4. A period which is not fixed in length but terminates with a fixed period after notice of termination from one of the parties.

It is, of course, also possible to have other solutions, combinations or variations of the different methods. In the fourth example it is, for instance, not unusual to have a minimum period, i.e. a period from the commencement of the contract period until a certain day during which a notice of termination from one of the parties is not valid.

When the system with notice of termination is used, the length of the period from notice until termination must also be agreed in a contract. The length of this notice period is sometimes short and in other cases very long, perhaps several years. In the latter case, where one has a long notice period, the notice period itself can be seen as the contract period which, as long as no notice of termination is given, is prolonged. The contract period is sometimes divided into part periods with individual terms. Especially in long term contracts such part periods are found within the total contract period and it is often the clauses about the owner's remuneration that vary from part period to part period.

Commencement and termination of the period. Borderline between part periods

It is usually not sufficient to describe the contract period as, for instance, "1993-01-01 to 1995-12-31". Each voyage covers a period of time and it should be established in a more precise way what event, or at what stage, it is in a voyage that determines whether a certain voyage is within the contract period or not. It is necessary to decide if a particular voyage, or part of a voyage, belongs to one stage or another of the contract. One way to do this is to add "*the first vessel to be loadready at the loading port in the period January 1–15, 1993, and the last vessel under the contract to be loadready at the loading port not later than December 1, 1995*" or a similar clause.

When the period is divided into part periods it is important that the contract establishes to which part period a certain voyage belongs. If uncertainty arises in this respect, the parties may have difficulty in establishing whether the freight rate for the first or the second part period shall apply for the voyage, whether the quantity on the voyage shall be referred to the first or the second part period, etc.

THE CARGO

Type of cargo

The problems and questions connected with the type of cargo in a CoA are basically the same as in other contracts of carriage. (See pages 184, 219.) The cargo is usually—and also when the CoA is based on time charter principles— defined in the CoA. Sometimes only one commodity is covered by the contract but other commodities are mentioned occasionally, either as planned alternatives or as possible completion cargoes.

Total quantity of cargo

It is not enough to state the contractual number of tons or other cargo units. The parties' respective obligations towards each other in connection with quantities are also important. When the cargo quantity is estimated and evaluated during the negotiation it is therefore necessary to analyse the contract from several aspects.

Any CoA can be classified as follows (each CoA will fall either under A or B in each group).

   1A. Quantity fixed
   1B. Quantity not fixed
   2A. Obligation on charterer's side to offer cargo to the owner
   2B. No obligation on charterer's side to offer cargo to the owner
   3A. Obligation on owner's side to carry cargo offered by the charterer
   3B. No obligation on owner's side to carry cargo offered by the charterer

Quantity fixed or not fixed. 1A or 1B

Sometimes the quantity covered by the contract is fixed in a very precise way, such as "*X metric tons*", "*Y units*". The quantity may also be fixed by a minimum and maximum like *"minimum X and maximum Y metric tons"*, *"between X and Y units"*. In both cases the word *"about"* or expressions like *"X percent more or less"* or *"X percent more or less in Owners' (Charterers') option"* or similar are often used to give more flexibility. Sometimes the quantity is described by reference to charterers' production during a certain period, like *"All Charterers' export on c.i.f. basis"* during a certain period or otherwise based on charterers' requirement. Such requirement can be more or less known beforehand depending on the type of commodity, the nature of the charterers' sales contracts, etc. *Requirement contracts* can be combined with minimum figures, maximum figures and sometimes both minimum and maximum figures like *"Charterers' production during 1994 up to X metric tons"*, *"Charterers' production 1994 not less than Y metric tons"*.

It is not always easy to find out whether the cargo quantity is fixed or not. When, for instance, the quantity of cargo is described as *"all Charterers' production of potato during the contract period"*, the quantity is in one way fixed but in another way is not. It is fixed to the quantity produced during the contract period, but as this quantity is not known beforehand when the contract is negotiated and concluded, it is for calculation purposes not fixed. The important thing during the negotiation is to ask how much cargo (maximum, minimum, expected quantity) is to be carried under the contract and then evaluate the answer together with other components of the contract.

Charterer's obligation to offer cargo. 2A or 2B

Sometimes the charterer only has the *option* to carry cargo with a particular owner's vessels. In other cases, it is the charterer's *obligation* to deliver cargo for shipment under the CoA and frequently the construction is that the charterer has an obligation to deliver a certain quantity and an option to deliver additional quantities. The expression "first refusal" is sometimes used as, for instance, *"Charterer to give Owners first refusal on all his shipments of potato from the Canadian Atlantic coast during 1994"*. Such an expression does not mean much unless it is combined with a contract containing the main terms such as freight, allocation of costs, functions, etc.

Owner's obligation to carry cargo. 3A or 3B

It is also important here to find out if the owner has an obligation to carry all cargo offered or if it is just a right for him to carry the cargo if he so wishes.

THE VESSEL

As the CoA is built up around the transportation of the cargo and not around the transportation of a cargo with a certain vessel, the ship or the ships are often not mentioned in the CoA. The owner shall see to it that the vessels used for transportation under the CoA are suitable for the cargo, the ports and the seaways. Sometimes the ships are specified directly or indirectly in the CoAs. This can be done in several ways as, for instance: *"Owners to nominate only vessels suitable for handling of palletized cargo"*, *"Owners to nominate only vessels of X-type"*, *"Owners to nominate only vessels flying British flag"* etc.

THE NOMINATION PROCEDURE

Under a CoA covering several shipments it is sometimes agreed from the beginning when the different loadings will take place and how much cargo each vessel under the contract will load. Usually the parties have, however, built in a certain flexibility, both as regards time for shipments and quantities lifted for each shipment. It is important that both parties are as flexible as possible. If one of the parties insists on a certain loading date, a certain quantity of cargo or something else which he, according to the contract, can request the cost for the other party may increase without corresponding savings for the one who insists. This will have a negative influence on the total economy.

Especially in long-term contracts it is difficult to agree beforehand exactly when the different shipments shall take place and what quantities will be lifted for each shipment. The parties therefore usually choose to agree about the framework and procedure for more detailed planning. This is sometimes done by using general expressions like *"The shipments under this contract shall be evenly (fairly) spread over the contract period"* or *"The 20 shipments under this contract shall be allocated as follows: 5 vessels to be presented loadready at loading port during the period January–March, 10 vessels during the period April–June and the remaining 5 vessels during the period July–December. All shipments to be evenly spread within each period"*.

The parties also have to agree about the procedure as to how to fix a more detailed schedule. This can, for instance, be done by a clause saying that the owner (or the charterer) at a certain date shall present a schedule including dates for loading and names of the ships intended. Sometimes the schedule is finally fixed in this way and sometimes the schedule is merely a base for a more detailed discussion between the parties.

When the schedule is established a system of notices often takes over. A clause dealing with such notices can have the following wording: *"The owners or the vessel to give ETA-notices 30, 15, 5 and 2 days prior to estimated time of loadreadiness at first port of loading. The owners to keep charterers informed about all changes in vessel's expected loadreadiness."*

Such notices often have different values. Expressions such as *"preliminary notices"*, *"definite notices"* are used without a clear understanding of what the different kinds of notices mean. To avoid misunderstanding it should be established to what extent the owner has the right to change the vessel's ETA and to what extent he is bound by a notice once given.

THE INDIVIDUAL CLAUSES

Notwithstanding the need for individual consideration of each component of a CoA, it is often possible to use standard forms or standard clauses as part of the contract. When the contract is a *"hybrid contract"*, one must, however, be very careful in order to avoid an inappropriate combination of clauses. One should also avoid using established shipping terms and concepts for other purposes than they are intended for. If the parties have found a solution which is unusual and/or specially designed for the contract, they should also give it a denomination that is special and not misleading.

Some clauses are of special importance in long-term contracts. We have already mentioned that the clauses dealing with the nomination of the vessel and the cargo are more complicated than in charter-parties covering one voyage only. Other important clauses are currency clauses, escalation clauses and clauses of a *force majeure* nature. For currency and escalation clauses, we refer to page 164ff., section "Effect of Cost Variations on the Contractual Relationship". *Force majeure* clauses are not specially dealt with in this book, but we refer to the comments about War Risk clauses and War Cancellation clauses (page 160ff.), and also to the comments about the Doctrine of Frustration (page 154).

Finally, it should be mentioned that the parties in a CoA sometimes agree to average the effect of certain circumstances or clauses. It is not unusual that laytime calculations are seen as a whole for the contract period or for a part of the contract period. Demurrage/despatch is calculated voyage by voyage but the final settlement is not done until the average result of all voyages is known.

CONCLUDING REMARKS

We feel it is necessary once more to stress that the reader who wants detailed and precise information on individual disputes will have to find specialized literature. The above aims at giving the reader a basis for making charter calculations, for evaluating the meaning of a number of clauses in frequent use, for making an effort to translate the legal implications of certain clauses into the financial calculations and for having an intelligible discussion with an opposite party when a dispute arises. For the interested reader we suggest perusal of the Bibliography on p. xixf.

APPENDICES

APPENDIX I*

GENCON*

* Reproduced by kind permission of BIMCO.

1. Shipbroker	RECOMMENDED THE BALTIC AND INTERNATIONAL MARITIME CONFERENCE UNIFORM GENERAL CHARTER (AS REVISED 1922 and 1976) INCLUDING "F.I.O." ALTERNATIVE, ETC. (To be used for trades for which no approved form is in force) CODE NAME: "GENCON" Part I
	2. Place and date
3. Owners/Place of business (Cl. 1)	4. Charterers/Place of business (Cl. 1)
5. Vessel's name (Cl. 1)	6. GRT/NRT (Cl. 1)
7. Deadweight cargo carrying capacity in tons (abt.) (Cl. 1)	8. Present position (Cl. 1)
9. Expected ready to load (abt.) (Cl. 1)	
10. Loading port or place (Cl. 1)	11. Discharging port or place (Cl. 1)

12. Cargo (also state quantity and margin in Owners' option, if agreed; if full and complete cargo not agreed state "part cargo") (Cl. 1)

13. Freight rate (also state if payable on delivered or intaken quantity) (Cl. 1)	14. Freight payment (state currency and method of payment; also beneficiary and bank account) (Cl. 4)
15. Loading and discharging costs (state alternative (a) or (b) of Cl. 5; also indicate if vessel is gearless)	16. Laytime (if separate laytime for load. and disch. is agreed, fill in a) and b). If total laytime for load. and disch., fill in c) only) (Cl. 6)
	a) Laytime for loading
17. Shippers (state name and address) (Cl. 6)	b) Laytime for discharging
	c) Total laytime for loading and discharging
18. Demurrage rate (loading and discharging) (Cl. 7)	19. Cancelling date (Cl. 10)

20. Brokerage commission and to whom payable (Cl. 14)

21. Additional clauses covering special provisions, if agreed.

It is mutually agreed that this Contract shall be performed subject to the conditions contained in this Charter which shall include Part I as well as Part II. In the event of a conflict of conditions, the provisions of Part I shall prevail over those of Part II to the extent of such conflict.

Signature (Owners)	Signature (Charterers)

PART II
"Gencon" Charter (As Revised 1922 and 1976)
Including "F.I.O." Alternative, etc.

1. It is agreed between the party mentioned in Box 3 as Owners of the 1
steamer or motor-vessel named in Box 5, of the gross/nett Register 2
tons indicated in Box 6 and carrying about the number of tons of 3
deadweight cargo stated in Box 7, now in position as stated in Box 8 4
and expected ready to load under this Charter about the date in- 5
dicated in Box 9, and the party mentioned as Charterers in Box 4 6
that: 7
The said vessel shall proceed to the loading port or place stated 8
in Box 10 or so near thereto as she may safely get and lie always 9
afloat, and there load a full and complete cargo (if shipment of deck 10
cargo agreed same to be at Charterers' risk) as stated in Box 11 11
(Charterers to provide all mats and/or wood for dunnage and any 12
separations required, the Owners allowing the use of any dunnage 13
wood on board if required) which the Charterers bind themselves to 14
ship, and being so loaded the vessel shall proceed to the discharg- 15
ing port or place stated in Box 11 as ordered on signing Bills of 16
Lading or so near thereto as she may safely get and lie always 17
afloat and there deliver the cargo on being paid freight on delivered 18
or intaken quantity as indicated in Box 13 at the rate stated in 19
Box 13. 20

2. Owners' Responsibility Clause
Owners are to be responsible for loss of or damage to the goods 21
or for delay in delivery of the goods only in case the loss, damage 22
or delay has been caused by the improper or negligent stowage of 23
the goods (unless stowage performed by shippers/Charterers or their 24
stevedores or servants) or by personal want of due diligence on the 25
part of the Owners or their Manager to make the vessel in all respects 26
seaworthy and to secure that she is properly manned, equipped and 27
supplied or by the personal act or default of the Owners or their 28
Manager. 29
And the Owners are responsible for no loss or damage or delay 30
arising from any other cause whatsoever, even from the neglect or 31
default of the Captain or crew or some other person employed by the 32
Owners on board or ashore for whose acts they would, but for this 33
clause, be responsible, or from unseaworthiness of the vessel on 34
loading or commencement of the voyage or at any time whatsoever. 35
Damage caused by contact with or leakage, smell or evaporation 36
from other goods or by the inflammable or explosive nature or in- 37
sufficient package of other goods not to be considered as caused 38
by improper or negligent stowage, even if in fact so caused. 39
 40

3. Deviation Clause
The vessel has liberty to call at any port or ports in any order, for 41
any purpose, to sail without pilots, to tow and/or assist vessels in 42
all situations, and also to deviate for the purpose of saving life and/ 43
or property. 44
 45

4. Payment of Freight
The freight to be paid in the manner prescribed in Box 14 in cash 46
without discount on delivery of the cargo at mean rate of exchange 47
ruling on day or days of payment, the receivers of the cargo being 48
bound to pay freight on account during delivery, if required by Cap- 49
tain or Owners. 50
Cash for vessel's ordinary disbursements at port of loading to be 51
advanced by Charterers if required at highest current rate of ex- 52
change, subject to two per cent. to cover insurance and other ex- 53
penses. 54
 55

5. Loading/Discharging Costs
* (a) Gross Terms 56
The cargo to be brought alongside in such a manner as to enable 57
vessel to take the goods with her own tackle. Charterers to procure 58
and pay the necessary men on shore or on board the lighters to do 59
the work there, vessel only heaving the cargo on board. 60
If the loading takes place by elevator, cargo to be put free in vessel's 61
holds. Owners only paying trimming expenses. 62
Any pieces and/or packages of cargo over two tons weight, shall be 63
loaded, stowed and discharged by Charterers at their risk and expense. 64
The cargo to be received by Merchants at their risk and expense 65
alongside the vessel not beyond the reach of her tackle. 66
 67
* (b) F.i.o. and free stowed/trimmed 68
The cargo shall be brought into the holds, loaded, stowed and/or trim- 69
med and taken from the holds and discharged by the Charterers or 70
their Agents, free of any risk, liability and expense whatsoever to the 71
Owners. 72
The Owners shall provide winches, motive power and winchmen from 73
the Crew if requested and permitted; if not, the Charterers shall 74
provide and pay for winchmen from shore and/or cranes, if any. (This 75
provision shall not apply if vessel is gearless and stated as such in 76
Box 15). 77
* indicate alternative (a) or (b), as agreed, in Box 15. 78

6. Laytime 79
* (a) Separate laytime for loading and discharging 80
The cargo shall be loaded within the number of running hours as 81
indicated in Box 16, weather permitting, Sundays and holidays ex- 82
cepted, unless used, in which event time actually used shall count. 83
The cargo shall be discharged within the number of running hours 84
as indicated in Box 16, weather permitting, Sundays and holidays ex- 85
cepted, unless used, in which event time actually used shall count. 86
 87
* (b) Total laytime for loading and discharging 88
The cargo shall be loaded and discharged within the number of total 89
running hours as indicated in Box 16, weather permitting, Sundays and 90
holidays excepted, unless used, in which event time actually used 91
shall count. 92
(c) Commencement of laytime (loading and discharging) 93
Laytime for loading and discharging shall commence at 1 p.m. if 94
notice of readiness is given before noon, and at 6 a.m. next working 95
day if notice given during office hours after noon. Notice at loading 96
port to be given to the Shippers named in Box 17. 97
Time actually used before commencement of laytime shall count. 98
Time lost in waiting for berth to count as loading or discharging 99
time, as the case may be. 100
* indicate alternative (a) or (b) as agreed, in Box 16.

7. Demurrage 101
Ten running days on demurrage at the rate stated in Box 18 per 102
day or pro rata for any part of a day, payable day by day, to be 103
allowed Merchants altogether at ports of loading and discharging. 104

8. Lien Clause 105
Owners shall have a lien on the cargo for freight, dead-freight, 106
demurrage and damages for detention. Charterers shall remain re- 107
sponsible for dead-freight and demurrage (including damages for 108
detention), incurred at port of loading. Charterers shall also remain 109
responsible for freight and demurrage (including damages for deten- 110
tion) incurred at port of discharge, but only to such extent as the 111
Owners have been unable to obtain payment thereof by exercising 112
the lien on the cargo. 113

9. Bills of Lading 114
The Captain to sign Bills of Lading at such rate of freight as 115
presented without prejudice to this Charterparty, but should the 116
freight by Bills of Lading amount to less than the total chartered 117
freight the difference to be paid to the Captain in cash on signing 118
Bills of Lading. 119

10. Cancelling Clause 120
Should the vessel not be ready to load (whether in berth or not) on 121
or before the date indicated in Box 19, Charterers have the option 122
of cancelling this contract, such option to be declared, if demanded, 123
at least 48 hours before vessel's expected arrival at port of loading. 124
Should the vessel be delayed on account of average or otherwise, 125
Charterers to be informed as soon as possible, and if the vessel is 126
delayed for more than 10 days after the day she is stated to be 127
expected ready to load, Charterers have the option of cancelling this 128
contract, unless a cancelling date has been agreed upon. 129

11. General Average 130
General average to be settled according to York-Antwerp Rules, 131
1974. Proprietors of cargo to pay the cargo's share in the general 132
expenses even if same have been necessitated through neglect or 133
default of the Owners' servants (see clause 2). 134

12. Indemnity 135
Indemnity for non-performance of this Charterparty, proved damages, 136
not exceeding estimated amount of freight. 137

13. Agency 138
In every case the Owners shall appoint his own Broker or Agent both 139
at the port of loading and the port of discharge. 140

14. Brokerage 141
A brokerage commission at the rate stated in Box 20 on the freight 142
earned is due to the party mentioned in Box 20. 143
In case of non-execution at least ⅓ of the brokerage on the estimated 144
amount of freight and dead-freight to be paid by the Owners to the 145
Brokers as indemnity for the latter's expenses and work. In case of 146
more voyages the amount of indemnity to be mutually agreed. 147

15. GENERAL STRIKE CLAUSE 148
Neither Charterers nor Owners shall be responsible for the con- 149
sequences of any strikes or lock-outs preventing or delaying the 150
fulfilment of any obligations under this contract. 151
If there is a strike or lock-out affecting the loading of the cargo, 152
or any part of it, when vessel is ready to proceed from her last port 153
or at any time during the voyage to the port or ports of loading or 154
after her arrival there, Captain or Owners may ask Charterers to 155
declare, that they agree to reckon the laydays as if there were no 156
strike or lock-out. Unless Charterers have given such declaration in 157
writing (by telegram, if necessary) within 24 hours, Owners shall 158
have the option of cancelling this contract. If part cargo has already 159
been loaded, Owners must proceed with same, (freight payable on 160
loaded quantity only) having liberty to complete with other cargo 161
on the way for their own account. 162
If there is a strike or lock-out affecting the discharge of the cargo 163
on or after vessel's arrival at or off port of discharge and same has 164
not been settled within 48 hours, Receivers shall have the option of 165
keeping vessel waiting until such strike or lock-out is at an end 166
against paying half demurrage after expiration of the time provided 167
for discharging, or of ordering the vessel to a safe port where she 168
can safely discharge without risk of being detained by strike or lock- 169
out. Such orders to be given within 48 hours after Captain or Owners 170
have given notice to Charterers of the strike or lock-out affecting 171
the discharge. On delivery of the cargo at such port, all conditions 172
of this Charterparty and of the Bill of Lading shall apply and vessel 173
shall receive the same freight as if she had discharged at the 174
original port of destination, except that if the distance of the sub- 175
stituted port exceeds 100 nautical miles, the freight on the cargo 176
delivered at the substituted port to be increased in proportion. 177

16. War Risks ("Voywar 1950") 178
(1) In these clauses "War Risks" shall include any blockade or any 179
action which is announced as a blockade by any Government or by any 180
belligerent or by any organized body, sabotage, piracy, and any actual 181
or threatened war, hostilities, warlike operations, civil war, civil com- 182
motion or revolution. 183

(2) If at any time before the Vessel commences loading, it appears that 184
performance of the contract will subject the Vessel or her Master and 185
crew or her cargo to war risks at any stage of the adventure, the Owners 186
shall be entitled by letter or telegram despatched to the Charterers, to 187
cancel this Charter. 188

(3) The Master shall not be required to load cargo or to continue 189
loading or to proceed on or to sign Bill(s) of Lading for any adventure 190
on which or any port at which it appears that the Vessel, her Master 191
and crew or her cargo will be subjected to war risks. In the event of 192
the exercise by the Master of his right under this Clause after part or 193
full cargo has been loaded, the Master shall be at liberty either to 194
discharge such cargo at the loading port or to proceed therewith. 195
In the latter case the Vessel shall have liberty to carry other cargo 196
for Owners' benefit and accordingly to proceed to and load or 197
discharge such other cargo at any other port or ports whatsoever, 198
backwards or forwards, although in a contrary direction to or out of 199
beyond the ordinary route. In the event of the Master electing to 200
proceed with part cargo under this Clause freight shall in any case 201
be payable on the quantity delivered. 202

(4) If at the time the Master elects to proceed with part or full cargo 203
under Clause 3, or after the Vessel has left the loading port, or the 204

PART II
"Gencon" Charter (As Revised 1922 and 1976)
Including "F.I.O." Alternative, etc.

last of the loading ports, if more than one, it appears that further 205
performance of the contract will subject the Vessel, her Master and 206
crew or her cargo, to war risks, the cargo shall be discharged, or if 207
the discharge has been commenced shall be completed, at any safe 208
port in vicinity of the port of discharge as may be ordered by the 209
Charterers. If no such orders shall be received from the Charterers 210
within 48 hours after the Owners have despatched a request by 211
telegram to the Charterers for the nomination of a substitute discharg- 212
ing port, the Owners shall be at liberty to discharge the cargo at 213
any safe port which they may, in their discretion, decide on and such 214
discharge shall be deemed to be due fulfilment of the contract of 215
affreightment. In the event of cargo being discharged at any such 216
other port, the Owners shall be entitled to freight as if the discharge 217
had been effected at the port or ports named in the Bill(s) of Lading 218
or to which the Vessel may have been ordered pursuant thereto. 219

(5) (a) The Vessel shall have liberty to comply with any directions 220
or recommendations as to loading, departure, arrival, routes, ports 221
of call, stoppages, destination, zones, waters, discharge, delivery or 222
in any other wise whatsoever (including any direction or recom- 223
mendation not to go to the port of destination or to delay proceeding 224
thereto or to proceed to some other port) given by any Government or 225
by any belligerent or by any organized body engaged in civil war, 226
hostilities or warlike operations or by any person or body acting or 227
purporting to act as or with the authority of any Government or 228
belligerent or of any such organized body or by any committee or 229
person having under the terms of the war risks insurance on the 230
Vessel, the right to give any such directions or recommendations. If, 231
by reason of or in compliance with any such direction or recom- 232
mendation, anything is done or is not done, such shall not be deemed 233
a deviation. 234

(b) If, by reason of or in compliance with any such directions or re- 235
commendations, the Vessel does not proceed to the port or ports 236
named in the Bill(s) of Lading or to which she may have been 237
ordered pursuant thereto, the Vessel may proceed to any port as 238
directed or recommended or to any safe port which the Owners in 239
their discretion may decide on and there discharge the cargo. Such 240
discharge shall be deemed to be due fulfilment of the contract of 241
affreightment and the Owners shall be entitled to freight as if 242
discharge had been effected at the port or ports named in the Bill(s) 243
of Lading or to which the Vessel may have been ordered pursuant 244
thereto. 245

(6) All extra expenses (including insurance costs) involved in discharg- 246
ing cargo at the loading port or in reaching or discharging the cargo 247
at any port as provided in Clauses 4 and 5 (b) hereof shall be paid 248
by the Charterers and or cargo owners, and the Owners shall have 249
a lien on the cargo for all moneys due under these Clauses. 250

17. GENERAL ICE CLAUSE 251
Port of loading 252

(a) In the event of the loading port being inaccessible by reason of 253
ice when vessel is ready to proceed from her last port or at any 254
time during the voyage or on vessel's arrival or in case frost sets in 255
after vessel's arrival, the Captain for fear of being frozen in is at 256
liberty to leave without cargo, and this Charter shall be null and 257
void. 258

(b) If during loading the Captain, for fear of vessel being frozen in, 259
deems it advisable to leave, he has liberty to do so with what cargo 260
he has on board and to proceed to any other port or ports with 261
option of completing cargo for Owners' benefit for any port or ports 262
including port of discharge. Any part cargo thus loaded under this 263
Charter to be forwarded to destination at vessel's expense but 264
against payment of freight, provided that no extra expenses be 265
thereby caused to the Receivers, freight being paid on quantity 266
delivered (in proportion if lumpsum), all other conditions as per 267
Charter. 268

(c) In case of more than one loading port, and if one or more of 269
the ports are closed by ice, the Captain or Owners to be at liberty 270
either to load the part cargo at the open port and fill up elsewhere 271
for their own account as under section (b) or to declare the Charter 272
null and void unless Charterers agree to load full cargo at the open 273
port. 274

(d) This Ice Clause not to apply in the Spring. 275

Port of discharge 276

(a) Should ice (except in the Spring) prevent vessel from reaching 277
port of discharge Receivers shall have the option of keeping vessel 278
waiting until the re-opening of navigation and paying demurrage, or 279
of ordering the vessel to a safe and immediately accessible port 280
where she can safely discharge without risk of detention by ice. 281
Such orders to be given within 48 hours after Captain or Owners 282
have given notice to Charterers of the impossibility of reaching port 283
of destination. 284

(b) If during discharging the Captain for fear of vessel being frozen 285
in deems it advisable to leave, he has liberty to do so with what 286
cargo he has on board and to proceed to the nearest accessible 287
port where she can safely discharge. 288

(c) On delivery of the cargo at such port, all conditions of the Bill 289
of Lading shall apply and vessel shall receive the same freight as 290
if she had discharged at the original port of destination, except that if 291
the distance of the substituted port exceeds 100 nautical miles, the 292
freight on the cargo delivered at the substituted port to be increased 293
in proportion. 294

APPENDIX II

LINERTIME

1. Shipbroker			THE BALTIC AND INTERNATIONAL MARITIME CONFERENCE Deep Sea Time Charter (Box Layout 1974) CODE NAME: "LINERTIME" PART I
			2. Place and date
3. Owners/Place of business			4. Charterers/Place of business
5. Vessel's name	6. GRT/NRT	7. Class	8. Indicated horse power
9. Total tons d.w. (abt.) on summer freeboard		10. Quantity of stores, provisions and fresh water not exceeding (tons)	
11. Cubic-feet grain/bale capacity available for cargo		12. Permanent bunkers (abt.)	
13. Speed capability in knots (abt.) on a consumption per 24 hours of (abt.)		14. Present position	
15. Period of hire (Cl. 1)		16. Port of delivery (also indicate alternative (a) or (b)) (Cl. 1)	
		17. Time for delivery (Cl. 1)	
18. Number of days' notice of expected date of delivery (Cl. 1)		19. Cancelling date (Cl. 2)	
20. Trade limits (also indicate alternative (a) or (b)) (Cl. 3)			
21. Injurious, inflammable or dangerous goods limited to (also state name of authorities concerned) (Cl. 3)		22. Vessel's cargo handling gear (Cl. 5)	
23. Fuel consumption in port per 24 hours (abt.) (Cl. 5)		24. Bunker price (indicate alternative (a) or (b) and fixed price if agreed) (Cl. 6)	
25. Bunkers on delivery (state min. and max. quantities) (Cl. 6)		26. Bunkers on re-delivery (state min. and max. quantities) (Cl. 6)	
27. Charter hire (also indicate alternative (a) or (b)) (Cl. 7)		28. Hire payment (state currency, mode and place of payment; also beneficiary and bank account) (Cl. 7)	
29. Place or range of re-delivery (Cl. 8)		30. Number of days' preliminary and final notice of port and date of re-delivery (Cl. 8)	
31. Suspension of hire etc. (indic. no. of consecutive hours) (Cl. 14 (A))		32. Cleaning of boilers etc. (indicate number of hours) (Cl. 15)	
33. Advances (only to be filled in if special agreement made) (Cl. 16)		34. Overtime (state lumpsum or if other special agreement made) (Cl. 19)	
35. War (only to be filled in if Section (C) agreed) (Cl. 23)		36. General average to be settled in (Cl. 24)	
37. Supercargo (state price agreed) (Cl. 27)		38. Meals (state price agreed) (Cl. 28)	
39. Brokerage commission and to whom payable (Cl. 33)			
40. Numbers of additional clauses covering special provisions, if agreed			

It is mutually agreed that this Contract shall be performed subject to the conditions contained in this Charter which shall include Part I as well as Part II. In the event of a conflict of conditions, the provisions of Part I shall prevail over those of Part II to the extent of such conflict.

Signature (for the Owners)	Signature (for the Charterers)

Printed and sold by Fr. G. Knudtzon Ltd., 55. Toldbodgade, Copenhagen.
by authority of The Baltic and International Maritime Conference, Copenhagen.

PART II

"LINERTIME" Deep Sea Time Charter   Page 2

It is agreed between the party mentioned in Box 3 as Owners of the 1
Vessel named in Box 5 of the gross/net Register tons indicated in 2
Box 6, classed as stated in Box 7 and of indicated horse power as 3
stated in Box 8, carrying about the number of tons deadweight in- 4
dicated in Box 9 on about summer freeboard inclusive of bunkers, as well 5
as stores, provisions and fresh water not exceeding the number of 6
tons indicated in Box 10 having a cubic-feet grain/bale capacity 7
available for cargo as stated in Box 11, exclusive of permanent 8
bunkers, which contain about the number of tons stated in Box 12, 9
and fully loaded capable of steaming about the number of knots 10
indicated in Box 13 in good weather and smooth water on a con- 11
sumption of about the number of tons stated in Box 13 per 24 hours, 12
now in position as stated in Box 14, and the party mentioned as 13
Charterers in Box 4, as follows 14

1. Period and Port of Delivery

The Owners let, and the Charterers hire the Vessel for a period of 15
the number of calendar months indicated in Box 15 from the time 16
(not a Sunday or a legal Holiday unless taken over) the Vessel is 17
delivered and placed at the disposal of the Charterers between 7 a.m. 18
and 10 p.m., or between 7 a.m. and noon if on Saturday, at the port 19
stated in Box 16 in such ready berth where she can safely lie 20

(a) always afloat* 21

(b) always afloat or safely aground where it is customary for vessels 22
of similar size and draught to be safe aground* 23

as the Charterers may direct, she being in every way fitted for 24
ordinary dry cargo service with cargo holds well swept, cleaned 25
and ready to receive cargo before delivery under this Charter. 26
(* state alternative agreed in Box 16) 27

Time for Delivery

The Vessel to be delivered not before the date indicated in Box 17. 29
The Owners to give the Charterers not less than the number of days' 30
notice stated in Box 18 of the date on which the Vessel is expected 31
to be ready for delivery. 32
The Owners to keep the Charterers closely advised of possible 33
changes in Vessel's position. 34

2. Cancelling

Should the Vessel not be delivered by the date indicated in Box 19, 36
the Charterers to have the option of cancelling. 37
If the Vessel cannot be delivered by the cancelling date, the Char- 38
terers, if required, to declare within 48 hours (Sundays and Holidays 39
excluded) after receiving notice thereof whether they cancel or will 40
take delivery of the Vessel. 41

3. Trade

The Vessel to be employed in lawful trades for the carriage of lawful 43
merchandise only between good and safe ports or places where she 44
can safely lie 45

(a) always afloat* 46

(b) always afloat or safely aground where it is customary for vessels 47
of similar size and draught to be safe aground* 48

within the limits as stated in Box 20 49
(* state alternative agreed in Box 20) 50

No live stock, sulphur and pitch in bulk to be shipped. Injurious, 52
inflammable or dangerous goods (such as acids, explosives, calcium 53
carbide, ferro silicon, naphta, motor spirit, tar, or any of their 54
products) to be limited to the number of tons stated in Box 21 and 55
same to be packed, loaded, stowed and discharged in accordance 56
with the regulations of the local authorities and Board of Trade 57
as specified in Box 21, and if any special measures have to be 58
taken by reason of having this cargo aboard including cost of 59
erection and dismantling magazines, etc., same to be at Charterers' 60
expense and in Charterers' time. 61

Nuclear Fuel

Notwithstanding any other provisions contained in this Charter it is 63
agreed that nuclear fuels or radioactive products or waste are 64
specifically excluded from the cargo permitted to be loaded or 65
carried under this Charter. This exclusion does not apply to radio- 66
isotopes used or intended to be used for any industrial, commercial, 67
agricultural, medical or scientific purposes provided the Owners' 68
prior approval has been obtained to loading thereof. 69

4. Owners to Provide

The Owners to provide and pay for all provisions and wages, for 70
insurance of the Vessel, for all deck and engine-room stores and 71
maintain her in a thoroughly efficient state in hull and machinery 72
during service. 74
The Owners to provide one winchman per working hatch. In lieu of 75
winchmen the Charterers are entitled to ask for two watchmen. If 76
further winchmen or watchmen are required, or if the stevedores 77
refuse or are not permitted to work with the Crew, the Charterers to 78
provide and pay qualified men. The gangway watchman to be provided 79
by the Owners but where compulsory to employ gangway watchmen 80
from shore, the expenses to be for the Charterers' account 81

5. Charterers to Provide

The Charterers to pay all dock, harbour, light and tonnage dues at 83
the ports of delivery and re-delivery (unless incurred through cargo 84
carried before delivery or after re-delivery). 85
Whilst on hire the Charterers to provide and pay for all fuel, water 86
for boilers, port charges, pilotages (whether compulsory or not), 87
canal steersmen, boatage, lights, tug-assistance, consular charges 88
(except those payable to the consulates of the country of the Vessel's 89
flag) canal, dock and other dues and charges, including any foreign 90
general municipality or state taxes, agencies, commissions, also to 91
arrange and pay for loading, trimming, stowing (including dunnage 92
and shifting boards, excepting any already on board), unloading, 93
weighing, tallying and delivery of cargoes, surveys on hatches, any 94
other survey on cargo, meals supplied to officials and men in their 95
service at the rate per man per meal indicated in Boxes 37 and 38, 96
respectively, and all other charges and expenses whatsoever. 97

Cargo Gear

All ropes, slings and special runners actually used for loading and 99
discharging and any special gear, including special ropes, hawsers 100
and chains required by the custom of the port for mooring to be for 101
the Charterers' account unless already on board. The Vessel is fitted 102
with cargo handling gear as specified in Box 22. 103
This gear is to be kept in full working order for immediate use, the 104
Charterers however to give sufficient notice of their intention to use 105
heavy lift gear 106

Cargo Gear Certificate

The Owners guarantee the Vessel possesses cargo gear register and 108
certificates in compliance with requirement of International Labour 109
Organization. Convention No. 32. 110

Fuel Consumption in Port

The Vessel's normal fuel consumption whilst in port working all 112
cargo gear is about the number of tons stated in Box 23 per 24 hours 113

6. Bunkers

The Charterers at port of delivery and the Owners at port of re- 115
delivery to take over and pay for all fuel remaining in the Vessel's 116
bunkers at 117

(a) current price, at the respective ports* 118

(b) a fixed price per ton* 119

(* state alternative agreed in Box 24*). 120

The Vessel to be delivered with no. less than the number of tons 121
and not exceeding the number of tons stated in Box 25 in the 122
Vessel's bunkers. 123
The Vessel to be re-delivered with not less than the number of tons 124
and not exceeding the number of tons stated in Box 26 in the 125
Vessel's bunkers. 126

7. Hire

The Charterers to pay as hire the rate stated in Box 27 128

(a) per 30 days* 129

(b) per day* 130

commencing in accordance with Clause 1 until her re-delivery to the 131
Owners. 132
(* state alternative agreed in Box 27). 133

Payment

Payment of hire to be made in cash, in the currency stated in Box 28 135
without discount, every 30 days, in advance, and in the manner 136
prescribed in Box 28. 137
In default of payment the Owners to have the right of withdrawing 138
the Vessel from the service of the Charterers, without noting any 139
protest and without interference by any court or any other formality 140
whatsoever and without prejudice to any claim the Owners may 141
otherwise have on the Charterers under the Charter. 142

Last Hire Payment

Should the Vessel be on her voyage towards port of re-delivery at 144
time a payment of hire is due, said payment to be made for such 145
length of time as the Owners or their Agents and the Charterers or 146
their Agents may agree upon as estimated time necessary to com- 147
plete the voyage, taking into account bunkers to be taken over by 148
the Vessel and estimated disbursements for Owners' account 149
before re-delivery and when the Vessel is re-delivered any difference 150
to be refunded by the Owners or paid by the Charterers, as the case 151
may require 152

8. Re-delivery

The Vessel to be re-delivered on the expiration of the Charter in 154
the same good order as when delivered to the Charterers (fair wear 155
and tear excepted) at a safe and ice-free port in the Charterers' 156
option in the place or within the range stated in Box 29 between 157
7 a.m. and 10 p.m., and 7 a.m. and noon on Saturday, but the day 158
of re-delivery shall not be a Sunday or legal Holiday. 159
Repairs for the Charterers' account as far as possible to be effected 160
simultaneously with dry-docking or annual repairs, respectively: if 161
any further repairs are required, for time occupied in effecting 162
such repairs the Owners to receive compensation at the hire agreed 163
in this Charter. The Charterers always to be properly notified of the 164
time and place when and where repairs for their account will be 165
performed 166

Notice

The Charterers to give the Owners not less than the number of days' 168
preliminary and the number of days' final notice as stated in Box 30 169
of the port of re-delivery and the date on which the Vessel is ex- 170
pected to be ready for re-delivery. The Charterers to keep the Owners 171
closely advised of possible changes in the Vessel's position. 172
Should the Vessel be ordered on a voyage by which the Charter 173
period may be exceeded the Charterers to have the use of the Vessel 174
to enable them to complete the voyage, provided it could be reason- 175
ably calculated that the voyage would allow re-delivery about the 176
time fixed for the termination of the Charter, but for any time 177
exceeding the termination date the Charterers to pay the market rate 178
if higher than the rate stipulated herein. 179

9. Cargo Space

The whole reach and burden of the Vessel, including lawful deck- 181
capacity to be at the Charterers' disposal, reserving proper and suf- 182
ficient space for the Vessel's Master, Officers, Crew, tackle, apparel, 183
furniture, provisions and stores. 184

10. Master

The Charterers to give the necessary sailing instructions, subject to 186
the limits of the Charter. 187
The Master to be under the orders of the Charterers as regards em- 188
ployment, agency, or other arrangements. The Master to prosecute 189
all voyages with the utmost despatch and render customary as- 190
sistance with the Vessel's Crew. 191
The Master and Engineer to keep full and correct logs including 192
scrap logs accessible to the Charterers or their Agents. 193
If the Charterers have reason to be dissatisfied with the conduct of 194
the Master, Officers, or Engineers, the Owners on receiving parti- 195
culars of the complaint, promptly to investigate the matter, and, if 196
necessary and practicable, to make a change in the appointments. 197

11. Bills of Lading

The Charterers to have the option of using their own regular Bill of 199
Lading form. The Bill of Lading to contain Paramount Clause in- 200
corporating Hague Rules legislation, the Amended Jason Clause and 201
the Both-to-Blame Collision Clause. 202

12. Responsibility

The Charterers shall keep and care for the cargo at loading and 204
discharging ports, arrange for any transhipment, and deliver the 205
cargo at destination. 206

"LINERTIME" Deep Sea Time Charter Page 3

The Charterers shall load, stow, trim and discharge the cargo at 207
their expense under supervision of the Master who shall sign Bills 208
of Lading as presented, in conformity with Mate's or tally clerk's 209
receipts. The Charterers shall be responsible for the accuracy of 210
all statements of fact in such Bills of Lading. 211
The Owners shall be liable for claims in respect of cargo arising or 212
resulting from: 213
a) Failure on their part properly and carefully to carry, keep and 214
care for the cargo while on board. 215
b) Unreasonable deviation from the voyage described in the Bills of 216
Lading unless such deviation is ordered or approved by the Char- 217
terers. 218
c) Lack of due diligence on their part before and at the beginning 219
of each voyage to make the Vessel seaworthy but claims arising or 220
resulting from faulty preparation of the holds and/or tanks of the 221
Vessel or from bad stowage of the cargo not affecting the trim or 222
stability of the Vessel on sailing shall be the Charterers' liability. 223
Except as aforesaid the Charterers shall be liable for all cargo 224
claims. 225
If the cargo is the property of the Charterers, the Owners shall have 226
the same responsibility as they would have had under this Clause 227
had the cargo been the property of a third party and carried under 228
a Bill of Lading incorporating the Hague Rules. 229
The Charterers shall be liable for Customs or other fines or penalties, 230
whether or not lawfully levied or imposed, relating to the cargo or 231
other property or persons carried with Charterers' approval or to 232
the acts or omissions of the owners of the cargo. 233
Claims for death and personal injury shall be borne by the Owners 234
unless caused by the act, neglect or default of the Charterers, their 235
servants or agents including stevedores and all others for whom 236
Charterers are responsible under this Charter. 237
If for any reason the Owners or the Charterers are obliged to pay 238
any claims, Customs or other fines or penalties, for which the other 239
party has assumed liability as above, that other party hereby agrees 240
to indemnify the Owners or Charterers as the case may be against 241
all loss, damage or expenses arising or resulting from such claims. 242
However, the Owners' indemnity to the Charterers under this clause 243
shall be restricted in that amount to which the Owners' liability 244
would have been limited had they been sued directly. 245

13. Exceptions 246
As between the Charterers and the Owners, the responsibility for 247
any loss, damage, delay or failure in performance of this Charter, 248
not dealt with in Clause 12, to be subject to the following mutual 249
exceptions: 250
Act of God, act of war, civil commotions, strikes, lock-outs, restraint 251
of princes and rulers, quarantine restrictions. 252
Further, such responsibility upon the Owners to be subject to the 253
following exceptions: 254
Any act or neglect by the Master, pilots or other servants of the 255
Owners in the navigation or management of the Vessel, fire or ex- 256
plosion not due to the personal fault of the Owners or their Manager, 257
collision or stranding, unforeseeable breakdown or any latent defect 258
in the Vessel's hull, equipment or machinery. 259
The above provisions in no way to affect the provisions as to sus- 260
pension of hire in this Charter. 261

14. Suspension of Hire, etc. 262
(A) In the event of dry-docking or other necessary measures to main- 263
tain the efficiency of the Vessel, deficiency of men or Owners' stores, 264
strike of Master, Officers and Crew, breakdown of machinery, damage 265
to hull or other accident, either hindering or preventing the working 266
of the Vessel and continuing for more than the number of con- 267
secutive hours indicated in Box 31, no hire to be paid in respect of 268
any time lost thereby during the period in which the Vessel is unable 269
to perform the service immediately required. 270
Should the Vessel deviate or put back during a voyage, contrary to 271
the orders or directions of the Charterers, for any reason other than 272
accident to the Cargo, the hire to be suspended from the time of 273
her deviating or putting back until she is again in the same or 274
equidistant position from the destination and the voyage resumed 275
therefrom. 276

Winch Breakdown 277
In the event of a breakdown of a winch or winches, not caused by 278
carelessness of shore labourers, the time lost to be calculated pro 279
rata for the period of such inefficiency in relation to the number of 280
winches required for work. If the Charterers elect to continue work, 281
the Owners are to pay for shore appliances in lieu of the winches, 282
but in such cases the Charterers to pay full hire. 283
Any hire paid in advance to be adjusted accordingly. 284

Detention for Charterers' Account 285
(B) In the event of the Vessel being driven into port or to anchorage 286
through stress of weather, trading to shallow harbours or to rivers 287
or ports with bars or suffering an accident to her cargo, any de- 288
tention of the Vessel and/or expenses resulting from such detention 289
to be for the Charterers' account even if such detention and/or 290
expenses, or the cause by reason of which either is incurred, be 291
due to, or be contributed to by, the negligence of the Owners' 292
servants. 293

Dry-docking 294
Owners to give the Charterers at least four weeks notice of their 295
intention of dry-docking the ship for bottom painting and normal 296
maintenance work and actual time and place for such dry-docking 297
to be mutually agreed. 298

15. Cleaning Boilers, etc. 299
Cleaning of boilers or opening of pistons whenever possible to be 300
done during service, but if impossible the Charterers to give the 301
Owners necessary time for such work at an interval of not less than 302
three months for this purpose. Should the Vessel be detained beyond 303
the number of hours stated in Box 32 hire to cease until again 304
ready. The Owners or the Master to give the Charterers reasonable 305
notice of their intention to clean boilers or open pistons. 306

16. Advances 307
The Charterers or their Agents to advance to the Master, if required, 308
necessary funds for ordinary disbursements for the Vessel's account 309
at any port charging only one per cent. commission, such advances 310
to be deducted from hire, unless other agreement is made according 311
to Box 33. 312

17. Excluded Ports 313
The Vessel not to be ordered to nor bound to enter: 314

a) any place where fever or epidemics are prevalent or to which the 315
Master, Officers and Crew by law are not bound to follow the Vessel; 316

Ice 317
b) any ice-bound place or any place where lights, lightships, marks 318
and buoys are or are likely to be withdrawn by reason of ice on the 319
Vessel's arrival or where there is risk that ordinarily the Vessel will not 320
be able on account of ice to reach the place or to get out after 321
having completed loading or discharging. The Vessel not to be 322
obliged to force ice, nor to follow ice-breakers when inwards bound. 323
If on account of ice the Master considers it dangerous to remain 324
at the loading or discharging place for fear of the Vessel being 325
frozen in and/or damaged, he has liberty to sail to a convenient 326
open place and await the Charterers' fresh instructions. 327
Detention through any of above causes to be for the Charterers' 328
account. 329

18. Loss of Vessel 330
Should the Vessel be lost or missing, hire to cease from the date 331
when she was lost. If the date of loss cannot be ascertained half 332
hire to be paid from the date the Vessel was last reported until the 333
calculated date of arrival at the destination. Any hire paid in ad- 334
vance to be adjusted accordingly. 335

19. Overtime 336
The Vessel to work day and night if required. The Charterers to pay 337
Owners a lumpsum per 30 days as indicated in Box 34 or pro rata 338
for any overtime to Officers and Crew, unless other agreement is 339
made according to Box 34. 340

20. Lien 341
The Owners to have a lien upon all cargoes and sub-freights be- 342
longing to the Time-Charterers and any Bill of Lading freight for 343
all claims under this Charter, and the Charterers to have a lien on 344
the Vessel for all moneys paid in advance and not earned. 345
The Charterers will not suffer, nor permit to be continued any lien 346
or encumbrance incurred by them or their Agents, which might have 347
priority over the title and interest of the Owners in the Vessel. 348

21. Salvage 349
All salvage and assistance to other vessels to be for the Owners' 350
and the Charterers' equal benefit after deducting the Master's and 351
Crew's proportion and all legal and other expenses including hire 352
paid under the Charter for time lost in the salvage, also repairs of 353
damage and fuel consumed. The Charterers to be bound by all 354
measures taken by the Owners in order to secure payment of salvage 355
and to fix its amount. 356

22. Sublet 357
The Charterers to have the option of subletting the Vessel, giving 358
due notice to the Owners, but the original Charterers always to 359
remain responsible to the Owners for due performance of the 360
Charter. 361

23. War 362
(A) The Vessel unless the consent of the Owners be first obtained 363
not to be ordered nor continue to any place or on any voyage nor 364
be used on any service which will bring her within a zone which 365
is dangerous as the result of any actual or threatened act of war, 366
war, hostilities, warlike operations, acts of piracy or of hostility or 367
malicious damage against this or any other vessel or its cargo by 368
any person, body or State whatsoever, revolution, civil war, civil 369
commotion or the operation of international law, nor be exposed in 370
any way to any risks or penalties whatsoever consequent upon the 371
imposition of Sanctions, nor carry any goods that may in any way 372
expose her to any risks of seizure, capture, penalties or any other 373
interference of any kind whatsoever by the belligerent or fighting 374
powers or parties or by any Government or Ruler. 375
(B) Should the Vessel approach or be brought or ordered within 376
such zone, or be exposed in any way to the said risks, 377
1) the Owners to be entitled from time to time to insure their interests 378
in the Vessel and/or hire and/or any of the risks likely to be in- 379
volved thereby on such terms as they shall think fit, the Charterers 380
to make a refund to the Owners of the premium on demand; and 381
2) notwithstanding the terms of Clause 14 hire to be paid for all 382
time lost including any lost owing to loss of or injury to the Master, 383
Officers or Crew or to the action of the Crew in refusing to proceed 384
to such zone or to be exposed to such risks. 385
(C)In the event of the wages and/or war bonus of the Master, Officers 386
and or Crew or the cost of provisions and/or stores for deck and/or 387
engine room and/or insurance and or war risk insurance premiums 388
being increased by reason of or during the existence of any of the 389
matters mentioned in Section (A) the amount of any increase to be 390
added to the hire and paid by the Charterers on production of the 391
Owners account therefor, such account being rendered monthly. 392
(D) The Vessel to have liberty to comply with any orders or directions 393
as to departure, arrival, routes, ports of call, stoppages, destination, 394
delivery or in any other wise whatsoever given by the Government 395
of the nation under whose flag the Vessel sails or any other Govern- 396
ment or any person (or body) acting or purporting to act with the 397
authority of such Government or by any committee or person having 398
under the terms of the war risks insurance on the Vessel the right 399
to give any such orders or directions. 400
(E) in the event of the outbreak of war (whether there be a declara- 401
tion of war or not) between any two or more of the following coun- 402
tries: the United Kingdom, the United States of America, France, the 403
Union of Soviet Socialist Republics, the People's Republic of China 404
or 405
in the event of the nation under whose flag the Vessel sails be- 406
coming involved in war (whether there be a declaration of war 407
or not) 408
either the Owners or the Charterers may cancel this Charter, where- 409
upon the Charterers shall re-deliver the Vessel to the Owners in ac- 410
cordance with Clause 8, if she has cargo on board after discharge 411
thereof at destination or if debarred under this clause from reaching 412
or entering it at a near open and safe port as directed by the 413
Owners, or if she has no cargo on board, at the port at which she 414
then is or if at sea at a near open and safe port as directed by the 415
Owners. In all cases hire shall continue to be paid in accordance 416
with Clause 7 and except as aforesaid all other provisions of this 417
Charter shall apply until re-delivery. 418
(F) If in compliance with the provisions of this clause anything is 419
done or is not done, such not to be deemed a deviation. 420
Section (C) is optional and should be considered deleted unless 421
agreed according to Box 35. 422

"LINERTIME" Deep Sea Time Charter   Page 4

24. General Average   423

General Average to be settled in the place stated in Box 36 according 424
to York/Antwerp Rules, 1974. Hire not to contribute to General 425
Average.   426

25. Fumigation   427

Expenses in connection with fumigations and/or quarantine ordered 428
because of cargoes carried or ports visited while the Vessel is 429
employed under this Charter to be for the Charterers' account. Ex- 430
penses in connection with all other fumigations and/or quarantine 431
to be for the Owners' account.   432

26. Funnel Mark   433

The Charterers to have the option of painting the Vessel's funnel 434
in their own colours, but the Vessel to be re-delivered with the 435
Owners' colours. Painting and repainting to be for the Charterers' 436
account and time to count. The Charterers also to have the option 437
of flying their house flag during the currency of this Charter. 438

27. Supercargo   439

The Charterers to have the option of placing a Supercargo on board, 440
they paying the price stated in Box 37 per day for lodging and 441
victualling at the Master's table.   442

28. Meals   443

The Owners to victual pilots and Customs officers and also, when 444
authorised by Charterers or their Agents, to victual tally clerks, 445
stevedores' foremen, Charterers' guests, etc., the Charterers paying 446
the price stated in Box 38 per man per meal, for all such victualling. 447

29. Light   448

The Owners to supply light on deck and in holds, as on board at 449
all times, free of expense to the Charterers, unless electrical clusters 450
from shore are compulsory, in which case same to be for the 451
Charterers' account.   452

30. Stevedoring Damage   453

The Owners to instruct the Master to report in writing to the Super- 454
cargo, if on board, and to the Charterers and/or their Agents at the 455
port involved, about any stevedoring damage caused to the Vessel, 456
Such reports to be made immediately after the damage is done 457
unless the damage could not be detected at once in spite of close 458
supervision of the stevedoring.   459

31. Ballast   460

If any ballast is required, all expenses for same, including time used 461
in loading and discharging, to be for the Owners' account. 462

32. Arbitration   463

Any dispute arising under the Charter to be referred to arbitration 464
in London, one Arbitrator to be nominated by the Owners and the 465
other by the Charterers, and in case the Arbitrators shall not agree 466
then to the decision of an Umpire to be appointed by them, the 467
award of the Arbitrators or the Umpire to be final and binding upon 468
both parties.   469
If either of the appointed Arbitrators refuses to act, or is incapable 470
of acting, or dies, the party who appointed him may appoint a new 471
Arbitrator in his place.   472
If one party fails to appoint an Arbitrator, either originally, or by 473
way of substitution as aforesaid, for seven clear days after the other 474
party, having appointed his Arbitrator, has served the party making 475
default with notice to make the appointment, the party who has 476
appointed an Arbitrator may appoint that Arbitrator to act as sole 477
Arbitrator in the reference and his award shall be binding on both 478
parties as if he had been appointed by consent.   479

33. Commission   480

The Owners to pay a commission at the rate stated in Box 39 to the 481
party mentioned in Box 39 on any hire paid under the Charter but 482
in no case less than is necessary to cover the actual expenses of 483
the Brokers and a reasonable fee for their work. If the full hire is 484
not paid owing to breach of Charter by either of the parties the 485
party liable therefor to indemnify the Brokers against their loss of 486
commission.   487
Should the parties agree to cancel the Charter, the Owners to in- 488
demnify the Brokers against any loss of commission but in such 489
case the commission not to exceed the brokerage on one year's 490
hire.   491

APPENDIX III

CONLINEBILL*

* Reproduced by kind permission of BIMCO.

LINER BILL OF LADING

Page 1

(Liner terms approved by The Baltic and International Maritime Conference)

Code Name: "CONLINEBILL"

Amended January 1st, 1950, August 1st, 1952, January 1st, 1973, July 1st, 1974, August 1st, 1976, January 1st 1978.

1. **Definition.**
Wherever the term "Merchant" is used in this Bill of Lading, it shall be deemed to include the Shipper, the Receiver, the Consignee, the Holder of the Bill of Lading and the Owner of the cargo.

2. **General Paramount Clause.**
The Hague Rules contained in the International Convention for the Unification of certain rules relating to Bills of Lading, dated Brussels the 25th August 1924 as enacted in the country of shipment shall apply to this contract. When no such enactment is in force in the country of shipment, the corresponding legislation of the country of destination shall apply, but in respect of shipments to which no such enactments are compulsorily applicable, the terms of the said Convention shall apply.
Trades where Hague-Visby Rules apply.
In trades where the International Brussels Convention 1924 as amended by the Protocol signed at Brussels on February 23rd 1968 The Hague-Visby Rules – apply compulsorily, the provisions of the respective legislation shall be considered incorporated in this Bill of Lading. The Carrier takes all reservations possible under such applicable legislation, relating to the period before loading and after discharging and while the goods are in the charge of another Carrier, and to deck cargo and live animals.

3. **Jurisdiction.**
Any dispute arising under this Bill of Lading shall be decided in the country where the carrier has his principal place of business, and the law of such country shall apply except as provided elsewhere herein.

4. **Period of Responsibility.**
The Carrier or his Agent shall not be liable for loss of or damage to the goods during the period before loading and after discharge from the vessel, howsoever such loss or damage arises.

5. **The Scope of Voyage.**
As the vessel is engaged in liner service the intended voyage shall not be limited to the direct route but shall be deemed to include any proceeding or returning to or stopping or slowing down at or off any ports or places for any reasonable purpose connected with the service including maintenance of vessel and crew.

6. **Substitution of Vessel, Transhipment and Forwarding.**
Whether expressly arranged beforehand or otherwise, the Carrier shall be at liberty to carry the goods to their port of destination by the said or other vessel or vessels either belonging to the Carrier or others, or by other means of transport, proceeding either directly or indirectly to such port and to carry the goods or part of them beyond their port of destination, and to tranship, land and store the goods either on shore or afloat and reship and forward the same at Carrier's expense but at Merchant's risk. When the ultimate destination at which the Carrier may have engaged to deliver the goods is other than the vessel's port of discharge, the Carrier acts as Forwarding Agent only.
The responsibility of the Carrier shall be limited to the part of the transport performed by him on vessels under his management and no claim will be acknowledged by the Carrier for damage or loss arising during any other part of the transport even though the freight for the whole transport has been collected by him.

7. **Lighterage.**
Any lightering in or off ports of loading or ports of discharge to be for the account of the Merchant.

8. **Loading, Discharging and Delivery**
of the cargo shall be arranged by the Carrier's Agent unless otherwise agreed.
Landing, storing and delivery shall be for the Merchant's account.
Loading and discharging may commence without previous notice.
The Merchant or his Assign shall tender the goods when the vessel is ready to load and as fast as the vessel can receive and – but only if required by the Carrier – also outside ordinary working hours notwithstanding any custom of the port. Otherwise the Carrier shall be relieved of any obligation to load such cargo and the vessel may leave the port without further notice and deadfreight is to be paid.
The Merchant or his Assign shall take delivery of the goods and continue to receive the goods as fast as the vessel can deliver and – but only if required by the Carrier – also outside ordinary working hours notwithstanding any custom of the port. Otherwise the Carrier shall be at liberty to discharge the goods and any discharge to be deemed a true fulfilment of the contract, or alternatively to act under Clause 16.
The Merchant shall bear all overtime charges in connection with tendering and taking delivery of the goods as above.
If the goods are not applied for within a reasonable time, the Carrier may sell the same privately or by auction.
The Merchant shall accept his reasonable proportion of unidentified loose cargo.

9. **Live Animals and Deck Cargo**
shall be carried subject to the Hague Rules as referred to in Clause 2 hereof with the exception that notwithstanding anything contained in Clause 19 the Carrier shall not be liable for any loss or damage resulting from any act, neglect or default of his servants in the management of such animals and deck cargo.

10. **Options.**
The port of discharge for optional cargo must be declared to the vessel's Agents at the first of the optional ports not later than 48 hours before the vessel's arrival there. In the absence of such declaration the Carrier may elect to discharge at the first or any other optional port and the contract of carriage shall then be considered as having been fulfilled. Any option can be exercised for the total quantity under this Bill of Lading only.

11. **Freight and Charges.**
(a) Prepayable freight, whether actually paid or not, shall be considered as fully earned upon loading and non-returnable in any event. The Carrier's claim for any charges under this contract shall be considered definitely payable in like manner as soon as the charges have been incurred.
Interest at 5 per cent., shall run from the date when freight and charges are due.
(b) The Merchant shall be liable for expenses of fumigation and of gathering and sorting loose cargo and of weighing onboard and expenses incurred in repairing damage to and replacing of packing due to excepted causes and for all expenses caused by extra handling of the cargo for any of the aforementioned reasons.
(c) Any dues, duties, taxes and charges which under any denomination may be levied on any basis such as amount of freight, weight of cargo or tonnage of the vessel shall be paid by the Merchant.
(d) The Merchant shall be liable for all fines and or losses which the Carrier, vessel or cargo may incur through non-observance of Custom House and or import or export regulations.
(e) The Carrier is entitled in case of incorrect declaration of contents, weights, measurements or value of the goods to claim double the amount of freight which would have been due if such declaration had been correctly given. For the purpose of ascertaining the actual facts, the Carrier reserves the right to obtain from the Merchant the original invoice and to have the contents inspected and the weight, measurement or value verified.

12. **Lien.**
The Carrier shall have a lien for any amount due under this contract and costs of recovering same and shall be entitled to sell the goods privately or by auction to cover any claims.

13. **Delay.**
The Carrier shall not be responsible for any loss sustained by the Merchant through delay of the goods unless caused by the Carrier's personal gross negligence.

14. **General Average and Salvage.**
General Average to be adjusted at any port or place at Carrier's option and to be settled according to the York-Antwerp Rules 1974. In the event of accident, danger, damage or disaster before or after commencement of the voyage resulting from any cause whatsoever, whether due to negligence or not, for which or for the consequence of which the Carrier is not responsible by statute, contract or otherwise, the Merchant shall contribute with the Carrier in General Average to the payment of any sacrifice, losses or expenses of a General Average nature that may be made or incurred, and shall pay salvage and special charges incurred in respect of the goods. If a salving vessel is owned or operated by the Carrier, salvage shall be paid for as fully as if the salving vessel or vessels belonged to strangers.

15. **Both-to-Blame Collision Clause.** (This clause to remain in effect even if unenforcible in the Courts of the United States of America).
If the vessel comes into collision with another vessel as a result of the negligence of the other vessel and any act, negligence or default of the Master, Mariner Pilot or the servants of the Carrier in the navigation or in the management of the vessel, the Merchant will indemnify the Carrier against all loss or liability to the other or non-carrying vessel or her Owner in so far as such loss or liability represents loss of or damage to or any claim whatsoever of the owner of the said goods paid or payable by the other or non-carrying vessel or her Owner to the owner of said cargo and set-off, or recouped or recovered by the other or non-carrying vessel or her Owner as part of his claim against the carrying vessel or Carrier. The foregoing provisions shall also apply where the Owner, operator or those in charge of any vessel or vessels or objects other than, or in addition to, the colliding vessels or objects are at fault in respect of a collision or contact.

16. **Government directions, War, Epidemics, Ice, Strikes, etc.**
(a) The Master and the Carrier shall have liberty to comply with any order or directions or recommendations in connection with the transport under this contract given by any Government or Authority, or anybody acting or purporting to act on behalf of such Government or Authority, or having under the terms of the insurance on the vessel the right to give such orders or directions or recommendations.
(b) Should it appear that the performance of the transport would expose the vessel or any goods onboard to risk of seizure or damage or delay, resulting from war, warlike operations, blockade, riots, civil commotions or piracy, or any person onboard to the risk of loss of life or freedom, or that any such risk has increased, the Master may discharge the cargo at port of loading or any other safe and convenient port.
(c) Should it appear that epidemics, quarantine, ice – labour troubles, labour obstructions, strikes, lockouts, any of which onboard or on shore – difficulties in loading or discharging would prevent the vessel from leaving the port of loading or reaching or entering the port of discharge or there discharging in the usual manner and leaving again, all of which safely and without delay, the Master may discharge the cargo at port of loading or any other safe and convenient port.
(d) The discharge under the provisions of this clause of any cargo for which a Bill of Lading has been issued shall be deemed due fulfilment of the contract. If in connection with the exercise of any liberty under this clause any extra expenses are incurred, they shall be paid by the Merchant in addition to the freight, together with return freight if any and a reasonable compensation for any extra services rendered to the goods.
(e) If any situation referred to in this clause may be anticipated, or if for any such reason the vessel cannot safely and without delay reach or enter the loading port or must undergo repairs, the Carrier may cancel the contract before the Bill of Lading is issued.
(f) The Merchant shall be informed if possible.

17. **Identity of Carrier.**
The Contract evidenced by this Bill of Lading is between the Merchant and the Owner of the vessel named herein (or substitute) and it is therefore agreed that said Shipowner only shall be liable for any damage or loss due to any breach or non-performance of any obligation arising out of the contract of carriage, whether or not relating to the vessel's seaworthiness. If, despite the foregoing, it is adjudged that any other is the Carrier and/or bailee of the goods shipped hereunder, all limitations of, and exonerations from, liability provided for by law or by this Bill of Lading shall be available to such other.
It is further understood and agreed that as the Line Company or Agents who has executed this Bill of Lading for and on behalf of the Master is not a principal in the transaction, said Line, Company or Agents shall not be under any liability arising out of the contract of carriage, nor as Carrier nor bailee of the goods.

18. **Exemptions and Immunities of all servants and agents of the Carrier.**
It is hereby expressly agreed that no servant or agent of the Carrier (including every independent contractor from time to time employed by the Carrier) shall in any circumstances whatsoever be under any liability whatsoever to the Merchant for any loss damage or delay arising or resulting directly or indirectly from any act, neglect or default on his part while acting in the course of or in connection with his employment and, but without prejudice to the generality of the foregoing provisions in this clause, every exemption, limitation, condition and liberty herein contained and every right, exemption from liability, defence and immunity of whatsoever nature applicable to the Carrier or to which the Carrier is entitled hereunder shall also be available and shall extend to protect every such servant or agent of the Carrier acting as aforesaid and for the purpose of all the foregoing provisions of this clause the Carrier is or shall be deemed to be acting as agent or trustee on behalf of and for the benefit of all persons who are or might be his servants or agents from time to time (including independent contractors as aforesaid) and all such persons shall to this extent be or be deemed to be parties to the contract evidenced by this Bill of Lading.
The Carrier shall be entitled to be paid by the Merchant on demand any sum recovered or recoverable by the Merchant or any other from such servant or agent of the Carrier for any such loss, damage or delay or otherwise.

19. **Optional Stowage. Unitization.**
(a) Goods may be stowed by the Carrier as received, or, at Carrier's option, by means of containers, or similar articles of transport used to consolidate goods.
(b) Containers, trailers and transportable tanks, whether stowed by the Carrier or received by him in a stowed condition from the Merchant, may be carried on or under deck without notice to the Merchant.
(c) The Carrier's liability for cargo stowed as aforesaid shall be governed by the Hague Rules as defined above notwithstanding the fact that the goods are being carried on deck and the goods shall contribute to general average and shall receive compensation in general average.

ADDITIONAL CLAUSES

(To be added if required in the contemplated trade).

A. Demurrage.
The Carrier shall be paid demurrage at the daily rate per ton of the vessel's gross register tonnage as indicated on Page 2 if the vessel is not loaded or discharged with the dispatch set out in Clause 8, any delay in waiting for berth at or off port to count. Provided that if the delay is due to causes beyond the control of the Merchant, 24 hours shall be deducted from the time on demurrage.
Each Merchant shall be liable towards the Carrier for a proportionate part of the total demurrage due, based upon the total freight on the goods to be loaded or discharged at the port in question.
No Merchant shall be liable in demurrage for any delay arisen only in connection with goods belonging to other Merchants.
The demurrage in respect of each parcel shall not exceed its freight.
(This Clause shall only apply if the Demurrage Box on Page 2 is filled in).

B. U.S. Trade. Period of Responsibility.
In case the Contract evidenced by this Bill of Lading is subject to the U.S. Carriage of Goods by Sea Act, then the provisions stated in said Act shall govern before loading and after discharge and throughout the entire time the goods are in the Carrier's custody.

Shipper	**LINER BILL OF LADING**	**Page 2**
		B/L No.
	Reference No.	

Consignee

Notify address

Pre-carriage by*	Place of receipt by pre-carrier*
Vessel	Port of loading
Port of discharge	Place of delivery by on-carrier*

| Marks and Nos | Number and kind of packages. description of goods | Gross weight | Measurement |

Particulars furnished by the Merchant

Freight details. charges etc	
	SHIPPED on board in apparent good order and condition, weight, measure, marks, numbers, quality, contents and value unknown, for carriage to the Port of Discharge or so near thereunto as the Vessel may safely get and lie always afloat, to be delivered in the like good order and condition at the aforesaid Port unto Consignees or their Assigns, they paying freight as indicated to the left plus other charges incurred in accordance with the provisions contained in this Bill of Lading. In accepting this Bill of Lading the Merchant expressly accepts and agrees to all its stipulations on both pages, whether written, printed, stamped or otherwise incorporated, as fully as if they were all signed by the Merchant. One original Bill of Lading must be surrendered duly endorsed in exchange for the goods or delivery order. IN WITNESS whereof the Master of the said Vessel has signed the number of original Bills of Lading stated below, all of this tenor and date. one of which being accomplished, the others to stand void.
Daily demurrage rate (additional Clause A)	

| * Applicable only when document used as a Through Bill of Lading | Freight payable at | Place and date of issue |
| | Number of original Bs L | Signature |

Printed and sold
by Fr. G. Knudtzon. Ltd . 55. Toldbodgade. Copenhagen.
by authority of The Baltic and International Maritime Conference
(BIMCO). Copenhagen

APPENDIX IV

NEW YORK PRODUCE
EXCHANGE FORM 1993*

* Reproduced by kind permission of
the Association of Ship Brokers and Agents (U.S.A.) Inc.

Code Name: "NYPE 93"
Recommended by:
The Baltic and International Maritime Council (BIMCO)
The Federation of National Associations of
Ship Brokers and Agents (FONASBA)

TIME CHARTER©
New York Produce Exchange Form
Issued by the Association of Ship Brokers and Agents (U.S.A.), Inc.

November 6th, 1913 - Amended October 20th, 1921; August 6th, 1931; October 3rd, 1946;
Revised June 12th, 1981; September 14th 1993.

THIS CHARTER PARTY, made and concluded in	1
this ....day of.......................................19...	2
Between..	3
....	4
<u>Owners</u> of the Vessel described below, and..	5
....	6
....	7
<u>Charterers</u>.	8
<u>Description of Vessel</u>	9

Name .... Flag .... Built ....(year).	10
Port and number of Registry	11
Classed...in...	12
Deadweight.......................................long*/metric* tons (cargo and bunkers, including freshwater and	13
stores not exceeding .... long*/metric* tons) on a salt water draft of	14
on summer freeboard.	15
Capacity .... cubic feet grain..................................cubic feet bale space.	16
Tonnage... GT/GRT.	17
Speed about .... knots, fully laden, in good weather conditions up to and including maximum	18
Force .... on the Beaufort wind scale, on a consumption of about .... long*/metric*	19
tons of.......................................	20

* *Delete as appropriate.*	21
For further description see Appendix "A" (if applicable)	22

1. <u>Duration</u>	23
The Owners agree to let and the Charterers agree to hire the Vessel from the time of delivery for a period	24
of..	25
....	26
....	27
....within below mentioned trading limits.	28

2.   <u>Delivery</u>   29

The Vessel shall be placed at the disposal of the Charterers at 30

.... 31

.... 32

.... The Vessel on her delivery 33

shall be ready to receive cargo with clean-swept holds and tight, staunch, strong and in every way fitted 34

for ordinary cargo service, having water ballast and with sufficient power to operate all cargo-handling gear 35

simultaneously.   36

The Owners shall give the Charterers not less than ....days notice of expected date of 37

delivery.   38

3.   <u>On-Off Hire Survey</u>   39

Prior to delivery and redelivery the parties shall, unless otherwise agreed, each appoint surveyors, for their 40

respective accounts, who shall not later than at first loading port/last discharging port respectively, conduct 41

joint on-hire/off-hire surveys, for the purpose of ascertaining quantity of bunkers on board and the condition 42

of the Vessel. A single report shall be prepared on each occasion and signed by each surveyor, without 43

prejudice to his right to file a separate report setting forth items upon which the surveyors cannot agree. 44

If either party fails to have a representative attend the survey and sign the joint survey report, such party 45

shall nevertheless be bound for all purposes by the findings in any report prepared by the other party. 46

On-hire survey shall be on Charterers' time and off-hire survey on Owners' time.   47

4.   <u>Dangerous Cargo/Cargo Exclusions</u>   48

(a) The Vessel shall be employed in carrying lawful merchandise excluding any goods of a dangerous, 49

injurious, flammable or corrosive nature unless carried in accordance with the requirements or 50

recommendations of the competent authorities of the country of the Vessel's registry and of ports of 51

shipment and discharge and of any intermediate countries or ports through whose waters the Vessel must 52

pass. Without prejudice to the generality of the foregoing, in addition the following are specifically 53

excluded: livestock of any description, arms, ammunition, explosives, nuclear and radioactive materials, 54

.... 55

.... 56

.... 57

.... 58

.... 59

.... 60

.... 61

.... 62

.... 63

.... 64

(b) If IMO-classified cargo is agreed to be carried, the amount of such cargo shall be limited to 65

.... tons and the Charterers shall provide the Master with any evidence he may 66

reasonably require to show that the cargo is packaged, labelled, loaded and stowed in accordance with IMO 67

regulations, failing which the Master is entitled to refuse such cargo or, if already loaded, to unload it at 68

the Charterers' risk and expense.   69

5.   <u>Trading Limits</u>   70

The Vessel shall be employed in such lawful trades between safe ports and safe places   71
within..   72
....excluding   73
....   74
....   75
....as the Charterers shall direct.   76

6.   <u>Owners to Provide</u>   77

The Owners shall provide and pay for the insurance of the Vessel, except as otherwise provided, and for   78
all provisions, cabin, deck, engine-room and other necessary stores, including boiler water; shall pay for   79
wages, consular shipping and discharging fees of the crew and charges for port services pertaining to the   80
crew; shall maintain the Vessel's class and keep her in a thoroughly efficient state in hull, machinery and   81
equipment for and during the service, and have a full complement of officers and crew.   82

7.   <u>Charterers to Provide</u>   83

The Charterers, while the Vessel is on hire, shall provide and pay for all the bunkers except as otherwise   84
agreed; shall pay for port charges (including compulsory watchmen and cargo watchmen and compulsory   85
garbage disposal), all communication expenses pertaining to the Charterers' business at cost, pilotages,   86
towages, agencies, commissions, consular charges (except those pertaining to individual crew members   87
or flag of the Vessel), and all other usual expenses except those stated in Clause 6, but when the Vessel   88
puts into a port for causes for which the Vessel is responsible (other than by stress of weather), then all   89
such charges incurred shall be paid by the Owners. Fumigations ordered because of illness of the crew   90
shall be for the Owners' account. Fumigations ordered because of cargoes carried or ports visited while   91
the Vessel is employed under this Charter Party shall be for the Charterers' account. All other fumigations   92
shall be for the Charterers' account after the Vessel has been on charter for a continuous period of six   93
months or more.   94

The Charterers shall provide and pay for necessary dunnage and also any extra fittings requisite for a   95
special trade or unusual cargo, but the Owners shall allow them the use of any dunnage already aboard   96
the Vessel. Prior to redelivery the Charterers shall remove their dunnage and fittings at their cost and in   97
their time.   98

8.   <u>Performance of Voyages</u>   99

(a) The Master shall perform the voyages with due despatch, and shall render all customary assistance   100
with the Vessel's crew.   The Master shall be conversant with the English language and (although   101
appointed by the Owners) shall be under the orders and directions of the Charterers as regards   102
employment and agency; and the Charterers shall perform all cargo handling, including but not limited to   103
loading, stowing, trimming, lashing, securing, dunnaging, unlashing, discharging, and tallying, at their risk   104
and expense, under the supervision of the Master.   105

(b) If the Charterers shall have reasonable cause to be dissatisfied with the conduct of the Master or   106
officers, the Owners shall, on receiving particulars of the complaint, investigate the same, and, if   107
necessary, make a change in the appointments.   108

9.   **Bunkers**   109

(a) The Charterers on delivery, and the Owners on redelivery, shall take over and pay for all fuel and   110
diesel oil remaining on board the Vessel as hereunder.   The Vessel shall be delivered with: 111
.... long*/metric* tons of fuel oil at the price of .... per ton;   112
.....................................tons of diesel oil at the price of .... per ton. The vessel shall   113
be redelivered with: .... tons of fuel oil at the price of................................... per ton;   114
.... tons of diesel oil at the price of .... per ton.   115

* *Same tons apply throughout this clause.*   116

(b) The Charterers shall supply bunkers of a quality suitable for burning in the Vessel's engines and   117
auxiliaries and which conform to the specification(s) as set out in Appendix A.   118

The Owners reserve their right to make a claim against the Charterers for any damage to the main engines   119
or the auxiliaries caused by the use of unsuitable fuels or fuels not complying with the agreed   120
specification(s). Additionally, if bunker fuels supplied do not conform with the mutually agreed   121
specification(s) or otherwise prove unsuitable for burning in the Vessel's engines or auxiliaries, the Owners   122
shall not be held responsible for any reduction in the Vessel's speed performance and/or increased bunker   123
consumption, nor for any time lost and any other consequences.   124

10.   **Rate of Hire/Redelivery Areas and Notices**   125

The Charterers shall pay for the use and hire of the said Vessel at the rate of $....................................   126
U.S. currency, daily, **or** $.................................. U.S. currency per ton on the Vessel's total deadweight   127
carrying capacity, including bunkers and stores, on .... summer freeboard, per 30 days,   128
commencing on and from the day of her delivery, as aforesaid, and at and after the same rate for any part   129
of a month; hire shall continue until the hour of the day of her redelivery in like good order and condition,   130
ordinary wear and tear excepted, to the Owners (unless Vessel lost) at....................................   131
....   132
....   133
.... unless otherwise mutually agreed.   134

The Charterers shall give the Owners not less than .... days notice of the Vessel's   135
expected date and probable port of redelivery.   136

For the purpose of hire calculations, the times of delivery, redelivery or termination of charter shall be   137
adjusted to GMT.   138

11.   **Hire Payment**   139

(a)   *Payment*   140

Payment of Hire shall be made so as to be received by the Owners or their designated payee in   141
...., viz..   142
....   143
....   144
....in   145

.... currency, or in United States Currency, in funds available to the   146
Owners on the due date, 15 days in advance, and for the last month or part of same the approximate   147
amount of hire, and should same not cover the actual time, hire shall be paid for the balance day by day   148
as it becomes due, if so required by the Owners. Failing the punctual and regular payment of the hire,   149
or on any fundamental breach whatsoever of this Charter Party, the Owners shall be at liberty to   150
withdraw the Vessel from the service of the Charterers without prejudice to any claims they (the Owners)   151
may otherwise have on the Charterers.   152

At any time after the expiry of the grace period provided in Sub-clause 11 (b) hereunder and while the   153
hire is outstanding, the Owners shall, without prejudice to the liberty to withdraw, be entitled to withhold   154
the performance of any and all of their obligations hereunder and shall have no responsibility whatsoever   155
for any consequences thereof, in respect of which the Charterers hereby indemnify the Owners, and hire   156
shall continue to accrue and any extra expenses resulting from such withholding shall be for the   157
Charterers' account.   158

(b)   _Grace Period_   159

Where there is failure to make punctual and regular payment of hire due to oversight, negligence, errors   160
or omissions on the part of the Charterers or their bankers, the Charterers shall be given by the Owners   161
.... clear banking days (as recognized at the agreed place of payment) written notice to rectify the   162
failure, and when so rectified within those .... days following the Owners' notice, the payment shall   163
stand as regular and punctual.   164

Failure by the Charterers to pay the hire within .... days of their receiving the Owners' notice as   165
provided herein, shall entitle the Owners to withdraw as set forth in Sub-clause 11 (a) above.   166

(c)   _Last Hire Payment_   167

Should the Vessel be on her voyage towards port of redelivery at the time the last and/or the penultimate   168
payment of hire is/are due, said payment(s) is/are to be made for such length of time as the Owners and   169
the Charterers may agree upon as being the estimated time necessary to complete the voyage, and taking   170
into account bunkers actually on board, to be taken over by the Owners and estimated disbursements for   171
the Owners' account before redelivery. Should same not cover the actual time, hire is to be paid for the   172
balance, day by day, as it becomes due. When the Vessel has been redelivered, any difference is to be   173
refunded by the Owners or paid by the Charterers, as the case may be.   174

(d)   _Cash Advances_   175

Cash for the Vessel's ordinary disbursements at any port may be advanced by the Charterers, as required   176
by the Owners, subject to 2½ percent commission and such advances shall be deducted from the hire.   177
The Charterers, however, shall in no way be responsible for the application of such advances.   178

12.   **Berths**   179

The Vessel shall be loaded and discharged in any safe dock or at any safe berth or safe place that   180
Charterers or their agents may direct, provided the Vessel can safely enter, lie and depart always afloat   181
at any time of tide.   182

13.   Spaces Available   183

(a) The whole reach of the Vessel's holds, decks, and other cargo spaces (not more than she can   184
reasonably and safely stow and carry), also accommodations for supercargo, if carried, shall be at the   185
Charterers' disposal, reserving only proper and sufficient space for the Vessel's officers, crew, tackle,   186
apparel, furniture, provisions, stores and fuel.   187

(b) In the event of deck cargo being carried, the Owners are to be and are hereby indemnified by the   188
Charterers for any loss and/or damage and/or liability of whatsoever nature caused to the Vessel as a   189
result of the carriage of deck cargo and which would not have arisen had deck cargo not been loaded.   190

14.   Supercargo and Meals   191

The Charterers are entitled to appoint a supercargo, who shall accompany the Vessel at the Charterers'   192
risk and see that voyages are performed with due despatch. He is to be furnished with free   193
accommodation and same fare as provided for the Master's table, the Charterers paying at the rate of   194
.... per day. The Owners shall victual pilots and customs officers, and also, when   195
authorized by the Charterers or their agents, shall victual tally clerks, stevedore's foreman, etc.,   196
Charterers paying at the rate of .... per meal for all such victualling.   197

15.   Sailing Orders and Logs   198

The Charterers shall furnish the Master from time to time with all requisite instructions and sailing   199
directions, in writing, in the English language, and the Master shall keep full and correct deck and engine   200
logs of the voyage or voyages, which are to be patent to the Charterers or their agents, and furnish the   201
Charterers, their agents or supercargo, when required, with a true copy of such deck and engine logs,   202
showing the course of the Vessel, distance run and the consumption of bunkers. Any log extracts   203
required by the Charterers shall be in the English language.   204

16.   Delivery/Cancelling   205

If required by the Charterers, time shall not commence before .... and should the   206
Vessel not be ready for delivery on or before..but not later than...........hours,   207
the Charterers shall have the option of cancelling this Charter Party.   208

Extension of Cancelling   209

If the Owners warrant that, despite the exercise of due diligence by them, the Vessel will not be ready   210
for delivery by the cancelling date, and provided the Owners are able to state with reasonable certainty   211
the date on which the Vessel will be ready, they may, at the earliest seven days before the Vessel is   212
expected to sail for the port or place of delivery, require the Charterers to declare whether or not they will   213
cancel the Charter Party. Should the Charterers elect not to cancel, or should they fail to reply within two   214
days or by the cancelling date, whichever shall first occur, then the seventh day after the expected date   215
of readiness for delivery as notified by the Owners shall replace the original cancelling date. Should the   216
Vessel be further delayed, the Owners shall be entitled to require further declarations of the Charterers   217
in accordance with this Clause.   218

17. __Off Hire__ 219

In the event of loss of time from deficiency and/or default and/or strike of officers or crew, or deficiency 220
of stores, fire, breakdown of, or damages to hull, machinery or equipment, grounding, detention by the 221
arrest of the Vessel, (unless such arrest is caused by events for which the Charterers, their servants, 222
agents or subcontractors are responsible), or detention by average accidents to the Vessel or cargo unless 223
resulting from inherent vice, quality or defect of the cargo, drydocking for the purpose of examination or 224
painting bottom, or by any other similar cause preventing the full working of the Vessel, the payment of 225
hire and overtime, if any, shall cease for the time thereby lost. Should the Vessel deviate or put back 226
during a voyage, contrary to the orders or directions of the Charterers, for any reason other than accident 227
to the cargo or where permitted in lines 257 to 258 hereunder, the hire is to be suspended from the time 228
of her deviating or putting back until she is again in the same or equidistant position from the destination 229
and the voyage resumed therefrom. All bunkers used by the Vessel while off hire shall be for the Owners' 230
account. In the event of the Vessel being driven into port or to anchorage through stress of weather, 231
trading to shallow harbors or to rivers or ports with bars, any detention of the Vessel and/or expenses 232
resulting from such detention shall be for the Charterers' account. If upon the voyage the speed be 233
reduced by defect in, or breakdown of, any part of her hull, machinery or equipment, the time so lost, and 234
the cost of any extra bunkers consumed in consequence thereof, and all extra proven expenses may be 235
deducted from the hire. 236

18. __Sublet__ 237

Unless otherwise agreed, the Charterers shall have the liberty to sublet the Vessel for all or any part of 238
the time covered by this Charter Party, but the Charterers remain responsible for the fulfillment of this 239
Charter Party. 240

19. __Drydocking__ 241

The Vessel was last drydocked 242

*(a) The Owners shall have the option to place the Vessel in drydock during the currency of this Charter 243
at a convenient time and place, to be mutually agreed upon between the Owners and the Charterers, for 244
bottom cleaning and painting and/or repair as required by class or dictated by circumstances. 245

*(b) Except in case of emergency no drydocking shall take place during the currency of this Charter 246
Party. 247

* *Delete as appropriate* 248

20. __Total Loss__ 249

Should the Vessel be lost, money paid in advance and not earned (reckoning from the date of loss or 250
being last heard of) shall be returned to the Charterers at once. 251

21. __Exceptions__ 252

The act of God, enemies, fire, restraint of princes, rulers and people, and all dangers and accidents of the 253
seas, rivers, machinery, boilers, and navigation, and errors of navigation throughout this Charter, always 254
mutually excepted. 255

22.   **Liberties**   256

The Vessel shall have the liberty to sail with or without pilots, to tow and to be towed, to assist vessels   257
in distress, and to deviate for the purpose of saving life and property.   258

23.   **Liens**   259

The Owners shall have a lien upon all cargoes and all sub-freights and/or sub-hire for any amounts due   260
under this Charter Party, including general average contributions, and the Charterers shall have a lien on   261
the Vessel for all monies paid in advance and not earned, and any overpaid hire or excess deposit to be   262
returned at once.   263

The Charterers will not directly or indirectly suffer, nor permit to be continued, any lien or encumbrance,   264
which might have priority over the title and interest of the Owners in the Vessel. The Charterers   265
undertake that during the period of this Charter Party, they will not procure any supplies or necessaries   266
or services, including any port expenses and bunkers, on the credit of the Owners or in the Owners' time.   267

24.   **Salvage**   268

All derelicts and salvage shall be for the Owners' and the Charterers' equal benefit after deducting   269
Owners' and Charterers' expenses and crew's proportion.   270

25.   **General Average**   271

General average shall be adjusted according to York-Antwerp Rules 1974, as amended 1990, or any   272
subsequent modification thereof, in .... and settled in   273
currency.   274

The Charterers shall procure that all bills of lading issued during the currency of the Charter Party will   275
contain a provision to the effect that general average shall be adjusted according to York-Antwerp Rules   276
1974, as amended 1990, or any subsequent modification thereof and will include the "New Jason   277
Clause" as per Clause 31.   278

Time charter hire shall not contribute to general average.   279

26.   **Navigation**   280

Nothing herein stated is to be construed as a demise of the Vessel to the Time Charterers. The Owners   281
shall remain responsible for the navigation of the Vessel, acts of pilots and tug boats, insurance, crew,   282
and all other matters, same as when trading for their own account.   283

27.   **Cargo Claims**   284

Cargo claims as between the Owners and the Charterers shall be settled in accordance with the Inter-Club   285
New York Produce Exchange Agreement of February 1970, as amended May, 1984, or any subsequent   286
modification or replacement thereof.   287

28.   **Cargo Gear and Lights**   288

The Owners shall maintain the cargo handling gear of the Vessel which is as follows:..........................   289
....   290
....   291
....   292
providing gear (for all derricks or cranes) capable of lifting capacity as described. The Owners shall also   293
provide on the Vessel for night work lights as on board, but all additional lights over those on board shall   294
be at the Charterers' expense. The Charterers shall have the use of any gear on board the Vessel. If   295
required by the Charterers, the Vessel shall work night and day and all cargo handling gear shall be at the   296
Charterers' disposal during loading and discharging. In the event of disabled cargo handling gear, or   297
insufficient power to operate the same, the Vessel is to be considered to be off hire to the extent that   298
time is actually lost to the Charterers and the Owners to pay stevedore stand-by charges occasioned   299
thereby, unless such disablement or insufficiency of power is caused by the Charterers' stevedores. If   300
required by the Charterers, the Owners shall bear the cost of hiring shore gear in lieu thereof, in which   301
case the Vessel shall remain on hire.   302

29.   **Crew Overtime**   303

In lieu of any overtime payments to officers and crew for work ordered by the Charterers or their agents,   304
the Charterers shall pay the Owners, concurrently with the hire ....per month   305
or pro rata.   306

30.   **Bills of Lading**   307

(a) The Master shall sign the bills of lading or waybills for cargo as presented in conformity with mates   308
or tally clerk's receipts. However, the Charterers may sign bills of lading or waybills on behalf of the   309
Master, with the Owner's prior written authority, always in conformity with mates or tally clerk's receipts.   310

(b) All bills of lading or waybills shall be without prejudice to this Charter Party and the Charterers shall   311
indemnify the Owners against all consequences or liabilities which may arise from any inconsistency   312
between this Charter Party and any bills of lading or waybills signed by the Charterers or by the Master   313
at their request.   314

(c) Bills of lading covering deck cargo shall be claused: "Shipped on deck at Charterers', Shippers' and   315
Receivers' risk, expense and responsibility, without liability on the part of the Vessel, or her Owners for   316
any loss, damage, expense or delay howsoever caused."   317

31.   **Protective Clauses**   318

This Charter Party is subject to the following clauses all of which are also to be included in all bills of   319
lading or waybills issued hereunder: 320

(a)   CLAUSE PARAMOUNT   321
"This bill of lading shall have effect subject to the provisions of the Carriage of Goods by Sea Act of the   322
United States, the Hague Rules, or the Hague-Visby Rules, as applicable, or such other similar national   323
legislation as may mandatorily apply by virtue of origin or destination of the bills of lading, which shall   324
be deemed to be incorporated herein and nothing herein contained shall be deemed a surrender by the   325

carrier of any of its rights or immunities or an increase of any of its responsibilities or liabilities under said 326
applicable Act. If any term of this bill of lading be repugnant to said applicable Act to any extent, such 327
term shall be void to that extent, but no further." 328

and 329

(b)   BOTH-TO-BLAME COLLISION CLAUSE 330
"If the ship comes into collision with another ship as a result of the negligence of the other ship and any 331
act, neglect or default of the master, mariner, pilot or the servants of the carrier in the navigation or in 332
the management of the ship, the owners of the goods carried hereunder will indemnify the carrier against 333
all loss or liability to the other or non-carrying ship or her owners insofar as such loss or liability represents 334
loss of, or damage to, or any claim whatsoever of the owners of said goods, paid or payable by the other 335
or non-carrying ship or her owners to the owners of said goods and set off, recouped or recovered by the 336
other or non-carrying ship or her owners as part of their claim against the carrying ship or carrier. 337

The foregoing provisions shall also apply where the owners, operators or those in charge of any ships or 338
objects other than, or in addition to, the colliding ships or objects are at fault in respect to a collision or 339
contact." 340

and 341

(c)   NEW JASON CLAUSE 342
"In the event of accident, danger, damage or disaster before or after the commencement of the voyage 343
resulting from any cause whatsoever, whether due to negligence or not, for which, or for the 344
consequences of which, the carrier is not responsible, by statute, contract, or otherwise, the goods, 345
shippers, consignees, or owners of the goods shall contribute with the carrier in general average to the 346
payment of any sacrifices, losses, or expenses of a general average nature that may be made or incurred, 347
and shall pay salvage and special charges incurred in respect of the goods. 348

If a salving ship is owned or operated by the carrier, salvage shall be paid for as fully as if salving ship 349
or ships belonged to strangers. Such deposit as the carrier or his agents may deem sufficient to cover 350
the estimated contribution of the goods and any salvage and special charges thereon shall, if required, 351
be made by the goods, shippers, consignees or owners of the goods to the carrier before delivery." 352

and 353

(d)   U.S. TRADE - DRUG CLAUSE 354
"In pursuance of the provisions of the U.S. Anti Drug Abuse Act 1986 or any re-enactment thereof, the 355
Charterers warrant to exercise the highest degree of care and diligence in preventing unmanifested 356
narcotic drugs and marijuana to be loaded or concealed on board the Vessel. 357

Non-compliance with the provisions of this clause shall amount to breach of warranty for consequences 358
of which the Charterers shall be liable and shall hold the Owners, the Master and the crew of the Vessel 359
harmless and shall keep them indemnified against all claims whatsoever which may arise and be made 360
against them individually or jointly. Furthermore, all time lost and all expenses incurred, including fines, 361
as a result of the Charterers' breach of the provisions of this clause shall be for the Charterer's account 362
and the Vessel shall remain on hire. 363

Should the Vessel be arrested as a result of the Charterers' non-compliance with the provisions of this   364
clause, the Charterers shall at their expense take all reasonable steps to secure that within a reasonable   365
time the Vessel is released and at their expense put up the bails to secure release of the Vessel.   366

The Owners shall remain responsible for all time lost and all expenses incurred, including fines, in the   367
event that unmanifested narcotic drugs and marijuana are found in the possession or effects of the   368
Vessel's personnel."   369

and   370

(e)   WAR CLAUSES   371
"(i) No contraband of war shall be shipped. The Vessel shall not be required, without the consent of the   372
Owners, which shall not be unreasonably withheld, to enter any port or zone which is involved in a state   373
of war, warlike operations, or hostilities, civil strife, insurrection or piracy whether there be a declaration   374
of war or not, where the Vessel, cargo or crew might reasonably be expected to be subject to capture,   375
seizure or arrest, or to a hostile act by a belligerent power (the term "power" meaning any de jure or de   376
facto authority or any purported governmental organization maintaining naval, military or air forces).   377

(ii) If such consent is given by the Owners, the Charterers will pay the provable additional cost of insuring   378
the Vessel against hull war risks in an amount equal to the value under her ordinary hull policy but not   379
exceeding a valuation of.. In addition, the Owners may purchase and the   380
Charterers will pay for war risk insurance on ancillary risks such as loss of hire, freight disbursements,   381
total loss, blocking and trapping, etc. If such insurance is not obtainable commercially or through a   382
government program, the Vessel shall not be required to enter or remain at any such port or zone.   383

(iii) In the event of the existence of the conditions described in (i) subsequent to the date of this Charter,   384
or while the Vessel is on hire under this Charter, the Charterers shall, in respect of voyages to any such   385
port or zone assume the provable additional cost of wages and insurance properly incurred in connection   386
with master, officers and crew as a consequence of such war, warlike operations or hostilities.   387

(iv) Any war bonus to officers and crew due to the Vessel's trading or cargo carried shall be for the   388
Charterers' account."   389

32.   War Cancellation   390

In the event of the outbreak of war (whether there be a declaration of war or not) between any two or   391
more of the following countries:...   392
....   393
....   394
....   395
either the Owners or the Charterers may cancel this Charter Party. Whereupon, the Charterers shall   396
redeliver the Vessel to the Owners in accordance with Clause 10; if she has cargo on board, after   397
discharge thereof at destination, or, if debarred under this Clause from reaching or entering it, at a near   398
open and safe port as directed by the Owners; or, if she has no cargo on board, at the port at which she   399
then is; or, if at sea, at a near open and safe port as directed by the Owners. In all cases hire shall   400
continue to be paid in accordance with Clause 11 and except as aforesaid all other provisions of this   401
Charter Party shall apply until redelivery.   402

33.   <u>Ice</u>   403

The Vessel shall not be required to enter or remain in any icebound port or area, nor any port or area   404
where lights or lightships have been or are about to be withdrawn by reason of ice, nor where there is   405
risk that in the ordinary course of things the Vessel will not be able on account of ice to safely enter and   406
remain in the port or area or to get out after having completed loading or discharging. Subject to the   407
Owners' prior approval the Vessel is to follow ice-breakers when reasonably required with regard to her   408
size, construction and ice class.   409

34.   <u>Requisition</u>   410

Should the Vessel be requisitioned by the government of the Vessel's flag during the period of this Charter   411
Party, the Vessel shall be deemed to be off hire during the period of such requisition, and any hire paid   412
by the said government in respect of such requisition period shall be retained by the Owners. The period   413
during which the Vessel is on requisition to the said government shall count as part of the period provided   414
for in this Charter Party.   415

If the period of requisition exceeds .... months, either party shall have the option   416
of cancelling this Charter Party and no consequential claim may be made by either party.   417

35.   <u>Stevedore Damage</u>   418

Notwithstanding anything contained herein to the contrary, the Charterers shall pay for any and all   419
damage to the Vessel caused by stevedores provided the Master has notified the Charterers and/or their   420
agents in writing as soon as practical but not later than 48 hours after any damage is discovered. Such   421
notice to specify the damage in detail and to invite Charterers to appoint a surveyor to assess the extent   422
of such damage.   423

(a) In case of any and all damage(s) affecting the Vessel's seaworthiness and/or the safety of the crew   424
and/or affecting the trading capabilities of the Vessel, the Charterers shall immediately arrange for repairs   425
of such damage(s) at their expense and the Vessel is to remain on hire until such repairs are completed   426
and if required passed by the Vessel's classification society.   427

(b) Any and all damage(s) not described under point (a) above shall be repaired at the Charterers' option,   428
before or after redelivery concurrently with the Owners' work. In such case no hire and/or expenses will   429
be paid to the Owners except and insofar as the time and/or the expenses required for the repairs for   430
which the Charterers are responsible, exceed the time and/or expenses necessary to carry out the   431
Owners' work.   432

36.   <u>Cleaning of Holds</u>   433

The Charterers shall provide and pay extra for sweeping and/or washing and/or cleaning of holds between   434
voyages and/or between cargoes provided such work can be undertaken by the crew and is permitted by   435
local regulations, at the rate of................................ per hold.   436

In connection with any such operation, the Owners shall not be responsible if the Vessel's holds are not   437
accepted or passed by the port or any other authority. The Charterers shall have the option to re-deliver   438
the Vessel with unclean/unswept holds against a lumpsum payment of......................in lieu of cleaning.   439

37.   **Taxes**   440

Charterers to pay all local, State, National taxes and/or dues assessed on the Vessel or the Owners   441
resulting from the Charterers' orders herein, whether assessed during or after the currency of this Charter   442
Party including any taxes and/or dues on cargo and/or freights and/or sub-freights and/or hire (excluding   443
taxes levied by the country of the flag of the Vessel or the Owners).   444

38.   **Charterers' Colors**   445

The Charterers shall have the privilege of flying their own house flag and painting the Vessel with their   446
own markings. The Vessel shall be repainted in the Owners' colors before termination of the Charter   447
Party. Cost and time of painting, maintaining and repainting those changes effected by the Charterers   448
shall be for the Charterers' account.   449

39.   **Laid Up Returns**   450

The Charterers shall have the benefit of any return insurance premium receivable by the Owners from their   451
underwriters as and when received from underwriters by reason of the Vessel being in port for a minimum   452
period of 30 days if on full hire for this period or pro rata for the time actually on hire.   453

40.   **Documentation**   454

The Owners shall provide any documentation relating to the Vessel that may be required to permit the   455
Vessel to trade within the agreed trade limits, including, but not limited to certificates of financial   456
responsibility for oil pollution, provided such oil pollution certificates are obtainable from the Owners'   457
 P & I club, valid international tonnage certificate, Suez and Panama tonnage certificates, valid certificate   458
of registry and certificates relating to the strength and/or serviceability of the Vessel's gear.   459

41.   **Stowaways**   460

(a)   (i) The Charterers warrant to exercise due care and diligence in preventing stowaways in gaining   461
           access to the Vessel by means of secreting away in the goods and/or containers shipped by the   462
           Charterers.   463

           (ii) If, despite the exercise of due care and diligence by the Charterers, stowaways have gained   464
           access to the Vessel by means of secreting away in the goods and/or containers shipped by the   465
           Charterers, this shall amount to breach of charter for the consequences of which the Charterers   466
           shall be liable and shall hold the Owners harmless and shall keep them indemnified against all   467
           claims whatsoever which may arise and be made against them. Furthermore, all time lost and all   468
           expenses whatsoever and howsoever incurred, including fines, shall be for the Charterers' account   469
           and the Vessel shall remain on hire.   470

           (iii) Should the Vessel be arrested as a result of the Charterers' breach of charter according to   471
           sub-clause (a)(ii) above, the Charterers shall take all reasonable steps to secure that, within a   472
           reasonable time, the Vessel is released and at their expense put up bail to secure release of the   473
           Vessel.   474

(b)   (i) If, despite the exercise of due care and diligence by the Owners, stowaways have gained   475
access to the Vessel by means other than secreting away in the goods and/or containers shipped   476
by the Charterers, all time lost and all expenses whatsoever and howsoever incurred, including   477
fines, shall be for the Owners' account and the Vessel shall be off hire.   478

(ii) Should the Vessel be arrested as a result of stowaways having gained access to the Vessel   479
by means other than secreting away in the goods and/or containers shipped by the Charterers,   480
the Owners shall take all reasonable steps to secure that, within a reasonable time, the Vessel   481
is released and at their expense put up bail to secure release of the Vessel.   482

42.   Smuggling   483

In the event of smuggling by the Master, Officers and/or crew, the Owners shall bear the cost of any   484
fines, taxes, or imposts levied and the Vessel shall be off hire for any time lost as a result thereof.   485

43.   Commissions   486

A commission of........................ percent is payable by the Vessel and the Owners to..........................   487
....   488
....   489
....   490
on hire earned and paid under this Charter, and also upon any continuation or extension of this Charter.   491

44.   Address Commission   492

An address commission of .... percent is payable to..   493
....   494
....   495
....on hire earned and paid under this Charter.   496

45.   Arbitration   497

(a)   NEW YORK   498
All disputes arising out of this contract shall be arbitrated at New York in the following manner, and   499
subject to U.S. Law: 500

One Arbitrator is to be appointed by each of the parties hereto and a third by the two so chosen. Their   501
decision or that of any two of them shall be final, and for the purpose of enforcing any award, this   502
agreement may be made a rule of the court. The Arbitrators shall be commercial men, conversant with   503
shipping matters. Such Arbitration is to be conducted in accordance with the rules of the Society of   504
Maritime Arbitrators Inc.   505

For disputes where the total amount claimed by either party does not exceed US $ ....**   506
the arbitration shall be conducted in accordance with the Shortened Arbitration Procedure of the Society   507
of Maritime Arbitrators Inc.   508

(b)   LONDON   509
All disputes arising out of this contract shall be arbitrated at London and, unless the parties agree   510
forthwith on a single Arbitrator, be referred to the final arbitrament of two Arbitrators carrying on business   511
in London who shall be members of the Baltic Mercantile & Shipping Exchange and engaged in Shipping,   512
one to be appointed by each of the parties, with power to such Arbitrators to appoint an Umpire. No   513
award shall be questioned or invalidated on the ground that any of the Arbitrators is not qualified as   514
above, unless objection to his action be taken before the award is made. Any dispute arising hereunder   515
shall be governed by English Law.   516

For disputes where the total amount claimed by either party does not exceed US $ ....**   517
the arbitration shall be conducted in accordance with the Small Claims Procedure of the London Maritime   518
Arbitrators Association.   519

* Delete para (a) or (b) as appropriate   520

** Where no figure is supplied in the blank space this provision only shall be void but the other provisions   521
of this clause shall have full force and remain in effect.   522

If mutually agreed, clauses .... to ...., both inclusive, as attached hereto are fully   523
incorporated in this Charter Party.   524

APPENDIX "A"

525

To Charter Party dated 526
Between...Owners 527
and .... Charterers 528

Further details of the Vessel: 529

530

APPENDIX V

SHELLTIME 4*

Code word for this Charter Party
"SHELLTIME 4"

Issued December 1984

Time Charter Party

LONDON,   19

	IT IS THIS DAY AGREED between	1
	of (hereinafter referred to as "Owners"), being owners of the	2
	good vessel called	3
	(hereinafter referred to as "the vessel") described as per Clause 1 hereof and	4
	of (hereinafter referred to as "Charterers"):	5

Description and Condition of Vessel	1. At the date of delivery of the vessel under this charter	6
	(a) she shall be classed;	7
	(b) she shall be in every way fit to carry crude petroleum and/or its products;	8
	(c) she shall be tight, staunch, strong, in good order and condition, and in every way fit for the	9
	service, with her machinery, boilers, hull and other equipment (including but not limited to hull stress calculator	10
	and radar) in a good and efficient state;	11
	(d) her tanks, valves and pipelines shall be oil-tight;	12
	(e) she shall be in every way fitted for burning	13
	at sea – fueloil with a maximum viscosity of Centistokes at 50 degrees Centigrade/any	14
	commercial grade of fueloil ("ACGFO") for main propulsion, marine diesel oil/ACGFO	15
	for auxiliaries	16
	in port – marine diesel oil/ACGFO for auxiliaries;	17
	(f) she shall comply with the regulations in force so as to enable her to pass through the Suez and	18
	Panama Canals by day and night without delay;	19
	(g) she shall have on board all certificates, documents and equipment required from time to time by	20
	any applicable law to enable her to perform the charter service without delay;	21
	(h) she shall comply with the description in Form B appended hereto, provided however that if there	22
	is any conflict between the provisions of Form B and any other provision, including this Clause 1, of this charter	23
	such other provision shall govern.	24

Shipboard Personnel and their Duties	2. (a) At the date of delivery of the vessel under this charter	25
	(i) she shall have a full and efficient complement of master, officers and crew for a vessel of her	26
	tonnage, who shall in any event be not less than the number required by the laws of the flag state and who shall be	27
	trained to operate the vessel and her equipment competently and safely;	28
	(ii) all shipboard personnel shall hold valid certificates of competence in accordance with the	29
	requirements of the law of the flag state;	30
	(iii) all shipboard personnel shall be trained in accordance with the relevant provisions of the	31
	International Convention on Standards of Training, Certification and Watchkeeping for Seafarers, 1978;	32
	(iv) there shall be on board sufficient personnel with a good working knowledge of the English	33
	language to enable cargo operations at loading and discharging places to be carried out efficiently and safely and	34
	to enable communications between the vessel and those loading the vessel or accepting discharge therefrom to be	35
	carried out quickly and efficiently.	36
	(b) Owners guarantee that throughout the charter service the master shall with the vessel's officers	37
	and crew, unless otherwise ordered by Charterers,	38
	(i) prosecute all voyages with the utmost despatch;	39
	(ii) render all customary assistance; and	40
	(iii) load and discharge cargo as rapidly as possible when required by Charterers or their agents	41
	to do so, by night or by day, but always in accordance with the laws of the place of loading or discharging (as the	42
	case may be) and in each case in accordance with any applicable laws of the flag state.	43

Duty to Maintain	3. (i) Throughout the charter service Owners shall, whenever the passage of time, wear and tear or any	44
	event (whether or not coming within Clause 27 hereof) requires steps to be taken to maintain or restore the	45
	conditions stipulated in Clauses 1 and 2(a), exercise due diligence so to maintain or restore the vessel.	46
	(ii) If at any time whilst the vessel is on hire under this charter the vessel fails to comply with the	47
	requirements of Clauses 1, 2(a) or 10 then hire shall be reduced to the extent necessary to indemnify Charterers	48
	for such failure. If and to the extent that such failure affects the time taken by the vessel to perform any services	49
	under this charter, hire shall be reduced by an amount equal to the value, calculated at the rate of hire, of the time	50
	so lost.	51
	Any reduction of hire under this sub-Clause (ii) shall be without prejudice to any other remedy	52
	available to Charterers, but where such reduction of hire is in respect of time lost, such time shall be excluded	53
	from any calculation under Clause 24.	54
	(iii) If Owners are in breach of their obligation under Clause 3(i) Charterers may so notify Owners in	55
	writing; and if, after the expiry of 30 days following the receipt by Owners of any such notice, Owners have failed	56
	to demonstrate to Charterers' reasonable satisfaction the exercise of due diligence as required in Clause 3(i), the	57
	vessel shall be off-hire, and no further hire payments shall be due, until Owners have so demonstrated that they	58
	are exercising such due diligence.	59
	Furthermore, at any time while the vessel is off-hire under this Clause 3 Charterers have the	60
	option to terminate this charter by giving notice in writing with effect from the date on which such notice of	61
	termination is received by Owners or from any later date stated in such notice. This sub-Clause (iii) is without	62
	prejudice to any rights of Charterers or obligations of Owners under this charter or otherwise (including without	63
	limitation Charterers' rights under Clause 21 hereof).	64

2

Period Trading Limits	4. Owners agree to let and Charterers agree to hire the vessel for a period of commencing from the time and date of delivery of the vessel, for the purpose of carrying all lawful merchandise (subject always to Clause 28) including in particular	65 66 67

in any part of the world, as Charterers shall direct, subject to the limits of the current British Institute Warranties and any subsequent amendments thereof. Notwithstanding the foregoing, but subject to Clause 35, Charterers may order the vessel to ice-bound waters or to any part of the world outside such limits provided that Owners consent thereto (such consent not to be unreasonably withheld) and that Charterers pay for any insurance premium required by the vessel's underwriters as a consequence of such order. 68
69
70
71
72

Charterers shall use due diligence to ensure that the vessel is only employed between and at safe places (which expression when used in this charter shall include ports, berths, wharves, docks, anchorages, submarine lines, alongside vessels or lighters, and other locations including locations at sea) where she can safely lie always afloat. Notwithstanding anything contained in this or any other clause of this charter, Charterers do not warrant the safety of any place to which they order the vessel and shall be under no liability in respect thereof except for loss or damage caused by their failure to exercise due diligence as aforesaid. Subject as above, the vessel shall be loaded and discharged at any places as Charterers may direct, provided that Charterers shall exercise due diligence to ensure that any ship-to-ship transfer operations shall conform to standards not less than those set out in the latest published edition of the ICS/OCIMF Ship-to-Ship Transfer Guide. 73
74
75
76
77
78
79
80
81

The vessel shall be delivered by Owners at a port in 82

at Owners' option and redelivered to Owners at a port in 83

at Charterers' option. 84

Laydays/ Cancelling	5. The vessel shall not be delivered to Charterers before and Charterers shall have the option of cancelling this charter if the vessel is not ready and at their disposal on or before	85 86
Owners to Provide	6. Owners undertake to provide and to pay for all provisions, wages, and shipping and discharging fees and all other expenses of the master, officers and crew; also, except as provided in Clauses 4 and 34 hereof, for all insurance on the vessel, for all deck, cabin and engine-room stores, and for water; for all drydocking, overhaul, maintenance and repairs to the vessel; and for all fumigation expenses and de-rat certificates. Owners' obligations under this Clause 6 extend to all liabilities for customs or import duties arising at any time during the performance of this charter in relation to the personal effects of the master, officers and crew, and in relation to the stores, provisions and other matters aforesaid which Owners are to provide and pay for and Owners shall refund to Charterers any sums Charterers or their agents may have paid or been compelled to pay in respect of any such liability. Any amounts allowable in general average for wages and provisions and stores shall be credited to Charterers insofar as such amounts are in respect of a period when the vessel is on-hire.	87 88 89 90 91 92 93 94 95 96
Charterers to Provide	7. Charterers shall provide and pay for all fuel (except fuel used for domestic services), towage and pilotage and shall pay agency fees, port charges, commissions, expenses of loading and unloading cargoes, canal dues and all charges other than those payable by Owners in accordance with Clause 6 hereof, provided that all charges for the said items shall be for Owners' account when such items are consumed, employed or incurred for Owners' purposes or while the vessel is off-hire (unless such items reasonably relate to any service given or distance made good and taken into account under Clause 21 or 22); and provided further that any fuel used in connection with a general average sacrifice or expenditure shall be paid for by Owners.	97 98 99 100 101 102 103
Rate of Hire	8. Subject as herein provided, Charterers shall pay for the use and hire of the vessel at the rate of per day, and pro rata for any part of a day, from the time and date of her delivery (local time) until the time and date of her redelivery (local time) to Owners.	104 105 106
Payment of Hire	9. Subject to Clause 3 (iii), payment of hire shall be made in immediately available funds to:	107

Account 108
in   per calendar month in advance, less: 109
(i)   any hire paid which Charterers reasonably estimate to relate to off-hire periods, and 110
(ii) any amounts disbursed on Owners' behalf, any advances and commission thereon, and charges which are for Owners' account pursuant to any provision hereof, and 111
112
(iii) any amounts due or reasonably estimated to become due to Charterers under Clause 3 (ii) or 24 hereof, 113
114

any such adjustments to be made at the due date for the next monthly payment after the facts have been ascertained. Charterers shall not be responsible for any delay or error by Owners' bank in crediting Owners' account provided that Charterers have made proper and timely payment. 115
116
117

In default of such proper and timely payment, 118
(a) Owners shall notify Charterers of such default and Charterers shall within seven days of receipt of such notice pay to Owners the amount due including interest, failing which Owners may withdraw the vessel from the service of Charterers without prejudice to any other rights Owners may have under this charter or otherwise; and 119
120
121
122

(b) Interest on any amount due but not paid on the due date shall accrue from the day after that date up to and including the day when payment is made, at a rate per annum which shall be 1% above the U.S. Prime Interest Rate as published by the Chase Manhattan Bank in New York at 12.00 New York time on the due date, or, if no such interest rate is published on that day, the interest rate published on the next preceding day on which such a rate was so published, computed on the basis of a 360 day year of twelve 30-day months, compounded semi-annually. 123
124
125
126
127
128

APPENDIX V

3

Space Available to Charterers	10. The whole reach. burthen and decks of the vessel and any passenger accommodation (including Owners' suite) shall be at Charterers' disposal. reserving only proper and sufficient space for the vessel's master. officers. crew. tackle. apparel. furniture. provisions and stores. provided that the weight of stores on board shall not. unless specially agreed. exceed tonnes at any time during the charter period.	129 130 131 132
Overtime	11. Overtime pay of the master. officers and crew in accordance with ship's articles shall be for Charterers' account when incurred. as a result of complying with the request of Charterers or their agents. for loading. discharging. heating of cargo. bunkering or tank cleaning.	133 134 135
Instructions and Logs	12. Charterers shall from time to time give the master all requisite instructions and sailing directions. and he shall keep a full and correct log of the voyage or voyages. which Charterers or their agents may inspect as required. The master shall when required furnish Charterers or their agents with a true copy of such log and with properly completed loading and discharging port sheets and voyage reports for each voyage and other returns as Charterers may require. Charterers shall be entitled to take copies at Owners' expense of any such documents which are not provided by the master.	136 137 138 139 140 141

Bills of Lading	13. (a) The master (although appointed by Owners) shall be under the orders and direction of Charterers as regards employment of the vessel. agency and other arrangements. and shall sign bills of lading as Charterers or their agents may direct (subject always to Clauses 35(a) and 40) without prejudice to this charter. Charterers hereby indemnify Owners against all consequences or liabilities that may arise
	      (i) from signing bills of lading in accordance with the directions of Charterers or their agents. to the extent that the terms of such bills of lading fail to conform to the requirements of this charter. or (except as provided in Clause 13(b)) from the master otherwise complying with Charterers' or their agents' orders:
	      (ii) from any irregularities in papers supplied by Charterers or their agents.
	     (b) Notwithstanding the foregoing. Owners shall not be obliged to comply with any orders from Charterers to discharge all or part of the cargo
	      (i) at any place other than that shown on the bill of lading and/or
	      (ii) without presentation of an original bill of lading
	unless they have received from Charterers both written confirmation of such orders and an indemnity in a form acceptable to Owners.
		142 143 144 145 146 147 148 149 150 151 152 153 154 155

Conduct of Vessel's Personnel	14. If Charterers complain of the conduct of the master or any of the officers or crew. Owners shall immediately investigate the complaint. If the complaint proves to be well founded. Owners shall. without delay. make a change in the appointments and Owners shall in any event communicate the result of their investigations to Charterers as soon as possible.	156 157 158 159
Bunkers at Delivery and Redelivery	15. Charterers shall accept and pay for all bunkers on board at the time of delivery. and Owners shall on redelivery (whether it occurs at the end of the charter period or on the earlier termination of this charter) accept and pay for all bunkers remaining on board. at the then-current market prices at the port of delivery or redelivery. as the case may be. or if such prices are not available payment shall be at the then-current market prices at the nearest port at which such prices are available; provided that if delivery or redelivery does not take place in a port payment shall be at the price paid at the vessel's last port of bunkering before delivery or redelivery. as the case may be. Owners shall give Charterers the use and benefit of any fuel contracts they may have in force from time to time. if so required by Charterers. provided suppliers agree.	160 161 162 163 164 165 166 167

Stevedores. Pilots. Tugs	16. Stevedores when required shall be employed and paid by Charterers. but this shall not relieve Owners from responsibility at all times for proper stowage. which must be controlled by the master who shall keep a strict account of all cargo loaded and discharged. Owners hereby indemnify Charterers. their servants and agents against all losses. claims. responsibilities and liabilities arising in any way whatsoever from the employment of pilots. tugboats or stevedores. who although employed by Charterers shall be deemed to be the servants of and in the service of Owners and under their instructions (even if such pilots. tugboat personnel or stevedores are in fact the servants of Charterers their agents or any affiliated company): provided. however. that
	      (i) the foregoing indemnity shall not exceed the amount to which Owners would have been entitled to limit their liability if they had themselves employed such pilots. tugboats or stevedores. and
	      (ii) Charterers shall be liable for any damage to the vessel caused by or arising out of the use of stevedores. fair wear and tear excepted. to the extent that Owners are unable by the exercise of due diligence to obtain redress therefor from stevedores.
		168 169 170 171 172 173 174 175 176 177 178 179

Supernumeraries	17. Charterers may send representatives in the vessel's available accommodation upon any voyage made under this charter. Owners finding provisions and all requisites as supplied to officers. except liquors. Charterers paying at the rate of per day for each representative while on board the vessel.	180 181 182
Sub-letting	18. Charterers may sub-let the vessel. but shall always remain responsible to Owners for due fulfilment of this charter.	183 184

Final Voyage	19. If when a payment of hire is due hereunder Charterers reasonably expect to redeliver the vessel before the next payment of hire would fall due. the hire to be paid shall be assessed on Charterers' reasonable estimate of the time necessary to complete Charterers' programme up to redelivery. and from which estimate Charterers may deduct amounts due or reasonably expected to become due for
	      (i) disbursements on Owners' behalf or charges for Owners' account pursuant to any provision hereof. and
	      (ii) bunkers on board at redelivery pursuant to Clause 15.
	     Promptly after redelivery any overpayment shall be refunded by Owners or any underpayment made good by Charterers.
	     If at the time this charter would otherwise terminate in accordance with Clause 4 the vessel is on a ballast voyage to a port of redelivery or is upon a laden voyage. Charterers shall continue to have the use of the vessel at the same rate and conditions as stand herein for as long as necessary to complete such ballast voyage. or to complete such laden voyage and return to a port of redelivery as provided by this charter. as the case may be.
		185 186 187 188 189 190 191 192 193 194 195 196 197

4

Loss of Vessel	20. Should the vessel be lost, this charter shall terminate and hire shall cease at noon on the day of her loss; should the vessel be a constructive total loss, this charter shall terminate and hire shall cease at noon on the day on which the vessel's underwriters agree that the vessel is a constructive total loss: should the vessel be missing, this charter shall terminate and hire shall cease at noon on the day on which she was last heard of. Any hire paid in advance and not earned shall be returned to Charterers and Owners shall reimburse Charterers for the value of the estimated quantity of bunkers on board at the time of termination, at the price paid by Charterers at the last bunkering port.	198 199 200 201 202 203 204
Off-hire	21. (a) On each and every occasion that there is loss of time (whether by way of interruption in the vessel's service or, from reduction in the vessel's performance, or in any other manner)	205 206

Loss of
Vessel

20. Should the vessel be lost, this charter shall terminate and hire shall cease at noon on the day of her loss; should the vessel be a constructive total loss, this charter shall terminate and hire shall cease at noon on the day on which the vessel's underwriters agree that the vessel is a constructive total loss: should the vessel be missing, this charter shall terminate and hire shall cease at noon on the day on which she was last heard of. Any hire paid in advance and not earned shall be returned to Charterers and Owners shall reimburse Charterers for the value of the estimated quantity of bunkers on board at the time of termination, at the price paid by Charterers at the last bunkering port.

198
199
200
201
202
203
204

Off-hire

21. (a) On each and every occasion that there is loss of time (whether by way of interruption in the vessel's service or, from reduction in the vessel's performance, or in any other manner)
    (i) due to deficiency of personnel or stores; repairs; gas-freeing for repairs; time in and waiting to enter dry dock for repairs; breakdown (whether partial or total) of machinery, boilers or other parts of the vessel or her equipment (including without limitation tank coatings); overhaul, maintenance or survey; collision, stranding, accident or damage to the vessel; or any other similar cause preventing the efficient working of the vessel; and such loss continues for more than three consecutive hours (if resulting from interruption in the vessel's service) or cumulates to more than three hours (if resulting from partial loss of service); or
    (ii) due to.industrial action, refusal to sail, breach of orders or neglect of duty on the part of the master, officers or crew; or
    (iii) for the purpose of obtaining medical advice or treatment for or landing any sick or injured person (other than a Charterers' representative carried under Clause 17 hereof) or for the purpose of landing the body of any person (other than a Charterers' representative), and such loss continues for more than three consecutive hours; or
    (iv) due to any delay in quarantine arising from the master, officers or crew having had communication with the shore at any infected area without the written consent or instructions of Charterers or their agents, or to any detention by customs or other authorities caused by smuggling or other infraction of local law on the part of the master, officers, or crew; or
    (v) due to detention of the vessel by authorities at home or abroad attributable to legal action against or breach of regulations by the vessel, the vessel's owners, or Owners (unless brought about by the act or neglect of Charterers); then
    without prejudice to Charterers' rights under Clause 3 or to any other rights of Charterers hereunder or otherwise the vessel shall be off-hire from the commencement of such loss of time until she is again ready and in an efficient state to resume her service from a position not less favourable to Charterers than that at which such loss of time commenced; provided, however, that any service given or distance made good by the vessel whilst off-hire shall be taken into account in assessing the amount to be deducted from hire.
    (b) If the vessel fails to proceed at any guaranteed speed pursuant to Clause 24, and such failure arises wholly or partly from any of the causes set out in Clause 21(a) above, then the period for which the vessel shall be off-hire under this Clause 21 shall be the difference between
    (i) the time the vessel would have required to perform the relevant service at such guaranteed speed, and
    (ii) the time actually taken to perform such service (including any loss of time arising from interruption in the performance of such service).
    For the avoidance of doubt, all time included under (ii) above shall be excluded from any computation under Clause 24.
    (c) Further and without prejudice to the foregoing, in the event of the vessel deviating (which expression includes without limitation putting back, or putting into any port other than that to which she is bound under the instructions of Charterers) for any cause or purpose mentioned in Clause 21(a), the vessel shall be off-hire from the commencement of such deviation until the time when she is again ready and in an efficient state to resume her service from a position not less favourable to Charterers than that at which the deviation commenced, provided, however, that any service given or distance made good by the vessel whilst so off-hire shall be taken into account in assessing the amount to be deducted from hire. If the vessel, for any cause or purpose mentioned in Clause 21 (a), puts into any port other than the port to which she is bound on the instructions of Charterers, the port charges, pilotage and other expenses at such port shall be borne by Owners. Should the vessel be driven into any port or anchorage by stress of weather hire shall continue to be due and payable during any time lost thereby.
    (d) If the vessel's flag state becomes engaged in hostilities, and Charterers in consequence of such hostilities find it commercially impracticable to employ the vessel and have given Owners written notice thereof then from the date of receipt by Owners of such notice until the termination of such commercial impracticability the vessel shall be off-hire and Owners shall have the right to employ the vessel on their own account.
    (e) Time during which the vessel is off-hire under this charter shall count as part of the charter period.

205
206
207
208
209
210
211
212
213
214
215
216
217
218
219
220
221
222
223
224
225
226
227
228
229
230
231
232
233
234
235
236
237
238
239
240
241
242
243
244
245
246
247
248
249
250
251
252
253
254
255
256

Periodical
Drydocking

22. (a) Owners have the right and obligation to drydock the vessel at regular intervals of On each occasion Owners shall propose to Charterers a date on which they wish to drydock the vessel, not less than before such date, and Charterers shall offer a port for such periodical drydocking and shall take all reasonable steps to make the vessel available as near to such date as practicable.
    Owners shall put the vessel in drydock at their expense as soon as practicable after Charterers place the vessel at Owners' disposal clear of cargo other than tank washings and residues. Owners shall be responsible for and pay for the disposal into reception facilities of such tank washings and residues and shall have the right to retain any monies received therefor, without prejudice to any claim for loss of cargo under any bill of lading or this charter.
    (b) If a periodical drydocking is carried out in the port offered by Charterers (which must have suitable accommodation for the purpose and reception facilities for tank washings and residues), the vessel shall be off-hire from the time she arrives at such port until drydocking is completed and she is in every way ready to resume Charterers' service and is at the position at which she went off-hire or a position no less favourable to Charterers, whichever she first attains. However,
    (i) provided that Owners exercise due diligence in gas-freeing, any time lost in gas-freeing to the standard required for entry into drydock for cleaning and painting the hull shall not count as off-hire, whether lost on passage to the drydocking port or after arrival there (notwithstanding Clause 21), and

257
258
259
260
261
262
263
264
265
266
267
268
269
270
271
272
273
274

5

(ii)   any additional time lost in further gas-freeing to meet the standard required for hot work or
entry to cargo tanks shall count as off-hire. whether lost on passage to the drydocking port or after arrival there.
        Any time which, but for sub-Clause (i) above, would be off-hire, shall not be included in any
calculation under Clause 24.
        The expenses of gas-freeing, including without limitation the cost of bunkers, shall be for
Owners account.
        (c)   If Owners require the vessel, instead of proceeding to the offered port, to carry out periodical
drydocking at a special port selected by them, the vessel shall be off-hire from the time when she is released to
proceed to the special port until she next presents for loading in accordance with Charterers' instructions,
provided, however, that Charterers shall credit Owners with the time which would have been taken on passage at
the service speed had the vessel not proceeded to drydock. All fuel consumed shall be paid for by Owners but
Charterers shall credit Owners with the value of the fuel which would have been used on such notional passage
calculated at the guaranteed daily consumption for the service speed, and shall further credit Owners with any
benefit they may gain in purchasing bunkers at the special port.
        (d)   Charterers shall, insofar as cleaning for periodical drydocking may have reduced the amount of
tank-cleaning necessary to meet Charterers' requirements, credit Owners with the value of any bunkers which
Charterers calculate to have been saved thereby, whether the vessel drydocks at an offered or a special port.

Ship Inspection   23.   Charterers shall have the right at any time during the charter period to make such inspection of the
vessel as they may consider necessary. This right may be exercised as often and at such intervals as Charterers in
their absolute discretion may determine and whether the vessel is in port or on passage. Owners affording all
necessary co-operation and accommodation on board provided, however,
        (i)   that neither the exercise nor the non-exercise, nor anything done or not done in the exercise
or non-exercise, by Charterers of such right shall in any way reduce the master's or Owners' authority over, or
responsibility to Charterers or third parties for, the vessel and every aspect of her operation, nor increase
Charterers' responsbilities to Owners or third parties for the same; and
        (ii)   that Charterers shall not be liable for any act, neglect or default by themselves, their
servants or agents in the exercise or non-exercise of the aforesaid right.

Detailed   24.   (a)   Owners guarantee that the speed and consumption of the vessel shall be as follows:-
Description
and Performance

Average speed	Maximum average bunker consumption	
in knots	main propulsion – auxiliaries	
	fuel oil/diesel oil	fuel oil/diesel oil
Laden	tonnes	tonnes

Ballast

The foregoing bunker consumptions are for all purposes except cargo heating and tank cleaning
and shall be pro-rated between the speeds shown.
        The service speed of the vessel is   knots laden and   knots in ballast and in the absence
of Charterers' orders to the contrary the vessel shall proceed at the service speed. However if more than one
laden and one ballast speed are shown in the table above Charterers shall have the right to order the vessel to
steam at any speed within the range set out in the table (the "ordered speed").
        If the vessel is ordered to proceed at any speed other than the highest speed shown in the table,
and the average speed actually attained by the vessel during the currency of such order exceeds such ordered
speed plus 0.5 knots (the "maximum recognised speed"), then for the purpose of calculating any increase or
decrease of hire under this Clause 24 the maximum recognised speed shall be used in place of the average speed
actually attained.
        For the purposes of this charter the "guaranteed speed" at any time shall be the then–current
ordered speed or the service speed, as the case may be
        The average speeds and bunker consumptions shall for the purposes of this Clause 24 be
calculated by reference to the observed distance from pilot station to pilot station on all sea passages during each
period stipulated in Clause 24 (c), but excluding any time during which the vessel is (or but for Clause 22 (b) (i)
would be) off-hire and also excluding "Adverse Weather Periods", being (i) any periods during which reduction
of speed is necessary for safety in congested waters or in poor visibility (ii) any days, noon to noon, when winds
exceed force 8 on the Beaufort Scale for more than 12 hours.

6

(b)   If during any year from the date on which the vessel enters service (anniversary to anniversary) the vessel falls below or exceeds the performance guaranteed in Clause 24(a) then if such shortfall or excess results

(i)   from a reduction or an increase in the average speed of the vessel, compared to the speed guaranteed in Clause 24(a), then an amount equal to the value at the hire rate of the time so lost or gained, as the case may be, shall be deducted from or added to the hire paid;

(ii)   from an increase or a decrease in the total bunkers consumed, compared to the total bunkers which would have been consumed had the vessel performed as guaranteed in Clause 24(a), an amount equivalent to the value of the additional bunkers consumed or the bunkers saved, as the case may be, based on the average price paid by Charterers for the vessel's bunkers in such period, shall be deducted from or added to the hire paid.

The addition to or deduction from hire so calculated for laden and ballast mileage respectively shall be adjusted to take into account the mileage steamed in each such condition during Adverse Weather Periods, by dividing such addition or deduction by the number of miles over which the performance has been calculated and multiplying by the same number of miles plus the miles steamed during the Adverse Weather Periods, in order to establish the total addition to or deduction from hire to be made for such period.

Reduction of hire under the foregoing sub-Clause (b) shall be without prejudice to any other remedy available to Charterers.

(c)   Calculations under this Clause 24 shall be made for the yearly periods terminating on each successive anniversary of the date on which the vessel enters service, and for the period between the last such anniversary and the date of termination of this charter if less than a year. Claims in respect of reduction of hire arising under this Clause during the final year or part year of the charter period shall in the first instance be settled in accordance with Charterers' estimate made two months before the end of the charter period. Any necessary adjustment after this charter terminates shall be made by payment by Owners to Charterers or by Charterers to Owners as the case may require.

Payments in respect of increase of hire arising under this Clause shall be made promptly after receipt by Charterers of all the information necessary to calculate such increase.

Salvage   25.   Subject to the provisions of Clause 21 hereof, all loss of time and all expenses (excluding any damage to or loss of the vessel or tortious liabilities to third parties) incurred in saving or attempting to save life or in successful or unsuccessful attempts at salvage shall be borne equally by Owners and Charterers provided that Charterers shall not be liable to contribute towards any salvage payable by Owners arising in any way out of services rendered under this Clause 25.

All salvage and all proceeds from derelicts shall be divided equally between Owners and Charterers after deducting the master's, officers' and crew's share.

Lien   26.   Owners shall have a lien upon all cargoes and all freights, sub-freights and demurrage for any amounts due under this charter; and Charterers shall have a lien on the vessel for all monies paid in advance and not earned, and for all claims for damages arising from any breach by Owners of this charter.

Exceptions   27.   (a)   The vessel, her master and Owners shall not, unless otherwise in this charter expressly provided, be liable for any loss or damage or delay or failure arising or resulting from any act, neglect or default of the master, pilots, mariners or other servants of Owners in the navigation or management of the vessel; fire, unless caused by the actual fault or privity of Owners; collision or stranding; dangers and accidents of the sea; explosion, bursting of boilers, breakage of shafts or any latent defect in hull, equipment or machinery; provided, however, that Clauses 1, 2, 3 and 24 hereof shall be unaffected by the foregoing. Further, neither the vessel, her master or Owners, nor Charterers shall, unless otherwise in this charter expressly provided, be liable for any loss or damage or delay or failure in performance hereunder arising or resulting from act of God, act of war, seizure under legal process, quarantine restrictions, strikes, lock-outs, riots, restraints of labour, civil commotions or arrest or restraint of princes, rulers or people.

(b)   The vessel shall have liberty to sail with or without pilots, to tow or go to the assistance of vessels in distress and to deviate for the purpose of saving life or property.

(c)   Clause 27(a) shall not apply to or affect any liability of Owners or the vessel or any other relevant person in respect of

(i)   loss or damage caused to any berth, jetty, dock, dolphin, buoy, mooring line, pipe or crane or other works or equipment whatsoever at or near any place to which the vessel may proceed under this charter, whether or not such works or equipment belong to Charterers, or

(ii)   any claim (whether brought by Charterers or any other person) arising out of any loss of or damage to or in connection with cargo. All such claims shall be subject to the Hague-Visby Rules or the Hague Rules, as the case may be, which ought pursuant to Clause 38 hereof to have been incorporated in the relevant bill of lading (whether or not such Rules were so incorporated) or, if no such bill of lading is issued, to the Hague-Visby Rules.

(d)   In particular and without limitation, the foregoing subsections (a) and (b) of this Clause shall not apply to or in any way affect any provision in this charter relating to off-hire or to reduction of hire.

Injurious Cargoes   28.   No acids, explosives or cargoes injurious to the vessel shall be shipped and without prejudice to the foregoing any damage to the vessel caused by the shipment of any such cargo, and the time taken to repair such damage, shall be for Charterers' account. No voyage shall be undertaken, nor any goods or cargoes loaded, that would expose the vessel to capture or seizure by rulers or governments.

Grade of Bunkers   29.   Charterers shall supply marine diesel oil/fuel oil with a maximum viscosity of   Centistokes at 50 degrees Centigrade/ACGFO for main propulsion and diesel oil/ACGFO for the auxiliaries. If Owners require the vessel to be supplied with more expensive bunkers they shall be liable for the extra cost thereof.

Charterers warrant that all bunkers provided by them in accordance herewith shall be of a quality complying with the International Marine Bunker Supply Terms and Conditions of Shell International Trading Company and with its specification for marine fuels as amended from time to time.

Disbursements   30.   Should the master require advances for ordinary disbursements at any port, Charterers or their agents shall make such advances to him, in consideration of which Owners shall pay a commission of two and a half per cent, and all such advances and commission shall be deducted from hire.

327
328
329
330
331
332
333
334
335
336
337
338
339
340
341
342
343
344
345
346
347
348
349
350
351
352
353
354
355
356
357
358
359
360
361
362
363
364
365
366
367
368
369
370
371
372
373
374
375
376
377
378
379
380
381
382
383
384
385
386
387
388
389
390
391
392
393
394
395
396
397
398
399

7

Laying-up	31. Charterers shall have the option. after consultation with Owners. of requiring Owners to lay up the	400

Laying-up   31.   Charterers shall have the option. after consultation with Owners. of requiring Owners to lay up the   400
vessel at a safe place nominated by Charterers. in which case the hire provided for under this charter shall be   401
adjusted to reflect any net increases in expenditure reasonably incurred or any net saving which should   402
reasonably be made by Owners as a result of such lay-up. Charterers may exercise the said option any number of   403
times during the charter period.   404

Requisition   32.   Should the vessel be requisitioned by any government. de facto or de jure. during the period of this   405
charter. the vessel shall be off-hire during the period of such requisition. and any hire paid by such government in   406
respect of such requisition period shall be for Owners' account. Any such requisition period shall count as part of   407
the charter period.   408

Outbreak of War   33.   If war or hostilities break out between any two or more of the following countries: U.S.A.. U.S.S.R..   409
P.R.C.. U.K.. Netherlands–both Owners and Charterers shall have the right to cancel this charter.   410

Additional War   34.   If the vessel is ordered to trade in areas where there is war (de facto or de jure) or threat of war.   411
Expenses   Charterers shall reimburse Owners for any additional insurance premia. crew bonuses and other expenses which   412
are reasonably incurred by Owners as a consequence of such orders. provided that Charterers are given notice of   413
such expenses as soon as practicable and in any event before such expenses are incurred. and provided further   414
that Owners obtain from their insurers a waiver of any subrogated rights against Charterers in respect of any   415
claims by Owners under their war risk insurance arising out of compliance with such orders.   416

War Risks   35.   (a)   The master shall not be required or bound to sign bills of lading for any place which in his or   417
Owners' reasonable opinion is dangerous or impossible for the vessel to enter or reach owing to any blockade.   418
war. hostilities. warlike operations. civil war. civil commotions or revolutions.   419
(b)   If in the reasonable opinion of the master or Owners it becomes. for any of the reasons set out in   420
Clause 35(a) or by the operation of international law. dangerous. impossible or prohibited for the vessel to reach   421
or enter. or to load or discharge cargo at. any place to which the vessel has been ordered pursuant to this charter   422
(a "place of peril"). then Charterers or their agents shall be immediately notified by telex or radio messages. and   423
Charterers shall thereupon have the right to order the cargo. or such part of it as may be affected. to be loaded or   424
discharged. as the case may be. at any other place within the trading limits of this charter (provided such other   425
place is not itself a place of peril). If any place of discharge is or becomes a place of peril. and no orders have been   426
received from Charterers or their agents within 48 hours after dispatch of such messages. then Owners shall be at   427
liberty to discharge the cargo or such part of it as may be affected at any place which they or the master may in   428
their or his discretion select within the trading limits of this charter and such discharge shall be deemed to be due   429
fulfilment of Owners' obligations under this charter so far as cargo so discharged is concerned.   430
(c)   The vessel shall have liberty to comply with any directions or recommendations as to departure.   431
arrival. routes. ports of call. stoppages. destinations. zones. waters. delivery or in any other wise whatsoever   432
given by the government of the state under whose flag the vessel sails or any other government or local authority   433
or by any person or body acting or purporting to act as or with the authority of any such government or local   434
authority including any de facto government or local authority or by any person or body acting or purporting to   435
act as or with the authority of any such government or local authority or by any committee or person having under   436
the terms of the war risks insurance on the vessel the right to give any such directions or recommendations. If by   437
reason of or in compliance with any such directions or recommendations anything is done or is not done. such   438
shall not be deemed a deviation.   439
If by reason of or in compliance with any such direction or recommendation the vessel does not   440
proceed to any place of discharge to which she has been ordered pursuant to this charter. the vessel may proceed   441
to any place which the master or Owners in his or their discretion select and there discharge the cargo or such part   442
of it as may be affected. Such discharge shall be deemed to be due fulfilment of Owners' obligations under this   443
charter so far as cargo so discharged is concerned.   444
Charterers shall procure that all bills of lading issued under this charter shall contain the Chamber of   445
Shipping War Risks Clause 1952.   446

Both to Blame   36.   If the liability for any collision in which the vessel is involved while performing this charter falls to be   447
Collision Clause   determined in accordance with the laws of the United States of America. the following provision shall apply: 448
"If the ship comes into collision with another ship as a result of the negligence of the other ship and any   449
act. neglect or default of the master. mariner. pilot or the servants of the carrier in the navigation or in the   450
management of the ship. the owners of the cargo carried hereunder will indemnify the carrier against all loss. or   451
liability to the other or non-carrying ship or her owners in so far as such loss or liability represents loss of. or   452
damage to. or any claim whatsoever of the owners of the said cargo. paid or payable by the other or non-carrying   453
ship or her owners to the owners of the said cargo and set off. recouped or recovered by the other or non-carrying   454
ship or her owners as part of their claim against the carrying ship or carrier."   455
"The foregoing provisions shall also apply where the owners. operators or those in charge of any ship   456
or ships or objects other than. or in addition to. the colliding ships or objects are at fault in respect of a collision or   457
contact."   458
Charterers shall procure that all bills of lading issued under this charter shall contain a provision in the   459
foregoing terms to be applicable where the liability for any collision in which the vessel is involved falls to be   460
determined in accordance with the laws of the United States of America.   461

New Jason   37.   General average contributions shall be payable according to the York/Antwerp Rules. 1974. and shall   462
Clause   be adjusted in London in accordance with English law and practice but should adjustment be made in accordance   463
with the law and practice of the United States of America. the following provision shall apply: 464
"In the event of accident. danger. damage or disaster before or after the commencement of the   465
voyage. resulting from any cause whatsoever. whether due to negligence or not. for which. or for the   466
consequence of which. the carrier is not responsible by statute. contract or otherwise. the cargo. shippers.   467
consignees or owners of the cargo shall contribute with the carrier in general average to the payment of any   468
sacrifices. losses or expenses of a general average nature that may be made or incurred and shall pay salvage and   469
special charges incurred in respect of the cargo."   470
"If a salving ship is owned or operated by the carrier. salvage shall be paid for as fully as if the said   471
salving ship or ships belonged to strangers. Such deposit as the carrier or his agents may deem sufficient to cover   472

8

the estimated contribution of the cargo and any salvage and special charges thereon shall, if required, be made by the cargo, shippers, consignees or owners of the cargo to the carrier before delivery." 473 474

Charterers shall procure that all bills of lading issued under this charter shall contain a provision in the foregoing terms, to be applicable where adjustment of general average is made in accordance with the laws and practice of the United States of America. 475 476 477

**Clause
Paramount**

38. Charterers shall procure that all bills of lading issued pursuant to this charter shall contain the following clause: 478 479

"(1) Subject to sub-clause (2) hereof, this bill of lading shall be governed by, and have effect subject to, the rules contained in the International Convention for the Unification of Certain Rules relating to Bills of Lading signed at Brussels on 25th August 1924 (hereafter the "Hague Rules") as amended by the Protocol signed at Brussels on 23rd February 1968 (hereafter the "Hague-Visby Rules"). Nothing contained herein shall be deemed to be either a surrender by the carrier of any of his rights or immunities or any increase of any of his responsibilities or liabilities under the Hague-Visby Rules." 480 481 482 483 484 485

"(2) If there is governing legislation which applies the Hague Rules compulsorily to this bill of lading, to the exclusion of the Hague-Visby Rules, then this bill of lading shall have effect subject to the Hague Rules. Nothing herein contained shall be deemed to be either a surrender by the carrier of any of his rights or immunities or an increase of any of his responsibilities or liabilities under the Hague Rules." 486 487 488 489

"(3) If any term of this bill of lading is repugnant to the Hague-Visby Rules, or Hague Rules if applicable, such term shall be void to that extent but no further." 490 491

"(4) Nothing in this bill of lading shall be construed as in any way restricting, excluding or waiving the right of any relevant party or person to limit his liability under any available legislation and/or law." 492 493

TOVALOP

39. Owners warrant that the vessel is: 494
   (i) a tanker in TOVALOP and 495
   (ii) properly entered in   P & I Club 496

and will so remain during the currency of this charter. 497

When an escape or discharge of Oil occurs from the vessel and causes or threatens to cause Pollution Damage, or when there is the threat of an escape or discharge of Oil (i.e. a grave and imminent danger of the escape or discharge of Oil which, if it occurred, would create a serious danger of Pollution Damage, whether or not an escape or discharge in fact subsequently occurs), then Charterers may, at their option, upon notice to Owners or master, undertake such measures as are reasonably necessary to prevent or minimise such Pollution Damage or to remove the Threat, unless Owners promptly undertake the same. Charterers shall keep Owners advised of the nature and result of any such measures taken by them and, if time permits, the nature of the measures intended to be taken by them. Any of the aforementioned measures taken by Charterers shall be deemed taken on Owners' authority as Owners' agent, and shall be at Owners' expense except to the extent that: 498 499 500 501 502 503 504 505 506

(1) any such escape or discharge or Threat was caused or contributed to by Charterers, or 507

(2) by reason of the exceptions set out in Article III, paragraph 2, of the 1969 International Convention on Civil Liability for Oil Pollution Damage, Owners are or, had the said Convention applied to such escape or discharge or to the Threat, would have been exempt from liability for the same, or 508 509 510

(3) the cost of such measures together with all other liabilities, costs and expenses of Owners arising out of or in connection with such escape or discharge or Threat exceeds one hundred and sixty United States Dollars (US $160) per ton of the vessel's Tonnage or sixteen million eight hundred thousand United States Dollars (US $16,800,000), whichever is the lesser, save and insofar as Owners shall be entitled to recover such excess under either the 1971 International Convention on the Establishment of an International Fund for Compensation for Oil Pollution Damage or under CRISTAL; 511 512 513 514 515 516

PROVIDED ALWAYS that if Owners in their absolute discretion consider said measures should be discontinued, Owners shall so notify Charterers and thereafter Charterers shall have no right to continue said measures under the provisions of this Clause 39 and all further liability to Charterers under this Clause 39 shall thereupon cease. 517 518 519 520

The above provisions are not in derogation of such other rights as Charterers or Owners may have under this charter or may otherwise have or acquire by law or any International Convention or TOVALOP. 521 522

The term "TOVALOP" means the Tanker Owners' Voluntary Agreement Concerning Liability for Oil Pollution dated 7th January 1969, as amended from time to time, and the term "CRISTAL" means the Contract Regarding an Interim Supplement to Tanker Liability for Oil Pollution dated 14th January 1971, as amended from time to time. The terms "Oil", "Pollution Damage", and "Tonnage" shall for the purposes of this Clause 39 have the meanings ascribed to them in TOVALOP. 523 524 525 526 527

**Export
Restrictions**

40. The master shall not be required or bound to sign bills of lading for the carriage of cargo to any place to which export of such cargo is prohibited under the laws, rules or regulations of the country in which the cargo was produced and/or shipped. 528 529 530

Charterers shall procure that all bills of lading issued under this charter shall contain the following clause: 531 532

"If any laws rules or regulations applied by the government of the country in which the cargo was produced and/or shipped, or any relevant agency thereof, impose a prohibition on export of the cargo to the place of discharge designated in or ordered under this bill of lading, carriers shall be entitled to require cargo owners forthwith to nominate an alternative discharge place for the discharge of the cargo, or such part of it as may be affected, which alternative place shall not be subject to the prohibition, and carriers shall be entitled to accept orders from cargo owners to proceed to and discharge at such alternative place. If cargo owners fail to nominate an alternative place within 72 hours after they or their agents have received from carriers notice of such prohibition, carriers shall be at liberty to discharge the cargo or such part of it as may be affected by the prohibition at any safe place on which they or the master may in their or his absolute discretion decide and which is not subject to the prohibition, and such discharge shall constitute due performance of the contract contained in this bill of lading so far as the cargo so discharged is concerned". 533 534 535 536 537 538 539 540 541 542 543 544

The foregoing provision shall apply mutatis mutandis to this charter, the references to a bill of lading being deemed to be references to this charter. 545 546

9

**Law and
Litigation**

41. (a) This charter shall be construed and the relations between the parties determined in accordance with the laws of England.

(b) Any dispute arising under this charter shall be decided by the English Courts to whose jurisdiction the parties hereby agree.

(c) Notwithstanding the foregoing. but without prejudice to any party's right to arrest or maintain the arrest of any maritime property. either party may. by giving written notice of election to the other party. elect to have any such dispute referred to the arbitration of a single arbitrator in London in accordance with the provisions of the Arbitration Act 1950. or any statutory modification or re-enactment thereof for the time being in force.

    (i)   A party shall lose its right to make such an election only if:

        (a)   it receives from the other party a written notice of dispute which –

            (1)   states expressly that a dispute has arisen out of this charter;

            (2)   specifies the nature of the dispute; and

            (3)   refers expressly to this clause 41(c)

        and

        (b)   it fails to give notice of election to have the dispute referred to arbitration not later than 30 days from the date of receipt of such notice of dispute.

    (ii)   The parties hereby agree that either party may –

        (a)   appeal to the High Court on any question of law arising out of an award;

        (b)   apply to the High Court for an order that the arbitrator state the reasons for his award;

        (c)   give notice to the arbitrator that a reasoned award is required; and

        (d)   apply to the High Court to determine any question of law arising in the course of the reference.

(d) It shall be a condition precedent to the right of any party to a stay of any legal proceedings in which maritime property has been. or may be. arrested in connection with a dispute under this charter. that that party furnishes to the other party security to which that other party would have been entitled in such legal proceedings in the absence of a stay.

Construction

42. The side headings have been included in this charter for convenience of reference and shall in no way affect the construction hereof.

547
548
549
550
551
552
553
554
555
556
557
558
559
560
561
562
563
564
565
566
567
568
569
570
571
572
573

574
575

FORM B
(April 1987)

PARTICULARS OF VESSEL

This form is to be completed and returned to Charterers as soon as possible after charter negotiations are commenced. When completed and agreed the form will eventually be incorporated into any Charter Party ultimately concluded and the particulars contained therein will be taken as representations by Owners in reliance upon which Charterers will enter into such Charter Party. The acceptance of the particulars on this form and of plans of the vessel by Charterers shall not relieve Owners in any way of their responsibilities under the Charter Party.

	Particulars to be Completed
1. (a) Ship's Name	
(b) Yard & Hull No.	
(c) Year Built	
(d) Type of vessel as per International Oil Pollution Prevention Certificate	
2. DEADWEIGHT on:	
(a) Statutory Minimum Summer Freeboard	Tonnes
(b) Assigned Summer Freeboard	Tonnes
3. DIMENSIONS	
(a) Length Overall	Metres
(b) Distance by which bulbous bow extends forward of the forecastle	Metres
(c) Length between Perpendiculars	Metres
(d) Beam Extreme	Metres
(e) Draft on:	
(1) Statutory Minimum Summer Freeboard	Metres
(2) Assigned Summer Freeboard	Metres
(f) Moulded Depth	Metres
(g) Distance from underside of keel to highest fixed point on vessel	Metres
4. MACHINERY	
(a) Type of Propelling Machinery & Make	
(b) Maximum continuous H.P. & R.P.M.	H.P. @ R.P.M.
(c) Proposed service H.P. & R.P.M.	H.P. @ R.P.M.
(d) Type and make of prime mover for electrical generating plant	
(1) In Port	
(2) At Sea	
5. BOILER AND STEAM OUTPUT	
(a) Number & type of main and auxiliary boilers	
(b) Maximum steam output available	Kg. per hr.
(c) Type and capacity of waste heat boiler (if fitted)	Kg. per hr.
(d) (Steam Ships only) Normal service output corresponding to 4 (c)	Kg. per hr.
(e) Estimated steam required to maintain cargo heating in accordance with 14 (g)	Kg. per hr.
(f) Estimated steam required in port for auxiliaries and ships service including deck machinery but excluding all cargo and ballast pumps	Kg. per hr.

FORM B (continued)

Particulars to be
Completed

6. BUNKERS

    (a) Grade of Bunkers for Main Engine on passage...

    (b) Grade of Bunkers for Main Engine manoeuvring ....

    (c) Grade of Bunkers for Auxiliaries ....

Tonnes per hr

    (d) Maximum rates at which lines will receive bunkers...   Fuel   Diesel

    (e) Bunker consumption per tonne of water evaporated ....   Tonnes

    (f) Capacity of primary grade bunker tanks (98% Full) ....   Tonnes

    (g) Capacity of auxiliary grade bunker tanks (98% Full)..   Tonnes

7. FRESH WATER

    (a) Is vessel equipped with fresh water generating capacity (and sterilising equipment where necessary) sufficient to meet all needs of boilers, washing and potable purposes?....................

    (b) Capacity of water tanks (100% Full) ....   Tonnes

    (c) Daily consumption of boilers..   Tonnes

    (d) Daily consumption other purposes ....   Tonnes

    (e) Number of evaporators fitted ....

    (f) Total evaporator capacity per day ....   Tonnes

    (g) Is reverse osmosis equipment fitted ....

    (h) Is sterilising equipment fitted ....

LOADING/DISCHARGING ARRANGEMENTS

8. CARGO TANKS

    (a) Number of compartments (Including slop tank) ....

    (b) Total capacity (98% Full) ....   m'

    (c) Number of grades which the vessel can segregate with two valve separation ....   Grades

    (d) Can vessel fulfil requirements of Item 7 in the Digest*?...

    (e) Can vessel load discharge cargo with up to 14lbs Reid's vapour pressure? ....

    (f) Identify which tanks (if any) are coated..

    (g) Type of tank coating ....

    (h) Is vessel fitted with an approved Crude Oil Washing System ....

FORM B (continued)

Particulars to be
Completed

9. CARGO PUMPS

(a) Number...

(b) Make..

(c) Capacity of each pump in cubic metres per hour and the guaranteed discharge head at the manifold corresponding to this capacity ....

C.M.P.H. @
metres

(d) Prime mover type (steam turbine/reciprocating/diesel/electric/hydraulic) ....

(e) Estimated power consumption of each pump when discharging as in 9(c) above ....

HP KW Kg Steam hr.

(f) Type of cargo pump centralised self-priming system, if fitted ....

(g) Does the vessel fulfil the requirements of Item 9 in the Digest*? ....

10. STRIPPING PUMPS

(a) Number and Size..

(b) Design capacity of each pump in cubic metres per hour and discharge pressure at the pump ....

C.M.P.H. @
kgs. per Cm

11. BALLASTING SYSTEM

(a) Is vessel a Segregated Ballast Tanker or a Dedicated Clean Ballast Tanker in accordance with MARPOL? If so, state which applies ....

(b) State total cubic capacity of vessel's ballast tanks ....

m

(c) Number of pumps for dedicated handling ballast as in (b)..

(d) Capacity of each pump in cu. metres/hr & design head at pump corresponding to this capacity ....

C.M.P.H. @
metres

(e) Prime mover type (steam turbine/reciprocating/diesel/electric/hydraulic) ....

(f) Estimated power consumption of each pump when discharging to capacity as 11(d) above ....

HP KW Kg Steam hr.

12. CARGO LOADING PERFORMANCE

(a) Maximum rate at which vessel can load a homogeneous cargo ....

m per hr.

(b) Maximum rate at which vessel can load each grade when loading two grades simultaneously ....

m per hr.

FORM B (continued)

Particulars to be
Completed

13. CARGO AND BUNKERING MANIFOLDS

    (a) What is the distance of centre of manifold from amidships
       (from mid length position)?...   metres

    (b) Distance of manifold flanges from ship's side ....   metres

    (c) Height of centres of flanges above deck or working platform ....   metres

    (d) Distance between centres of manifold flanges...   metres

    (e) Specify number and size of reducing pieces on board...

    (f) Number of loading/discharging lines that the vessel can connect on each side......................

    (g) Number and position of bunkering connections relative to loading/discharging
       manifolds ....

    (h) Do loading and discharging manifold arrangements comply with all other requirements of
       Item 8 in the Digest*..

    (i) State the number of grades of cargo the vessel can load/discharge simultaneously through
       amidship connection with two valve separation without risk of contamination ....   Grades

14. HEATING COILS

    (a) Type of coils/heaters and material of which manufactured..

    (b) Type of heating fluid ....

    (c) Ratio of tank heating surface/volume (in case of coils) ....

       (1) Centre tanks... m^2/m^3

       (2) Side tanks... m^2/m^3

       (3) Slop tanks.. m^2/m^3

    (d) Height of coils from tank bottoms ....   metres

    (e) Maximum output available ....   KW

    (f) Does the vessel fulfil all the requirements of Items 10 and 12 of the Digest*? ....

    (g) The vessel is capable at all times of heating and maintaining the entire cargo
       at a temperature of at least ....   °C

15. INERT GAS

    (a) Manufacturer of Inert Gas System ....

    (b) Source of Inert Gas (Generator/Boiler) ....

    (c) If source of Inert Gas is Generator, state fuel grade used ....

    (d) Can vessel inert all cargo tanks? ....

    (e) Total capacity of Inert Gas fans .... m^3 per hr.

    (f) Number of Inert Gas mains ....

    (g) Can each tank be isolated from its Inert Gas Main?..

    (h) Is there pressure/vacuum protection for tanks which can be so isolated?...............................

16. SLOP TANKS AND TANK CLEANING

    (a) Is vessel fitted with slop tank(s) ....

    (b) Type of tank cleaning equipment fitted...

    (c) Type of gas extraction equipment fitted..

Particulars to be
Completed

17. MOORING AND LIFTING EQUIPMENT

(a) Does vessel conform with Item 13 in the Digest*? ....

(b) Safe working load of lifting equipment in way of manifold ....   Tonnes

(c) Safe working load of lifting equipment for handling forehold cargo ....   Tonnes

(d) Safe working load of lifting equipment on poop deck for handling stern hoses ....   Tonnes

(e) Number and brake holding power of each mooring winch ....   Number   Tonnes

(f) Type of deck machinery (steam/electric/hydraulic) ....

(g) Number, length, type and breaking strength of wires/ropes fitted ....

18. GENERAL

(a) Are hull stress calculators fitted? ....

(b) Cubic capacity of forehold ....   m

(c) Is forehold registered for volatile cargoes? ....

(d) Type of submerged log fitted? ....

(e) Does the vessel comply with Items 4, 11, 14 and 15 of the Digest*? ....

(f) Is Suez Canal Projector fitted? ....

(g) If vessel's dimensions compatible with Panama Canal transit will she comply with Panama Canal Regulations for the carriage of:- ....

    (1) Grade 'A' cargoes..

    (2) Grade 'B' cargoes..

    (3) Grade 'C' cargoes..

    (4) Grade 'D' cargoes..

N.B. When submitting this Form the following documents must be attached:-

    (1) General Arrangement and Capacity Plans ....

    (2) Detailed Cargo Manifold Arrangement Drawing ....

    (3) Cargo Pumping and Pipeline Arrangement Plans (Types of Valves fitted to be clearly shown) ....

    (4) Plan of Cargo Tank Ventilating and Inert Gas Systems..

    (5) Mooring Arrangements Plan and a completed Mooring Questionnaire ....

    (6) The current Shell Freight Trading Questionnaire ....

*Digest refers to Shell International Marine Limited's Digest of Charterers' Requirements dated April 1987 and any subsequent amendments thereto.

APPENDIX VI

SHELLVOY 5*

* Reproduced by kind permission of
Shell International Shipping Limited

Code word for this Charter Party

"SHELLVOY 5"

Issued July 1987

Voyage Charter Party
LONDON,   19

PREAMBLE	1

IT IS THIS DAY AGREED between   2

of   (hereinafter referred to as "Owners") being owners/disponent owners of the   3

motor/steam tank vessel called   4

(hereinafter referred to as "the vessel")   .5

and   of   6

(hereinafter referred to as "Charterers")   7

that the service for which provision is herein made shall be subject to the terms and conditions of this charter   8
which includes Part I and Part II. In the event of any conflict between the provisions of Part I and Part II hereof,   9
the provisions of Part I shall prevail.   10

PART I   11

(A) Description   Owners guarantee that at the date hereof the vessel:-   12
of vessel   13

(i)   Is classed   14

(ii)   Has a deadweight of   tonnes (1000 kg.) on a salt-water draft on assigned summer freeboard   15
         of   m.   16

(iii)   Has a capacity available for the cargo of   tonnes (1000 kg.) 5% more or less in Owners'   17
         option.   18

(iv)   Is fully fitted with heating systems for all cargo tanks capable of maintaining cargo at a temperature of up   19
         to   degrees Celsius.   20

(v)   Has tanks coated as follows:-   21

(vi)   Is equipped with cranes/derricks capable of lifting to and supporting at the vessel's port and starboard   22
         manifolds submarine hoses of up to   tonnes (1000 kg.) in weight.   23

(vii)   Has cargo pumps capable of discharging a full cargo within   hours or maintaining a back   24
         pressure of   at the vessel's manifold (provided shore facilities permit and the cargo does not   25
         have a kinematic viscosity exceeding 600 centistokes at the discharge temperature required by   26
         Charterers).   27

(viii) Has or will have carried the following three cargoes immediately prior to loading under this charter:-   28

         Last   29

         2.   30

         3.   31

(ix)   Has a crude oil washing system complying with the requirements of the International Convention for the   32
         Prevention of Pollution from Ships 1973 as modified by the Protocol of 1978 ("MARPOL 73/78").   33

(x)   Has an operational inert gas system.   34

(xi)   Has on board all papers and certificates required by any applicable law, in force as at the date of this   35
         charter, to enable the vessel to perform the charter service without any delay.   36

(xii)   Is entered in   P&I Club.   37

(B) Position/   Now   Expected ready to load   38
Readiness   39

(C) Laydays   Commencing Noon Local Time on   (Commencement Date)   40

         Terminating Noon Local Time on   (Termination Date)   41

Issued July 1987
                                                                "SHELLVOY 5"
PART I
                                                                PAGE 2

(D) Loading
    Port(s)/   42
    Range   43
                                    one or more ports at Charterers' option   44

(E) Discharging
    Port(s)/   45
    Range   46
                                    one or more ports at Charterers' option   47

(F) Cargo   48
    description   Charterers' option   49

    Maximum temperature on loading   degrees Celsius   50

(G) Freight rate   At   % of the rate for the voyage as provided for in the Worldwide Tanker Nominal Freight Scale current at   51
                    the date of commencement of loading (hereinafter referred to as "Worldscale") per ton (2240lbs)/tonne   52
                    (1000Kg).   53

(H) Freight
    payable to   54
                                                                                55

(I) Laytime   running hours   56

(J) Demurrage
    per day (or   57
    pro rata)   58
                                                                                59

(K) ETAs   All radio messages sent by the master to Charterers shall be addressed to   60

(L) Special
    provisions   61
                                                                                62

Signatures   **IN WITNESS WHEREOF**, the parties have caused this charter consisting of the Preamble, Parts I and II to be   63
             executed as of the day and year first above written.   64

                        By   65

                        By   66

APPENDIX VI

1

Issued July 1987

PART II

Condition of vessel	1. Owners shall exercise due diligence to ensure that from the time when the obligation to proceed to the loading port(s) attaches and throughout the charter service –
	    (a) the vessel and her hull, machinery, boilers, tanks, equipment and facilities are in good order and condition and in every way equipped and fit for the service required; and
	    (b) the vessel has a full and efficient complement of master, officers and crew;
	 and to ensure that before and at the commencement of any laden voyage the vessel is in all respects fit to carry the cargo specified in Part I(F).
		67
		68
		69
		70
		71
		72
		73
		74

Cleanliness of tanks	2. Whilst loading, carrying and discharging cargo the master shall at all times use due diligence to keep the tanks, lines and pumps of the vessel clean for the cargo specified in Part I(F). It shall be for the master alone to decide whether the vessel's tanks, lines and pumps are suitably clean. However, the decision of the master shall be without prejudice to the right of Charterers, should any contamination or damage subsequently be found, to contend that the same was caused by inadequate cleaning and/or some breach of this or any other Clause of this charter.	75 76 77 78 79 80
Voyage	3. Subject to the provisions of this charter the vessel shall perform her service with utmost despatch and shall proceed to such berths as Charterers may specify, in any port or ports within Part I(D) nominated by Charterers, or so near thereunto as she may safely get and there, always safely afloat, load a full cargo, but not in excess of the maximum quantity consistent with the International Load Line Convention for the time being in force and, being so loaded, proceed as ordered on signing bills of lading to such berths as Charterers may specify, in any port or ports within Part I(E) nominated by Charterers, or so near thereunto as she may safely get and there, always safely afloat, discharge the cargo.	81 82 83 84 85 86 87
	Charterers shall nominate loading and discharging ports, and shall specify loading and discharging berths, in sufficient time to avoid delay or deviation to the vessel. Subject to the foregoing, and provided it does not cause delay or deviation to the vessel, Charterers shall have the option of ordering the vessel to safe areas at sea for wireless orders.	88 89 90 91
	In this charter, "berth" means any berth, wharf, dock, anchorage, submarine line, a position alongside any vessel or lighter or any other loading or discharging point whatsoever to which Charterers are entitled to order the vessel hereunder, and "port" means any port or location at sea to which the vessel may proceed in accordance with the terms of this charter.	92 93 94 95
Safe berth	4. Charterers shall exercise due diligence to order the vessel only to ports and berths which are safe for the vessel and to ensure that transhipment operations conform to standards not less than those set out in the latest edition of ICS/OCIMF Ship-to-Ship Transfer Guide (Petroleum). Notwithstanding anything contained in this charter, Charterers do not warrant the safety of any port, berth or transhipment operation and Charterers shall not be liable for loss or damage arising from any unsafety if they can prove that due diligence was exercised in the giving of the order.	96 97 98 99 100 101
Freight	5. Freight shall be earned concurrently with delivery of cargo at the nominated discharging port or ports and shall be paid by Charterers to Owners without any deductions in United States Dollars at the rate(s) specified in Part I(G) on the gross Bill of Lading quantity as furnished by the shipper (subject to Clauses 8 and 40), upon receipt by Charterers of notice of completion of final discharge of cargo, provided that no freight shall be payable on any quantity in excess of the maximum quantity consistent with the International Load Line Convention for the time being in force.	102 103 104 105 106 107
	If the vessel is ordered to proceed on a voyage for which a fixed differential is provided in Worldscale, such fixed differential shall be payable without applying the percentage referred to in Part I(G).	108 109
	If cargo is carried between ports and/or by a route for which no freight rate is expressly quoted in Worldscale, then the parties shall, in the absence of agreement as to the appropriate freight rate, apply to Worldscale Association (London) Ltd., or Worldscale Association (NYC) Inc, for the determination of an appropriate Worldscale freight rate.	110 111 112 113
	Save in respect of the time when freight is earned, the location of any transhipment at sea pursuant to Clause 26(2) shall not be an additional nominated port for the purposes of this charter (including this Clause 5) and the freight rate for the voyage shall be the same as if such transhipment had not taken place.	114 115 116
Dues and other charges	6. Dues and other charges upon the vessel, including those assessed by reference to the quantity of cargo loaded or discharged, and any taxes on freight whatsoever shall be paid by Owners, and dues and other charges upon the cargo shall be paid by Charterers. However, notwithstanding the foregoing, where under a provision of Worldscale a due or charge is expressly for the account of Owners or Charterers then such due or charge shall be payable in accordance with such provision.	117 118 119 120 121
Loading and discharging cargo	7. The cargo shall be loaded into the vessel at the expense of Charterers and, up to the vessel's permanent hose connections, at Charterers' risk. The cargo shall be discharged from the vessel at the expense of Owners and, up to the vessel's permanent hose connections, at Owners' risk. Owners shall, unless otherwise notified by Charterers or their agents, supply at Owners' expense all hands, equipment and facilities required on board for mooring and unmooring and connecting and disconnecting hoses for loading and discharging.	122 123 124 125 126
Deadfreight	8. Charterers need not supply a full cargo, but if they do not freight shall nevertheless be paid as if the vessel had been loaded with a full cargo.	127 128
	The term "full cargo" as used throughout this charter means a cargo which, together with any collected washings (as defined in Clause 40) retained on board pursuant to the requirements of MARPOL 73/78, fills the vessel to either her applicable deadweight or her capacity stated in Part I(A)(iii), whichever is less, while leaving sufficient space in the tanks for the expansion of cargo.	129 130 131 132

2

Shifting	9. Charterers shall have the right to require the vessel to shift at ports of loading and/or discharging from a loading or discharging berth within port limits and back to the same or to another such berth once or more often on payment of all additional expenses incurred. For the purposes of freight payment and shifting the places grouped in Port and Terminal Combinations in Worldscale are to be considered as berths within a single port. If at any time before cargo operations are completed it becomes dangerous for the vessel to remain at the specified berth as a result of wind or water conditions, Charterers shall pay all additional expenses of shifting from any such berth and back to that or any other specified berth within port limits (except to the extent that any fault of the vessel contributed to such danger).	133 134 135 136 137 138 139 140

Subject to Clause 14(a) and (c) time spent shifting shall count against laytime or if the vessel is on demurrage for demurrage.

141
142

Charterers' failure to give orders	10. If the vessel is delayed due to Charterers' breach of Clause 3 Charterers shall, subject to the terms hereof, compensate Owners in accordance with Clause 15(1) and (2) as if such delay were time exceeding the laytime.	143 144 145

The period of such delay shall be calculated

(i)   from 6 hours after Owners notify Charterers that the vessel is delayed awaiting nomination of loading port until such nomination has been received by Owners, or

(ii)   from 6 hours after the vessel gives notice of readiness at the loading port until commencement of loading

as the case may be, subject always to the same exceptions as those set out in Clause 14. Any period of delay in respect of which Charterers pay compensation pursuant to this Clause 10 shall be excluded from any calculation of time for laytime or demurrage made under any other Clause of this charter.

146
147
148
149
150
151
152
153

Periods of delay hereunder shall be cumulative for each port, and Owners may demand compensation after the vessel has been delayed for a total of 20 running days, and thereafter after each succeeding 5 running days of delay and at the end of any delay. Each such demand shall show the period in respect of which compensation is claimed and the amount due. Charterers shall pay the full amount due within 14 days after receipt of Owners' demand. Should Charterers fail to make any such payments Owners shall have the right to terminate this charter by giving written notice to Charterers or their agents, without prejudice to any claims which Charterers or Owners may have against each other under this charter or otherwise.

154
155
156
157
158
159
160

Laydays/ Termination	11. Should the vessel not be ready to load by noon local time on the termination date set out in Part I(C) Charterers shall have the option of terminating this charter unless the vessel has been delayed due to Charterers' change of orders pursuant to Clause 26, in which case the laydays shall be extended by the period of such delay.	161 162 163 164

However, if Owners reasonably conclude that, despite the exercise of due diligence, the vessel will not be ready to load by noon on the termination date, Owners may, as soon as they are able to state with reasonable certainty a new date when the vessel will be ready, give notice to Charterers declaring the new readiness date and asking Charterers to elect whether or not to terminate this charter. Unless Charterers within 4 days after such notice or within 2 days after the termination date (whichever is earlier) declare this charter terminated, Part I(C) shall be deemed to be amended such that the new readiness date stated shall be the commencement date and the second day thereafter shall be the termination date.

165
166
167
168
169
170
171

The provisions of this Clause and the exercise or non-exercise by Charterers of their option to terminate shall not prejudice any claims which Charterers or Owners may have against each other.

172
173

Laytime	12. The laytime for loading, discharging and all other Charterers' purposes whatsoever shall be the number of running hours specified in Part I(I). Charterers shall have the right to load and discharge at all times, including night, provided that they shall pay for all extra expenses incurred ashore.	174 175 176

Notice of readiness/ Running time	13. (1) Subject to the provisions of Clauses 13(3) and 14, if the vessel loads or discharges cargo other than by transhipment at sea	177 178 179

(a)   Time at each loading or discharging port shall commence to run 6 hours after the vessel is in all respects ready to load or discharge and written notice thereof has been tendered by the master or Owners' agents to Charterers or their agents and the vessel is securely moored at the specified loading or discharging berth. However, if the vessel does not proceed immediately to such berth time shall commence to run 6 hours after (i) the vessel is lying in the area where she was ordered to wait or, in the absence of any such specific order, in a usual waiting area and (ii) written notice of readiness has been tendered and (iii) the specified berth is accessible. A loading or discharging berth shall be deemed inaccessible only for so long as the vessel is or would be prevented from proceeding to it by bad weather, tidal conditions, ice, awaiting daylight pilot or tugs, or port traffic control requirements (except those requirements resulting from the unavailability of such berth or of the cargo).

180
181
182
183
184
185
186
187
188
189
190

If Charterers fail to specify a berth at any port, the first berth at which the vessel loads or discharges the cargo or any part thereof shall be deemed to be the specified berth at such port for the purposes of this Clause.

191
192
193

Notice shall not be tendered before commencement of laydays and notice tendered by radio shall qualify as written notice provided it is confirmed in writing as soon as reasonably possible.

194
195
196

(b)   Time shall continue to run

(i)   until cargo hoses have been disconnected, or

197
198

(ii)   if the vessel is delayed for Charterers' purposes for more than one hour after disconnection of cargo hoses, until the termination of such delay provided that if the vessel waits at any place other than the berth, time on passage to such other place, from disconnecting of hoses to remooring/anchorage at such other place, shall not count.

199
200
201
202

3

(2) If the vessel loads or discharges cargo by transhipment at sea time shall count from the arrival of the vessel at the transhipment area or from commencement of the laydays, whichever is later, and, subject to Clause 14(c), shall run until transhipment has been completed and the vessels have separated.

(3) Notwithstanding anything else in this Clause 13, if Charterers start loading or discharging the vessel before time would otherwise start to run under this charter, time shall run from commencement of such loading or discharging.

(4) For the purposes of this Clause 13 and of Clause 14 "time" shall mean laytime or time counting for demurrage, as the case may be.

Suspension of time

14. Time shall not count when

    (a) spent on inward passage from the vessel's waiting area to the loading or discharging berth specified by Charterers, even if lightening occurred at such waiting area; or

    (b) spent in handling ballast except to the extent that cargo operations are carried on concurrently and are not delayed thereby; or

    (c) lost as a result of
        (i) breach of this Charter by Owners; or
        (ii) any cause attributable to the vessel, including breakdown or inefficiency of the vessel; or
        (iii) strike, lock-out, stoppage or restraint of labour of master, officers or crew of the vessel or tug boats or pilot.

Demurrage

15. (1) Charterers shall pay demurrage at the rate specified in Part I(J).

If the demurrage rate specified in Part I(J) is expressed as a percentage of Worldscale such percentage shall be applied to the demurrage rate applicable to vessels of a similar size to the vessel as provided in Worldscale or, for the purpose of clause 10 and/or if this charter is terminated prior to the commencement of loading, in the Worldwide Tanker Nominal Freight Scale current at the termination date specified in Part I(C).

Demurrage shall be paid per running day or pro rata for part thereof for all time which, under the provisions of this charter, counts against laytime or for demurrage and which exceeds the laytime specified in Part I(I). Charterers' liability for exceeding the laytime shall be absolute and shall not in any case be subject to the provisions of Clause 32.

(2) If, however, all or part of such demurrage arises out of or results from fire or explosion at ports of loading and/or discharging in or about the plant of Charterers, shippers or consignees of the cargo (not being a fire or explosion caused by the negligence or wilful act or omission of Charterers, shippers or consignees of the cargo or their respective servants or agents), act of God, act of war, riot, civil commotion, or arrest or restraint of princes rulers or peoples, the rate of demurrage shall be reduced by half for such demurrage or such part thereof.

(3) Owners shall notify Charterers within 60 days after completion of discharge if demurrage has been incurred and any demurrage claim together with supporting documentation shall be submitted within 90 days after completion of discharge. If Owners fail to give notice of or to submit any such claim within the time limits aforesaid, Charterers' liability for such demurrage shall be extinguished.

Vessel inspection

16. Charterers shall have the right, but no duty, to have a representative attend on board the vessel at any loading and/or discharging ports (except locations at sea) and the master and Owners shall co-operate to facilitate his inspection of the vessel and observation of cargo operations. However, such right, and the exercise or non-exercise thereof, shall in no way reduce the master's or Owners' authority over, or responsibility to Charterers and third parties for, the vessel and every aspect of her operation, nor increase Charterers' responsibilities to Owners or third parties for the same.

Cargo inspection

17. Without prejudice to Clause 2 hereof, Charterers shall have the right to require inspection of the vessel's tanks at loading and/or discharging ports (except locations at sea) to ascertain the quantity and quality of the cargo, water and residues on board. Depressurisation of the tanks to permit inspection and/or ullaging shall be carried out in accordance with the recommendations in the latest edition of the International Safety Guide for Oil Tankers and Terminals. Charterers shall also have the right to inspect and take samples from the bunker tanks and other non-cargo spaces. Any delay to the vessel caused by such inspection and measurement or associated depressurising/repressurising of tanks shall count against laytime, or if the vessel is on demurrage, for demurrage.

Cargo measurement

18. The master shall ascertain the contents of all tanks before and after loading and before and after discharging, and shall prepare tank-by-tank ullage reports of the cargo, water and residues on board which shall be promptly made available to Charterers or their representative if requested. Each such ullage report shall show actual ullage/dips, and densities at observed and standard temperature (15°Celsius). All quantities shall be expressed in cubic metres at both observed and standard temperature.

Inert gas

19. The vessel's inert gas system (if any) shall comply with Regulation 62, Chapter II-2 of the 1974 Safety of Life at Sea Convention as modified by the Protocol of 1978 and Owners warrant that such system shall be operated in accordance with the guidance given in the IMO publication "Inert Gas Systems (1983)". Should the inert gas system fail, Section 8 (Emergency Procedures) of the said IMO publication shall be strictly adhered to and time lost as a consequence of such failure shall not count against laytime or, if the vessel is on demurrage, for demurrage.

Crude oil washing

20. If the vessel is equipped for crude oil washing Charterers shall have the right to require the vessel to crude oil wash those tanks in which the cargo is carried. If crude oil washing is required by Charterers or any competent authority, any additional discharging time thereby incurred shall count against laytime or, if the vessel is on demurrage, for demurrage, and the number of hours specified in Part I(A)(vii) shall be increased by 0.75 hours per cargo tank washed.

4

Over age insurance	21. Any additional insurance on the cargo required because of the age of the vessel shall be for Owners' account.	270 271
Ice	22. The vessel shall not be required to force ice or to follow icebreakers. If the master finds that a nominated port is inaccessible due to ice, the master shall immediately notify Charterers requesting revised orders and shall remain outside the ice-bound area; and if after arrival at a nominated port there is danger of the vessel being frozen in, the vessel shall proceed to the nearest safe and ice free position and at the same time request Charterers to give revised orders.	272 273 274 275 276

In either case if the affected port is
- (i) the first or only loading port and no cargo has been loaded, Charterers shall either nominate another port, or give notice cancelling this charter in which case they shall pay at the demurrage rate in Part I(J) for the time from the master's notification aforesaid or from notice of readiness on arrival, as the case may be, until the time such cancellation notice is given;
- (ii) a loading port and part of the cargo has been loaded, Charterers shall either nominate another port, or order the vessel to proceed on the voyage without completing loading in which case Charterers shall pay for any deadfreight arising therefrom;
- (iii) a discharging port, Charterers shall either nominate another port or order the vessel to proceed to or return to and discharge at the nominated port. If the vessel is ordered to proceed to or return to a nominated port, Charterers shall bear the risk of the vessel being damaged whilst proceeding to or returning to or at such port, and the whole period from the time when the master's request for revised orders is received by Charterers until the vessel can safely depart after completion of discharge shall count against laytime or, if the vessel is on demurrage, for demurrage.

277
278
279
280
281
282
283
284
285
286
287
288
289
290

If, as a consequence of Charterers revising orders pursuant to this clause, the nominated port(s) or the number or rotation of ports is changed freight, shall nevertheless be paid for the voyage which the vessel would otherwise have performed had the orders not been so revised, such freight to be increased or reduced by the amount by which, as a result of such revision of orders,
- (a) the time used including any time awaiting revised orders (which shall be valued at the demurrage rate in Part I(J)),
- (b) the bunkers consumed (which shall be valued at the bunker costs at the port at which bunkers were last taken) and
- (c) the port charges

for the voyage actually performed are greater or less than those that would have been incurred on the voyage which, but for the revised orders under this Clause, the vessel would have performed.

291
292
293
294
295
296
297
298
299
300
301

Quarantine	23. Time lost due to quarantine shall not count against laytime or for demurrage unless such quarantine was in force at the time when the affected port was nominated by Charterers.	302 303
Agency	24. The vessel's agents shall be nominated by Charterers at nominated ports of loading and discharging.	304
	Such agents, although nominated by Charterers, shall be employed and paid by Owners.	305
Charterers' obligation at shallow draft port/ Lightening in port	25. (1) (a) If the vessel, with the quantity of cargo then on board, is unable due to inadequate depth of water in the port safely to reach any specified discharging berth and discharge the cargo there always safely afloat, Charterers shall specify a location within port limits where the vessel can discharge sufficient cargo into vessels or lighters to enable the vessel safely to reach and discharge cargo at such discharging berth, and the vessel shall lighten at such location.	306 307 308 309 310
	(b) If the vessel is lightened pursuant to Clause 25(1)(a) then, for the purposes of the calculation of laytime and demurrage, the lightening place shall be treated as the first discharging berth within the port where such lightening occurs.	311 312 313
Charterers' orders/ Change of orders/ Part cargo transhipment	26. (1) If, after loading and/or discharging ports have been nominated, Charterers wish to vary such nominations or their rotation, Charterers may give revised orders subject to Part I(D) and/or (E), as the case may be. Charterers shall reimburse Owners at the demurrage rate provided in Part I(J) for any deviation or delay which may result therefrom and shall pay at replacement price for any extra bunkers consumed.	314 315 316 317
	Charterers shall not be liable for any other loss or expense which is caused by such variation unless promptly on receipt of the revised orders Owners notify Charterers of the expectation of such loss or expense in which case, unless Charterers promptly revoke such orders, Charterers shall be liable to reimburse Owners for any such loss or expense proven.	318 319 320 321
	(2) Subject to Clause 33(6), Charterers may order the vessel to load and/or discharge any part of the cargo by transhipment at sea in the vicinity of any nominated port or en route between two nominated ports, in which case Charterers shall reimburse Owners at the demurrage rate specified in Part I(J) for any additional steaming time and/or delay which may be incurred as a consequence of proceeding to and from the location at sea of such transhipment and, in addition, Charterers shall pay at replacement price for any extra bunkers consumed.	322 323 324 325 326
Heating of cargo	27. If Charterers require cargo heating the vessel shall, on passage to and whilst at discharging port(s), maintain the cargo at the loaded temperature or at the temperature stated in Part I(A)(iv), whichever is the lower. Charterers may request that the temperature of the cargo be raised above or lowered below that at which it was loaded, in which event Owners shall use their best endeavours to comply with such request and Charterers shall pay at replacement price for any additional bunkers consumed and any consequential delay to the vessel shall count against laytime or, if the vessel is on demurrage, for demurrage.	327 328 329 330 331 332

5

ETA

28. Owners undertake that, unless Charterers require otherwise, the master shall:

    (a) advise Charterers by radio immediately on leaving the final port of call on the previous voyage or within 48 hours after the time and date of this charter, whichever is the later, of the time and date of the vessel's expected arrival at the first loading port or, if the loading range is in the Arabian Gulf, the time of her expected arrival off Quoin Island;

    (b) confirm or amend such advice not later than 72 hours and again not later than 24 hours before the vessel is due at the first loading port or, in the case of a loading range in the Arabian Gulf, off Quoin Island;

    (c) advise Charterers by radio immediately after departure from the final loading port, of the vessel's expected time of arrival at the first discharging port or the area at sea to which the vessel has been instructed to proceed for wireless orders, and confirm or amend such advice not later than 72 hours and again not later than 24 hours before the vessel is due at such port or area;

    (d) immediately radio any variation of more than six hours from expected times of arrival at loading or discharging ports, Quoin Island or such area at sea to Charterers;

    (e) address all radio messages in accordance with Part I(K).

Owners shall be responsible for any consequences or additional expenses arising as a result of non-compliance with this Clause.

Packed cargo

29. Charterers have the option of shipping products and/or general cargo in available dry cargo space, the quantity being subject to the master's discretion. Freight shall be payable at the bulk rate in accordance with Clause 5 and Charterers shall pay in addition all expenses incurred solely as a result of the packed cargo being carried. Delay occasioned to the vessel by the exercise of such option shall count against laytime or, if the vessel is on demurrage, for demurrage.

Subletting/ Assignment

30. Charterers shall have the option of sub-chartering the vessel and/or of assigning this charter to any person or persons, but Charterers shall always remain responsible for the due fulfilment of all the terms and conditions of this charter.

Liberty

31. The vessel shall be at liberty to tow or be towed, to assist vessels in all positions of distress, to call at any port or ports for bunkers, to sail without pilots, and to deviate for the purpose of saving life or property or for the purpose of embarking or disembarking persons spares or supplies by helicopter or for any other reasonable purpose.

Exceptions

32. (a) The vessel, her master and Owners shall not, unless otherwise in this charter expressly provided, be liable for any loss or damage or delay or failure arising or resulting from any act, neglect or default of the master, pilots, mariners or other servants of Owners in the navigation or management of the vessel; fire unless caused by the actual fault or privity of Owners; collision or stranding; dangers and accidents of the sea; explosion, bursting of boilers, breakage of shafts or any latent defect in hull, equipment or machinery; provided, however, that Part I(A) and Clauses 1 and 2 hereof shall be unaffected by the foregoing. Further, neither the vessel, her master or Owners, nor Charterers shall, unless otherwise in this charter expressly provided, be liable for any loss or damage or delay or failure in performance hereunder arising or resulting from act of God, act of war, act of public enemies, seizure under legal process, quarantine restrictions, strikes, lock-outs, restraints of labour, riots, civil commotions or arrest or restraint of princes rulers or people.

    (b) Nothing in this charter shall be construed as in any way restricting, excluding or waiving the right of Owners or of any other relevant persons to limit their liability under any available legislation or law.

    (c) Clause 32(a) shall not apply to or affect any liability of Owners or the vessel or any other relevant person in respect of

        (i) loss of or damage caused to any berth, jetty, dock, dolphin, buoy, mooring line, pipe or crane or other works or equipment whatsoever at or near any port to which the vessel may proceed under this charter, whether or not such works or equipment belong to Charterers, or

        (ii) any claim (whether brought by Charterers or any other person) arising out of any loss of or damage to or in connection with the cargo. Any such claim shall be subject to the Hague-Visby Rules or the Hague Rules, as the case may be, which ought pursuant to Clause 37 hereof to have been incorporated in the relevant bill of lading (whether or not such Rules were so incorporated), or, if no such bill of lading is issued, to the Hague-Visby Rules.

Bills of lading

33. (1) Subject to the provisions of this Clause Charterers may require the master to sign lawful bills of lading for any cargo in such form as Charterers direct.

    (2) The signing of bills of lading shall be without prejudice to this charter and Charterers hereby indemnify Owners against all liabilities that may arise from signing bills of lading to the extent that the same impose liabilities upon Owners in excess of or beyond those imposed by this charter.

    (3) All bills of lading presented to the master for signature, in addition to complying with the requirements of Clauses 35, 36 and 37, shall include or effectively incorporate clauses substantially similar to the terms of Clauses 22, 33(7) and 34.

    (4) All bills of lading presented for signature hereunder shall show a named port of discharge. If when bills of lading are presented for signature discharging port(s) have been nominated hereunder, the discharging port(s) shown on such bills of lading shall be in conformity with the nominated port(s). If at the time of such presentation no such nomination has been made hereunder, the discharging port(s) shown on such bills of lading must be within Part I(E) and shall be deemed to have been nominated hereunder by virtue of such presentation.

    (5) Article III Rules 3 and 5 of the Hague-Visby Rules shall apply to the particulars included in the bills of lading as if Charterers were the shippers, and the guarantee and indemnity therein contained shall apply to the description of the cargo furnished by or on behalf of Charterers.

6

(6)   Notwithstanding any other provisions of this charter, Owners shall not be obliged to comply with any orders from Charterers to discharge all or part of the cargo

    (i)   at any port other than that shown on the bills of lading (except as provided in Clauses 22 or 34) and/or

    (ii) without presentation of an original bill of lading

unless they have received from Charterers both written confirmation of such orders and an indemnity acceptable to Owners.

(7)   The master shall not be required or bound to sign bills of lading for any blockaded port or for any port which the master or Owners in his or their discretion consider dangerous or impossible to enter or reach.

(8)   Charterers hereby warrant that on each and every occasion that they issue orders under Clauses 22, 26, 34 or 38 they will have the authority of the holders of the bills of lading to give such orders, and that such bills of lading will not be transferred to any person who does not concur therein.

War risks

34.   (1)   If

    (a) any loading or discharging port to which the vessel may properly be ordered under the provisions of this charter or bills of lading issued pursuant to this charter be blockaded, or

    (b) owing to any war, hostilities, warlike operation, civil commotions, revolutions, or the operation of international law (i) entry to any such loading or discharging port or the loading or discharging of cargo at any such port be considered by the master or Owners in his or their discretion dangerous or prohibited or (ii) it be considered by the master or Owners in his or their discretion dangerous or impossible or prohibited for the vessel to reach any such loading or discharging port,

Charterers shall have the right to order the cargo or such part of it as may be affected to be loaded or discharged at any other loading or discharging port within the ranges specified in Part I(D) or (E) respectively (provided such other port is not blockaded and that entry thereto or loading or discharging of cargo thereat or reaching the same is not in the master's or Owners' opinion dangerous or impossible or prohibited).

(2)   If no orders be received from Charterers within 48 hours after they or their agents have received from Owners a request for the nomination of a substitute port, then

    (a) if the affected port is the first or only loading port and no cargo has been loaded, this charter shall terminate forthwith;

    (b) if the affected port is a loading port and part of the cargo has already been loaded, the vessel may proceed on passage and Charterers shall pay for any deadfreight so incurred;

    (c) if the affected port is a discharging port, Owners shall be at liberty to discharge the cargo at any port which they or the master may in their or his discretion decide on (whether within the range specified in Part I(E) or not) and such discharging shall be deemed to be due fulfilment of the contract or contracts of affreightment so far as cargo so discharged is concerned.

(3)   If in accordance with Clause 34(1) or (2) cargo is loaded or discharged at any such other port, freight shall be paid as for the voyage originally nominated, such freight to be increased or reduced by the amount by which, as a result of loading or discharging at such other port,

    (a) the time on voyage including any time awaiting revised orders (which shall be valued at the demurrage rate in Part I(J)),

    (b) the bunkers consumed (which shall be valued at the bunker costs at the port at which bunkers were last taken), and

    (c) the port charges

for the voyage actually performed are greater or less than those which would have been incurred on the voyage originally nominated Save as aforesaid, the voyage actually performed shall be treated for the purpose of this Charter as if it were the voyage originally nominated.

(4)   The vessel shall have liberty to comply with any directions or recommendations as to departure, arrival, routes, ports of call, stoppages, destinations, zones, waters, delivery or in any otherwise whatsoever given by the government of the nation under whose flag the vessel sails or any other government or local authority including any de facto government or local authority or by any person or body acting or purporting to act as or with the authority of any such government or authority or by any committee or person having under the terms of the war risks insurance on the vessel the right to give any such directions or recommendations. If by reason of or in compliance with any such directions or recommendations anything is done or is not done, such shall not be deemed a deviation.

If by reason of or in compliance with any such directions or recommendations the vessel does not proceed to the discharging port or ports originally nominated or to which she may have been properly ordered under the provisions of this charter or bills of lading issued pursuant to this charter, the vessel may proceed to any discharging port on which the master or Owners in his or their discretion may decide and there discharge the cargo. Such discharging shall be deemed to be due fulfilment of the contract or contracts of affreightment and Owners shall be entitled to freight as if discharging had been effected at the port or ports originally nominated or to which the vessel may have been properly ordered under the provisions of this charter or bills of lading issued pursuant to this charter. All extra expenses involved in reaching and discharging the cargo at any such other discharging port shall be paid by Charterers and Owners shall have a lien on the cargo for all such extra expenses.

7

Both to blame clause	35. If the liability for any collision in which the vessel is involved while performing this charter falls to be determined in accordance with the laws of the United States of America, the following clause, which shall be included in all bills of lading issued pursuant to this charter shall apply:–	467 468 469

"If the vessel comes into collision with another vessel as a result of the negligence of the other vessel and any act, neglect or default of the master, mariner, pilot or the servants of the Carrier in the navigation or in the management of the vessel, the owners of the cargo carried hereunder will indemnify the Carrier against all loss or liability to the other or non-carrying vessel or her owners in so far as such loss or liability represents loss of, or damage to, or any claim whatsoever of the owners of the said cargo, paid or payable by the other or non-carrying vessel or her owners to the owners of the said cargo and set off, recouped or recovered by the other or non-carrying vessel or her owners as part of their claim against the carrying vessel or the Carrier.

470
471
472
473
474
475
476

The foregoing provisions shall also apply where the owners, operators or those in charge of any vessel or vessels or objects other than, or in addition to, the colliding vessels or objects are at fault in respect of a collision or contact."

477
478
479

General average/ New Jason Clause	36. General average shall be payable according to the York/Antwerp Rules, 1974, and shall be adjusted in London, but should the adjustment be made in accordance with the law and practice of the United States of America, the following clause, which shall be included in all bills of lading issued pursuant to this charter, shall apply:–	480 481 482 483

"In the event of accident, danger, damage or disaster before or after the commencement of the voyage, resulting from any cause whatsoever, whether due to negligence or not, for which, or for the consequence of which, the Carrier is not responsible, by statute, contract or otherwise, the cargo, shippers, consignees or owners of the cargo shall contribute with the Carrier in general average to the payment of any sacrifices, losses or expenses of a general average nature that may be made or incurred and shall pay salvage and special charges incurred in respect of the cargo.

484
485
486
487
488
489

If a salving vessel is owned or operated by the Carrier, salvage shall be paid for as fully as if the said salving vessel or vessels belonged to strangers. Such deposit as the Carrier or its agents may deem sufficient to cover the estimated contribution of the cargo and any salvage and special charges thereon shall, if required, be made by the cargo, shippers, consignees or owners of the cargo to the Carrier before delivery."

490
491
492
493

Clause paramount	37. The following clause shall be included in all bills of lading issued pursuant to this charter:–	494 495 496

"CLAUSE PARAMOUNT

(1) Subject to sub-clause (2) hereof, this bill of lading shall be governed by, and have effect subject to, the rules contained in the International Convention for the Unification of Certain Rules relating to Bills of Lading signed at Brussels on 25th August 1924 (hereafter the "Hague Rules") as amended by the Protocol signed at Brussels on 23rd February 1968 (hereafter the "Hague-Visby Rules"). Nothing herein contained shall be deemed to be either a surrender by the Carrier of any of his rights or immunities or an increase of any of his responsibilities or liabilities under the Hague-Visby Rules.

497
498
499
500
501
502

(2) If there is governing legislation which applies the Hague Rules compulsorily to this bill of lading, to the exclusion of the Hague-Visby Rules, then this bill of lading shall have effect subject to the Hague Rules. Nothing herein contained shall be deemed to be either a surrender by the Carrier of any of his rights or immunities or an increase of any of his responsibilities or liabilities under the Hague Rules.

503
504
505
506

(3) If any term of this bill of lading is repugnant to the Hague-Visby Rules, or the Hague Rules if applicable, such term shall be void to that extent but no further.

507
508

(4) Nothing in this bill of lading shall be construed as in any way restricting, excluding or waiving the right of any relevant party or person to limit his liability under any available legislation and/or law."

509
510

Back loading	38. Charterers may order the vessel to load a part cargo at any nominated discharging port, and to discharge such part cargo at a port(s) to be nominated by Charterers within the range specified in Part I(E) and within the rotation of the discharging ports previously nominated, provided that such part cargo is of the description specified in Part I(F) and that the master in his absolute discretion determines that this cargo can be loaded, segregated and discharged without risk of contamination by, or of, any other cargo remaining on board.	511 512 513 514 515

Charterers shall pay a lump sum freight in respect of such part cargo calculated at the demurrage rate specified in Part I(J) on any additional time used by the vessel as a result of loading, carrying or discharging such part cargo.

516
517
518

Any additional expenses, including port charges, incurred as a result of loading or discharging such part cargo shall be for Charterers' account.

519
520

Bunkers	39. Owners shall give Charterers or any other company in the Royal Dutch/Shell Group of Companies first option to quote for the supply of bunker requirements for the performance of this charter.	521 522

Oil pollution prevention	40. (1) Owners shall ensure that the master shall:–	523
	(a) comply with MARPOL 73/78 including in particular and without limitation Regulation 9, Chapter II of the International Convention for the Prevention of Pollution from Ships 1973;	524 525
	(b) collect the drainings and any tank washings into a suitable tank or tanks and, after maximum separation of free water, discharge the bulk of such water overboard, consistent with the above regulations; and	526 527 528
	(c) thereafter notify Charterers promptly of the amounts of oil and free water so retained on board and details of any other washings retained on board from earlier voyages (together called the "collected washings").	529 530 531

(2)   On being so notified, Charterers, in accordance with their rights under this Clause (which shall include without limitation the right to determine the disposal of the collected washings), shall before the vessel's arrival at the loading berth (or if already arrived as soon as possible thereafter) give instructions as to how the collected washings shall be dealt with. Owners shall ensure that the master on the vessel's arrival at the loading berth (or if already arrived as soon as possible thereafter) shall arrange in conjunction with the cargo suppliers for the measurement of the quantity of the collected washings and shall record the same in the vessel's ullage record.

(3)   Charterers may require the collected washings to be discharged ashore at the loading port, in which case no freight shall be payable on them.

(4)   Alternatively Charterers may require either that the cargo be loaded on top of the collected washings and the collected washings be discharged with the cargo, or that they be kept separate from the cargo in which case Charterers shall pay for any deadfreight incurred thereby in accordance with Clause 8 and shall, if practicable, accept discharge of the collected washings at the discharging port or ports.

In either case, provided that the master has reduced the free water in the collected washings to a minimum consistent with the retention on board of the oil residues in them and consistent with sub-Clause (1)(a) above, freight in accordance with Clause 5 shall be payable on the quantity of the collected washings as if such quantity were included in a bill of lading and the figure therefor furnished by the shipper provided, however, that

> (i)   if there is provision in this charter for a lower freight rate to apply to cargo in excess of an agreed quantity, freight on the collected washings shall be paid at such lower rate (provided such agreed quantity of cargo has been loaded) and
>
> (ii) if there is provision in this charter for a minimum cargo quantity which is less than a full cargo, then whether or not such minimum cargo quantity is furnished, freight on the collected washings shall be paid as if such minimum cargo quantity had been furnished, provided that no freight shall be payable in respect of any collected washings which are kept separate from the cargo and not discharged at the discharge port.

(5)   Whenever Charterers require the collected washings to be discharged ashore pursuant to this Clause, Charterers shall provide and pay for the reception facilities, and the cost of any shifting therefor shall be for Charterers' account. Any time lost discharging the collected washings and/or shifting therefor shall count against laytime or, if the vessel is on demurrage, for demurrage.

TOVALOP

41.   Owners warrant that the vessel:
> (i)   is a tanker owned by a Participating Owner in TOVALOP
>   and
> (ii) is entered in the P&I Club stated in Part I(A)(xii)
and will so remain during the currency of this charter.

When an escape or discharge of Oil occurs from the vessel and causes or threatens to cause Pollution Damage, or when there is the Threat of an escape or discharge of Oil (i.e. a grave and imminent danger of the escape or discharge of Oil which, if it occurred, would create a serious danger of Pollution Damage, whether or not an escape or discharge in fact subsequently occurs), then Charterers may, at their option upon notice to Owners or master, undertake such measures as are reasonably necessary to prevent or minimise such Pollution Damage or to remove the Threat, unless Owners promptly undertake the same. Charterers shall keep Owners advised of the nature and result of any such measures taken by them and, if time permits, the nature of the measures intended to be taken by them. Any of the aforementioned measures taken by Charterers shall be deemed taken on Owners' authority and as Owners' agents, and shall be at Owners' expense except to the extent that:

> (1)   any such escape or discharge or Threat was caused or contributed to by Charterers, or
> (2)   by reason of the exceptions set out in Article III, paragraph 2, of the 1969 International Convention on Civil Liability for Oil Pollution Damage or any protocol thereto, Owners are or, had the said Convention applied to such escape or discharge or to the Threat, would have been, exempt from liability for the same, or
> (3)   the cost of such measures together with all other liabilities, costs and expenses of Owners arising out of or in connection with such escape or discharge or Threat exceeds the maximum liability applicable to the vessel under TOVALOP as at the time of such escape or discharge or threat, save and insofar as Owners shall be entitled to recover such excess under either the 1971 International Convention on the Establishment of an International Fund for Compensation for Oil Pollution Damage or under CRISTAL

PROVIDED ALWAYS that if Owners in their absolute discretion consider said measures should be discontinued, Owners shall so notify Charterers and thereafter Charterers shall have no right to continue said measures under the provisions of this Clause and all further liability to Charterers under this Clause shall thereupon cease.

The above provisions are not in derogation of such other rights as Charterers or Owners may have under this charter or may otherwise have or acquire by law or any international convention or TOVALOP.

The term "TOVALOP" means the Tanker Owners' Voluntary Agreement Concerning Liability for Oil Pollution dated 7th January 1969, as amended from time to time, and the term "CRISTAL" means the Contract Regarding an Interim Supplement to Tanker Liability for Oil Pollution dated 14th January 1971, as amended from time to time. The terms "Participating Owner", "Oil" and, "Pollution Damage" shall for the purposes of this clause have the meanings ascribed to them in TOVALOP.

Lien

42.   Owners shall have an absolute lien upon the cargo and all subfreights for all amounts due under this charter and the cost of recovery thereof including any expenses whatsoever arising from the exercise of such lien.

	532
	533
	534
	535
	536
	537
	538
	539
	540
	541
	542
	543
	544
	545
	546
	547
	548
	549
	550
	551
	552
	553
	554
	555
	556
	557
	558
	559
	560
	561
	562
	563
	564
	565
	566
	567
	568
	569
	570
	571
	572
	573
	574
	575
	576
	577
	578
	579
	580
	581
	582
	583
	584
	585
	586
	587
	588
	589
	590
	591
	592
	593
	594
	595
	596
	597
	598
	599

9

Law and litigation	43. (a) This charter shall be construed and the relations between the parties determined in accordance with the laws of England.

    (b) any dispute arising under this charter shall be decided by the English Courts to whose jurisdiction the parties hereby agree.

    (c) Notwithstanding the foregoing, but without prejudice to any party's right to arrest or maintain the arrest of any maritime property, either party may, by giving written notice of election to the other party, elect to have any such dispute referred to the arbitration of a single arbitrator in London in accordance with the provisions of the Arbitration Act 1950, or any statutory modification or re-enactment thereof for the time being in force.

    (i) A party shall lose its right to make such an election only if:
      (a) it receives from the other party a written notice of dispute which –
        (1) states expressly that a dispute has arisen out of this charter;
        (2) specifies the nature of the dispute; and
        (3) refers expressly to this clause 43(c) and;
      (b) it fails to give notice of election to have the dispute referred to arbitration not later than 30 days from the date of receipt of such notice of dispute.

    (ii) the parties hereby agree that either party may –
      (a) appeal to the High Court on any question of law arising out of an award;
      (b) apply to the High Court for an order that the arbitrator state the reasons for his award;
      (c) give notice to the arbitrator that a reasoned award is required; and
      (d) apply to the High Court to determine any question of law arising in the course of the reference.

    (d) It shall be a condition precedent to the right of any party to a stay of any legal proceedings in which maritime property has been, or may be, arrested in connection with a dispute under this charter, that that party furnishes to the other party security to which that other party would have been entitled in such legal proceedings in the absence of a stay.

Construction	44. The side headings have been included in this charter for convenience of reference only and shall in no way affect the construction hereof.

600
601

602
603

604
605
606
607
608

609
610
611
612
613
614
615

616
617
618
619
620
621

622
623
624
625

626
627

APPENDIX VII

LETTER OF CREDIT—THE FUNCTION OF THE BILL OF LADING

LETTER OF CREDIT—
THE FUNCTION OF THE
BILL OF LADING

COMMENTS TO THE ILLUSTRATION

1. According to the Sales Agreement a parcel of 5,000 metric tons of potatoes in bags of 50 kilos, has been sold for an agreed price of USD 1,100,000 CIF. The Seller and the Buyer have agreed that the payment (USD 1,100,000) shall be transferred via a Letter of Credit.

2. The Buyer contacts his bank and gives them instructions about the relevant parts of the Sales Agreement, usually the commodity (5,000 metric tons of potatoes in bags of 50 kilos), the price, time for shipment, necessary certificates, etc.

3. The Buyer's bank forwards the instructions to the Seller's bank.

4. The vessel arrives at the port of loading and loading commences. During the loading the cargo is tallied and a superficial inspection is made.

5. When the whole cargo is loaded the Master issues a Bill of Lading (usually the Bill of Lading is drawn up by the agent and controlled/signed by the Master). The Bill of Lading states inter alia the type of cargo, quantity, marks and also includes a statement saying that "the cargo has been loaded in apparent good order and condition". If the cargo was not in apparent good order and condition the Master should insert a remark about the quality.

6. The Seller/Shipper checks the Bill of Lading.

7. The Seller takes the Bill of Lading to the bank where it is controlled and compared with the instructions coming from the Buyer via his bank.

8. If the Bill of Lading passes the control in the bank, the bank pays the purchase price (USD 1,100,000) to the Seller/Shipper.

9. The Seller's bank forwards the original Bill of Lading to the Buyer's bank.

10. Meanwhile the vessel has left the port of loading and is on her way to the port of discharge.

11. Normally the freight is paid during the voyage, i.e. sometime between the completion of loading and before the commencement of discharge.

12. Normally the original Bills of Lading have arrived at the Buyer's bank who informs the Buyer that the Bills of Lading can be collected.

13. The Buyer goes to the bank and checks that the Bills of Lading are in accordance with the Sales Agreement and with his instructions to the bank.

14. If the Bills of Lading pass the Buyer's control he transfers the purchase price (USD 1,100,000) to his bank.

15. The Buyer's bank gives the original Bills of Lading to the Buyer.

16. The Buyer's bank transfers the purchase price to the Seller's bank.

17. The vessel arrives at port of discharge. Normally the agents have informed the Buyer of the ETA beforehand.

18. The Buyer goes to the vessel's agent (or to the Master) and delivers at least one of the original Bills of Lading.

19. The agent (or the Master) checks that the receiver's identity is in conformity with the Bill of Lading.

20. The cargo is discharged and delivered to the receiver.

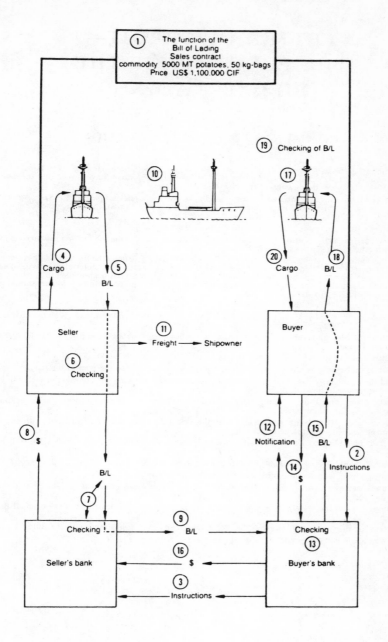

APPENDIX VIII

SALEFORM 1993*

MEMORANDUM OF AGREEMENT

Norwegian Shipbrokers' Association's Memo-
randum of Agreement for sale and purchase of
ships. Adopted by The Baltic and International
Maritime Council (BIMCO) in 1956.
Code-name
SALEFORM 1993
Revised 1966, 1983 and 1986/87.

Dated:

hereinafter called the Sellers, have agreed to sell, and	1
hereinafter called the Buyers, have agreed to buy	2
Name:	3
Classification Society/Class:	4
Built: By:	5
Flag: Place of Registration:	6
Call Sign: Grt/Nrt:	7
Register Number:	8
hereinafter called the Vessel, on the following terms and conditions:	9

Definitions   10

"Banking days" are days on which banks are open both in the country of the currency   11
stipulated for the Purchase Price in Clause 1 and in the place of closing stipulated in Clause 8.   12

"In writing" or "written" means a letter handed over from the Sellers to the Buyers or vice versa,   13
a registered letter, telex, telefax or other modern form of written communication.   14

"Classification Society" or "Class" means the Society referred to in line 4.   15

1.   Purchase Price   16

2.   Deposit   17

As security for the correct fulfilment of this Agreement the Buyers shall pay a deposit of 10 %   18
(ten per cent) of the Purchase Price within   banking days from the date of this   19
Agreement. This deposit shall be placed with   20

and held by them in a joint account for the Sellers and the Buyers, to be released in accordance   21
with joint written instructions of the Sellers and the Buyers. Interest, if any, to be credited to the   22
Buyers. Any fee charged for holding the said deposit shall be borne equally by the Sellers and the   23
Buyers.   24

3.   Payment   25

The said Purchase Price shall be paid in full free of bank charges to   26

on delivery of the Vessel, but not later than 3 banking days after the Vessel is in every respect   27
physically ready for delivery in accordance with the terms and conditions of this Agreement and   28
Notice of Readiness has been given in accordance with Clause 5.   29

4.   Inspections   30

a)*   The Buyers have inspected and accepted the Vessel's classification records. The Buyers   31
have also inspected the Vessel at/in   on   32
and have accepted the Vessel following this inspection and the sale is outright and definite,   33
subject only to the terms and conditions of this Agreement.   34

b)*   The Buyers shall have the right to inspect the Vessel's classification records and declare   35
whether same are accepted or not within   36

The Sellers shall provide for inspection of the Vessel at/in   37

The Buyers shall undertake the inspection without undue delay to the Vessel. Should the   38
Buyers cause undue delay they shall compensate the Sellers for the losses thereby incurred.   39
The Buyers shall inspect the Vessel without opening up and without cost to the Sellers.   40
During the inspection, the Vessel's deck and engine log books shall be made available for   41
examination by the Buyers. If the Vessel is accepted after such inspection, the sale shall   42
become outright and definite, subject only to the terms and conditions of this Agreement,   43
provided the Sellers receive written notice of acceptance from the Buyers within 72 hours   44
after completion of such inspection.   45
Should notice of acceptance of the Vessel's classification records and of the Vessel not be   46
received by the Sellers as aforesaid, the deposit together with interest earned shall be   47
released immediately to the Buyers, whereafter this Agreement shall be null and void.   48

*   4 a) and 4b) are alternatives; delete whichever is not applicable. In the absence of deletions,   49
alternative 4a) to apply.   50

5.   Notices, time and place of delivery   51

a)   The Sellers shall keep the Buyers well informed of the Vessel's itinerary and shall   52
provide the Buyers with   ,   , and   days notice of the estimated time of arrival at the   53
intended place of drydocking/underwater inspection/delivery. When the Vessel is at the place   54
of delivery and in every respect physically ready for delivery in accordance with this   55
Agreement, the Sellers shall give the Buyers a written Notice of Readiness for delivery.   56

b)   The Vessel shall be delivered and taken over safely afloat at a safe and accessible berth or   57
anchorage at/in   58

in the Sellers' option.   59

Expected time of delivery: 60

Date of cancelling (see Clauses 5 c), 6 b) (iii) and 14):   61

c)   If the Sellers anticipate that, notwithstanding the exercise of due diligence by them, the   62
Vessel will not be ready for delivery by the cancelling date they may notify the Buyers in   63
writing stating the date when they anticipate that the Vessel will be ready for delivery and   64
propose a new cancelling date. Upon receipt of such notification the Buyers shall have the   65
option of either cancelling this Agreement in accordance with Clause 14 within 7 running   66
days of receipt of the notice or of accepting the new date as the new cancelling date. If the   67
Buyers have not declared their option within 7 running days of receipt of the Sellers'   68
notification or if the Buyers accept the new date, the date proposed in the Sellers' notification   69
shall be deemed to be the new cancelling date and shall be substituted for the cancelling   70
date stipulated in line 61.   71

If this Agreement is maintained with the new cancelling date all other terms and conditions   72
hereof including those contained in Clauses 5 a) and 5 c) shall remain unaltered and in full   73
force and effect. Cancellation or failure to cancel shall be entirely without prejudice to any   74
claim for damages the Buyers may have under Clause 14 for the Vessel not being ready by   75
the original cancelling date.   76

d)   Should the Vessel become an actual, constructive or compromised total loss before delivery   77
          the deposit together with interest earned shall be released immediately to the Buyers   78
          whereafter this Agreement shall be null and void.   79

6.   Drydocking/Divers Inspection   80

a)**   The Sellers shall place the Vessel in drydock at the port of delivery for inspection by the   81
          Classification Society of the Vessel's underwater parts below the deepest load line, the   82
          extent of the inspection being in accordance with the Classification Society's rules. If the   83
          rudder, propeller, bottom or other underwater parts below the deepest load line are found   84
          broken, damaged or defective so as to affect the Vessel's class, such defects shall be made   85
          good at the Sellers' expense to the satisfaction of the Classification Society without   86
          condition/recommendation*.   87

b)**   (i)   The Vessel is to be delivered without drydocking. However, the Buyers shall   88
          have the right at their expense to arrange for an underwater inspection by a diver approved   89
          by the Classification Society prior to the delivery of the Vessel. The Sellers shall at their 90
          cost make the Vessel available for such inspection. The extent of the inspection and the   91
          conditions under which it is performed shall be to the satisfaction of the Classification   92
          Society. If the conditions at the port of delivery are unsuitable for such inspection, the   93
          Sellers shall make the Vessel available at a suitable alternative place near to the delivery   94
          port.   95

          (ii)   If the rudder, propeller, bottom or other underwater parts below the deepest load line 96
          are found broken, damaged or defective so as to affect the Vessel's class, then unless   97
          repairs can be carried out afloat to the satisfaction of the Classification Society, the Sellers 98
          shall arrange for the Vessel to be drydocked at their expense for inspection by the   99
          Classification Society of the Vessel's underwater parts below the deepest load line, the   100
          extent of the inspection being in accordance with the Classification Society's rules. If the   101
          rudder, propeller, bottom or other underwater parts below the deepest load line are found   102
          broken, damaged or defective so as to affect the Vessel's class, such defects shall be made   103
          good by the Sellers at their expense to the satisfaction of the Classification Society   104
          without condition/recommendation*. In such event the Sellers are to pay also for the cost of 105
          the underwater inspection and the Classification Society's attendance.   106

          (iii)   If the Vessel is to be drydocked pursuant to Clause 6 b) (ii) and no suitable dry-   107
          docking facilities are available at the port of delivery, the Sellers shall take the Vessel   108
          to a port where suitable drydocking facilities are available, whether within or outside the   109
          delivery range as per Clause 5 b). Once drydocking has taken place the Sellers shall deliver   110
          the Vessel at a port within the delivery range as per Clause 5 b) which shall, for the   111
          purpose of this Clause, become the new port of delivery. In such event the cancelling date   112
          provided for in Clause 5 b) shall be extended by the additional time required for the   113
          drydocking and extra steaming, but limited to a maximum of 14 running days.   114

c)   If the Vessel is drydocked pursuant to Clause 6 a) or 6 b) above   115

          (i)   the Classification Society may require survey of the tailshaft system, the extent of 116
          the survey being to the satisfaction of the Classification surveyor. If such survey is not   117
          required by the Classification Society, the Buyers shall have the right to require the tailshaft 118
          to be drawn and surveyed by the Classification Society, the extent of the survey being in   119
          accordance with the Classification Society's rules for tailshaft survey and consistent with   120
          the current stage of the Vessel's survey cycle. The Buyers shall declare whether they   121
          require the tailshaft to be drawn and surveyed not later than by the completion of the   122
          inspection by the Classification Society. The drawing and refitting of the tailshaft shall be 123
          arranged by the Sellers. Should any parts of the tailshaft system be condemned or found   124
          defective so as to affect the Vessel's class, those parts shall be renewed or made good at   125
          the Sellers' expense to the satisfaction of the Classification Society without   126
          condition/recommendation*.   127

(ii)   the expenses relating to the survey of the tailshaft system shall be borne   128
by the Buyers unless the Classification Society requires such survey to be carried out, in   129
which case the Sellers shall pay these expenses. The Sellers shall also pay the expenses   130
if the Buyers require the survey and parts of the system are condemned or found defective   131
or broken so as to affect the Vessel's class*.   132

(iii)   the expenses in connection with putting the Vessel in and taking her out of   133
drydock, including the drydock dues and the Classification Society's fees shall be paid by   134
the Sellers if the Classification Society issues any condition/recommendation* as a result   135
of the survey or if it requires survey of the tailshaft system. In all other cases the Buyers   136
shall pay the aforesaid expenses, dues and fees.   137

(iv)   the Buyers' representative shall have the right to be present in the drydock, but   138
without interfering with the work or decisions of the Classification surveyor.   139

(v)   the Buyers shall have the right to have the underwater parts of the Vessel   140
cleaned and painted at their risk and expense without interfering with the Sellers' or the   141
Classification surveyor's work, if any, and without affecting the Vessel's timely delivery. If,   142
however, the Buyers' work in drydock is still in progress when the Sellers have   143
completed the work which the Sellers are required to do, the additional docking time   144
needed to complete the Buyers' work shall be for the Buyers' risk and expense. In the event   145
that the Buyers' work requires such additional time, the Sellers may upon completion of the   146
Sellers' work tender Notice of Readiness for delivery whilst the Vessel is still in drydock   147
and the Buyers shall be obliged to take delivery in accordance with Clause 3, whether   148
the Vessel is in drydock or not and irrespective of Clause 5 b).   149

*   Notes, if any, in the surveyor's report which are accepted by the Classification Society   150
without condition/recommendation are not to be taken into account.   151

**   6 a) and 6 b) are alternatives; delete whichever is not applicable. In the absence of deletions,   152
alternative 6 a) to apply.   153

7.   Spares/bunkers, etc.   154

The Sellers shall deliver the Vessel to the Buyers with everything belonging to her on board and on   155
shore. All spare parts and spare equipment including spare tail-end shaft(s) and/or spare   156
propeller(s)/propeller blade(s), if any, belonging to the Vessel at the time of inspection used or   157
unused, whether on board or not shall become the Buyers' property, but spares on order are to be   158
excluded. Forwarding charges, if any, shall be for the Buyers' account. The Sellers are not required to   159
replace spare parts including spare tail-end shaft(s) and spare propeller(s)/propeller blade(s) which   160
are taken out of spare and used as replacement prior to delivery, but the replaced items shall be the   161
property of the Buyers. The radio installation and navigational equipment shall be included in the sale   162
without extra payment if they are the property of the Sellers. Unused stores and provisions shall be   163
included in the sale and be taken over by the Buyers without extra payment.   164

The Sellers have the right to take ashore crockery, plates, cutlery, linen and other articles bearing the   165
Sellers' flag or name, provided they replace same with similar unmarked items. Library, forms, etc.,   166
exclusively for use in the Sellers' vessel(s), shall be excluded without compensation. Captain's,   167
Officers' and Crew's personal belongings including the slop chest are to be excluded from the sale,   168
as well as the following additional items (including items on hire):   169

The Buyers shall take over the remaining bunkers and unused lubricating oils in storage tanks and   170
sealed drums and pay the current net market price (excluding barging expenses) at the port and date   171
of delivery of the Vessel.   172
Payment under this Clause shall be made at the same time and place and in the same currency as   173
the Purchase Price.   174

8.   Documentation   175

The place of closing: 176

In exchange for payment of the Purchase Price the Sellers shall furnish the Buyers with delivery   177
documents, namely: 178

a)   Legal Bill of Sale in a form recordable in   (the country in which the Buyers are   179
        to register the Vessel), warranting that the Vessel is free from all encumbrances, mortgages   180
        and maritime liens or any other debts or claims whatsoever, duly notarially attested and   181
        legalized by the consul of such country or other competent authority.   182

b)   Current Certificate of Ownership issued by the competent authorities of the flag state of   183
        the Vessel.   184

c)   Confirmation of Class issued within 72 hours prior to delivery.   185

d)   Current Certificate issued by the competent authorities stating that the Vessel is free from   186
        registered encumbrances.   187

e)   Certificate of Deletion of the Vessel from the Vessel's registry or other official evidence of   188
        deletion appropriate to the Vessel's registry at the time of delivery, or, in the event that the   189
        registry does not as a matter of practice issue such documentation immediately, a written   190
        undertaking by the Sellers to effect deletion from the Vessel's registry forthwith and furnish a   191
        Certificate or other official evidence of deletion to the Buyers promptly and latest within 4   192
        (four) weeks after the Purchase Price has been paid and the Vessel has been delivered.   193

f)   Any such additional documents as may reasonably be required by the competent authorities   194
        for the purpose of registering the Vessel, provided the Buyers notify the Sellers of any such   195
        documents as soon as possible after the date of this Agreement.   196

At the time of delivery the Buyers and Sellers shall sign and deliver to each other a Protocol of   197
Delivery and Acceptance confirming the date and time of delivery of the Vessel from the Sellers to the   198
Buyers.   199

At the time of delivery the Sellers shall hand to the Buyers the classification certificate(s) as well as all   200
plans etc., which are on board the Vessel. Other certificates which are on board the Vessel shall also   201
be handed over to the Buyers unless the Sellers are required to retain same, in which case the   202
Buyers to have the right to take copies. Other technical documentation which may   203
be in the Sellers' possession shall be promptly forwarded to the Buyers at their expense, if they so   204
request. The Sellers may keep the Vessel's log books but the Buyers to have the right to take   205
copies of same.   206

9.   Encumbrances   207

The Sellers warrant that the Vessel, at the time of delivery, is free from all charters, encumbrances,   208
mortgages and maritime liens or any other debts whatsoever. The Sellers hereby undertake   209
to indemnify the Buyers against all consequences of claims made against the Vessel which have   210
been incurred prior to the time of delivery.   211

10.   Taxes, etc.   212

Any taxes, fees and expenses in connection with the purchase and registration under the Buyers' flag   213
shall be for the Buyers' account, whereas similar charges in connection with the closing of the Sellers'   214
register shall be for the Sellers' account.   215

11.   Condition on delivery   216

The Vessel with everything belonging to her shall be at the Sellers' risk and expense until she is   217
delivered to the Buyers, but subject to the terms and conditions of this Agreement she shall be   218
delivered and taken over as she was at the time of inspection, fair wear and tear excepted.   219
However, the Vessel shall be delivered with her class maintained without condition/recommendation*,   220
free of average damage affecting the Vessel's class, and with her classification certificates and   221
national certificates, as well as all other certificates the Vessel had at the time of inspection, valid and   222
unextended without condition/recommendation* by Class or the relevant authorities at the time of   223
delivery.   224
"Inspection" in this Clause 11, shall mean the Buyers' inspection according to Clause 4 a) or 4 b), if   225
applicable, or the Buyers' inspection prior to the signing of this Agreement. If the Vessel is taken over   226
without inspection, the date of this Agreement shall be the relevant date.   227

*   Notes, if any, in the surveyor's report which are accepted by the Classification Society   228
       without condition/recommendation are not to be taken into account.   229

12.   Name/markings   230

Upon delivery the Buyers undertake to change the name of the Vessel and alter funnel markings.   231

13.   Buyers' default   232

Should the deposit not be paid in accordance with Clause 2, the Sellers have the right to cancel this   233
Agreement, and they shall be entitled to claim compensation for their losses and for all expenses   234
incurred together with interest.   235
Should the Purchase Price not be paid in accordance with Clause 3, the Sellers have the right to   236
cancel the Agreement, in which case the deposit together with interest earned shall be released to the   237
Sellers. If the deposit does not cover their loss, the Sellers shall be entitled to claim further   238
compensation for their losses and for all expenses incurred together with interest.   239

14.   Sellers' default   240

Should the Sellers fail to give Notice of Readiness in accordance with Clause 5 a) or fail to be ready   241
to validly complete a legal transfer by the date stipulated in line 61 the Buyers shall have   242
the option of cancelling this Agreement provided always that the Sellers shall be granted a   243
maximum of 3 banking days after Notice of Readiness has been given to make arrangements   244
for the documentation set out in Clause 8. If after Notice of Readiness has been given but before   245
the Buyers have taken delivery, the Vessel ceases to be physically ready for delivery and is not   246
made physically ready again in every respect by the date stipulated in line 61 and new Notice of   247
Readiness given, the Buyers shall retain their option to cancel. In the event that the Buyers elect   248
to cancel this Agreement the deposit together with interest earned shall be released to them   249
immediately .   250
Should the Sellers fail to give Notice of Readiness by the date stipulated in line 61 or fail to be ready   251
to validly complete a legal transfer as aforesaid they shall make due compensation to the Buyers for   252
their loss and for all expenses together with interest if their failure is due to proven   253
negligence and whether or not the Buyers cancel this Agreement.   254

15.   Buyers' representatives   255

After this Agreement has been signed by both parties and the deposit has been lodged, the Buyers   256
have the right to place two representatives on board the Vessel at their sole risk and expense upon   257
arrival at   on or about   258
These representatives are on board for the purpose of familiarisation and in the capacity of   259
observers only, and they shall not interfere in any respect with the operation of the Vessel. The   260
Buyers' representatives shall sign the Sellers' letter of indemnity prior to their embarkation.   261

16.   Arbitration   262

a)*   This Agreement shall be governed by and construed in accordance with English law and   263
any dispute arising out of this Agreement shall be referred to arbitration in London in   264
accordance with the Arbitration Acts 1950 and 1979 or any statutory modification or   265
re-enactment thereof for the time being in force, one arbitrator being appointed by each   266
party. On the receipt by one party of the nomination in writing of the other party's arbitrator,   267
that party shall appoint their arbitrator within fourteen days, failing which the decision of the   268
single arbitrator appointed shall apply. If two arbitrators properly appointed shall not agree   269
they shall appoint an umpire whose decision shall be final.   270

b)*   This Agreement shall be governed by and construed in accordance with Title 9 of the   271
United States Code and the Law of the State of New York and should any dispute arise out of   272
this Agreement, the matter in dispute shall be referred to three persons at New York, one to   273
be appointed by each of the parties hereto, and the third by the two so chosen; their   274
decision or that of any two of them shall be final, and for purpose of enforcing any award, this   275
Agreement may be made a rule of the Court.   276
The proceedings shall be conducted in accordance with the rules of the Society of Maritime   277
Arbitrators, Inc. New York.   278

c)*   Any dispute arising out of this Agreement shall be referred to arbitration at   279
                                   , subject to the procedures applicable there.   280
The laws of   shall govern this Agreement.   281

*   16 a), 16 b) and 16 c) are alternatives; delete whichever is not applicable. In the absence of   282
deletions, alternative 16 a) to apply.   283

INDEX